Setting the Desert on Fire

Also by James Barr

The Bow Group: A History

Setting the Desert on Fire

T. E. Lawrence and Britain's Secret War
in Arabia, 1916–1918

James Barr

W. W. NORTON & COMPANY

NEW YORK   LONDON

For information about permission to reproduce
selections from this book, write to Permissions,
W. W. Norton & Company, Inc.,
500 Fifth Avenue, New York, NY 10110

For information about special discounts for bulk purchases, please contact
W. W. Norton Special Sales at specialsales@wwnorton.com or 800-233-4830

Manufacturing by RR Donnelley, Harrisonburg
Book design by Iris Weinstein
Production manager: Julia Druskin

Library of Congress Cataloging-in-Publication Data

Barr, James, 1976–
Setting the desert on fire : T.E. Lawrence and Britain's secret
war in Arabia, 1916/1918 / James Barr. — 1st American ed.
p. cm.
Includes bibliographical references and index.
ISBN 978-0-393-06040-9 (hardcover)
1. World War, 1914–1918—Campaigns—Arab countries.
2. World War, 1914–1918—Campaigns—Arabian Peninsula.
3. Arab countries—Politics and government—20th century.
4. Lawrence, T. E. (Thomas Edward), 1888–1935. I. Title.
D568.4.B37 2008
940.4'15092—dc22

2007039274

W. W. Norton & Company, Inc.
500 Fifth Avenue, New York, N.Y. 10110
www.wwnorton.com

W. W. Norton & Company Ltd.
Castle House, 75/76 Wells Street, London W1T 3QT

1 2 3 4 5 6 7 8 9 0

Contents

Key Figures in This Book

Abdullah ibn Husein (1882–1951) Husein's second son. He was the ambitious power behind his father, and his own aspirations hinged on joining the Hijaz to Yemen and staving off the threat posed by Ibn Saud. Recognized by the British as emir of Transjordan in May 1923, he was assassinated in Jerusalem.

Allenby, Sir Edmund (1861–1936) Commander in chief of the British Third Army in France from October 1915. Sent to Egypt in June 1917 following his perceived failure at Arras, he brought a sense of purpose to the demoralized Egyptian Expeditionary Force. Best known for capturing Jerusalem in December 1917, he served as high commissioner in Egypt in difficult circumstances after the war, from March 1919.

Asquith, Herbert (1852–1928) British Liberal prime minister, 1908 until December 1916.

Auda abu Tayi (died 1924) Sheikh of the Huwaytat. Auda was an infamous raider well known to prewar European travelers to the region. Outlawed by the Ottomans after he had murdered two tax collectors, he seemed to the British a natural supporter of the Arab revolt.

Balfour, Arthur (1848–1930) Former prime minister (1902–5) whom Lloyd George brought back as foreign secretary in December 1916. Published the Balfour Declaration in November 1917. Resigned in 1922.

Brémond, Edouard (1868–1948) Commanded an infantry unit in France before he was wounded, and then was nominated as chief of the French military mission to the Hijaz in August 1916, on the strength of his extensive prewar experience in North Africa. Recalled December 1917.

Chamberlain, Sir Austen (1863–1937) Secretary of state for India from May 1915 to July 1917. Initially against British intervention in the Hijaz, he increasingly feared the consequences if the Ottomans recaptured Mecca, and supported sending British troops. Forced to resign in July 1917 over a damning report into the failed Indian army expedition to Baghdad that had met with disaster at Kut in 1916.

Clayton, Gilbert ("Bertie") (1875–1929) Director of military intelligence at British Army Headquarters, 1914–16; in charge of the Arab Bureau and Hijaz operations, 1916–17; chief political officer in Egyptian Expeditionary Force, 1917–18. Cautious, firm believer in the threat to Egypt posed by the Ottoman declaration of jihad.

Fakhreddin ("Fakhri") Pasha (1868–1948) Ottoman commander who was sent to defend Medina in late May 1916, following suspicions that a revolt was imminent. He held out until January 1919.

Feisal ibn Husein (1886–1933) Third son of Sharif Husein. The recipient of British support after showing a willingness to help the British that contrasted with the attitude of his two elder brothers. Forced out of Syria by the French in July 1919. Proclaimed king of Iraq in Baghdad by the British in August 1921.

Grey, Sir Edward (1862–1933) British foreign secretary, 1905–16. A dutiful, but increasingly uncertain, politician who willingly delegated responsibility for dealing with Sharif Husein to Henry McMahon in Cairo in 1915.

Haidar, Ali (1866–1935) Appointed emir of Mecca by the Ottoman government in June 1916 to replace Sharif Husein. Returned to Lebanon in March 1917 after eight months in Medina.

Hogarth, David (1862–1927) Arrived in Egypt in August 1915. Director of the Arab Bureau from its creation in spring 1916 until that autumn. Hogarth was a veteran archaeologist who volunteered his services following the outbreak of war. He was instrumental in bringing Lawrence into intelligence work in Cairo. He opposed large-scale intervention in the Hijaz.

Husein ibn Ali (1853–1931) Appointed emir of Mecca in 1908 by Sultan Abdul Hamid. Revolted against the Ottoman government in June 1916. Recognized as king of Hijaz in 1916, he abdicated in favor of his eldest son, Ali, in 1924. After Abdul Aziz ibn Saud overran the Hijaz in 1925, he spent the rest of his life in exile.

Ibn Saud, Abdul Aziz (1880–1953) Sultan of Najd, in central Arabia. Having captured Riyadh in 1902, he was allied to, and received assistance from, the British during the war. He defeated his rivals Ibn Rashid, 1921–22, and Sharif Husein's son Ali, in 1925.

Jafar Pasha al Askari (1885–1936) Ottoman army officer, held prisoner of war in Cairo. He had been captured by the British in February 1916 during their suppression of the Senussi's revolt, in which he was an agent provocateur. He was persuaded to serve with the Arab rebels, whom he joined in the summer of 1917. Born in Baghdad, he served twice as prime minister of Iraq, and several times as minister of defense between 1923 and 1936, when he was murdered in a coup.

Jemal Pasha, Ahmed (1872–1922) Commander of the Ottoman Fourth Army and military governor of Syria from December 1914. A secretive man, he orchestrated efforts to win Sharif Husein's support for an invasion of Egypt and then, when these failed, a crackdown on nascent Arab nationalism in Syria, which earned him the soubriquet the Blood-letter. Recalled following the loss of Jerusalem, December 1917.

Joyce, Pierce (1878–1965) Egyptian army officer. Arrived at Rabigh in November 1916, tasked with protecting the new British airfield, and effectively defending the village against Ottoman attack. Joyce rapidly became the organizational linchpin of operations in the Hijaz and at Aqaba. He was an adviser to the Iraqi army after the war.

Kitchener, Herbert (1850–1916) Secretary of state for war, 1914–16. Supported British encouragement of Sharif Husein's plans to revolt. His death at sea in June 1916 robbed the Arab revolt's enthusiasts of a key ally in Whitehall just when the revolt had run out of momentum.

Lawrence, Thomas Edward (T. E.) (1888–1935) Intelligence officer in Egypt, from December 1914 until November 1916, when he was formally transferred to the Arab Bureau to work on Hijaz operations. Lawrence was drawn into British intelligence following his work as an archaeologist in the region before the war. He was sent to the Hijaz in October 1916 to assess the deteriorating situation following contradictory reports.

Liman von Sanders, Otto (1855–1929) German commander of the Ottoman Fifth Army. Originally sent to Constantinople in December 1913 at the head of a German military mission to improve the Ottomans' armed forces, Liman von Sanders was given command of the combined Turkish and German forces in Palestine in February 1918.

Lloyd, George (1879–1941) Elected MP for West Staffordshire in 1910, Lloyd was attached to the Mediterranean Expeditionary Force as a Turkish-speaking intelligence officer in November 1914. Intermittently involved in the Arab Bureau, Lloyd took a close interest in economic and financial matters and was a fervent imperialist.

Lloyd George, David (1863–1945) Minister for munitions, May 1915–July 1916; secretary of state for war, July–December 1916. Lloyd George achieved his ambition when he became prime minister in December 1916 (to October 1922), his energy attracting Conservative and Unionist support. He hoped to colonize Palestine, and his support for an advance toward Jerusalem first served to help the Arabs, but ultimately let them down.

McMahon, Sir Henry (1862–1949) High commissioner in Egypt, 1914–16. Pursued a policy of ambiguity and procrastination when tasked with coming to an agreement with Sharif Husein by London in 1915.

Murray, Sir Archibald (1860–1945) Commander in chief of the Egyptian Expeditionary Force, January 1916–June 1917. Tasked with sending as many men as possible back to France to fight, he was vehemently opposed to sending British troops to the Hijaz to support Husein. He was eventually undone by conflicting political and military pressures and, following the unsuccessful second battle of Gaza, was recalled to Britain in June 1917.

Robertson, Sir William (1860–1933) Chief of the Imperial General Staff, January 1915–February 1918. Trenchant opponent of any military venture that might distract resources and attention from the western front. Once the Arabs made headway north, he became marginally less skeptical.

Said, Nuri (1888–1958) Arab Ottoman army officer. Joined Arab revolt in July 1916, acting as Jafar Pasha's chief of staff. He remained loyal to Feisal after the war, and—testimony to the region's political instability—served as prime minister of Iraq fourteen times between 1930 and 1958, when he was murdered in a coup.

Shaalan, Nuri (born ca. 1845, dead by 1927) Sheikh of the north Arabian Rwala Bedu. The Rwala were an important and wide-ranging constituent of the large Aniza tribe. Nuri Shaalan had murdered two brothers to assume his title. He was sought as an important, if volatile, ally by both Ottomans and British.

Stirling, Francis (1880–1958) Intelligence officer, who had been sent back to Egypt after being shell-shocked at Gallipoli in 1915. He served with the Arabs in the final stages of their campaign in July 1918 and after the war as a political officer in Cairo.

Storrs, Ronald (1881–1955) Oriental secretary at the British High Commission in Cairo 1909–17. Prickly, early enthusiast for encouraging Sharif Husein to revolt and seize the caliphate. Appointed "stopgap" military governor of Jerusalem in December 1917.

Sykes, Sir Mark (1879–1919) British MP for Hull (from 1911) and government adviser on the Middle East (from spring 1915). Closely involved in the discussions on the future of the Ottoman Empire in 1915, he was tasked with pursuing the agreement with France and Russia over the division of the Ottoman Empire in which France was allotted present-day Syria and Lebanon.

Weizmann, Chaim (1874–1952) A scientist for the British government, Weizmann was appointed head of the Zionist commission to Palestine in 1918. He met Feisal that May and eventually became the first president of Israel, 1949–52.

Wemyss, Rosslyn (1864–1933) Appointed commander of the Egyptian Squadron of the Royal Navy in January 1916 after service at Gallipoli. Supported efforts to supply the Arabs during the early stages of the revolt. Recalled to London in July 1917, where he was made first sea lord.

Wilson, Cyril (1873–1938) Appointed Britain's "pilgrimage officer" at Jeddah in June 1916, after serving as governor of the Red Sea Province of Sudan. Bluntly rejected Wingate's call for troops to be sent to help Husein, an intervention prompted by his overriding sense of duty to Britain.

Wilson, Sir Henry (1864–1922) A corps commander with the British Expeditionary Force in France in 1916. Wilson's lucid explanation of complex military issues and political awareness endeared him to Lloyd George, who promoted him to replace Robertson as chief of the Imperial General Staff in February 1918. Retired February 1922 and assassinated that June by Irish republicans.

Wingate, Sir Reginald (1861–1953) Governor-general of the Sudan, and sirdar of the Egyptian Army 1899–1916. Appointed high commissioner of Egypt, October 1916. Insistently proposed sending British troops to the Hijaz when the revolt's momentum failed. Replaced by Allenby in 1919.

Young, Sir Hubert (1885–1950) Assistant political officer and logistics officer in Mesopotamia, 1915–18. Transferred to help the Arabs in Syria in March 1918. Easily irascible, he served after the war in the Foreign and Colonial Offices.

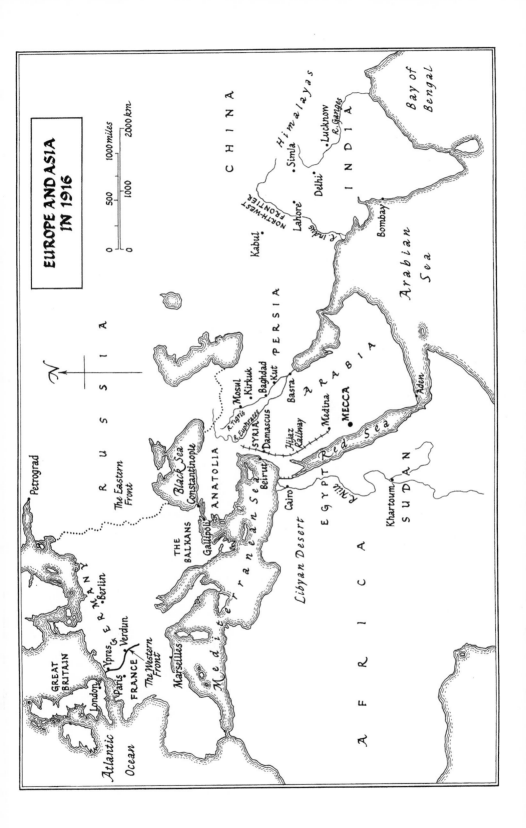

EUROPE AND ASIA
IN 1916

0   500   1000 miles
0   1000   2000 km.

Atlantic
Ocean

GREAT
BRITAIN

London

Paris
FRANCE

Verdun

Ypres
The Western
Front

Marseilles

Berlin

G E R M A N Y

Petrograd

R U S S I A

The Eastern
Front

THE
BALKANS

Gallipoli

Black Sea

Constantinople

ANATOLIA

M e d i t e r r a n e a n   S e a

Libyan Desert

EGYPT

Cairo

Khartoum

SUDAN

A F R I C A

Beirut

SYRIA

Damascus

R. Tigris
R. Euphrates

Mosul

Kirkuk

Baghdad

Kut

Basra

PERSIA

Hijaz Railway

Medina

MECCA

Red Sea

R. Nile

Aden

A R A B I A

Arabian
Sea

Kabul

Lahore

R. Indus

NORTH-WEST
FRONTIER

Delhi

Simla

Himalayas

Lucknow

R. Ganges

I N D I A

Bombay

Bay of
Bengal

C H I N A

N

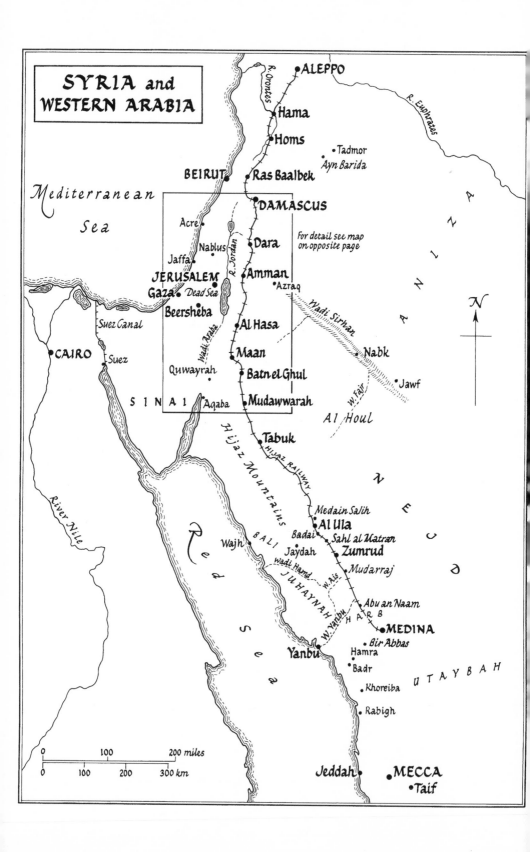

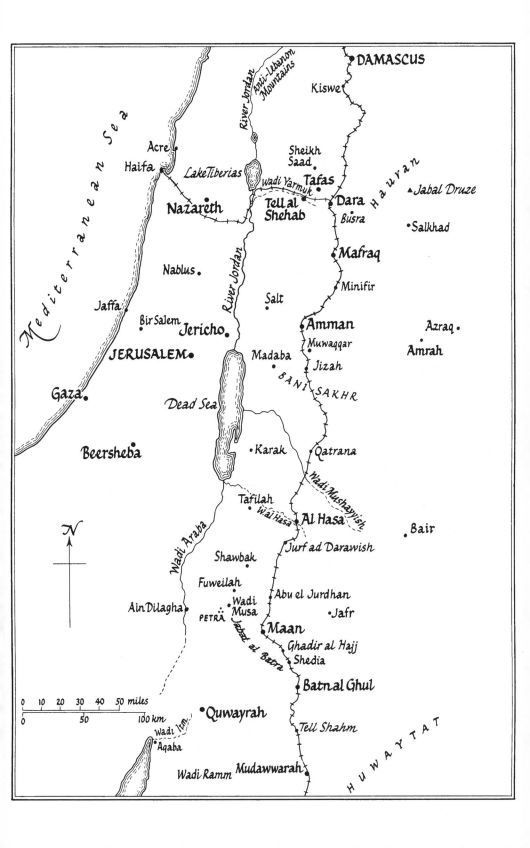

A Note on the Text

Because of the difficulty of transliterating Arabic words into English, the names of Arabs and places in this narrative were spelled in a wide variety of ways by the British at the time. I have standardized the spelling of place and personal names to a single form across the text and the quotations to avoid confusion, and dropped the definite article "Al" in many cases for simplicity. Major places are referred to by their Anglicized names. The spelling of all other place-names follows the most recent *The Times Atlas of the World*, minus the diacritical marks or accents. Like the British at the time, I have used the words Ottoman and Turk interchangeably. However, the Ottoman army included soldiers from around the empire, including Arabs.

All dialogue is quoted directly from official minutes or the reports and memoirs of those who witnessed the conversation. Its accuracy cannot be proven, but it is the best record we have of what was said at the time.

The exchange rate in 1916 meant that £1,000 was worth $4,800. The effect of inflation makes that $4,800 worth approximately $90,000 today, if we use consumer price index data as a basis. In other words, £1,000 is worth nearly $100,000.

Setting the Desert on Fire

Prologue

In a stony valley in the Hijaz mountains of western Saudi Arabia, one hundred miles north of Medina, stands a rust-brown steam engine. It rests ten yards off the railway embankment it once plied, its wheels half sunk in the drifting desert sand, pointing north. A few yards farther up the line, its tender is heading in the opposite direction. A jumble of skewed wheels is all that remains of two more cars. Like the railway track itself, their wooden sides have long since disappeared. Here,

Wrecked train, south of Wayban in the Hijaz.

**Damage to the footplate and
firebox was probably caused by a mine.**

among some stunted thornbushes and under the silty blue desert sky,
I found an unsettling scene of headlong disaster.[1] It was only March
2005, but nearly noon, and under the ferocious midday sun the heat on
my face felt as if it were roaring from an enormous, open oven.

A closer look among the wreckage provides the likely cause of this
catastrophe. A brutal dent in the back of the firebox and below it a
chunk of missing floor both suggest that it was an explosion beneath
the wheels that blasted this engine off the track. This train was probably mined. Today it is one of only four remaining wrecks along the long-
abandoned railway line, slowly disintegrating memorials to a secret
war, directed by the British, that began in June 1916.

The war in this harsh desert was fluid and fast moving, waged by
guerrillas who might travel to their targets by camel or by armored car.
Although its tactics were unorthodox, it remained, according to one
British officer who fought in it, a "very gentlemanly war" into which he
opposed introducing any "western frightfulness."[2] And by contrast to
the western front, it was small-scale. The heaviest artillery made avail-

able to the Arabs was about the lightest in use on the Somme.[3] The £1.5 million that the British spent to fight it in its first year was equivalent to "the cost of the war for about 7 hours," one civil servant reckoned.[4] And yet this smallest of wars was to have reverberations that can still be felt throughout the Middle East today. It was to find their origins that I started working on this book.

Seven hundred miles farther north and three years earlier, off a back street in the ancient city of Damascus—the capital of modern Syria—I had already discovered a line of similar, elderly steam engines, woven to some sidings by dry grass growing through their wheels. It was this glimpse that first sparked my curiosity. These were the shunting yards of the northern terminus of the Hijaz Railway, which once linked Damascus with the holy city of Medina, where the Prophet Muhammad, founder of Islam, is buried.

Begun in 1900, the Hijaz Railway was the brainchild of the Ottoman sultan Abdul Hamid, and it attracted British suspicions from the start. Before it was even finished, the hawkish foreign editor of the influential London newspaper the *Times*, Valentine Chirol, described the project as an effort by the sultan to "link up the seat of his temporal power as Sultan at Constantinople with the seat of his spiritual power as Caliph of Mecca." The sultan's strategy, he claimed, was designed to enhance "throughout the Mohammedan world the spiritual authority to which he lays claim as heir to the Caliphate of Islam."[5] The caliph—the deputy or successor to the Prophet Muhammad—was the title conferred on Muhammad's closest followers after his death; the caliphate, the extensive empire they went on to conquer. The title outlived the empire, which was overrun by the Mongols in the thirteenth century. It was appropriated by the Ottomans in the fifteenth century, just as their own empire was reaching its zenith, and came to signify the leadership of the now fragmented Islamic world and the hope that, one day, it might yet reunite.

From the beginning of the eighteenth century, however, the Ottomans' story was one of gradual, picturesque decline, which the British had initially tried to slow. In 1854 Britain went to war with Russia in the Crimea to preserve the Ottoman Empire as a buffer against Russian expansion. At that time the Ottomans still ran much of the eastern Mediterranean. Their possessions included their Anatolian heartland and much of the Balkans to the west, and Libya and Egypt to the south.

At the eastern end of the sea, Syria—which included Palestine—and Iraq were also Ottoman, as were the coastal fringes of Arabia, including the Hijaz, the holy land of Islam surrounding the sacred cities of Mecca and Medina. Greeks, Slavs, Armenians, Kurds, Jews, Circassians, and Arabs: all were ruled from Constantinople by a government dominated—from the Sultan downward—by Turks. Some, ambitious Arabs in particular, were aggrieved that their opportunities within the Ottoman Empire were so limited.

Yet the Ottoman sultan depended increasingly on Arabia. Not only did Islam provide a unifying force within his disparate empire, but its leadership—through the caliphate and control of the Hijaz—gave him an influence among Muslims throughout the world. The British initially encouraged him, thinking, wrongly, that as caliph the sultan's influence was spiritual, not political. They believed that the Ottomans were a stabilizing influence in an otherwise volatile region, and that a highly publicized friendship with the sultan might improve an uneasy relationship with their Muslim subjects, particularly the 60 million living in British India.

By the 1870s, however, British relations with the Ottomans had begun to cool. From its opening in 1869 the Suez Canal provided a bypass through the increasingly troubled Ottoman Empire, which defaulted on its loans in 1876. The default frightened away many British investors, and, without as great a financial stake, when Russia invaded Ottoman territory in the Balkans two years later, Britain did not intervene as forcefully as before. And the price of British willingness to help the Ottomans through their overwhelming financial problems was steep. Britain took over Cyprus in 1878 and occupied Egypt four years later after a breakdown in law and order directly threatened the security of the canal, by now a key strategic asset as Britain's economic and military dependence on India continued to grow.

Britain and the Ottoman Empire were growing apart. That might not have mattered had it not been becoming uncomfortably apparent that as caliph the sultan commanded much more than the religious loyalty of Muslims around the world. The evidence was widespread. When Greece clashed with the Ottomans in 1897, British officials in India observed with alarm how, even on the remote North–West Frontier, Muslims backed their co-religionists against the Greeks. In Egypt in 1906 the ruling British agent in Cairo received a letter, which was clearly sufficiently disconcerting to be carefully filed away. "The Caliph holds the sacred places and the noble relics," stated its anonymous author. "Though the Caliph were hapless as Bayazid, cruel as Murad or mad as Ibrahim,* he is the shadow of God, and every Moslem must leap up at his call as the willing servant to his master's work."[6]

At the *Times* Valentine Chirol believed that the sultan's power as caliph gave him a disturbing and disruptive political influence worldwide. He and others feared that the sultan would use his position to upset the stability of Britain's eastern empire, home to 100 million of the global population of nearly 300 million Muslims. And there was another European power that shared this belief. That power was Germany.

Convinced that Muslim unrest could turn the advantage of the British Empire's enormous size into a terrible liability, the Germans now also encouraged the Ottomans to exploit the caliphate. "The Sultan and the three hundred million Muslims who revere him as their leader should know that the German Emperor is their friend forever," declared the kaiser on a visit to Damascus in 1898.[7] To prove the point, and reveal a questionable sense of taste, he also gave the city an overblown gilt wreath to bolt onto the tomb of Saladin, the Muslim warrior lionized for defeating the Crusaders seven centuries before. Fancy metalwork continued to play an important role in the burgeoning German-Ottoman friendship: Germany supplied the engineering expertise the sultan needed to build the Hijaz Railway, its rails, and many of the trains that ran on them.

The sultan encouraged donations from Muslims around the world toward the railway. Muslims in India, the British government took note, gave generously. According to one official estimate five million rupees were sent from India toward the scheme, at a time when the average income of a Bombay family was fifty-two rupees a month.[8] Donations paid for one-third of the cost of the railway, which reached Medina in 1908, a year ahead of schedule.

For eight years afterward the Hijaz Railway transformed travel through the lawless Arabian hinterland. A forty-day desert march or an expensive voyage by sea down through the British-controlled Suez

---

* Three Ottoman sultans: Bayazid I (1389–1402) had plans to capture Constantinople, which were disrupted by the unexpected appearance of Tamerlaine, who enslaved him; Murad IV (1623–40) restored stability to the Ottoman state by killing 20,000 opponents; Ibrahim I (1640–48) was a lunatic.

Canal now took just three days by train. Yet this achievement brought the Ottomans into mounting conflict with the Bedu. These were the small and feuding tribes of violent nomadic herders who scratched a living in the desert by robbing one another and hiring camels and guides to travelers. Found throughout Arabia, the Bedu were, a British intelligence guide advised, "less to be trusted in Hijaz than in almost any other Arabian province," and with good reason.[9] The tribes of the Hijaz were small and fractured. Blood feuds between them perpetuated a continuous cycle of sporadic violence. Into this maelstrom was sucked the traffic of rich pilgrims through the Hijaz, for protection rackets and robbery were lucrative additional lines of business for the Bedu tribesmen, who also extorted money from the towns and villages in the Hijaz in return for peace and quiet. The Bedu's ancient way of life and death was now threatened by the train, the arrival of the Ottoman tax man who competed for the tributes the tribesmen had previously demanded, and the diseases that followed in the wake of the railway, like cholera, which devastated close-knit nomadic families. A period of severe drought at around this time made life in the

The Hijaz Railway under construction, near Amman.
The steam engine abruptly ended the Bedu's monopoly
on the transport of pilgrims and grain through the
desolate landscape of southern Syria and northwest Arabia.

The Bedu dancing, waving their rifles
and swords in the air. Impromptu celebrations
and spur-of-the-moment songs were regular
features of the nomads' harsh and unpredictable life.

desert even harder. Unsurprisingly, given their rapacious way of life, the plight of the Bedu attracted little sympathy. What mattered was that the pilgrimage to Mecca was now faster, cheaper, and safer than ever before. The sultan, as a consequence, basked in the gratitude of Muslims worldwide. His grip, which had been waning, seemed renewed; his influence, once limited, suddenly appeared to extend far beyond the crumbling borders of the shrinking Ottoman Empire.

Chirol predicted trouble. "The completion of the Hijaz Railway," he foresaw, "will in a large measure relieve the Sultan from the galling dependence upon friendly relations with Great Britain which the maintenance of his main line of communications with Arabia now necessitates."[10] And he was right. At the outbreak of war in 1914 the Ottomans joined the Germans' side. The breakdown of relations between the Ottomans and the British was complete: far from the trenches of the western front a desperate struggle for the loyalty of Muslims throughout the British Empire was just about to start.

My search for the arena of this struggle drew me from the crowded bazaars of Damascus deep into the stony deserts of Jordan and Saudi Arabia in 2004 and 2005. I traveled by car and on foot, searching for wrecked trains and ruined stations along the Hijaz Railway in Jordan and Saudi Arabia, and spent one balmy and memorable night trying and failing to sleep under the eerie yellow-gray moonlight in the southern Jordanian desert. I found locomotives lying where they were abandoned at the end of the war and stations pockmarked by gunfire. I saw jagged shards of rock set upright in the desert: the lonely tombstones of those who died in the fighting. I walked the humid streets of old Jeddah, wandered the ruins of ancient Petra at dawn, and sweated in the sweltering port of Aqaba, at the head of the Red Sea. It was about a month in all. I wanted a sense of what it would have been like to fight in these circumstances, and I wanted to see for myself the places that were pivotal to the story that I am about to tell.

1

A Clear-Thinking Hatchet Man

A gunshot and the tinkle of broken glass on the ship's deck abruptly ended Ronald Storrs's brief siesta.[1] It was his third trip down the Red Sea in five months, when he had been banking on no more than one. This time Storrs was heading for the port of Jeddah, gateway to the chain of sandpapery mountains that gave the edge of western Arabia its daunting name: the Hijaz, Arabic for "barrier." It was there that the "Great Arab Revolt," as he had encouraged the *Times* in London to dub it grandiosely, had started four months earlier. Now Storrs's ship, the *Lama*, was crammed dangerously full with secret supplies for this tribal uprising against the Ottomans, which had already begun to falter.

In his white tropical suit, damp with sweat and now stained red by the leather armchair in which he sat, with perspiration glistening on his balding head, the thirty-four-year-old Storrs must have looked the reluctant adventurer he was. "We are loaded with coal, ammunition etc over 2 feet above safety line," he had jotted nervously in his diary two days earlier as he left the port of Suez to go south.[2] Nor had the departure date reassured him. Friday, 13 October 1916, was, as the ship's captain admitted, an ominous day to sail. Within ten minutes of this observation two of the *Lama*'s boilers had burst, making full steam impossible and adding an extra day to a journey Storrs knew from experience he would find very dull. A prickly man, Storrs hated the boring company that he had been forced to endure on previous voyages down the Red Sea. And so he had been eagerly looking forward to sparkling conversation with the "super-cerebral companion" from the Intelligence Department whom he was traveling with this time.[3]

But the intelligence officer had other ideas. He proved unwilling to join Storrs in a sedentary discussion of the merits of Debussy. And to Storrs's great annoyance, he was amusing himself by shooting at a line of bottles balanced on the ship's handrail instead. At twenty-eight, this man was seven years Storrs's junior, too short to be a regular army officer, with fair hair and electric-blue eyes. Everyone always noticed his eyes. "Very, very blue," remembers Diana Elles, one of the handful of people alive today who knew him. Sitting in her elegant Westminster apartment within earshot of Big Ben, she told me how he had "a very keen face. You could see the pressure behind it."[4] In his right hand he held a large Browning pistol, which he deftly raised again to eye level. Another shot: another bottle evaporated from the rail. His name was Thomas Edward Lawrence. But, for his exploits in the desert over the next two years, he would emerge from the war as the famous "Lawrence of Arabia."

Storrs had gotten to know Lawrence only four months earlier, shortly after the Arab ruler of Mecca, Sharif Husein, had spurred the Bedu tribes of the Hijaz into revolt. Husein was a superficially charming, yet wily, obsessive, and reactionary, old man, whose authority among the Bedu arose from his claim to direct descent from the Prophet Muhammad, the prized ancestry denoted by his title, "sharif." The tribesmen had answered his call, and, helped by a British naval bombardment, they seized the port of Jeddah. But they could not repeat this quick success elsewhere. Two hundred miles to the north at Medina, they proved no match for the Ottoman garrison in open warfare. In Mecca it was only after weeks of desultory fighting and the arrival of British artillery that they had forced the Turks to surrender that July. The artillery broke a similar deadlock in the summer resort of Taif, high in the serrated mountains above the holy city, in September. Although Husein now controlled the three cities of the southern Hijaz and had taken over 5,000 Turkish soldiers prisoner, the momentum of his uprising had evaporated in the ferocious summer heat, his actions had been met with a mixture of anger and disbelief across the Islamic world, and in Medina the Turks, who by now boasted a force of about 12,000 men, were preparing to retake Mecca. The "Great Arab Revolt," so long in the planning, was going badly wrong.

While the uprising was unraveling, Storrs had decided to design some postage stamps to emphasize the independence of the Hijaz. He wanted them ready for the annual pilgrimage to Mecca, which fell at the start of October that year. The idea was typical of Storrs's devious brain: in his own words, "self-paying and incontrovertible" evidence that the revolt had been successful, which would be spread throughout the Muslim world by pilgrims' letters home.[5] Storrs had approached Husein for inspiration, but was disappointed by the rather modern image sent back by the sharif, which could easily be mistaken for an Ottoman design. So he sought the advice of the map-making section of the Intelligence Department that July 1916. It was there that he first encountered Lawrence, who was interested in printing. According to Storrs, the pair had passed an afternoon wandering the corridors of the Arab Museum in Cairo looking for traditional arabesque motifs they felt were more suitable for the Hijaz. The first stamps, cobalt-blue and each worth one piastre, were issued that August.[6]

Lawrence had been delighted to be asked to help. He was a brilliant medieval historian with a first-class degree from Oxford University and several years' experience managing Arab laborers on archaeological digs in Syria. He had injected these excavations with an excitement not usually associated with the world of archaeology by firing his pistol in the air whenever an interesting find was unearthed. The experience left him with a deep admiration for the Arabs, who were clearly enthusiastic in turn: Lawrence gained a reputation for "getting on very well with natives."[7] So it was hardly surprising that he was bored rigid by the mundane desk work allotted to him in the Intelligence Department, where he seemed to spend too much of his time answering the telephone. In the meantime two of his brothers had been killed on the western front. "They were both younger than I am," he wrote to a friend, "and it doesn't seem right, somehow, that I should go on living peacefully in Cairo."[8]

Lawrence had been itching for the British to take a more buccaneering approach within the Middle East in which he might play an active role. In particular he wondered whether the Bedu tribesmen he had met before the war might help defeat the Turks in that part of the world. "I want to pull them all together, & to roll up Syria by way of the Hijaz in the name of the Sharif," he wrote to his mentor, the Oxford University professor and Middle East expert David Hogarth, early in

T. E. Lawrence (left) and
David Hogarth (center)
with Alan Dawnay (right)
in Egypt, 1918.
The unorthodox approach
relished by Hogarth
and his former student,
Lawrence, contrasted
with Dawnay's textbook
professionalism.

1915. But it was not just the Ottomans he hoped to remove: with Husein as a figurehead, Lawrence believed, "we can rush right up to Damascus, & biff the French out of all hope of Syria."[9]

The French ambition to control Syria dated back to the Crusades. The Ottomans had then offered the French favorable trade terms in 1536, at the same time acknowledging France as the protector of Christians in the Holy Land. As a consequence of this nearly four-hundred-year-old treaty, French influence still manifested itself strongly: in 1914 no other country invested more in the Ottoman Empire, and French was the lingua franca of the Middle East. The French naturally assumed that after the war Syria would finally be theirs. This prospect appalled Lawrence, who felt that foreign influence vulgarized the Arabs. "If only you had seen the ruination caused by the French influence," he had written to his mother from Syria before the war, "you would never wish it to be extended. . . . Better a thousand times the Arab untouched."[10] Over the next four years denying the French the prize they presumed to win would become his driving obsession.

Early in 1916 Lawrence had begun moonlighting for the Arab Bureau, which was run from a suite of rooms in a Cairo hotel by Hogarth, who had by now been sucked into intelligence work himself. The bureau's role was twofold, an uneasy combination of intelligence analysis and policy-making. Its staff routinely condensed intelligence from around the Arab world into a frequent digest, the *Arab Bulletin*, which was issued to a small circle of senior officials interested in the region. Its other, harder task was to try to persuade British politicians and their officials in London, Cairo, and Delhi, who had all pursued divergent Middle Eastern policies, to support its policy of encouraging Sharif Husein to revolt. This was the purpose behind a revealing report that Lawrence wrote titled "The Politics of Mecca" in February 1916. In it he compared the effects of an armed uprising in Mecca to those of the fourteenth-century Western Schism on the Roman Catholic church:

> If we can arrange that this political change shall be a violent one, we will have abolished the threat of Islam, by dividing it against itself, in its very heart. There will then be a Khalifa in Turkey and a Khalifa in Arabia, in theological warfare, and Islam will be as little formidable as the Papacy when Popes lived in Avignon.[11]

The memorandum was to mark a turning point in Lawrence's life, because the man who supervised the bureau, the director of military intelligence in Cairo, Bertie Clayton, loved its analysis. "Lawrence is quite excellent on this and many other subjects, and you may take his stuff as being good," he told the director of intelligence in London.[12]

The problem was that in Britain's major colony, India, government officials had not been won over by the Arab Bureau's argument. The Indian army had invaded Ottoman-controlled Mesopotamia—now modern Iraq—in November 1914. Its original aim had been to secure the oil wells of southern Persia and Mesopotamia, but, like so many military ventures, its ambitions had stealthily grown to include the capture of Baghdad. To protect its southern flank while it pursued this goal, the Indian army had formed alliances with several Arab chiefs, including Ibn Saud, who would later found the state of Saudi Arabia. These chiefs, officials in India feared, would feel put out if Britain helped Husein to take the caliphate. They also worried about a backlash among Indian Muslims if British interference in such a sensitive

religious issue were discovered. Clayton, a patient, unflappable professional soldier in his early forties, whom Lawrence greatly admired
and later described as working "like water, or permeating oil, creeping
silently and insistently through everything," was undeterred.[13] When
an opportunity arose, he dispatched Lawrence to Basra, the Indian
army's base in Mesopotamia, on a mission to find evidence that would
both denigrate its intelligence capability and shore up the case for
backing Sharif Husein. In Basra, Lawrence uncovered in the files an
interesting letter of which the bureau had previously been unaware. "If
the Sultan of Turkey were to disappear," one Indian army officer who
had lived with Ibn Saud had written, "the Caliphate by common consent of Islam would fall to the family of the Prophet, the present representative of which is the Sharif of Mecca. In this case he would
command the support of the Ibn Saud."[14] Lawrence had also seen
enough to write a devastating critique of the Basra Intelligence
Department. Witheringly, he described its head as "very excellent but
he has never been in Turkey, or read about it, and he knows no Arabic.
This would not necessarily matter, but unfortunately his staff do not
supply the necessary knowledge."[15]

The contents of Lawrence's report rapidly assumed a legendary
notoriety in Cairo. "It was a violent criticism," recalled another intelligence officer: "We dared not show it to the C-in-C, but had to water it
down till it was considered fit for the great man's perusal."[16] On his
return to Cairo, Lawrence also embarked on a campaign of pedantry
designed to ensure he could transfer permanently from the Intelligence Department to the Arab Bureau. "I was all claws and teeth, and
had a devil," he later admitted of this period.[17] By the time he set out
for Jeddah with Storrs, the Intelligence Department was glad to see
the back of him, and he had earned a well-deserved name as a clear-
thinking hatchet man. As the revolt reached crisis point that autumn
and the British began to panic, it was this reputation that ensured
Lawrence a place with Storrs aboard the *Lama*. Lawrence, Storrs
wrote approvingly, liked "nonsense to be treated as nonsense, and not
civilly or dully accepted or dismissed."[18]

Yet, as he practiced his shooting on the *Lama* that October,
Lawrence was largely unknown outside the tight, closed club of military intelligence officers in Cairo. This was the reality to which Storrs
alluded when he admitted many years afterward that mentions of

Lawrence's name in his diary occurred until that point "with what must now seem a ludicrous infrequency and inadequacy," because Lawrence was too junior to have been part of the inner circle of officials who had steered British support for the revolt so far.[19]

≈❧≈

Ronald Storrs had been part of the inner circle from the start. He understood, better than anyone else, how a short and awkward conversation in Cairo over two years earlier, shortly before the outbreak of World War I, had led to Britain's shipping guns, ammunition, and money to fuel an uprising in the Hijaz in 1916. He had first suggested that the sixty-three-year-old sharif would be the ideal, pliant candidate to assume the caliphate once the Ottoman sultan had been deposed. The Turks' unexpected resilience, however, turned the tables. When it became clear that their attempt to knock the Turks out of the war had failed, the British began to hope instead that a revolt at the heart of Islam led by the sharif could blunt the Ottomans' call for a worldwide Islamic jihad, which threatened their eastern empire. But their calculations were suddenly upset by new and disconcerting intelligence suggesting that Husein's influence was much greater than they had previously believed, and that his support could not be taken for granted. The British now found themselves negotiating with the sharif from a position of weakness: they made some bold, glib promises that, mistakenly, they never expected they would have to honor.

At the beginning of 1914 Storrs was the oriental secretary at the British agency in Cairo, a hectic, cosmopolitan city, just as filthy as it is today. Egypt had gradually become the fulcrum of the British Empire because of the Suez Canal. The canal, which had been completed in 1869, transformed the Red Sea from a dead end into an artery through which pumped the blood of British imperial commerce. By 1914 India was Britain's most important export market, and, not surprisingly given Britain's economic interest in this traffic, political developments on both shores of the Red Sea assumed an increasing importance. When Sharif Husein's son Abdullah had appeared in April 1914, bemoaning the difficulties his father was experiencing with his Ottoman overlords, Storrs was delegated to meet him.

Years later Storrs could still vividly recall that meeting. "I found myself . . . being asked categorically whether Great Britain would present the Grand Sharif with a dozen, or even half a dozen machine guns," he wrote in his memoirs.[20] He rebuffed Abdullah's appeal to help his father resist the Ottomans, but in terms that did not preclude a later change of mind: "We could never entertain the idea of supplying arms to be used against a Friendly Power," Storrs had explained, choosing this last phrase carefully. "Abdullah can have expected no other reply, and we parted on the best of terms."

Storrs's sly point was that by 1914 the Ottomans were no longer a friendly power in more than name. The Turks' recent willingness to look to Germany for military support reflected the true state of affairs, and when, shortly after the start of the war, the Ottomans declared their support for Germany and Austro-Hungary, the British were disappointed, but not surprised. Of course, Storrs's cagey proviso to Abdullah lapsed at once.

Britain's wartime priority in the Middle East was to protect the main sea route to India through the Suez Canal and down the Red Sea, and it was partly because of this, and partly to inflame the tensions between the Arabs and the Turks, that the British quickly made overtures to Sharif Husein. They already knew of an ancient tenet—downplayed by the Ottomans because they did not meet it—that the caliph should come from the Quraysh, the Prophet Muhammad's own tribe, of which Abdullah and his father, Sharif Husein, were members.[21] With this in mind, at the end of October 1914 the secretary of state for war, Storrs's former boss, Lord Kitchener, dispatched a suggestive message to Husein via Storrs: "Till now we have defended and befriended Islam in the person of the Turks: henceforward it shall be in that of the noble Arab. It may be that an Arab of true race will assume the Caliphate at Mecca or Medina, and so good may come by the help of God out of all the evil which is now occurring."[22] But Husein had responded warily, and for a time the British did not further press the possibility that Kitchener had now raised.

The issue rapidly resurfaced in 1915, after the British government agreed to launch an offensive designed to knock the Ottomans out of the war. The plan was to seize the Ottoman Empire by the throat with a landing in the Dardanelles Strait, 150 miles southwest of the capital, Constantinople. British forces would fight their way up the Gallipoli Peninsula and into the capital, forcing the Ottomans to surrender and opening a new southern front against Austria and Germany in the process. Paying exemplary, if somewhat optimistic, attention to post-war planning, the British decided that once they had deposed the sultan his obvious successor as caliph was Sharif Husein. The sharif, in Storrs's opinion, was ideally suited for the role—"a hereditary spiritual Pope with no temporal power," a puppet who would be propped up by an annual subsidy from the British and whatever revenue he derived from the pilgrimage.[23] But the plan came to nothing. Premature naval action off Gallipoli alerted the Turks to British intentions, and with too little preparation, surprise, or firepower, the mainly Australian and New Zealander force that landed on the peninsula on 25 April suffered terrible casualties and was quickly fought to a standstill.

Searching for a way to end the deadlock, the British commander at Gallipoli cast around for ways to undermine his enemy. As his intelligence suggested that Arab troops composed a substantial proportion of the Ottoman force he faced, he too suggested that the British revive contact with Sharif Husein, as a way of encouraging the Arabs to desert. Kitchener's successor in Cairo, the high commissioner* Sir Henry McMahon, a slight and cautious civil servant, remembered what had happened next: "I was begged by the Foreign Office to take immediate action and draw the Arabs out of the war."[24] At the end of May he contacted Husein, telling the sharif that the British government wanted to communicate secretly with him.[25]

Concerns triggered by the deteriorating situation at Gallipoli would form the crucial backdrop to the negotiations with Husein that followed. Early that September the Foreign Office circulated a secret memorandum that considered for the first time the consequences of a British withdrawal from Gallipoli. The paper warned that if the British abandoned the peninsula, the Ottomans would be free to attack the Suez Canal again. The Turks had already tried to do so once, and intelligence suggested that they would now be able to attack in much greater numbers. In the meantime, Gallipoli had challenged the conventional wisdom that the Ottoman Empire was close to collapse and

---

* The title given to the official appointed by the British government to supervise the government of a British protectorate. In Egypt, McMahon was the first to occupy the post, as Britain made Egypt a protectorate only in 1914, after the Ottomans declared war. Yet, although his title was new, McMahon's role was much the same as Kitchener's (as consul general) had been before.

the British Empire nigh on invincible. The paper's author asked an awful question: Would the Arabs in Egypt, because of their Muslim faith, support the Ottomans if they attacked the canal a second time?

The uncertain strength of the Arab Egyptians' and other Muslim populations' loyalty to the British Empire had exercised the British from the moment when, on 14 November 1914, the Ottoman sultan had made an incendiary announcement. "Know that our state is today at war with the Governments of Russia, England and France and their allies, who are the mortal enemies of Islam," his spokesman dramatically proclaimed from Constantinople. "The commander of the Faithful, the Caliph of the Muslims, summons you to the jihad!"[26]

No matter how far-fetched it seems today, the idea that Muslims around the world might, regardless of their race or sect, respond violently en masse to the sultan's summons was one that mesmerized the British. The most famous evocation of the mood it caused is provided by the novelist John Buchan, who was then working in the Foreign Office in London. He vividly conveyed the tense atmosphere of that time in his thriller *Greenmantle*, which was first published in 1916. Following the call for jihad, in Buchan's spine-tingling phrase, there was "a dry wind blowing through the East and the parched grasses wait the spark."[27]

**The declaration of jihad on 14 November 1914
in Constantinople. The summons sparked British fears
that widespread Muslim unrest might follow.**

With what he described as a "discreditable army of agents," which now included "two amateur, but undeniable and unutterable, strumpets," Storrs tried to chase the rumors wafting through Cairo.[28] In the fraught days of early 1915, when the British were expecting the Turks to attack the Suez Canal at any time, he was passed a leaflet found circulating in the city's bazaar. "Peace be with you, Muslims of Egypt," it declared. "The Ottoman Army is coming to embrace you. Shortly, by the will of God, you will see its sharp swords and glittering bayonets thrust into the hearts of its enemies. . . . Prepare to welcome this Army which is composed of your brethren in blood and creed."[29] The city was awash with gossip: the Turks were ready to invade with four hundred thousand men; they would cross the canal by driving camels laden with dry cement into the water to form a causeway; India was in revolt, and the British army's Indian soldiers on the canal had joined the Turks. Another officer spoke of Cairo's being "honeycombed with seditious propaganda."[30]

Storrs defused the tension with black humor. He warned his servant "that upon the first attempt of him, or of his colleagues, to cut my throat (or even Cheetham's*), their wages [would] be reduced by half: dismissal to follow upon the second offence."[31] The Turks' anticipated attack on the canal in February 1915 did not succeed, and the population of Egypt remained quiescent. The nearest mutinies by Indian troops took place in Rangoon and Singapore, and both were easily quelled. And yet Storrs never discounted the threat of jihad, not least because that summer reports appeared that in the desert west of Cairo the Senussi—a tribe known for its religious fanaticism—were about to begin a disruptive campaign against the British, backed by Ottoman military advisers, guns, and money. The possibility of an uprising continued to stalk the British in Cairo.

With the benefit of hindsight, it is easy to dismiss the jihad as a chimera: frightening but unreal. Yet this is to miss the point. All the British had to go by at the time were perceptions shaped by their thinking, and not the reality, which is only clear in retrospect. Disturbing intelligence at the time—coming from across the Islamic world—seemed to confirm and corroborate existing British beliefs about the power the caliph wielded and the extraordinary unity among Muslims

---

* Milne Cheetham was another British official working in Cairo. He was senior to Storrs.

he commanded, and in this atmosphere the call to jihad explained and connected events that were in truth completely unrelated. There was a further reason, too, which was best encapsulated by *Greenmantle*'s fictional Foreign Office mandarin: "The war must be won or lost in Europe. Yes; but if the East blazes up, our effort will be distracted from Europe and the great *coup* may fail. The stakes are no less than victory and defeat."[32] It was not simply a question of whether the jihad *would* happen. It was whether it *could* happen, and whether the British could afford to choose between beating the Germans and losing the empire, if it did. The knowledge that they could not haunted Storrs and his colleagues throughout the correspondence with Husein that followed next. It would also pressure them into making a grandiose promise that they had no intention of keeping.

2

Will This Do?

By the summer of 1915 Sharif Husein's reservations about doing a deal with the British had faded. Now more worried about his own security, he was suddenly much keener to gain Britain's support. In the seven years since he had been appointed emir, or ruler, of Mecca, he found himself increasingly isolated. He owed his job to the then Sultan Abdul Hamid, but Abdul Hamid had been deposed in 1909, and the new "Young Turks" who took over viewed his appointee in Mecca suspiciously.

Scared of being deposed, Husein rarely left Mecca. He shored up his standing with the city's multinational population with grand displays of largesse, receiving and giving coffee to as many as three thousand Meccans in a day. He also played heavily on his ancestry, thinking that the government would balk at forcing out a descendant of Muhammad. So he left visitors with the impression of being enigmatic and very venerable: "more like an old Imam than a King" was one man's verdict.[1] He would speak slowly yet obscurely and dressed traditionally and austerely in a black robe and tarbush, around which a fine white turban was tightly swirled. The turban and his silky, almost pure white beard framed large brown eyes and a solemn, inscrutable expression. This was an image that softened slightly in private for, when it suited him, Husein would reach across the divide he had fashioned, patting his guests with his hand or putting his arm around their shoulders and calling them Ibni, My Son, or Habibi, My Dear.[2] "Such a nice old man, with a charming twinkle in his eye," wrote one man fooled by Husein's disarming

Sharif Husein ibn Ali
in December 1916. He
was "the most obstinate
old diplomat on earth"
according to D. G. Hogarth.

tactics and the stream of cups of cardamom-flavored coffee and glasses of sweet sherbet that accompanied meetings with the sharif.[3] But as another, more perceptive visitor noted, "for all his benignity and hand-patting and endearments," Husein was "the most obstinate old diplomat on earth and knows to an inch where he has you!"[4] The sharif, he added dryly, was a man who loved "to deal first hand with affairs."[5] For behind Husein's otherworldly façade lurked an obsessive, yet often indecisive, patriarch whose four sons, Ali, Abdullah, Feisal, and Zeid, signed themselves off in letters to him as his "slaves," who had reputedly ordered the murder of some of his opponents and kept others chained to the floor of a foul prison beneath his palace.[6]

Yet Husein knew that his beguiling tactics could do only so much. From Mecca he had been watching warily as, immediately to the east, a powerful rival emerged. Abdul Aziz Ibn Saud was a young, belligerent chieftain who had forged his reputation in 1902 by seizing the central Arabian town of Riyadh—then a collection of adobe forts, today the soulless skyscraper capital of modern Saudi Arabia. From Riyadh, Ibn Saud began to promote Wahhabism, a strongly puritanical form of Islam, across a swath of central Arabia. By 1912 he controlled the central region of Arabia known as the Najd. East of Riyadh the following year he expelled the Turks from the fertile coastal region of Al Hasa. This conquest gave him access to the Persian Gulf. Even before the discovery of oil beneath Al Hasa's sands, it turned him from one of many desert warlords into a major regional power.[7]

By 1915 Husein was increasingly exercised about the spread of Wahhabi ideas. These included a vehement insistence on the equality of all men before Allah, which did not bode well for the deference Husein expected and exploited as a sharif, and a violent dislike of the tombs and shrines dotting the Hijaz that attracted pilgrims but that the Wahhabis believed only encouraged idolatry.[8] Each winter, when the rains replenished the seasonal wells and revived the plants that provided widespread grazing, the Bedu tribesmen from around Mecca on whom Husein counted for support would wander deep into the desert. There they would come into contact with the Saudis, who offered them money, rifles, and land on which to settle if they took up the Wahhabi faith espoused by Ibn Saud. In difficult times the Bedu would naturally gravitate toward the strongest tribal leader. Amid recent drought, and the disease and economic turmoil caused by the arrival of the railway in the Hijaz, Husein worried that to the tribesmen Ibn Saud looked richer and stronger than he.[9] Nor was it long before he found himself being denounced by the Wahhabis as an "infidel."[10]

From the north another threat presented itself. The Ottoman government was putting Husein, as ruler of Mecca and a descendant of Muhammad, under mounting pressure to endorse the sultan's call for jihad. Aware of Ottoman plans to dispense with him if he refused, Husein, to play for time, sent his son Feisal to Constantinople to confront the government and to Damascus to discuss the terms of his support. It was in Damascus that Feisal was quietly approached by members of a secretive Arab cabal. They begged him to ask his father to champion their fight for greater recognition of Arabs within the Ottoman Empire.

Husein was flattered by the request. He was quite willing to adopt the Arab nationalists' modern vocabulary of rights, decentralization, and home rule, if it helped him strengthen his own dynastic struggle in the Hijaz. And he liked the idea of a realm encompassing Syria because it promised the self-sufficiency the Hijaz had never had. Reliant throughout its history on the outside world—especially India—for food and pilgrims, the Hijaz was badly affected by a war in which the British cut off both. Sugar trebled in price; rice and coffee almost disappeared.[11] In India much of the available shipping was requisitioned for military usage by the authorities, who, disturbed by the sultan's call for holy war, were in any case extremely reluctant to allow pilgrims to go anywhere they might pick up subversive ideas. By 1915 the number of pilgrims arriving in the Hijaz from abroad had fallen to less than a quarter of prewar levels, and the revenue they generated correspondingly fell away.[12] Gasoline was still imported to Arabia from abroad, and, as it and timber were scarce, Meccans were reduced to selling off their furniture and the ornately carved wooden doors and fretwork windows of their houses for firewood to feed themselves.[13] These screens shielded their womenfolk indoors from prying eyes: it was a deeply humiliating resort to have to take.

A devout, old-fashioned man who had never traveled farther than Constantinople, Husein believed, like many Muslims, that divine anger lay behind these signs of economic decline. He was convinced that it was the modernizing policies of the Ottoman government, which did not follow the dictates of the Quran, that were causing divine displeasure. Women working in the post office, for instance, whom he had been dismayed to encounter in Constantinople some years earlier, were "an evil that will greatly injure us if it increases."[14] Once he had control of Mecca after the uprising the following year, he would replace the Turkish legal code with religiously inspired sharia law, which sanctioned beheadings and amputations as punishments, and remains in place across the state of Saudi Arabia today. Under this new regime the city's cafés were also forced to shut at prayer times, and, among other things, alcohol and gramophones were banned.[15] But as he contemplated this drastic action to address the problems he perceived, Husein faced a dilemma. Muslim scripture was absolutely clear: to rise against the sultan-caliph was to rebel against Allah Himself.[16] Fortunately for his conscience, the fact that the Young Turk ruling party had seized most of the sultan's powers in 1909 offered him a convenient loophole. He could remain loyal to the sultan, while choosing, as he later put it, "either to please the gang who rule the Ottoman Empire and provoke the anger of God, or to provoke their anger and please God."[17]

Husein made up his mind on 13 July 1915, when, on the first day of Ramadan, he discovered that Ottoman soldiers in the Hijaz had been excused from the obligation of observing the monthlong daytime fast.[18] Afterward he would criticize this violation of one of Islam's five essential acts of faith, but soldiers serving on the front line are excused from the duty of fasting, and it may simply have dawned on him that what he had seen revealed the Ottomans' belief that he was their enemy. The following day he wrote to the British high commissioner in Egypt, Sir Henry McMahon, aggressively repeating the demands made to him by the Syrians his son Feisal had met. To secure Arab friendship the British would have to recognize "the independence of the Arab countries."[19] According to Husein, these included, in today's terms, the entire Arabian Peninsula (except Aden, which was then British), Israel, Jordan, Iraq, Lebanon, and Syria, as well as a horizontal sliver of southern Turkey running between the Mediterranean and the Iranian border. Britain would also have to agree to an Arab caliphate, receiving preferential economic treatment in return. In a covering note, which more accurately reflected the weakness of his position, Husein's son Abdullah pleaded for the resumption of the annual tributes of grain traditionally sent by the government of Egypt to the Hijaz for the poor of Mecca and Medina.

When he received Husein's letter in August, McMahon refused to take its demands seriously. The sharif's "pretensions are in every way exaggerated, no doubt considerably beyond his hope of acceptance," he informed the British foreign secretary, Sir Edward Grey, "but it seems very difficult to treat with him in detail without seriously discouraging him."[20] Worried about either overcommitting the British government or disappointing Husein, McMahon decided that the safest option was to procrastinate. He delegated to Ronald Storrs the task of drafting a response, telling Husein that it was too early to discuss the future settlement of an area still under Ottoman control.

What McMahon's dilatory answer lacked in encouragement, Storrs tried to make up for with flowery style: "To the excellent and well-born Sayyid, the descendant of the Sharifs, the Crown of the Proud, Scion of Muhammad's Tree and Branch of the Qurayshite Trunk," the opening of his reply began.[21] Husein, however, saw through this wordy greeting and, in his answer, accused McMahon of stalling: "The fact is," he replied, "the proposed frontiers and boundaries represent not the suggestions of one individual whose claim might well await the conclusion of the War, but the demands of our people who believe that

Sir Henry McMahon, the
British high commissioner
in Egypt. He offered Husein
a vaguely defined empire
assuming that the
commitment would never
have to be honored.

those frontiers form the minimum necessary to the establishment of the new order for which they are striving."[22]

Husein's dramatic claim to represent wider Arab demands, which was based only on the approach his son Feisal had received in Damascus, might have sounded ridiculous had it not been for the extraordinary coincidence that then occurred. Just before Husein's reply reached McMahon, a young Arab deserter from the Ottoman army arrived in Cairo. Muhammad al Faruqi was a junior staff officer at Gallipoli who had given himself up to the British. When he was interviewed by the director of military intelligence in Cairo, the genial Bertie Clayton, Faruqi claimed that nine out of ten Arab officers in the Ottoman army were members of a powerful and well-funded underground nationalist movement that was in the process of deciding whether to back the British or the Germans, depending on who would offer them more. Complete rubbish though this was—there were, it has since been established, never more than ninety active Arab nationalists within the Ottoman army, and they had already been widely dispersed by the suspicious Ottoman high command—the plausibility of the network Faruqi described soared when he disclosed that he knew that McMahon was negotiating with Husein.[23] The British were unnerved. Crucially, they convinced themselves that the very invisibility of the Arab movement was proof of its sophistication rather than an indication of its insignificance. Moreover, they were frightened that a call to back the Germans from an influential fellow Arab like Husein might galvanize the Arab Egyptian population, when the Turkish summons to jihad so far had not.

There were already concerns in Cairo that the government in London was not treating the threat posed by the jihad seriously enough. When the general staff asked Clayton for a note on the information he had gleaned from Faruqi, Clayton recognized he had been given a golden chance to make this point. "I shall take the opportunity of rubbing in the fact that if we definitely refuse to consider the aspirations of the Arabs," he wrote, "we are running a grave risk of throwing them into the arms of our enemies which would mean that the jihad which so far has been a failure would probably become a reality."[24]

This dire warning from the normally imperturbable Clayton could not be ignored, and it was wired straightaway to Kitchener in London. "You must do your best to prevent any alienation of the Arabs' traditional loyalty to England," Kitchener replied the following day.[25] Then, on 18 October, McMahon received Husein's reply. Husein's claim in it to be the spokesman of "our people" and Faruqi's story corroborated one another, and McMahon was forced to reconsider his previously dismissive view of the sharif. Convinced that the Arab network that Faruqi had described existed and that its leader, Sharif Husein, was on the brink of deciding whom to back, he immediately wired the Foreign Office to say that Husein was unhappy with his reply and that he had no choice but to negotiate. McMahon met Faruqi right away to discuss what terms the Arabs might be willing to accept. "From further conversation with Faruqi," he told Grey in another telegram that day, "it appears evident that Arab party are at parting of the ways and unless we can give them immediate assurance of nature to satisfy them they will throw themselves into the hands of Germany."[26]

McMahon's stark warning that the Arabs were on the verge of backing the Germans had an immediate effect in London. When the Dardanelles committee, an unwieldy coalition of British politicians steering the war effort, next met at 10 Downing Street, on 20 October, it was forced to decide how McMahon should respond to Husein. Circumstances conspired against a careful consideration of the problem. The prime minister was already ill with overwork. The loyalty of the Arabs was an arcane intrusion into an agenda dominated at that time by an argument over whether conscription should be introduced, which was tearing his party apart. It seems as if it was only shortly before discussion of the matter that day that the foreign secretary, Sir Edward Grey, hurriedly drafted instructions for McMahon. Grey too was suffering from the strain of war. His eyesight was failing, and since the outbreak of hostilities he had increasingly doubted whether he could make much difference to the war effort. The urgency of McMahon's request offered him the chance to pass the buck.

I found Grey's brief handwritten advice among the papers in Britain's National Archive, at Kew in the suburbs of southwest London. "The important thing is to give our assurances that will prevent Arabs from being alienated, and I must leave you discretion in the matter as it is urgent and there is not time to discuss an exact formula," Grey proposed telling McMahon.[27] "The simplest plan would be to give an assurance of Arab independence saying that we will proceed at once to discuss boundaries if they will send representatives for that purpose, but if something more precise than this is required you can give it." But it is Grey's hastily scribbled pencil message above these words, which he must have added just before he passed the note down the table to his colleague Kitchener, that is most revealing: "Lord K," it reads, "will this do? EG."

Kitchener evidently thought it would. After the meeting the two politicians had a short and very British discussion. Should they pass the sharif "warm" or "cordial" assurances? Kitchener, who had met Husein's son Abdullah before the war, favored "warm"; Grey, who had not, preferred the starchy "cordial." Grey's view prevailed. Later that day he wired McMahon, instructing him to give the sharif cordial assurances. With this essential detail covered, he delegated McMahon the responsibility for coming to an arrangement with Husein.

McMahon cannot have been pleased to receive Grey's telegram. Regarding himself as a wartime caretaker (in a war that was initially expected to be short), he had studiously avoided taking on more responsibility than he had to. Instead, he relied heavily on his advisers, one of whom described him as, with one exception, "quite the laziest man I have met."[28] Other men who knew him were only slightly more charitable. "He is a nice man and I like him very much, but his ability is of a very ordinary type," observed another former colleague.[29] Despite these reservations, McMahon had now been given what Clayton interpreted as "a free hand."[30]

One British official had some advice to offer on the conduct of the negotiations that Grey had authorized McMahon to open: "the position must be clearly understood from both the French and the Arab side from the outset, or we shall be heading straight for serious trouble."[31] But McMahon neither informed the French of his dealings with the sharif nor took Grey's advice to ask for representatives from the sharif for face-to-face talks. And most importantly, he quite deliberately never made it clear beyond doubt what he was offering to the Arabs.[32] Clever as this seemed at the time, this tactic would come back to bite the British, because, to this day, the meaning of McMahon's correspondence with Husein—particularly with regard to Palestine—continues to be the subject of a very bitter debate.

In a letter dated 24 October 1915, McMahon gave Husein a hazy declaration that Britain would recognize the majority of the area he demanded, but which excluded two of its most fertile zones. One was the bridgehead at the northern end of the Persian Gulf, which was already occupied by the Indian army. The other was a sketchily defined coastal portion of Syria. On Grey's advice he purposefully kept the boundaries of this area vague and added a further general qualification, the aim of which he then explained to Grey. "I am not aware of the extent of French claims in Syria, nor of how far His Majesty's Government have agreed to recognize them," he reminded the foreign secretary two days after writing to Husein:

Hence, while recognizing the towns of Damascus, Hama, Homs and Aleppo as being within the circle of Arab countries, I have endeavoured to provide for possible French pretensions for those places by a general modification to the effect that His Majesty's Government can only give assurances in regard to these territories "in which she can act without detriment to the interests of her ally France."[33]

This final phrase was a carefully crafted ambiguity, with which McMahon and Storrs were clearly both delighted. Although from the Arab point of view, it could be read as a confirmation that Britain was free to commit Syria to the Arabs, in reality the phrase was a qualification that made McMahon's offer provisional on the resolution of France's expansive, but as yet undefined, territorial ambitions in the Levant. These, as he would discover six months later, were about to be thrashed out, but McMahon was happy to remain ignorant of their scope so that he could preserve his ability to make an offer to Husein that, as he implied to Grey, he never expected the British would have to honor in full.[34]

McMahon thought that he could afford to be vague, because he believed that his work was a temporary expedient rather than a long-term commitment. It was an assumption that was widely shared. "After all, what harm can our acceptance of his [Husein's] proposals do?" asked Sir Reginald Wingate, the pocket-sized Machiavelli who was both governor-general of Sudan and sirdar, or commander, of the Egyptian army. "If the embryonic Arab State comes to nothing, all our promises vanish and we are absolved from them—if the Arab State becomes a reality, we have quite sufficient safeguards to control it. . . . In other words the cards seem to be in our hands and we have only to play them carefully."[35]

Similar assumptions underlay the negotiations over Syria that were about to start in London. The secret deal reached by the British and French governments, the Anglo-French agreement, is better known by the names of its negotiators, Sykes and Picot, who spent the winter of 1915–16 carving up the Middle East between them. Sir Mark Sykes was a rambunctious young Tory member of Parliament and witty caricaturist. He had sealed his reputation as "a world-famous authority on all Eastern questions" with the publication of a doorstopper history of the Ottoman Empire earlier in 1915.[36] He came to the negotiating table wanting only "a belt of English-controlled country between the Sharif of Mecca and the French" to keep Husein, whom he favored as the next caliph, out of the clutches of Paris.[37] His counterpart, François Georges-Picot, was the tall, thin former consul in Beirut who had been forced to leave his post in a hurry at the outbreak of war in 1914. He simply wanted Syria, and proved a tough negotiator whose tactic was "to give nothing and to claim everything," according to one British

The British member of Parliament Sir Mark Sykes.
On behalf of the British government he secretly
promised Lebanon and Syria to the French.

observer.[38] Picot flatly told the British that "France would never consent to offer independence to the Arabs."[39]

Picot's intransigence gave the British a headache, but one that was simply cured by Sykes, who said privately that his aim was "to get [the] Arabs to concede as much as possible to [the] French."[40] So, at the beginning of 1916 with Picot, Sykes overlaid a veneer of imperial influence, if not actual control, on the area that McMahon had just committed to Husein. The Sykes-Picot agreement parted this territory into northern and southern areas under French and British protection, respectively, which were divided by a diagonal line, "from the 'e' in Acre to the last 'k' in Kirkuk," to quote the words Sykes used as he sliced his finger across the map.[41] Adjacent to each area would be zones of control where Britain and France would be free to establish "such direct or indirect administration or control as they desire."[42] The "Blue" French zone filled the Syrian coastal area disputed by Husein and mushroomed north into Anatolia, while the "Red" British zone capped the Persian Gulf like the head of an unlit match. At Russian insistence Palestine would be internationally administered. It was designated the color brown. This scheme attracted skepticism from some.

"It seems to me we are rather in the position of the hunters who divided up the skin of the bear before they had killed it," the director of military intelligence in London remarked.[43]

The incongruity of the Sykes-Picot agreement with what McMahon had already offered Husein has been traditionally and charitably explained away as "a case of the left hand, Sir Mark Sykes, not knowing what the right hand, Lord Kitchener, had promised the Arabs."[44] But this is nonsense, for it is clear that Sykes knew exactly what had been promised to Husein from Cairo, and he disregarded it. As one entry in the index of his book—"Arab character: see also Treachery"[45]—lightheartedly makes clear, Sykes saw little need to keep faith with the Arabs, whose territorial ambitions he did not expect to be realized. "I am confident," he told a colleague, "that the suzerainty of the Sharif in Arabia proper will in practice be purely honorary."[46] Low expectations of the likelihood of Arab success meant that worries that McMahon's and Sykes's respective commitments were contradictory could be ignored—for the time being.

Husein knew nothing of the horse-trading going on in London. He was more immediately preoccupied by the threats posed by his rival Ibn Saud and by an imminent Ottoman crackdown on his powers than by the exact extent of a future Arab state in Syria, and because of this he made an unsuitable spokesman for the Syrian Arabs. Softened by the gift of £20,000 that McMahon dispatched with a further letter in December, Husein replied to McMahon that, though he still did not accept the British exclusion of the Syrian coast, he did not want to strain the Anglo-French alliance and that the dispute could be resolved after the war. For all his cunning, Husein implicitly believed throughout that an Englishman's word was his bond. "Great Britain may rest assured, that we shall adhere to our resolve . . . which was made known to Storrs—that able and accomplished man—two years ago," declared the sharif, in a hint at his violent plans: "We are only waiting for an opportunity in consonance with our situation."[47]

Then, on 18 February, believing that the Ottomans were about to send troops south to deal with him, Husein appealed to McMahon for food, £50,000 in gold, weapons, and ammunition. In return he promised that his son Feisal could raise a revolt of "not less than 100,000 people" in Syria.[48] A fortnight later Husein wrote again, raising this estimate to 250,000. Showing vastly unrealistic expectations of British resources, he also called on the British to land on the Syrian coast to help the uprising, and he asked them to blockade the Hijaz coast, hoping that, by blaming this action on the Ottomans' presence in the region, he could bully the merchants of Jeddah—who were firmly pro-Ottoman—into supporting him. For Clayton, Husein's spontaneous approach to McMahon was a crucial turning point. "The Sharif has definitely decided that his interests lie with the Allies and not with the Turks," he wrote at the beginning of March, before adding a telling indication of the limited importance he attached to the promises McMahon had made: "Whatever may be the outcome of the negotiations, it seems they have at least had the effect of preventing him from throwing in his lot on the side of our enemies."[49]

3

The Uprising Starts and Stutters

Mehmed Zia was crouched on the floor of the town hall in Mecca because it was too dangerous to stand up. Now and then bullets splurted through the building's tall wooden shutters and spat over his head. They left dust in the air, splinters of silvery sun-bleached timber on the floor, and an unfamiliar constellation of holes through which the molten daylight squinted. It was early in the morning of 10 June 1916, at the epicenter of the Muslim world.

The Holy Mosque in Mecca. Worshippers were killed
and the central building, the Kaaba, was slightly damaged
in the fighting that followed the outbreak of the revolt.

Zia, the Turkish commander of Ottoman forces in the holy city, considered his situation. Three weeks earlier, news had reached Mecca that the Ottomans' enemy, the British, had just begun to blockade the Red Sea. Reports of Britain's sudden move had sparked a panic about food in Mecca. The grand mufti, Mecca's highest authority on religious matters, then issued an apocalyptic warning to the inhabitants that they would starve unless they threw the Turks out of their city. Not entirely surprisingly, relations between the Ottomans and the townspeople then deteriorated abruptly. Gunfire had finally erupted at half past three that morning, just after the call to prayer at dawn had ululated through the city's close streets.

During the winter Zia might have had enough troops to stop the violence. But it was now the height of an Arabian summer, and over half the Ottoman soldiers who normally garrisoned Mecca were taking refuge from the ferocious summer heat forty miles east and four thousand feet higher in the mountain resort of Taif, up among the barren, serrated mountains of the Hijaz. Down in Mecca, where by midafternoon the temperature might reach forty-five degrees Celsius, Zia had been left behind to preserve order with about a thousand men. Almost all of these were across town in barracks on the Jeddah road, but there was also a handful of soldiers in the Jiyad fortress, which dominated the city from the south. However, sometime before dawn the previous day the water to the fortress and the telegraph cables to Jeddah, Medina, and Taif had all been cut. So too, Zia now discovered, had the telephone line from the barracks. When he resorted to sending orders by hand to his forces there, his messenger was shot within yards of leaving the town hall. The man now sprawled dead, his blood soaking into the earthen street outside.

Having gingerly examined the bullet holes perforating his office, Zia decided that the gunfire originated from the amphitheater of rocky, ocher hills above the city and that the Bedu, the wild nomadic tribesmen of the desert, were consequently responsible. Even by the low standards of Arabia, life in the Hijaz was especially violent—"The only things made in Mecca are swords, daggers and slippers for Arabs," one visitor remarked—and unrest among the tribes was commonplace, especially since the Hijaz Railway had reached Medina eight years earlier.[1] Since then disturbances by the Bedu had punctuated life in the region with growing frequency, but Zia knew that some concessions to the tribesmen would normally ensure a cease-fire. So he tugged the telephone toward himself to ring Number One Mecca and speak to Sharif Husein.[2]

As his telephone number suggested, if anyone could call the tribesmen off, it was Husein. The emir, or governor, of Mecca, Husein was not only respected as a sharif but feared for having quietly orchestrated the local tribesmen's violent campaign to stop the railway's being extended from Medina to Mecca, to which the Ottomans had given in. And averse as he was to the forces of progress, he nevertheless loved using the telephone.

"I called up the Emir," Zia remembered, "and asked what this all meant, saying at the same time, 'The Bedouins have revolted against the Government; find a way out.'"[3]

"Of course we shall," Husein replied enigmatically, before cutting Zia off.

It had been Husein himself, it later emerged, who had fired the shot that had tipped the holy city into chaos that morning. But though he may have had his finger on the trigger, his arm had been forced by a series of events to the north in Syria: he had been frightened into action prematurely.

Husein had become suspicious after Enver Pasha, the minister for war, and Jemal Pasha, the governor of Syria, took a train from Damascus to Medina that February, three months earlier, to press him for the troops he had promised for the jihad. Both men hoped that when they attacked the Suez Canal again, an Arab force within the Ottoman army would destabilize the Arab population of Cairo. Enver also explained his plans to send troops south through the Hijaz to Yemen to encourage an uprising among the Muslims in the Horn of Africa, which might assist the German forces fighting the British for control of East Africa. Their joint mission smacked of desperation, but Husein saw it as a threat.

When Jemal realized that no Arab troops would be forthcoming, his patience snapped. From letters seized when Picot had hurriedly left the French consulate in Beirut, he had known since the beginning of the war that some Arab nationalists had asked for French assistance to help them liberate Syria. But although he authorized the arrest of some of those implicated by the letters, he had taken no further action. To have done so, he later explained, would have undermined his campaign to win Arab support for the jihad. When it dawned on him that Husein had no intention of honoring his earlier promise, Jemal decided to take action against the nationalists. The first, a Christian Arab, was convicted of treason and hanged that April. Then, in May, Jemal ordered the trial of a larger group of well-known, and mostly Muslim, Arabs.

By now Husein had received a promise of sorts, money, and a first clandestine shipment of arms from the British. Wrongly believing that he also enjoyed widespread support in Syria, he rallied to the Arab nationalists' cause and overreached himself. He wired Enver with a provocative set of demands he wanted satisfied before he would support a holy war with troops. "If you want me to remain quiet," Jemal remembered Husein saying, "you must recognize my independence in the whole of the Hijaz—from Tabuk to Mecca—and create me hereditary prince there. You must also drop the prosecution of the guilty Arabs and proclaim a general amnesty for Syria and Iraq."[4]

Designed to provoke though it probably was, Husein's telegram was a bad miscalculation, based on his belief that his support was stronger than it was. It merely hardened the Ottomans' resolve and gave away his own intentions before he was ready to revolt. Early on 6 May twenty-one Arabs, convicted of association with the nationalist movements, were hanged in public in Beirut and Damascus. The executions convinced Husein that he could delay no longer. Suspecting that his son Feisal, who had been acting in Damascus as his envoy to the Ottomans, was now in danger, he recalled him to the Hijaz. Feisal made his excuses and hurriedly left for Mecca.

Events moved quickly after that. Jemal, who later said that he had underestimated Husein, ordered Turkish officials in Mecca to make local grandees swear an oath of allegiance and hand out money to various sheikhs—supposedly as gifts to the poor—in a thinly veiled effort to buy tribal loyalties. The British blockade of Jeddah, which began on 15 May, provoked uproar in the Hijaz and made that task much harder. To cope with panic buying, the Turks first shut and then—under pressure from Husein—reopened the city's main bazaar, a volte-face that not only enflamed local ill-feeling but revealed their own weakness. On 22 May, Jemal, who was also the commander of the Ottoman Fourth Army, based at Damascus, ordered Fakhreddin Pasha, who led the army's Twelfth Corps, to move to Medina. A zealous, intimidating man, Fakhri, as he was known to the British, had infamously been involved in the organization of the massacres of Christian Armenians in southern Anatolia the year before. He was proud to have been given responsibility for the holy city, and he promised he would report on the situation once he arrived.

Reacting to the news that Fakhri and his men were on their way to Medina, Husein sent a staccato message to McMahon, saying that he was about to revolt and asking for more money. This news, which arrived in Cairo on 23 May, "caused equal consternation and surprise," the director of the Arab Bureau, David Hogarth, admitted afterward, because "not nearly enough material and sinews of war had been put into [the] Hijaz, nor were we ready to co-operate in any other part of the Arab area."[5] Part of the reason for this was that the Arab Bureau's efforts to that point had been focused on persuading Husein to revolt but not on the logistical requirements that lay beyond. Partly too, Clayton was worried that Husein would simply waste any additional money he received on an uprising in Syria, which, he felt, was doomed to failure. He wanted to see concrete results before providing more assistance.[6] McMahon agreed and sent Storrs to the Hijaz with £10,000 in gold, which he was to hand over only when he was convinced that the revolt had indeed begun. The sharif's older sons were all hastily preparing to attack the principal cities of the Hijaz, and it was left to the youngest, Zeid, to meet Storrs at a brief rendezvous on a desolate beach not far from Jeddah. Zeid did not impress Storrs greatly—"obviously the Benjamin of the family," Storrs sniffed—but he convinced the British diplomat that the revolt had begun the previous day in Medina.[7] Storrs handed over the money he had brought and, in a cavalier moment, removed his gold watch and fastened it to Zeid's wrist, before gratefully returning to the safety of his ship offshore, where he composed a telegram to Cairo.

> Satisfactory meeting with Zeid and his cousin this morning. Rising began yesterday Monday at Medina but as all communications in Hijaz are cut no news. Other towns to rise on Saturday. Arabs hope to induce 800 Turks at Jeddah, 1,000 at Mecca, and 1,200 at Taif to surrender; otherwise they will kill them. . . . Please dispatch immediately 50,000 pounds now definitely promised but not payable until revolt satisfactorily ascertained to have begun.[8]

But the rising was not going according to plan. Fakhri had warned Damascus that trouble was imminent three days earlier. He was ready for the Arabs' attack when it finally came on 5 June. There was not much support for Husein or his family in a city that, owing to the new railway, was as close in spirit to Damascus as it was in miles to Mecca. And, unlike Mecca, the old city of Medina was walled, more self-reliant for food, and well defended by thousands of troops who were supported by artillery and machine guns in concrete, ziggurat-like forts dotted around the plain surrounding the city. Against these, the camel-mounted tribesmen led by Ali, Husein's eldest son, had an array of antique flintlocks and rifles, often with twisted barrels or held together with wire. Moreover, the elderly Japanese rifles the British had supplied in May belatedly revealed a disconcerting tendency to burst on firing.[9] Some of the ammunition turned out to be the wrong caliber. Ali and his men were forced to retreat.

To the north of Medina, Feisal tried to attack the railway connecting the city with the north, but, with no explosives to hand, all his tribesmen could do was tear up the track or pile rocks on the rails.[10] As the Ottoman government had hoped to extend the railway farther southward, there was a large hoard of track and ties in Medina. Using these where necessary, engineers in an armored train quickly repaired the damage, so that specialist reinforcements could be dispatched to the city.[11] Feisal joined Ali a safe distance from the city. They had no money to pay the tribesmen. To lend the opposite impression, Feisal later admitted, he had filled a chest with stones, and had it locked and guarded constantly.[12]

In Taif, above Mecca, the uprising also stalled. By the time Husein's son Abdullah arrived there on 9 June, the town was buzzing with rumors that violence was imminent. Many people had packed their belongings and were hurrying away. The Turks were fortifying the town, digging trenches outside the walls. Against advice Abdullah went to see Ghalib Pasha, the *vali*, or governor, of the Hijaz, in his office, leaving two friends outside the door. "If there was any trouble I was to shoot the *vali* in the room, and they were to dispatch anyone who tried to interfere outside," he wrote in his memoirs.[13] He tried to convince Ghalib that he was on a tribal raid beyond the town, but the *vali* did not believe him, turning gray and mumbling that he wished he had stayed in Mecca. Abdullah's attack shortly after midnight failed to capture Taif, but it did succeed in stopping the Turkish there from going down to Mecca to help their colleagues. As darkness fell the following day, Abdullah recalled, "we lit bonfires on the hills and kept up a continuous shouting and beating of drums to make the enemy believe that the tribes were gathering in great numbers."[14] The city would not be captured by the Arabs until Ghalib finally surrendered on 22 September.

The attack on Jeddah went rather better. On 9 June two British ships, the *Fox* and the *Hardinge*, arrived off the port, having been alerted by Storrs's telegram to Cairo that an attack was imminent. In a reflection of the low priority that British commanders in Egypt gave to helping Husein, neither vessel represented the cream of the British fleet: according to her short and energetic commander, "Ginger" Boyle, the *Fox* was "almost the slowest and oldest ship commanded by a Captain in the Navy," while the *Hardinge* had been lent from the Royal Indian Marine.[15] As planned, at nine o'clock that night both ships turned on their searchlights and began to fire the first of over seven hundred shells at Turkish positions outside the town. Then, early the following day, a force of about four thousand local tribesmen attacked the beleaguered port. "We were horrified at the Arab method of attack—they were simply advancing in a mass, quite openly some of them firing their rifles in the air," a British sailor recalled. "The Turks simply waited and then poured a withering fire into their ranks."[16] Trying to help the Arabs regain the initiative, the British became unwittingly embroiled in the port's highly factional politics when Boyle invited a local tribal leader aboard the *Fox* to point out possible targets inside the town that he could shell. Boyle became suspicious when the man identified some unlikely looking buildings. "Months after I heard that my picturesque sheikh was in reality a merchant of the town," he later wrote, surmising that the man "had taken advantage of this opportunity to rid himself of trade rivals."[17]

Jeddah surrendered to the Arabs on 16 June, but fifty miles east, the Turks' resistance in Mecca proved much tougher. Although most of the holy city was in the tribesmen's hands and at the town hall the Ottoman commander Zia was forced to surrender, his troops held out in their barracks and in the Jiyad fortress that overlooked the city. It was from here shortly afterward that they began to bombard the Kaaba, the sacred stone cube at the center of the Holy Mosque. The first shell left a footlong gash in the building. The second set fire to the kiswa, the Kaaba's black covering embroidered with extracts from the Quran.[18] Several worshippers in the central open area of the mosque were killed by flying shrapnel.

News of the bloodshed in the Hijaz quickly spread across the Muslim world. A report of British involvement in the violence was badly received by British officials in India, who had pointedly never endorsed the policy the Arab Bureau was following with the sharif. From his office overlooking the emerald lawns of Simla—summer capital of the government of India—the viceroy, Lord Chelmsford, dispatched an angry telegram to London on 13 June. "We are greatly disturbed," he wrote, using one of the ruder phrases the strangled intercourse of British diplomacy would permit, "by report of British naval activity off Jeddah," and asked for the news to be carefully suppressed in light of the impact it might have on Muslim opinion. "It appears very difficult to reconcile action taken with the pledge formally given," he observed, referring to the promise Britain had made not to violate the Hijaz when war broke out. He was, he added, opposed to any further action that would break the spirit of Britain's earlier commitment.[19]

In Cairo, Ronald Storrs took the opposite view. Dismissing what he called the "ill-informed criticism of Simla," he wanted the news of the revolt spread widely because it "struck what should be a fatal blow at the religious prestige of the Turk."[20] Only if the split between Sharif Husein and the sultan were made public would Muslims question whether, if Husein, scion of the Prophet and ruler of Mecca, had rejected the sultan's call, the jihad could possibly be justified. So he ignored the Government of India and on 21 June quietly leaked the story to the press.

Later the same day Reuters reported that an uprising had begun in the Hijaz. The "Startling" news of the "Great Arab Revolt," as Storrs had portrayed Husein's local uprising, was reported in the *Times* the following day, though British involvement was, naturally, not admitted. Faced with the now impossible task of stopping the story from seeping into the subcontinent, two days later the Government of India was forced to confirm that a rebellion in Mecca had broken out.

Just as Lord Chelmsford had feared they would, Muslims in India reacted vociferously. On the volatile North–West Frontier, the governor reported how Husein was being publicly cursed in the mosques for bringing violence on the Hijaz by revolting.[21] On 27 June in Lucknow, the All-India Muslim League met and condemned the sharif's action with a vitriolic resolution, the strength of which took Chelmsford aback. More disturbingly still, the Bombay Muslim League suggested that Husein's actions had given real cause for jihad.

The Muslim press called on the British not to intervene. "In these circumstances," the Lahore newspaper *Kisan* declared on 30 June, "the utmost that we can expect from our Government is that it will avoid making any interference in the matter and will take no step to encourage the Sharif of Mecca."[22] Later the same day in Jeddah the British landed explosives, 3,000 more rifles, six machine guns, 1.2 million rounds of ammunition, almost 600 tons of food, and a first batch of mountain guns. With these McMahon sent Egyptian gunners. "Care of course would be taken not to send anyone with religious scruples," he reassured the Foreign Office.[23]

It was the stealthy arrival of this Egyptian artillery in the Hijaz that broke the deadlock in Mecca. After five days of being pounded, the remaining Turkish soldiers in the barracks in Mecca surrendered on 10 July, exactly a month after the uprising began. Battling the summer heat—"almost unbearable," in their commander's words—it would take the Egyptians a further ten weeks to force a Turkish surrender at Taif.[24]

Lord Kitchener did not live to hear the news that the revolt had broken out. On 5 June, the same day that the uprising began in Medina, the ship on which he was sailing to Russia sank off northern Scotland, taking the patron of the Arabs' uprising with it. His body was never found. Kitchener's abrupt death deprived the Arabs of their greatest advocate in London; without his influence, other, more skeptical politicians began to question why Britain should be embroiled in the revolt at all. In Cairo these questions were to start a crisis.

4

The Blame Game Begins

For almost three weeks after the outbreak of the uprising, the British in Cairo remained under the false impression that all was going well in the Hijaz. On 1 July, T. E. Lawrence wrote to his mother apologizing that he was not allowed to tell her much about his job, but enclosing a copy of the Reuters telegram reporting the outbreak of the revolt to give her some idea. "It has taken a year and a half to do, but now is going very well," he believed.[1] He and his colleagues trusted rumors that Feisal had captured Medina, that his tribesmen had torn up a hundred miles of the railway, and that a second uprising had begun, in Syria.[2] As it started to become clear that nothing of the sort had happened, on 25 June the Arab Bureau issued a shrill analysis of what might follow if the sharif failed. "Accusations would be made that we had callously exploited Islam for our own purposes: we should be looked upon as a faithless friend and a feeble enemy," its author warned. "Our position in the Mohammedan world would deteriorate and other most unfortunate results might follow."[3]

The reality that the revolt was not the sudden, successful coup the British had wanted it to be threw another problem into sharp relief. Beyond the enormous, one-off shipment of arms and food that had been landed at Jeddah on 30 June, no thought had been given to sustaining the sharif's supporters in the future. "Don't start a battle you can't supply" is a basic rule of military strategy.[4] Yet that was precisely what the British had just done.

The fundamental problem was that no one man in Cairo was responsible for the revolt, which would need military support to achieve the complex political ends the British wanted from it. The high commissioner, Sir Henry McMahon, had been tasked only with coming to an agreement with Husein that would encourage him to take up arms. But as a diplomat reporting to the Foreign Office and not a soldier, he had no resources at his disposal to assist the uprising; even if he had, as the revolt descended into crisis, he wished he had never gotten involved at all. He was unable and unwilling to solve the growing crisis.

The military commander in Egypt, Sir Archibald Murray, was able but unwilling. A thoughtful, highly regarded officer, he had arrived that January charged with defending the Suez Canal and Egypt as well as reorganizing the army that had by now retreated from Gallipoli. He had the resources McMahon lacked and could have diverted supplies to help Husein, but his orders were to protect the canal with the smallest possible force, and he was warned by his boss in London, Sir William Robertson, not to intervene. As chief of the Imperial General Staff, Robertson was the overall British military commander and the prime minister's main adviser on military strategy. A very determined man, who remains the only British soldier to have risen from the lowest rank to the highest (he retired a field marshal), Robertson vehemently opposed any operation that would distract the war effort from the western front. In this, Husein's revolt could not have been worse timed, for it coincided almost perfectly with the run-up to the Somme offensive, an operation of unprecedented scale that was about to start in France. "My sole object is to win the war," Robertson later stated bluntly, "and we shall not do that in the Hijaz."[5]

The Arab Bureau, which stood awkwardly astride the political and military divide, had been given some responsibility for assisting Husein. But though its staff members were willing, they were proving to be incompetent. Experts on the region though they may have been, the intelligence officers were hopeless at logistics. From Jeddah, when only a tenth the number of bags of rice that the sharif had asked for arrived, Storrs's agent Ruhi commented plaintively, "It seem[s] that one nought was dropped off when calculating them. It is a pity to have things done like that."[6] The difficulty of communicating by encoded wireless telegraph with Jeddah was undoubtedly a factor in this type of error, but the bureau at this time was evidently in chaos. "The last two weeks we have lived in the middle of a storm of telegrams and conferences and excursions," Lawrence wrote in Cairo at the beginning of July.[7] "Unfortunately our clerical staff consists almost entirely of ladies who are not used to Government work," the bureau's deputy director admitted.[8] The secretaries at the bureau do not all appear to have been employed for their shorthand. "One of our typists, Miss MacKenzie, was the success of the evening," Hogarth told his wife, of a dance held later that year.[9] Of the others, Miss Clay was "very pretty," Miss Mason's qualifications included a spell as "a show-off skating girl for a rink," while Miss James, a "very cheeky" "honeypot," had instantly fallen for one of the new officers who then joined the bureau to improve logistics.[10] It took a long time for the situation to improve. "The confusion last month was great," the bureau's deputy director confessed that November, adding that his staff were learning—although "by experience of many mistakes."[11]

The aesthetics of the bureau's female staff and the excuses made on their behalf cut little ice with General Murray, who complained that the bureau was failing to send him copies of telegrams keeping him in touch with what was happening. As it became clear to him that the British were "in for a long, costly and difficult business" in the Hijaz, his willingness to offer even marginal support evaporated, and he instructed his staff, who apparently regarded the revolt as "a mess they do not wish to be mixed up in," not to help the Arab Bureau.[12] With the bureau's, and his own, competence under question, Clayton was forced to head to London to lobby for support.

Neither the civil nor the military authorities wanted to take control of matters, and the Arab Bureau, though willing, relied on ebbing military support. At a meeting of all three in Cairo on 28 June, Murray recommended to McMahon and Hogarth, the Arab Bureau's director and Lawrence's mentor, that while McMahon should retain political direction for Britain's involvement in the Hijaz, another man should take responsibility for the military aspects. The new recruit was Sir Reginald Wingate, the golf-playing, overspending, and freewheeling governor-general of the Sudan. Although this division of responsibility would prove to be unsustainable, Wingate's outspoken willingness that he would do whatever it took to ensure that the sharif succeeded seemed exactly what was needed at this moment.

An unabashed imperialist, Wingate had enthusiastically supported British interference in the Hijaz from the start. He saw the revolt as an opportunity for Britain to establish itself as the patron of the Arabs and for him to demonstrate his own abilities, which in his opinion were considerable yet not always appreciated in London. Obsequious to those in authority, overbearing to his juniors, who referred to him as "Master," Wingate was a man of modest talents who through hard work had elbowed his way to the top of the mediocre Egyptian army, of which he was now sirdar, or commander in chief. The governor-generalship, based in Sudan's capital, Khartoum, was his reward for service as the chief intelligence officer in Kitchener's successful reconquest of the region in 1898. It was an outpost so remote that Wingate took the view that he could do what he liked and inform London, if he was successful, afterward.

Wingate, characteristically, had not waited for permission before taking action. Fed up with being "bombarded with telegrams from all parts, none of which quite tally with each other," he had a fortnight earlier dispatched one of his officials, Colonel Cyril Wilson, to establish exactly what was going on in Jeddah.[13] The delivery of the massive shipment of food and weapons late in June gave Wilson an excuse to go ashore. Jeddah, which unlike Mecca or Medina was a commercial and not a

A typical street in Jeddah in October 1916. The port's merchants remained wary of Sharif Husein and the Bedu, despite the renewed trade that followed the revolt.

holy city, was clustered around its central market, but under the saggy awnings in the bazaar there was almost nothing to buy. "Everyone stares at you fixedly and silently," noted another visitor, who described Jeddah as a "strange uncanny place which breathes danger and death."[14]

I know the feeling. Unusually for modern Saudi Arabia, the old quarter of Jeddah today retains a strong sense of the dilapidated feel that Wilson must have experienced ninety years ago. The town's tall houses, white like ivory, list unsteadily: dead coral, though abundant, has never been an ideal building material. Their overbearing teak balconies, intricate fretwork, and ornately carved doors and shutters only add to the claustrophobic air of the twisting narrow alleys, where scrawny cats root among the trash cans. Old men in white robes and red keffiyehs lounge in plastic chairs on the street side, and—a constant reminder of the slave trade that thrived across the Red Sea until recently—black African faces mingle with Arab. Everywhere there is the fruity smell of sewage. Choice in the characterless central bazaar has hardly improved, though alongside endless ranks of leather sandals and women's outer clothing—in any color you like, so long as it's black—there was one stall at which you could buy gnarled sprigs of a sinister-looking plant used, so its owner explained, to "induce childbirth."

In his report to Wingate, Wilson bluntly described the tensions within the town. There were at least two factions in Jeddah: the tribesmen who had captured the town, led by the wiry Sharif Mohsen, a former smuggler with a penchant for torture, and the merchants, represented by Mohammed Nessif, a portly trader who wore gold-rimmed spectacles. Nessif lived in the center of Jeddah in a palatial house topped with plaster crenellations, which it is possible to look around today. In the privacy of one of the dark, grand upstairs rooms, furnished with Persian carpets and divans, Nessif confided to Wilson and a colleague that he dreaded being ruled by Husein because "the Sharifs in the country were all corrupt and unreliable."[15] It was an early sign that Sharif Husein did not command the broad respect the British thought he would.

Added to the factionalism within the port, Wilson suspected that Faruqi was stirring up anti-British sentiment and withholding information to protect his role as intermediary between the sharif and McMahon. Probably prompted by his ambitious chief, who was suggesting the same idea simultaneously to Robertson, Wilson recom-

mended that the roles of political and military support for the sharif be
held by one man who would communicate with the sharif through a
British officer posted to the Hijaz. "Unless there is some permanent
British representative at Jeddah the present confusion of the continual
requests for supplies . . . will continue," Wilson argued, effectively rec-
ommending himself for the job.[16]

And so it was that Wilson returned to Jeddah at the end of July to stay.
Over the British consulate a tatty Union Jack billowed languorously once
again. Wilson's guise was "Pilgrimage Officer," a title calculated by
Ronald Storrs to be colorless enough not to invite similar diplomatic
representatives from France or Italy, but apt because the annual pilgrimage to Mecca would take place in eight weeks' time. The British
government pledged £500,000 to make the ceremony the box-office
success Storrs wanted it to be. Husein's "first independent season," he
wrote from Cairo, should "open as brilliantly as possible; any row, scan-
dal, or epidemic, would react swiftly and discreditably upon the man-
agement, and discourage or even annihilate subsequent bookings."[17]

A professional soldier turned provincial governor in Sudan, Wilson
was, in several ways, an odd choice for what was essentially a demanding diplomatic role. He did not speak that much Arabic, and his hall-
mark was an honest bluntness quite at odds with the elliptical approach
to negotiations the Arabs preferred. He "maintained the habit," joked
a colleague, "of presenting facts in a manner abrupt and alarming to
the Oriental."[18] Determined though Wilson was, whether he was phys-
ically up to the task was also questionable. "I've never forgotten that illness Cyril had at Erkowit," his forceful wife, Beryl, fretted, for her
husband had been worn down by years of intermittent dysentery.[19]
Though only in his early forties, he "looked tired, like a man grappling
ceaselessly with insoluble problems," recalled another man who
worked with him: "he had a thankless task, which was performed with
unfailing good humor."[20] On the other hand, he reminded Storrs of "a
very low geared bicycle working at full speed day and night."[21]

Days after Wilson's arrival, on the evening of 1 August, the Ottoman
government's new emir of Mecca stepped off the train in Medina, two
hundred miles to the north of Jeddah. A plumper, glitzier version of
Sharif Husein, Sharif Ali Haidar had been appointed six weeks earlier
by the sultan, as soon as the Ottoman government had heard of the
revolt in the Hijaz. The Prophet Muhammad's descendants, the sha-

rifs, were divided into rival branches, the Aoun and the Zaid. The way-ward Sharif Husein led the Aoun; Sharif Ali Haidar, the Zaid. Ali Haidar was Husein's obvious replacement.[22]

Led from the station through crowds of onlookers, Ali Haidar's first destination was the Mosque of the Holy Tomb, Muhammad's place of burial, where he stopped to pray. Behind him a caravan followed bring-ing the tents and carpets needed by a tribal leader as well as the water filters and medicines required to preempt and ease the inevitable internal consequences of living in the East. He had also, strangely, been given a number of furs by the sultan, who had evidently never vis-ited the Hijaz in summer.

The Ottoman commander in Medina, Fakhri Pasha, seems to have wanted to install Ali Haidar in Mecca by the time of the pilgrimage, two months later. Two days after Ali Haidar's arrival, Fakhri launched a counterattack against Sharif Husein's forces on the road south toward Mecca. The running battle that followed lasted over twenty-four hours. Coincidentally, the following day in the Sinai Desert a Turkish force of about 18,000—double the number the British anticipated—clashed with British forces only twenty-five miles east of the Suez Canal. The British defeated the Turkish force, but at a cost of over 1,100 men killed and wounded. Worried about the febrile atmosphere in Egypt that enemy agents had worked up, Sir Archibald Murray ordered that the Ottoman prisoners of war be marched through the streets of Cairo to try to stop the spread of rumors of an imminent Turkish invasion.[23]

In Cairo the Arab Bureau hastily concocted a plan to relieve the pressure on the sharif, by raiding the Hijaz Railway from the Turkish-held port of Aqaba, at the foot of modern Jordan. Clayton, in London, lobbied for the idea, but it was quickly dismissed as impossible. Naval reconnaissance proved that Aqaba itself—then a run-down fort and a few houses among a shoreline palm grove—was better defended than expected, and, even if a landing there was successful, the sixty-mile trek to reach the railway passed through a stony desert roamed by two tribes, the Huwaytat and the Bani Atiyah, well known for their treach-ery and violence.[24] Finally there was predictable military opposition to the plan. From London Sir William Robertson wrote to Murray in August, telling him to concentrate on giving the Turks "a good hiding in the Sinai Peninsula"[25] and warning him, "We cannot go to Aqaba merely for the sake of helping the Sharif. We must be sure that the

operations will give us some definite advantage over the Turk, with special reference to the defence of Egypt. . . . One never knows where
these little expeditions may not lead us."[26]

Although Robertson's intervention scotched the Aqaba plan, Wingate
continued to entertain the idea that British troops might be sent to
help the sharif farther south, since Wilson reported from Jeddah that
he did not think that the Arabs alone could resist a concerted Ottoman
assault on Mecca. Wingate, in any case, wanted to expand his own role
in the revolt, but to send troops to the Hijaz would be controversial
because non-Muslims were not welcome in the region, and, in
Medina, Ali Haidar had already deftly exploited Husein's reliance on
support from Britain.

On 9 August, Ali Haidar had issued a proclamation in which he
accused his rival of naïveté for accepting British help and of "trying to
place the House of God, the Qibla* of Islam, and the tomb of the
Prophet, under the protection of a Christian Government."[27] Haidar
left the British with a difficult choice. To send troops would play into
his hands; not to, if Wilson's judgment was correct, risked the collapse
of the revolt. The potential aftereffects of either option were also
fiercely debated. From India, one provincial governor warned the
British government that "a flame of fire [would] undoubtedly be lit in
India" if any British soldier set foot in the Hijaz.[28] To Wingate, who was
partly worried about the loyalty of the Muslim Sudanese he ruled, the
danger of doing nothing looked just as great. He warned "that the collapse of the Sharif's movement will be a far more serious blow to British
prestige in the Islamic world than our failure in the Dardanelles or the
surrender at Kut"—a reference to the Mesopotamian town where, earlier that year, part of the Indian army had been forced to surrender after
being encircled by the Ottomans.[29] In a crisis Wingate expected the
sharif to allow British troops to land: "Religious prejudices, nationalis-
tic considerations and personal feelings go to the winds when the individual concerned is faced at close quarters with the alternatives of
success or defeat," he believed.[30] To test his boss's theory, Wilson
decided to sound out Husein's son Feisal on whether or not British troops
would be welcomed, but Husein refused to let him travel up the coast
to meet his son.

---

* The direction of prayer for all Muslims—toward Mecca.

Husein, indeed, was being generally difficult. He would not allow explosives to be offloaded, probably—the British speculated—because he feared an international backlash for ordering the destruction of the Hijaz Railway, for which so many Muslims had raised money a few years before. And he maintained an obsessive interest in Wilson's activities in Jeddah, calling at half-hourly intervals on the telephone from Mecca to check on progress.[31]

Under pressure from the Ottoman forces, who were consolidating their hold of the region around Medina, Husein eventually relented and allowed Wilson to go to Yanbu, the dilapidated little port where Feisal was based at the time. His decision was a relief for Wilson, who was finding the pace of work in Jeddah a strain. "I'm thankful to be going on this trip," Wilson wrote to Wingate, before adding that he blanched at the attire that Husein insisted he wear while out of town. "The Sharif is sending me down a silk scarf and the Bedouin rope thing which I will wear over my helmet," he reluctantly conceded. But "I absolutely refuse to disguise myself as an Arab," he declared: "if I'm scuppered I propose to be scuppered in my own uniform."[32]

Wilson was the first British officer to meet Feisal, at Yanbu on 27 August. It must have been an odd contrast: the short, trenchant Wilson, borrowed keffiyeh draped over his helmet, giving him the appearance of wearing an enormous red bonnet, beside the finely robed Feisal, a tall thin man in his early thirties whose long face, and the curved Arab dagger belted to his waist, gave him a medieval appearance. Wilson immediately liked Feisal.

Feisal explained to Wilson how he had left his tribesmen about forty miles east of Yanbu at Bir Abbas, a well in the last pass through the mountains separating Medina from the coast, through which the Turks were most likely to come. Hinting that he was rapidly losing face, he told Wilson that he would not return to his men until he could promise them men, money, and explosives to help them destroy the railway.

Feisal should blame his father for the shortage of dynamite, Wilson frankly replied: "60 odd boxes of bombs had been on board a warship for weeks," he explained. "Feisal," Wilson observed, "went as near cursing his saintly father as I suppose a son of a Grand Sharif could."[33]

"My father tries to do everything but is not a soldier," Feisal commented, with a sigh.

"Having had a month's experience of the old gentleman," Wilson wrote afterward, "I was able to agree cordially."

Wilson subsequently reported that Feisal had asked for three hundred men, but McMahon, who was dismayed to hear that Feisal was not leading from the front, raised this figure to a thousand. But finding such a large number of Muslim troops would not be easy. Wingate—in his role as sirdar—immediately volunteered Sudanese troops from the Egyptian army's ranks, provided these were replaced by regular British soldiers, who were much better trained. But the War Office in London saw through this self-serving offer and instantly rejected it.

The only other Muslim troops either were serving in East Africa or were Indians whose deployment to the Hijaz the Government of India would probably veto. That left the Arab prisoners of war who had been captured by the British in Mesopotamia. After a trawl of the prison camps, about seven hundred Arab former Ottoman soldiers were sent to the Hijaz in mid-July under Nuri Said, a young, elfin Iraqi officer who had defected to the Allies at the start of the war. A mixture of Syrians and Iraqis, they were "a scummy lot," said Wingate, disappointed that many of these former prisoners arrived in the Hijaz under the impression that they were being resettled, and proved unwilling to take up arms against the Ottomans.[34] Besides the brave few who did offer their services—risking their own and their families' lives if they were captured—there were also some volunteers from Mecca. As Wilson admitted toward the end of August, "the whole business of giving the Sharif military assistance bristles with difficulties; he has started, in a military sense, practically from bedrock."[35]

There was little time to train what recruits to Husein's cause there were. On 10 September, Cairo received a report that Turkish forces in Medina were building up and that a mahmal* had arrived in the city, the first hard evidence the British had received that the Turks hoped to recapture Mecca by the time of the pilgrimage. "I reckon that this will be all over by the middle of October," wrote Clayton the same day, though what he thought the final outcome would be he left unsaid.[36] Until then no one had seriously considered what might happen if the Turks recaptured Mecca. McMahon, who feared that the coup might

---

* A richly embroidered ceremonial litter used to transport the new kiswa, the black cloth covering the Kaaba, which was replaced each year during the pilgrimage.

galvanize Muslim unrest throughout the British Empire, convened a conference in Egypt to review the situation two days later on the twelfth. There he discussed the situation with Wilson, who had made the journey up from Jeddah specially, General Murray, and Admiral Wemyss, commander of the Red Sea fleet on which any support for the sharif depended.

Since the unusually frank minutes of this meeting survive, it is possible today to eavesdrop on the row that followed. "Something drastic" was needed, McMahon suggested, "to ensure that the Arabs keep their tails up through this critical period, which is not likely to, and cannot, last very long."[37] Wilson then described the three possible routes the Turks might take to Mecca. "What Feisal and the Arabs are very keen on," he explained, "is to see some regular troops." He went on to suggest a figure of between two and three thousand.

When Murray heard this number, he exploded. He had just received another demand for nearly three thousand troops to serve on the Balkan front, and this additional request was the final straw. Accusing Wilson of being "completely out of touch," Murray reminded the others present that his orders were to reduce the number of British troops in Egypt. Then he moved briskly on to other requests from the Hijaz he had recently received. "Take the telegram asking for two aeroplanes," he snapped at Wilson. "You talk as if two aeroplanes were two swallows, as if they could simply drop down there and do anything else you require."

When Murray had finally finished ranting, McMahon began to speak. "It was the most unfortunate date in my life when I was left in charge of this Arab movement," he complained; "it is nothing to do with me: it is a purely military business." Summing up the situation, he declared that it was time to weigh the consequences of the sharif's success or failure. Husein's success, he felt, would have very far-reaching results. McMahon feared that his failure, on the other hand, could have dire consequences, through the propaganda the Turks would generate if they retook the holy city. "The effect in India would be enormous," McMahon predicted. "I do not know how many troops it would take to clear that up."

The specter McMahon had raised, of having to divert thousands of troops to quell unrest in India, seemed to calm Murray. The general replied that he had finished grumbling and now wanted to arrive at some numbers of the troops he might be able to put on standby to help if necessary. Clayton inquired about the Sudanese troops whom Wingate had offered. Murray must have seen a flicker of concern cross Wilson's face, because he interrupted. "I think Colonel Wilson is right," he said. "If you are going to do it, do it with the proper coloured men; use white men."

"Of course there is a great religious difficulty about that," McMahon replied.

"I do not believe in sending black troops," said Murray. "They won't realize that the British Government is behind them unless they see British troops—white faced soldiers walking about and smoking."

"There is one more thing," McMahon added, bringing the discussion to a close. "If I cannot get these troops from the British Government I am reduced to getting them from the French. I could get them tomorrow but I do not want to do so," he said, referring to Britain's determination to shield Husein from French influence. "That is the alternative."

"I think we all learnt each other's minds and cleared the atmosphere somewhat," Wemyss noted in his diary.[38] But the fundamental question remained unanswered. Was it more risky to send troops or to watch the revolt fail—either of which might have unfathomed consequences across the Muslim world? And just in time to complicate the answer, as McMahon had alluded, came the arrival of the French.

5

The French Arrive

On 1 September 1916 a tall, broad-shouldered bear of a man disembarked at Alexandria. Colonel Edouard Brémond had a gray beard almost as long as his service in French North Africa. He had arrived in Egypt to take charge of France's military mission to the Hijaz. Less than a fortnight later, a second French delegation followed him. This turned out to be a flock of several hundred, mainly distinguished North African pilgrims led by the Moroccan sultan's head of protocol, a man named Ben Ghabrit, a former spy, in Storrs's opinion, with "a clever agreeable [and] utterly false face."[1] Brémond's arrival reflected the latent rivalry between Britain and France, allies that were already jockeying for position in the Middle East long before the war was even won.

When Husein's revolt began three months earlier, the French War Office had given it a guarded welcome, describing the uprising as "favorable to French interests to some extent," in that it might help pave the way for French intervention and hinder the Turks.[2] But in general the French viewed Arab success in the Hijaz quite differently from the British. Their North African colonies were also Arab, and the French government worried that if Husein succeeded they might find themselves "in the presence of an Arabised Islam that draws from its conquests new strength to expand and resist Christian power."[3] Nor did the idea that the sharif might assume the caliphate enchant them: Moroccans regarded the sultan of Morocco as their caliph, an arrangement the French were happy to leave undisturbed. That August the French government had decided to offer assistance so that it could keep a closer eye on what was happening in the Hijaz. The British government had no choice but to accept French help.

McMahon had received only sketchy details from the Foreign Office about the French mission, its members, and its purpose. As far as he was aware, a "Colonel Bredus" was on his way, who had no plans to venture closer to Arabia than Cairo. Displaying a touching faith in the Entente Cordiale, he believed this. Brémond rapidly corrected both his name and his remit on arrival, when he announced that he would be sailing to Jeddah in the middle of the month. His government, he explained, hoped to fix the notoriously volatile costs of the hajj to help their pilgrims and, by using a deputation of Muslim officers who could enter Mecca, establish directly from Husein exactly what he required.[4]

McMahon was unnerved when Brémond made it clear that the French were ready to send troops to support the sharif. The day after his acrimonious meeting with General Murray, at which he had raised the possibility that he might be forced to turn to the French for support, McMahon sent a panicky telegram to London. Describing the British as "morally committed" to support Husein and likely to be "held in a large measure responsible for his failure," he requested a brigade—just over four thousand men—to send to the coastal village of Rabigh, a hundred miles north of Jeddah. They could best stiffen Arab resistance there at the wells that made Rabigh the most likely route the Turks would take to Mecca. Were Britain unable to assist, he went on, "I know French Government is ready to offer to send French Moslem troops to Hijaz and this I greatly deprecate, as it will rob us of very great political advantages which Sharif's success will hereafter give us."[5] Murray, who met Brémond four days later, was equally concerned, for different reasons. Later the same day he wrote to Robertson, admitting that he would be "sorry if for political reasons the French render the Sharif material assistance," since if they did, the pressure on him to send British troops would only increase.[6]

On 15 September, Brémond left Egypt for the Hijaz together with the religious delegation, which took rose water for washing the Kaaba—a much sought-after task. They arrived off Jeddah five days later to a rapturous reception. Brémond soon spoke on the telephone to Husein, who immediately organized a dinner in his honor in the port the following night. It was a lavish affair, held in an enormous room decorated with French, British, and the sharif's crimson flags, and the hundred guests sat around a low table on borrowed carpets. Over the telephone Husein, who did not come down to Jeddah for the dinner, relayed more good news to Brémond. The Ottomans had finally surrendered at Taif, in the mountains above Mecca. This not only removed the final obstacle to the pilgrimage, by eliminating the threat posed by the closest Ottoman troops to Mecca, but also freed Abdullah to go north to help his brothers contain the Turks in Medina. Brémond happily relayed the message to Egypt, announcing that other pilgrims waiting in Egypt could depart for the Hijaz. Three days later a large tricolor was hoisted over the French consulate.

The fact that the French had instantly gained access to the sharif disturbed the British. In Cairo, McMahon's adviser Ronald Storrs decided it was time to make another trip down the Red Sea. Annoyed by Arab intermediaries who he believed could not pass on a message verbatim, Storrs was sufficiently anxious to speak to the sharif directly that he thought it might "even be worth the journey to Jeddah to talk with him awhile over the Jeddah–Mecca telephone."[7] An opportunity to do so arose when Storrs was detailed to accompany the Egyptian mahmal down to Jeddah aboard the Red Sea fleet's largest ship, HMS *Euryalus*. The British aim was clear: to land the mahmal with enough pomp to awe the Arabs and to trump the French.

Boarding the *Euryalus* on 22 September for his second mission to the Hijaz, Storrs discovered that he had been allotted the best berth aboard by the admiral, "Rosy" Wemyss. Early the following day, he had his bath to the sound of the Egyptian brass band doing its morning practice. To break up the monotony of the voyage, each day Storrs played chess with Wemyss on deck. The admiral, who wore a monocle, turned out to be a formidable opponent. In the background his gray parrot cawed "damn the Kaisah, damn the Kaisah" raucously.[8] Wemyss won every game; Storrs blamed the parrot for distracting him.

The *Euryalus* arrived off Jeddah on 26 September, joining a flotilla of British and French ships anchored off the port. Wemyss and Storrs went ashore the following morning, welcomed to the Hijaz first by a salute fired from some ancient mortars and then by a cluster of local dignitaries on the quayside. Among these were two familiar faces who, Storrs recorded, "appeared really glad to see us."[9] It was Wilson and Ruhi, Storrs's secret agent, whom he had lent to Wilson. After several stops for coffee and for what Wemyss described as the exchange of "flowery compliments," they called on Colonel Brémond and then headed for the British consulate.

Behind closed doors inside the consulate, Wilson assured Wemyss that the welcome, though elaborate, was genuine, and expressed his delight at the impact of the admiral's visit to Storrs. Wilson's own position, Storrs reported, had been "raised in a manner he had up to now scarcely dared to dream possible."[10] Despite the general expectation that the pilgrimage would trigger a Turkish attempt to recapture Mecca, Wilson seemed happier about the military situation as well. He "no longer believes in a Turkish advance south of Medina, and even speaks of reported withdrawals," noted Storrs in his diary. "If this means that it will no longer be necessary to send an English Brigade or French Batteries to Rabigh, it is a very deep relief to me."[11]

Like Brémond, Admiral Wemyss was invited to a dinner by Sharif Husein the following night, but as Husein would not be present, Wemyss thought it wiser to decline since he was anxious to visit Rabigh. Storrs spotted his opportunity and telephoned the sharif. A crossed line caused confusion, however, until Husein called through to the operator, Storrs recalled, "in stronger language than I had expected from so holy a man, ordering them to cut off everybody's instrument in the Hijaz excepting his own and mine for the next half-hour. This was instantly done and we conversed henceforth in a silence of death."[12]

Back aboard the *Euryalus* Wemyss also gave the Bedu leaders a tour of his flagship: "The big guns struck them so much that they could not at first believe them to be guns at all," observed Storrs, while "the size, comfort and cleanliness of the Admiral's cabin came in for admiring comment." But, he decided contentedly at the end of that day, "it was the guns in the end which produced the greatest effect."[13] After performing their prayers on the stern deck, the tribesmen departed "in a state of mind divided between awe, and intense satisfaction at having demonstrably espoused the winning cause." One of the party confided to Storrs that he had not, until then, believed that such a large ship could float.

The following morning the mahmal, carrying the new covering for the Kaaba, was landed in Jeddah. "Thousands . . . crammed the streets," said Brémond. "There was joy everywhere. 'The Harvest' had returned."[14] From a rooftop in the town one of Wilson's staff surveyed the scene. "Amidst a scene of wildest confusion," he later recalled, the mahmal was brought ashore, loaded onto a camel, and carried jauntily through the jostling spectators, many of whom carried black umbrellas to protect themselves from the morning sun.[15] The procession set out for Mecca the following morning, with "the stately mahmal and then the long string of dust-coloured camels passing into the pearly desert in the half light of dawn."

Leaving the *Euryalus* behind in Jeddah harbor for maximum effect, Wemyss and Storrs transferred to a smaller ship and headed one hundred miles up the coast to Rabigh. "Very hot, damp, windless and oppressive"[16] was Storrs's instant verdict on the fuggy climate of the desolate plain on which the village stood, at the edge of a lagoon in which sharks could occasionally be spotted. The hostile appearance of the area was deceptive, however, for the British believed that the wells at Rabigh provided the only fresh water for miles around. On this basis, the logic of defending the village was compelling: "Arab cause is successful if Mecca is denied to Turkish force," explained an intelligence officer: "According to all reports force must come by Rabigh and therefore if Rabigh is held Arab cause is won."[17] On the basis of this assumption, for the next three months Rabigh would become the eye of a tempestuous storm over whether or not troops should be sent to the Hijaz. Knowing that there was strong opposition to sending troops, Wemyss wanted to find out whether his ships' guns could defend the Arab forces that were camped around the wells, so, as the party walked away from the seashore, Storrs silently counted his paces.

The mud huts that made up Rabigh in 1916 have disappeared beneath a charmless seaside town today. When I visited in 2005, I was disappointed to find that the way onto the spit that separates the lagoon from the sea, then an empty whaleback of sand, is now blocked by an enormous oil terminal. A security fence and checkpoint made it impossible to go farther. But as I stood in the hot onshore breeze considering the situation something caught my eye inland. To the northeast, across the gently corrugated coastal plain, a distinctive two-horned mountain poking through the dirty desert haze indicates the direction from which the Turks, in 1916, were expected to come.

The War Committee first considered McMahon's request to send troops to Rabigh on 20 September, and decided to invite the views of officials in the Middle East on what might happen if the sharif were defeated. The responses discouraged the committee from approving McMahon's request. From Egypt, Murray argued that the sharif's failure might "have as little effect as evacuation of Gallipoli or surrender at Kut"—a deliberate reference to two raw defeats he hoped would discourage the politicians from intervening.[18] In India the viceroy, Lord Chelmsford, feared that, if British intervention became public knowledge, it would ruin Husein's claim to the caliphate and might even spark a jihad in Afghanistan. Even Cyril Wilson, when he was asked whether Mecca was in real danger, breezily replied, "No, not at the moment," though he added that if the Turks defeated the Arab forces in the Hijaz mountains and advanced closer to Rabigh, then the situation could become critical.[19] Chastened by the failure at Gallipoli and orchestrated by Robertson, members of the general staff in London also voiced their doubts. If the sharif was so precarious, they wondered, was a brigade of four thousand men enough to save him? "Their argument," reported one well-placed onlooker, "is that if we send a Brigade it may expand into a Division, then an Army Corps, and eventually an Expedition."[20]

The War Committee was swayed by these arguments and unconvinced by the pessimistic assessments made by McMahon and Wingate, who had both warned of Muslim agitation in Egypt, the Sudan, and India if the sharif were crushed. Buoyed too by news that the pilgrimage had gone well, the War Committee concluded on 3 October that the evidence "all pointed to the undesirability of sending any reinforcements to Rabigh beyond a flight of aeroplanes and such guns as might be eventually available."[21] Since Wemyss's reconnaissance ashore had demonstrated that Rabigh could be protected by naval barrage, the committee decided that naval assistance would be "sufficient if the local defence was properly organized."

Yet this decision was far from final. The War Committee had acted on the understanding that the situation in the Hijaz was improving, when in fact the reverse was true. The Turks began to attack the Arab positions at Bir Abbas, a well on the high pass on the road from Medina to Rabigh, the same day. The situation there was "not good at present," Wilson learned.[22] It worsened further when, two days later, the Turks captured Bir Abbas. From there it would be downhill all the way to Rabigh. With Feisal to the north, and Abdullah, who was supposedly on his way to Medina, but completely out of touch, it was clear that if the Turks now attacked Rabigh, they would capture the village and its water supply, and the way to Mecca would then be open.

At the same time the War Committee also decided to take responsibility for the political aspects of the revolt from McMahon and give them to Wingate. McMahon was stung by the implication that he was not up to the task, even though he had openly admitted he wanted no responsibility. In a telegram to London he now attacked Wingate. "The Sirdar shows a generous disposition to assume both political and military responsibilities which in my opinion his geographical position and the dearth of military resources rendered him and still render him incapable of discharging," he wrote, copying his forthright view to Wingate for good measure.[23] The government in London disagreed. On 9 October, encouraged by Murray, Grey told McMahon to give Wingate whatever political authority he needed. Two days later Wingate was also secretly offered McMahon's job as high commissioner in Egypt. Strangely, the War Committee had just promoted the very man who was most eager to send troops to help the sharif.

Flexing his new power from Khartoum, Wingate on 11 October seized on the report of the fighting at Bir Abbas to recommend "a British Brigade being at once placed under orders for Rabigh and all arrangements made for its immediate conveyance to that port."[24] He also announced his intention to see Rabigh for himself. It was a decision that would indirectly make another man, as yet unknown, a household name.

6

This Was the Man

It was Wingate's sudden suggestion that a delegation visit Jeddah and Rabigh that took T. E. Lawrence to Arabia. Clayton might have gone himself, but he was juggling his work with looking after his wife. She had just given birth to a son, who was desperately ill and would, ten days later, die. Wingate's own hopes of visiting Arabia were then squashed by the Foreign Office in London, where Grey feared that the appearance of so senior an official in the Hijaz would only fuel Arab suspicions of Britain's imperial ambitions there.[1] So in the end, Ronald Storrs went again, accompanied this time by Lawrence, who he claimed had "asked me point blank to take him down on my next voyage to Jeddah."[2] Lawrence later said that he had asked for "ten days' leave" to make the trip.[3] Neither story seems the full one, for Clayton almost certainly lurked behind Lawrence's abrupt departure for the Hijaz.

While he was away in London that summer, Clayton had been badly undermined by the infighting in Cairo over the revolt, and he returned to Egypt in the autumn to find that most of his staff had been poached to work at General Murray's headquarters. Murray himself was in the ascendant, having vetoed moves to send a raiding force to Aqaba and troops to Rabigh, and he was behind the defenestration of McMahon that October. By then Clayton, the "unfortunate shuttlecock" in the tension between Murray and McMahon, as Wingate put it, was in a very precarious position.[4]

Clayton's relationship with Wingate, once his boss, was also strained.

While Clayton and Murray had their differences over the Aqaba raid, they agreed that Wingate's support for sending troops to Rabigh was wrong. Here Clayton saw a chance to curry favor with the general. He wrote to Wingate on 12 October—the day before Storrs and Lawrence left for Jeddah—saying that it was pointless to send a brigade to defend Rabigh because, if it was sent in advance of the Turks' arrival, its appearance would upset the Arabs, whereas, if its dispatch was delayed until the Turks advanced, it would arrive too late to affect the outcome.[5] The argument was a strong one, but its inventors—Cyril Wilson and his colleague at Rabigh, Alfred Parker—were discredited. Murray certainly did not trust the judgment of either man, and it seems likely that his reservations were more widely shared.[6] From their opposing viewpoints, Wingate and Clayton both realized that to win the argument they each needed evidence from a more reliable eyewitness. That was why Wingate wanted to go to Rabigh himself and why, to outmaneuver Wingate, Clayton decided to send Lawrence. Lawrence agreed with Clayton that a brigade should not be sent, but, as his shooting practice once aboard the ship implied, he now entertained ideas that went well beyond the report that his chief wanted him to write.

⁂

Lawrence and Storrs finally landed at Jeddah early on Monday, 16 October. "When at last we anchored in the outer harbour, off the white town hung between the blazing sky and its reflection in the mirage," Lawrence later wrote, "then the heat of Arabia came out like a drawn sword and struck us speechless."[7]

The words, when Lawrence wrote them in the 1920s, were well thought out. While many of the other men who wrote powerfully of their experiences in the war never expected—or in several cases, lived—to see their work published, Lawrence had long been planning to write two books. One was to be on the Crusades—a favorite subject —the other on his travels in the Middle East, which he had already decided would be titled *Seven Pillars of Wisdom*, after a phrase in the Book of Proverbs.[8] Once in the Hijaz, he made detailed notes of the people he met, incidents, and his surroundings in a slim army notebook, which today is held in the British Library in London. Pasted in the back of this book he kept an elegiac newspaper cutting from the

Times about his younger brother, Will, a Royal Flying Corps observer, who had been missing since being shot down over France a year earlier. In the piece Will's Oxford tutor mourned the loss of so many of his students: "One by one they fall; great and strong and wise, they sleep deep the long sleep of death in gallant company," he wrote, describing his former student anonymously as "one of the noblest—if it be not a treason to discriminate—of all the dead one has known who have died for England."[9]

Pieced together from his notes and memories, *Seven Pillars of Wisdom* was to become Lawrence's story of what happened after he was first sent to Arabia. It was a book originally born of his anger at the unsatisfactory outcome of the revolt, which in time he softened into a private souvenir of a small war. Just two hundred lavishly illustrated copies were initially printed, most for subscribers who each paid thirty guineas for the book. "It does not pretend to be impartial," Lawrence wrote in a brief foreword in 1926, advising his readers to "take it as a personal narrative pieced out of memory."[10] Despite this caveat *Seven Pillars of Wisdom* remains an outstanding memoir, its accuracy usually corroborated by the other sources, both contemporary and subsequent, that since have come to light.

Lawrence found the atmosphere in the narrow streets of Jeddah close and tense. His uniform turned a deeper khaki from his sweat. Storrs strode ahead of him, oblivious that his own white suit was now stained red. At the British consulate Wilson ushered them into a dark room, shuttered against the heat. He did not trust Storrs, and his only previous contact with Lawrence had been a run-in over whether British officers should wear Arab dress about the town.

Wilson had only just learned through a telegram from Wingate that the government had decided not to send troops or airplanes after all. He had been under the impression all along that troops were being held in readiness, had told the sharif several times that aircraft were on their way, and was embarrassed that his ignorance was about to be exposed. The fact that it was Lawrence, a junior, amateur soldier, who was able to reveal to him the political badminton that had led to the dispatch of the brigade being sanctioned and canceled more than once, annoyed Wilson further. "Lawrence wants kicking and kicking *hard* at that then he would improve," he fulminated to Clayton, describing Lawrence as "a bumptious young ass who spoils his undoubted knowledge of Syrian Arabs etc by making himself out to be the only authority on war, engineering, running HM's ships and everything else. He put every single person's back up I've met, from the Admiral down to the most junior fellow."[11]

The feeling was mutual. As they had expected to, Storrs and Lawrence both quickly formed the impression that Wilson's judgment was poor and that the information he was passing back to Cairo was unreliable. "There are some personal remarks here about Colonel Wilson which I won't write down," Lawrence reported to Clayton, suggesting that he put "a few leading questions" to Storrs on his return.[12] We can guess what Storrs said from the comments he wrote in his diary. Wilson, he thought, was "irritable and aggressive, and totally unsuited for anything beyond provincial administration."[13] Terrified of being asked to replace Wilson, however, he kept his fiercest criticism private. Though "a good old boy who keeps British prestige fairly high in the Hijaz," Wilson, he told a friend, was "very stupid and knows no Arabic."[14]

Like Wilson, however, Storrs was mortified by the telegram canceling the airplanes, particularly as the ship that was carrying them had already arrived off Rabigh. Storrs was going to meet Abdullah at the consulate later that day for the first time since their initial, pregnant encounter in 1914. It would be a symbolic occasion, at which Storrs had been hoping to establish what Abdullah needed, not to tell him what he could not have. Instead, "it was our privilege," he wrote sarcastically, "to announce to Abdullah that the Brigade, more than once promised by HMG* would not be sent; and that the flight of aeroplanes, promised and dispatched to Rabigh was being withdrawn."[15] Nor could he provide the £10,000 Abdullah had asked for. "I felt myself therefore somewhat poorly equipped for the role of a *Deus ex Machina*," he later reminisced.[16]

Wilson read the news he had received aloud to Abdullah. "It was a lengthy telegram," Abdullah later recalled, "and the gist of it was that news of the Arab revolt had been received in India with the greatest indignation and that agents or friends of the Germans and the Turks there had made capital out of it, maintaining that the Allies had occupied sacred Muslim areas."[17] The British government, Wilson contin-

* His Majesty's Government.

Council of war at Jeddah,
October 1916. Either side
of the Arab officer behind
Sharif Abdullah (seated)
are Cyril Wilson (left) and
Ronald Storrs (right).

ued, could not risk trouble in India and had decided to restrict its help to arms, supplies, and money as before. Neither the troops nor the aircraft would now be sent. This news "was a heavy blow to me," Abdullah wrote later, "as we desperately needed aircraft, gunners and engineers."[18]

"Pardon me," Abdullah said, looking directly at Storrs, "it was your letter and your messages that began this thing with us, and you know it."[19] Abdullah "had us on toast now and then," Wilson reported honestly afterward, but there was nothing more that either Storrs or he could do.[20] Abdullah was forced to telephone his father with the bad news. After Abdullah had finished listening to his father's rant about the British change of mind, he handed the receiver to Storrs. "Storrs in full blast was a delight to listen to," wrote Lawrence, "a lesson to every Englishman alive on how to deal with suspicious or unwilling Orientals."[21] Within minutes of hinting that, with a clearer assessment of the situation, it might be possible to reverse the British government's decision, Storrs had managed to persuade the sharif that Lawrence should be allowed to visit Feisal in the mountains.

That evening Husein rang back. Would Storrs and his colleagues like to hear a recital by the Turkish brass band captured at Taif? "Sharif Husein laid his receiver on the table of his reception hall, and we, called solemnly one by one to the telephone, heard the band in the Palace at Mecca forty-five miles away," Lawrence recalled.[22]

Abdullah met Brémond early the following morning and told him the news that the British had withdrawn the airplanes and refused to send troops.

"I have heard nothing about this," Brémond told Abdullah, surprised that nothing had been said by Storrs or Lawrence at dinner the previous evening. "It is rather serious. What are you going to do?"

"It means concluding peace," Abdullah, according to Brémond, replied.[23]

Storrs's admission that the British would not be sending airplanes could not have been worse timed. Later that day Abdullah received a message from his brother Feisal, who was up in the hills on the road to Medina, telling him that he was now being bombed by Turkish aircraft. At about midday Sharif Husein made the first of many calls to Storrs, begging him to reverse the British government's decision. He continued "pitilessly without intermission to dominate and interrupt us," Storrs wrote at the end of that day, "till I had to remind him that we had not, unfortunately, got the British Army drawn up in the Consulate back garden."[24] When Storrs heard from Brémond that Abdullah had threatened to sue for peace, he rapidly arranged for McMahon to confirm to the sharif that supplies of food, weapons, and ammunition would continue to be sent. Abdullah, fortunately, saw this as a victory when, in fact, it was simply a restatement of the existing British policy.

Dinner that evening was a painful experience. Abdullah arrived with the bandsmen—"scarecrows," Lawrence called them—whom Husein had sent down to entertain the British. Reviews of the performance, which included a rendition of "Deutschland über Alles," were unanimous. "Somewhat discordant," said Wilson, in a moment of rare diplomacy.[25] "Excruciating" was the verdict of his colleague Young.[26] "Our ears ached with the noise," remembered Lawrence.[27] Storrs had been told that "there was a piece called *The Echo* they could render with great skill." The result, he later recalled, "was two notes of an ineffable *tristesse* on the trombone, followed by a pause in which we consumed more than half a course. Then a few more disjointed and incoherent notes from the rest of the orchestra, and so on *da capo*. Even the Egyptians—indeed all but Abdullah—were stricken with the horror of the melody."[28] Storrs himself was almost doubled up with laughter, desperately trying not to catch Lawrence's eye.

"Is not this the music that is played for the dead?" one Egyptian officer asked. "Storrs saved situation," Lawrence wrote in his army notebook, as his colleague skillfully made light of the comment, causing everyone to laugh.[29]

Lawrence was impatient. In a telegram that day to Clayton he brusquely summarized the day's discussions: "Nobody knew real situation Rabigh so much time wasted."[30] He would head for Rabigh only the following day, but his ideas about how to revive the revolt's momentum were already beginning to crystallize. Having listened to an Arab officer well acquainted with the situation, Lawrence increasingly took the view that, as money was likely to be the deciding factor in securing tribal support, it would be best in the future to pay Ali and Feisal directly, bypassing Husein, of whom they were "respectfully afraid" and who was "frightfully jealous of his purse-strings, and keeps his family annoyingly short."[31]

Lawrence knew, however, that any attempt to circumvent Husein's tightfistedness would never be sanctioned until someone had completed a more penetrating assessment of each of his sons' personalities than Wilson's, which only tended to reveal their author's reliance on degrees of the adjective "nice." To fill this gap, and to avoid having to return to Cairo with Storrs immediately, Lawrence spotted an opportunity for himself: "There is great need of some Intelligence work being done at Jeddah," he hinted heavily to Clayton. "If one stayed there, and worked, one would be able to appreciate the Hijaz situation quite well."[32]

Storrs and Lawrence anchored off Rabigh on 19 October, and Lawrence went ashore. "I can still see Lawrence . . . on the shore at Rabigh waving . . . as we left him there to return ourselves to Egypt," Storrs reminisced twenty years later.[33] Lawrence's first task was to meet Ali before riding inland to find Feisal. Ali was suffering from a relapse of his tuberculosis. He looked "a little old already," felt Lawrence, and, though conscientious, was "without force of character, nervous and rather tired."[34] Weak as he was, Ali was nevertheless extremely reluctant to allow Lawrence to head up-country, and he relented only on condition that Lawrence spoke to no one along the way. The local sheikh had an unresolved blood feud with Sharif Husein, and was correctly suspected to be in league with the Turks. With two guides from a friendly local tribe, Lawrence—dressed up in an Arab head scarf and cloak that Ali had lent to him to disguise his uniform—set out for Feisal's camp in the mountains after dark on 21 October. Knowing how some German sailors, who had attempted to travel up the Hijaz coast some months earlier, had been discovered afterward trussed up like chickens and minus their heads, he was well aware that he was about to embark on a dangerous journey.

Life at a desk in Cairo had barely prepared Lawrence for the slow journey by camel. Even in October his fair skin quickly blistered with sunburn, and his eyes ached from the glare of the sun reflecting off the coastal plain, the Tihamah. Bar the fast new highway that now follows the coast, the Tihamah has not changed in the intervening years. Unremittingly flat and bleak despite being so close to the sea, its miles of monotonous gravel flats are alleviated only by the occasional thorn tree, black as if burnt by the heat, and the gangs of Pakistani laborers, shoveling hot tarmac onto the road. "Hijaz sun does not scorch but slowly blackens and consumes anything—men or stones—subject to it," Lawrence ruefully observed at the time.[35]

It was halfway up this unpromising, coastal leg of the ride that Lawrence made his first significant discovery. His guides mentioned in passing that there were wells inland at Khoreiba, only twenty-five miles northeast of Rabigh. As Lawrence would stress on his return, the presence of abundant water so near undermined the point of sending men to defend the wells at Rabigh.

The guides led Lawrence east up Wadi Safra,* a narrowing rocky valley in which he passed through a series of settlements. Finally, after two days' riding, he reached Hamra, a large village surrounded by small gardens and a dense grove of date palms, sited on a bend in the valley that is about three hundred yards wide. I especially wanted to see this village and drove an hour or so down the road from Medina in 2005 until at last I found it. The old villages of Saudi Arabia are eerie places. Their dense clusters of mud-brick houses are separated by a

---

*Wadi: a dry and often sharply sided desert watercourse, which contains water only in periods after heavy rain. The term covers anything from a deep valley to a shallow channel. In Arabic, *safra* means "yellow."

maze of soundless alleyways and are largely empty, since the government used the profits of the oil boom to rehouse their inhabitants in the 1970s. Behind their disintegrating palm wood doors the dwellings are frequently chaotic, with jumbles of palm trunks that once supported the upper stories now collapsed under the winter rains. Today tumbledown and more or less deserted, the houses of Hamra in 1916 teemed with Feisal's supporters, who were camped there. Lawrence was led to one of the larger houses, where his guide spoke to a black slave standing guard with a sword, who in turn showed Lawrence into an inner courtyard. There, in a dark doorway, Lawrence remembered, was "a white figure waiting tensely for me. This was Feisal."[36] Feisal's dark hair, black hooded eyes, and strong nose reminded Lawrence the medieval scholar of someone. He described the sharif's son as looking "very like the monument of Richard I, at Fontevraud."[37]

"Do you like our place here in Wadi Safra?" Feisal asked.

"Well," replied Lawrence, "but it is far from Damascus." After the war he would boast that this pointed phrase fell on Feisal and his advisers "like a sword in their midst."[38] There was a pause as the Arabs considered the ambition and reproach implied by his answer. Then Feisal

Sharif Feisal ibn Husein,
pictured after the war at the
Paris peace conference.

looked up at Lawrence, smiled, and replied, "Praise be to God, there are Turks nearer us than that."[39]

"I felt at first glance," Lawrence wrote afterward, "that this was the man I had come to Arabia to seek."[40]

~⚹~

Back on the coast in the decrepit port of Yanbu two days later, Lawrence considered what he had seen. He began by writing up his impressions of each of the sharif's four sons. The youngest, the half brother of the others, Zeid, he arbitrarily dismissed: "His mother is Turkish and he takes after her."[41] Tuberculosis ruled out Ali. Abdullah, Lawrence decided, though likable, was too ambitious to be trustworthy. "The Arabs consider him a most astute politician, and a far-seeing statesman," he admitted, before adding mischievously, "he has possibly more of the former than of the latter in his composition."[42]

"Tall, graceful, vigorous, almost regal in appearance": Feisal was Lawrence's obvious preference.[43] He was "an absolute ripper," Lawrence told a colleague, in the eager language of that era.[44] Though Feisal had a hot temper, a short attention span, and a tendency to be rash, together with a mood that wildly fluctuated at times, he also had "far more personal magnetism and life than his brothers" and, promisingly, was "perhaps not over scrupulous." And he too had ambition: "full of dreams" was Lawrence's phrase, "with the capacity to realize them." Here was the answer. For what Lawrence believed the revolt had lacked, and that Feisal had, was "leadership: not intellect, nor judgment, nor political wisdom, but the flame of enthusiasm that would set the desert on fire."[45]

Since neither he nor Clayton wanted troops to be sent to the Hijaz, Lawrence also needed to undermine Wingate's disparaging view of the Bedu as "an untrained rabble, most of whom have never fired a rifle," who could never halt a Turkish advance alone.[46] Go just up the road beyond Hamra, the village where Lawrence first met Feisal, and ahead you can see two spiky peaks that dominate the climbing road to Medina. Lawrence, who saw this imposing view, argued that the Hijaz mountains presented a formidable barrier to Turkish ambitions to recapture Mecca. On the basis of a day's observation, he argued that the wiry, independent Bedu were "cheerful snipers" who were ideally

Two Bedu. "The term 'fighting man' in the Hijaz
meant anyone between twelve and sixty, sane
enough to shoot," wrote Lawrence.

suited to warfare in the mountains.[47] They had their limitations: they
would serve only under their own sheikhs and near their homes, and
they found artillery and airplanes terrifying. But they were "not afraid
of bullets, or of being killed—it is just the manner of death by artillery
that they cannot stand," he explained, in a reference to Muslims' belief
in bodily resurrection on the Day of Judgment, which being blown to
pieces would prejudice.

Lawrence's tribute to the Bedu's unorthodox military skills immediately met with skepticism. It was, one regular officer commented, "a
delightful theory" that did not bear clear reasoning. He believed that
Lawrence exaggerated the advantage the Bedu enjoyed in the mountains. "In India," he recalled from his own experience, "it has proved
that provided a force can move quickly enough it can carry out its
objective in the face of the opposition of a hill tribe, a more efficient
enemy than the Arab."[48]

Lawrence was determined to drive home the point that this war was,
for the British, entirely new: "The Hijaz war is one of dervishes against
regular troops—and we are on the side of the dervishes," he wrote from
Yanbu.[49] "Our text books do not apply to its conditions at all." This was
provocative and true. Both Wingate and Wilson had been involved in
fighting the dervishes at the end of the previous century, and the clas-
sic handbook on irregular warfare, *Small Wars*, made its loyalties clear
from the start: the forces opposing regular troops, its author, Charles
Callwell, stated, "whether guerrillas, savages or quasi-organized

armies, will be regarded as the enemy."[50] Though the book was already two decades old, Callwell had a timeless warning for his readers: "Guerrilla warfare is what the regular armies always have to dread, and when this is directed by a leader with a genius for war, an effective campaign becomes well-nigh impossible."[51] Lawrence was about to prove Callwell right again.

When, on 1 November, the *Suva* picked up Lawrence from Yanbu, its captain squinted at his disreputable-looking passenger. "I had heard of a Captain Lawrence being on the coast," he wrote in his memoirs: "I had assumed he was one of the military officers sent over and was a little astonished when a small, untidily dressed and most unmilitary figure strolled up to me on board the ship I was temporarily commanding and said, hands in pockets and so without a salute: 'I am going over to Port Sudan in this ship.'"[52]

7

Crisis over Rabigh

On 29 October in Jeddah, Cyril Wilson received a telegram from Abdullah, informing him that his father had been unanimously recognized as "King of the Arab Nation" by the people of Mecca. Wilson was stunned, and embarrassed that he had not known of the move beforehand. The news, he told McMahon, had come as a "complete surprise" and was "all the more astonishing" given that Storrs had done his best to discourage Abdullah from taking such a step.[1] Storrs had done so because he desperately wanted to avoid reopening the questions of over where exactly Husein would rule, and whether other Arab chiefs would accept him as their overlord.[2] Husein's bold claim to be king of the Arab nation now forced both issues. The British government would have to recognize Husein as king. But king of what?

The French had unwittingly made matters worse by appearing to endorse Husein. Some of their Muslim soldiers had been summoned to witness the announcement, which was made by a dignitary with frequent prompting from Abdullah. Unable to follow what was being said, the soldiers had assumed the ceremony was linked to the Islamic New Year the day before and, at its end, had followed the lead of the rest of the audience and cheered. It was only hours later that they found that "the talk of the town was that they had congratulated the Sharif on becoming King in the name of the French Republic," Wilson reported frantically days later.[3] The senior French Muslim officer, he added, had "now gone to bed with 'fever' until the decision of the French Government as to recognition is received."

Further confusion followed when Wilson telephoned Abdullah to ask him bluntly why he had not discussed his plans beforehand. Abdullah replied that negotiations on the announcement had been going on in secret between him and McMahon. This answer threw Wilson, and from London, Sir Edward Grey demanded an explanation. Unraveling the mystery in Cairo, Clayton discovered that in July Faruqi had told Husein that McMahon was willing to offer him the title "King of the Arabs."[4] To increase his own importance, Faruqi, Clayton established, was "apt to record purely imaginary conversations with the High Commissioner and sometimes to attribute to him somewhat remarkable statements."[5] This was an extraordinarily embarrassing admission because it was on information offered by Faruqi twelve months earlier that Clayton had based his shrill warning of the threat of jihad, which had in turn galvanized Grey into approving McMahon's approach to Husein.

Husein had agreed to the announcement only under pressure from his ambitious son Abdullah. Until then, in line with his justification that he was rebelling against the ruling Young Turk party, but not the sultan, he had rejected the idea of taking the title of king because it would implicitly challenge the sultan's authority. It was only when Abdullah raised the idea again, arguing that it would counter Ali Haidar's accusation that his father was a British puppet, and threatened to admit defeat unless the announcement was made, that Husein had given in. Abdullah worked feverishly late into the night after the declaration was made— "in my capacity as Foreign Minister," he later stated—telegraphing allied and neutral governments with the news, and concocting ready-made telegrams of congratulation to be distributed among the merchants in Jeddah for them to sign and return.[6]

Before the British government could do anything to stop them, their allies the Russian, Serbian, and Italian governments rapidly replied, offering their congratulations to the new monarch, which increased the pressure on Britain to do the same. Indeed, as Wilson recognized when he had recovered from the surprise, to recognize Husein in some way might help weaken the enemy claim that the British planned to rule the Hijaz. While it was agreed that, for the time being, Husein should be called "His Majesty the Sharif," the question of what to call him in the long run was a complicated one.

In London officials at the India Office said they did not mind recognizing Husein as "King of the Arabs," since the title conveyed a national, rather than territorial, claim, which did not impinge on their ally Ibn Saud. But the French, opposed to any title that might convey sovereignty over their Arab colonies in North Africa, preferred "King of the Holy Places." This the India Office rejected because it hinted at a spiritual supremacy too close to the caliphate for their comfort. Wingate meanwhile suggested "King of the Arabs in Hijaz," which McMahon, in the final days before he stepped down as high commissioner, boiled down to "King of the Hijaz." This was the narrow formula that was finally agreed and eventually announced to the wider world on 1 January 1917.[7] It was the first sign that, when put to the test, the British had no intention of honoring the commitments that McMahon, in the government's name, had made to Husein.

❦

By the time Lawrence reached Khartoum to report to Wingate on 6 November, bad news had already been received from the Hijaz. Feisal had abandoned his camp at Hamra and retreated farther down Wadi Safra toward the sea. The Turks had followed Feisal down the wadi and were now just three days' march from Rabigh. Lawrence told Wingate that, following his discovery that there were wells at Khoreiba, Rabigh could not be secured by the presence of British ships offshore: a large Turkish force could either outflank Rabigh altogether or use Khoreiba as a base for an overwhelming attack on the Arabs at Rabigh. Lawrence's view was that trying to defend Rabigh was pointless, but Wingate twisted Lawrence's point that ships could not defend the wells from an overwhelming attack, to reinforce the opinion he made in a report to the Foreign Office that it was necessary to land at least a brigade to defend the wells.[8]

At about the same time Wilson reported that Brémond had just told him that French troops earmarked for service in the Hijaz would arrive in Egypt in the middle of the month. This news only increased the pressure on Britain, just as Murray had predicted it would, for in London the French offer of help sparked concerns that, if the British did not match the French commitment, they would alone be blamed if the revolt collapsed.

Regardless of what their intervention might achieve, few politicians can resist the call that "something must be done" to counter accusations that they are doing nothing. This was the reflex that provoked the War Committee in London into reconsidering Wingate's view that a force should be sent to Rabigh.[9] On 10 November the prime minister asked Robertson to assess how many men would be needed to defend Rabigh.

Robertson, who thought he had already successfully buried the question of whether to send troops to Rabigh, was dismayed to witness the change in mood. Trying to discourage intervention, when he reported to the War Committee on 13 November, he suggested that a force of fifteen thousand troops—the same size as the Turkish garrison in Medina and more than three times the number Wingate had advised—would be required to defend the wells.

In Cairo, Murray, like Robertson, was concerned by the mounting political pressure for large-scale military intervention in the Hijaz. Not surprisingly, when he heard that Lawrence had just returned from Rabigh, he asked Lawrence's boss, Clayton, for a report on Lawrence's findings that he could then pass on to Robertson in London. Knowing the view it would contain, Clayton was only too willing to oblige.

Amid the confusion of the Arab Bureau's office, Lawrence wrote up his impressions of the situation in the Hijaz. In—his own words—"a violent memorandum," which largely embroidered Clayton's earlier view with his personal experience, he tore apart the arguments made for sending British troops to Rabigh.[10] The tribesmen, he said, were the backbone of the revolt, and, so long as they held out in the mountains, no British reinforcements were needed. If the tribesmen's resistance on the mountain road did collapse, unreliable communications with the Arabs and the fact that the Turks were now within a hundred miles of Rabigh meant that the British would have too little notice to deploy troops to Rabigh: they would have less time than it would take the Turks to advance to the coast. Any British attempt to preempt this sequence of events by landing a large number of troops while the Arabs were still holding out would have the opposite effect intended, Lawrence argued, because the Arabs were deeply suspicious of Britain's imperialist intentions in the Hijaz: "If the British, with or without the approval of the Sharif, disembarked an armed force at Rabigh powerful enough to take possession of the groves and organize a position there, they would, I am convinced, say 'We are betrayed' and scatter to their tents."[11] Having arrived in Rabigh, the British would be left holding a position on the coast, which the Turks, thanks to the wells at Khoreiba, could easily bypass. This, Lawrence continued, reaching the crux of his report, was exactly what the French wanted, because they did not want the Arab revolt to spread and challenge their own claim to Syria. "They say," Lawrence elaborated, "'Above all things, the Arabs must not take Medina. This can be assured if an allied force lands at Rabigh. The tribal contingents will go home, and we will be the sole bulwark of the Sharif in Mecca. At the end of the war we will give him Medina as a reward.'"[12] Having cast the French offer of help in a very unflattering light, he added that, given he had been allowed to go up-country, he believed that the reason for Arab animosity toward Christians' presence in the Hijaz was political rather than religious, and recommended that the British should limit their assistance to the airplanes that had been withdrawn and a handful of instructors, who would clearly represent no threat to the independence of the Hijaz. It was a contrived argument, for, as he later bluntly admitted, "the foreigner and Christian is not a popular person in Arabia."[13]

Robertson welcomed this helpful second opinion from Lawrence, whom Murray recommended as "an officer of great experience and knowledge of Arabs, who has just returned from a visit to Feisal's camp and also Rabigh."[14] He incorporated Lawrence's conclusions in a further report on 19 November. This covered Murray's plans to launch an offensive that would drive the Turks from the Sinai Desert east of the Suez Canal, which was designed to reduce the pressure on the Arabs in the Hijaz, and in it Robertson repeated his warning that a British force should not be sent to Rabigh.

Convinced by Lawrence's depiction of Brémond's agenda, officials in London pressed the French government on the behavior of its representative in the Hijaz. They evidently succeeded, for on 27 November the French commander in chief, Joffre, wired Brémond a message informing him that the French government supported the capture of Medina and telling him to change his attitude. However, as Brémond observed, this order was not followed by any of the artillery he had requested for Ali and Feisal. "One cannot capture a town with a telegram," he mused afterward.[15]

Clayton's astute support of Murray bolstered his own vulnerable position. Storrs told a friend admiringly how Clayton's "shares after having been forced down almost to zero . . . have now risen again together with those of the Arab Bureau, and are for the moment in some estimation."[16] Wingate, in the meantime, was forced to defend himself when the Foreign Office questioned the disparity between the opinion he had attributed to Lawrence in his telegram of 7 November and the views Lawrence had expressed in his own report ten days later, which Murray had then circulated widely. "I understood him to agree that in such an emergency the Arabs would welcome this help," Wingate weakly replied on the twenty-second.[17] Furious at the way in which he had been publicly outmaneuvered, Wingate could reveal his anger to Wilson only in private, criticizing Lawrence in a letter the following day as "a visionary" whose "amateur soldiering has evidently given him an exaggerated idea of the soundness of his views on purely military matters."[18] What was all the more galling was that he had already endorsed the suggestion of the chief of the Imperial General Staff, Sir William Robertson, that Lawrence return to the Hijaz.

With the blessing of Britain's most senior soldier, Lawrence was by 2 December back in Yanbu, the run-down port one hundred miles north of Rabigh. During his absence Feisal had retreated from Hamra, and that night Lawrence set out with a guide from the local Juhaynah tribe and rode through the night to find Feisal, who was now northeast of the port, in the fertile Wadi Yanbu.

Feisal's tribesmen were not far inland, and Lawrence reached their camp much sooner than he expected, in the middle of the night. "When we got near we saw through the palm trees the flame and smoke of many fires, and the whole valley was full of shouting, and rifle shots, and the roaring of camels," he wrote in his diary. "I have never seen so many camels together and the mess was indescribable."[19] Lawrence found Feisal sitting on a carpet in the middle of the wadi, reading reports and writing orders by lamplight. Feisal explained to him what had happened in the mountains after he had left his younger brother Zeid to guard the pass at Bir Abbas, on the mountain road from Medina to Rabigh. Under pressure from the advancing Turks, Zeid's force had disintegrated. His men, Lawrence would write, had become "a loose mob of fugitives" who were now either "riding wildly through the night towards Yanbu" or heading for their homes to protect their families from the Turks.[20]

The Turks' headway southwest from Medina was serious news, as it meant that they had effectively driven a wedge between Feisal's and Ali's forces at Yanbu and Rabigh, respectively. Having talked with Feisal almost until dawn, Lawrence then tried, and failed, to sleep. After an hour he got up: "it was too cold," he admitted, "to do anything else."[21] The mist had come down into the wadi, he was saturated, and, because Feisal's intelligence depended on the scattering tribesmen, wild, contradictory reports were coming in about Turkish movements. The Harb and Juhaynah, the two tribes on whom Feisal depended, were demoralized; their camp, Lawrence observed, was "not far off panic."[22]

After sunrise Feisal moved farther down the wadi toward the sea. The next day he offered Lawrence an odd gift. It was a British Lee-Enfield rifle that had been captured by the Turks at Gallipoli, engraved in golden Arabic, "Part of our booty in the battles for the Dardanelles," and then given by the Ottomans to Feisal. Lawrence carved the date—4 December 1916—into the stock and, apparently, carried the rifle throughout the rest of the war.[23] But he made no mention of the weapon in any of the reports he wrote immediately afterward, perhaps recognizing that the gift was a rather barbed one, since the fact that the rifle was Feisal's to give was the consequence of a terrible British military failure. Feisal also asked Lawrence to wear Arab garments, giving him some white silk robes embroidered with gold: wedding garments sent to him by an aunt in Mecca. Among the Bedu, who dressed in russet, brown, and indigo-dyed robes, these made Lawrence anything but inconspicuous—they were designed to give Lawrence a status that would make his permanent presence in the camp unquestionable.

Lawrence stayed two days with Feisal before returning to Yanbu. Back at the port, on 5 December he wrote to Hogarth with a downbeat report on Feisal's position, wondering whether his pessimism might be attributable to his having slept for a total of only three hours in the preceding three nights. "All the same," he admitted, "things are bad."[24]

There were telltale signs that Feisal's tribal coalition was under strain. The Juhaynah chiefs, Lawrence reported, were jealous of the influence Feisal was exerting on their kinsmen, and Feisal worried that the Harb and Juhaynah might turn on each other. Feisal himself, said Lawrence, was fast becoming a "tribal leader not a leader of tribes," a phrase that Wingate speedily appropriated to advance his own case for sending troops.[25] That the tribesmen were now drifting away, Lawrence admitted frankly, meant that "the shield of Rabigh on which, in my old report, I relied for all the defensive work is now gone."[26] Nothing now stood in the Turks' way except Ali's force in Rabigh, which Lawrence dismissed as "anaemic," and the threat posed to their supply line and rear by the Harb in the mountains and by Feisal in Wadi Yanbu. In his own notebook Lawrence recorded Feisal's bleak appraisal of the impact of the Turkish advance on the ambitious ideas they had already discussed: "Impossible go S[outh] Syria while Turks free attack Mecca: he would chuck the N[orth] and go south with Bisha and Hudheil to die in its defence"—a reference to two loyal tribes Feisal felt he could trust in the last resort.[27] With the Turks pressing the tribesmen down both Wadi Yanbu and Wadi Safra toward the sea, Feisal "has now swung round to the belief in a British force at Rabigh," Lawrence reported to Hogarth early in December,

The Arabs' camp in the mouth of Wadi Yanbu at the nadir
of the revolt in December 1916. Lawrence was nevertheless
very pleased with this photograph, which he took himself.

admitting, "I see myself that the arguments have force."[28]

Feisal rapidly followed Lawrence down to the sea. The day after Lawrence had left Feisal's damp campsite in Wadi Yanbu, the Turks had attacked. While the artillery the British had supplied made, in Lawrence's words, "an immense noise, most excellent for tribal work," the guns had not been supplied with sights or any of the range-finding equipment needed to make them effective, and the ancient shells that came with them had fuses damp with fungus.[29] Cosmetic in value, the artillery proved of little use in the battle that followed. The tribesmen were routed, and Feisal was forced to flee down the wadi to Yanbu itself. When asked by Feisal why his kinsmen had retreated, the Juhaynah's sheikh Abdel Kerim replied that his men were tired and thirsty and wanted to brew some coffee. After the war Lawrence remembered their reaction when Feisal recounted this excuse: "Feisal and I lay back and laughed: then we went to see what could be done to save the town."[30]

Faced with an imminent Turkish attack, the Arabs in Yanbu were frantically trying to improve the town's defenses. Coordinating the effort was Herbert Garland, a tall, sardonic metallurgist, who had worked before the war preserving ancient Egyptian tools. In wartime the conservationist had metamorphosed into bomb maker. Thousands of "Garland grenades"—a type of mortar shell—were manufactured and shipped to Gallipoli. Garland himself was shipped to the Hijaz in September 1916 to assist in training the Bedu in the use of explosives. "The barren, jagged, uninviting mountains of the Hijaz do not . . . display any apparent attractions which would indicate why Muhammad, or any less important person, should wish to visit them," he dryly observed, noting disparagingly of his pupils, "A robber in the Hijaz has his lot cast amongst such experts that his profession must be difficult to follow."[31]

The Juhaynah tribesmen, who deemed hard work beneath them, rounded up the townspeople of Yanbu to dig a trench in front of the town. Garland found an old Turkish cannon at the fort, but as it "was apt to fire astern instead of forward we relied on its warlike appearance to help us scare off the Turks."[32] More usefully, out at sea behind the town, five ships sent by the British scoured the Yanbu plain with their searchlights by night. One of the Turks' own Bedu guides later admitted that the Turks had faltered when the slow sweep of the searchlights revealed the barren openness of the plain they would have to cross to attack the little port.[33] Bright light alone saved Yanbu from a Turkish attack—which never did materialize.

Lawrence also found an unwelcome letter from Cyril Wilson awaiting him in Yanbu. Wilson was now in charge of the two branches of British activity in the Hijaz. One at Rabigh comprised the flight of British biplanes, which had just been returned to the Hijaz, protected by a detachment of Egyptian soldiers under Colonel Pierce Joyce. The other was a small military mission of officers, experts in artillery and demolitions who were about to arrive in the Hijaz. They would be led by Colonel Stewart Newcombe. Lawrence's place in this military hierarchy had never been made clear—a fact that reflected the unorthodox genesis of his initial visit to Arabia—but now, Wilson explained, a job had been found for him: Wingate wanted him to manage the supplies into the port. It was a prospect that Lawrence found deeply uncongenial, since he regarded himself as "primarily Intelligence Officer, or liaison with Feisal."[34]

Taking advantage of the ambiguity of his situation, Lawrence tried to wriggle out of obeying Wingate's order, which may well have been designed to clip his wings.[35] "I do not quite understand what the Sirdar can mean by my superintending the 'supply question,'" he replied to Wilson, arguing—inconsistently—that the Arabs were best left to manage supplies themselves and that Garland was better qualified for the role. To emphasize the point, he added that he was so bogged down by "coding and decoding, and local work" that he had been "unable to write a word of a report" on his visit to Feisal.[36] In fact, he had already written in detail on the precarious situation for the Arab Bureau director David Hogarth's benefit the day before.

In his letter to Wilson, Lawrence also requested an urgent aerial reconnaissance of Wadi Safra to establish how far down the wadi the Turks had reached. The biplanes, which could supply the accurate and up-to-date information on Turkish movements that had so far been lacking, would give the British an enormous advantage. But the results of their aerial reconnaissance, which was made on 8 December, were alarming. The series of photographs that Wilson received revealed that a small Turkish force had reached the wells at Bir Said, a village halfway between Wadi Yanbu and Wadi Safra, about twenty miles from the sea and just forty-five from Yanbu.

From the photographs, Colonel Pierce Joyce decided, it looked as if the Turks had made up their minds to "dispatch Feisal."[37] A brusque, west-coast Irishman, a "giant of a man" at over six feet four inches tall, Joyce was a professional soldier who walked stiffly as a result of a bad wound he had received during the Boer War. He had arrived at Rabigh a month earlier tasked by Wingate with protecting the biplanes and deciding how best to defend the wells, and he was unimpressed by what he found there. The trenches dug by the Arabs were "mere scratchings," he wrote to Wilson in Jeddah, and his men were having to sleep under blankets because the "*Minerva* brought us 10 tents *minus* the poles so of course they are useless."[38] With frequent heavy rain and hail at night, the lack of shelter was a serious problem: "I'd like to wring somebody's neck over it for it simply means that someone has been damn careless and we suffer in consequence."

Huddled under the soaking blankets were the 450 soldiers from the Egyptian army whom Joyce commanded. The Egyptians' job was to protect the new British airstrip beside the lagoon, but Joyce had little faith in them if the Turks made it as far as Rabigh, for the Egyptian army was, purposefully, no invincible military machine. A force of Egyptian and Sudanese troops, whose senior officers were all British, it had been designed by the British to be strong enough to defend the frontiers of Egypt and Sudan but weak enough not to be able to mount a coup. Brémond thought that the British officers always answered yes a little too fast when he asked them whether they trusted their Egyptian men.[39]

Nor was Joyce happy about the quality of the other Arab troops in the camp inland beside the wells at Rabigh, which Ali, whom he branded "a little shit," would not let him visit.[40] The Bedu were "doubtful allies putting up the rottenest fight," he complained, who would "melt away like snow when a few Turks appear" while the "so-called regular troops," by which he meant the Arab former prisoners of war and a few local men who had volunteered to fight, were "so eaten up with intrigue that it is very doubtful if they will fight either, or on which side."[41] Rampant intrigue was the most obvious of the Arabs' problems, but not the only one. At the end of January 1917, Joyce put in an order for ten thousand mercury pills to treat the syphilis rife among Ali's men.[42]

Further aerial reconnaissance confirmed that the Turks were steadily advancing down Wadi Yanbu toward Yanbu, and from Bir Said southwest toward the sea, in a move that threatened to cut Feisal's tribesmen in Yanbu off from Ali's in Rabigh.[43] In Yanbu, Feisal told Lawrence that he expected the revolt to collapse within three weeks.[44] And when Storrs visited the little port on 13 December, he reported "a regular panic ashore" and that Feisal had taken up residence aboard HMS *Hardinge* in anticipation of an imminent Turkish assault on the port.[45] Feisal was hardly showing the leadership that Lawrence had supposedly identified just six weeks earlier, but, luckily for the Arabs and their British advisers, the situation was about to change.

8

Turning Point

"Rabigh has been a perfect nuisance during the last few weeks but I have been as stubborn as a donkey and so far have succeeded in getting my way," Sir William Robertson wrote on 1 December.[1] He wanted to divert no troops to Rabigh, but he spoke too soon. The weakness of Lawrence's arguments had been rudely exposed by news that the Turks were nearing the coast. The Turks' advance and political crisis in London combined to revive the case for sending a force to the Hijaz. When, on 5 December, Herbert Asquith resigned as prime minister following a collapse in confidence over his conduct of the war, the secretary of state for India, Sir Austen Chamberlain, immediately buttonholed the energetic new prime minister, David Lloyd George, about whether to send troops to Rabigh.[2] "I disliked stirring up the Sharif," Chamberlain wrote in a private minute to his advisers, "but since he was egged on by Lord Kitchener and Egypt, I dislike still more the prospect of seeing him go under."[3]

Nudged by Chamberlain, the War Cabinet discussed the issue of sending troops to Rabigh again on 4 December, to Robertson's dismay.[4] Unwilling to appear to be doing nothing, it cautiously agreed that, if Husein applied for troops in writing, then a force could in principle be sent. "We do not wish to land troops in Hijaz except in last extremity, but Sharif must be saved from destruction if possible," the Foreign Office informed Wingate later the same day, adding that if a brigade was enough to hold Rabigh, "we authorize you to dispatch these troops from Suez whenever you receive a request from Sharif . . . but you must be satisfied that the force is sufficient and that it can be supplied with water and all necessities."[5]

By chance in Khartoum Wingate had received just such an appeal from the sharif, who had reluctantly handed Wilson a request for help in Jeddah the night before. Wingate immediately telegraphed the Foreign Office early on 11 December to say that Husein had finally asked for six thousand men. Husein would prefer Muslims, he reported, but if none were available, he had no objection to British troops instead.[6] His telegram crossed with the Foreign Office message authorizing dispatch.

Overnight, however, Husein changed his mind. He had been swayed by a report in the Medina-based Turkish propaganda newspaper, *Hijaz*, which alleged that he had already promised the region to the British after the war, and was unwilling to play further into the hands of his would-be replacement, Ali Haidar.[7]

At three o'clock on the afternoon of 12 December, Wingate was obliged to ask London to ignore his earlier message, explaining that Husein preferred to keep a force—which must comprise Muslim troops alone—on standby at either Suez or Port Sudan. Angry with the sharif, he drafted a telegram that night asking Wilson to try to force Husein to acknowledge his responsibility, should the Turks recapture Mecca.[8] He also asked for, and received, permission from London to issue an ultimatum to Husein, telling him that he had to accept troops now, or never. Husein, however, refused to be browbeaten.

Storrs arrived in Jeddah the same day. He was in a buoyant mood, having remembered to bring a gramophone with him on his latest voyage and, with the cool boom of Wagner in the background, had this time defeated the ship's paymaster "dreadfully" at chess.[9] Arriving ashore, Storrs wandered through the city's twisting streets to the tall, whitewashed palace where Husein was staying. Pushing his way through the large and noisy crowd that had gathered outside, he went inside with Wilson to meet Husein for the first time.

Husein was taller and more impressive than Storrs had expected. He had "a captivating sincerity of utterance, enhanced by a benignant, noble simplicity of demeanour," recorded Storrs, a man who never used a short word when a longer one might better demonstrate his intellect.[10] Under the glare of an acetylene lamp, Wilson and Storrs discussed the military situation with Husein late into the night. Wilson presented Husein with Feisal's prediction—reported by Lawrence—

that the revolt would collapse within three weeks. But the sharif was in a combative mood. Referring to the somewhat speculative request he had first made that March, he reproached Storrs for Britain's failure to land in Syria and cut the Hijaz Railway to support him. Gripping the young diplomat by the lapels of his jacket, Husein reminded Storrs of the importance of McMahon's letters. "The High Commissioner is the justification of my action," he said, "and wherever I meet him I will grasp him like this, claiming him as my witness."[11] It was becoming clear to the British that Husein invested considerably more faith in the correspondence than they did. And he did so from a position of considerable power. Husein was, wrote another British officer, "quite acute enough to realize that he . . . is rendering important services to the British in this theatre of the war" by "immobilizing the best part of two Turkish divisions," and expected to be treated if not as an equal then as more than "a mere suppliant in receipt of favours."[12]

In fact, tensions within the Ottoman government and army played just as important a part as Husein in bringing about the crucial turning point in the Arab revolt. Following the outbreak of the uprising, the Turkish minister for war, Enver Pasha, had originally planned to send an expeditionary force to the Hijaz to retake Mecca. But, according to the chief German military adviser to the Ottoman government, Otto Liman von Sanders, the "organization of this expedition, in which Christians could not be permitted to participate, was found so difficult by the Turks, that it was dropped in the fall."[13] Liman von Sanders had played his own part in ensuring that the expedition never set out, because he had evidence that British troops were now advancing eastward through the Sinai Desert and would shortly attack Palestine. He urged Jemal Pasha, the governor of Syria and commander of the Ottoman Fourth Army based there, to concentrate all his available resources on repelling the British offensive he expected. Disregarding the religious significance of holding on to Medina, he took the view that the holy city had no strategic value whatsoever and told Jemal to forget Fakhri, whose frequent pleas for supplies he dismissed as "customary Turkish exaggeration."[14]

Fakhri was not exaggerating, however, because supplies in Medina began to dwindle. Inside the city Ali Haidar complained that there was barely enough food for the townspeople and that the army's pack animals were starving.[15] Outside the city the Turks foraged for food in the mountains between their front line and Medina but, in doing so, incurred the hostility of the local Harb tribesmen whose livestock they were pilfering.[16] The Harb increasingly raided Turkish supply lines, which stretched for more than fifty miles through the mountain passes, on one occasion capturing three hundred camels.[17] Then, early in January, Husein's son Abdullah inflicted a lucky but significant defeat on the Turks when he encountered a column of Turkish troops near the railway and, after a fierce gun battle, captured its commander, artillery, and machine guns as well as a substantial sum of gold. Finding that the commander had left a letter to Fakhri explaining what had happened pinned to a telegraph pole beside the track, Abdullah added a note expressing his astonishment that Fakhri had "handed such a treasure to a company sent on such a hazardous expedition."[18]

The vast sums of British gold arriving in Jeddah meant that the Turks also had trouble buying ebbing tribal support with their comparatively worthless paper money. By the end of 1916 the British had paid the sharif nearly one million gold sovereigns—known colloquially as the "Cavalry of St. George" after the design on their reverse—and there are plenty of anecdotes to suggest that the Hijaz was awash with British coin.[19] One naval officer watched an Arab offer one of his men a sovereign (worth £1) in exchange for a packet of cigarette papers: "the sailor, although surprised, rose to the occasion," he remembered, followed swiftly by "other members of the boat's crew who were fortunate enough to have cigarette papers on them."[20] It was "the fattest time the tribes have ever known," said Lawrence.[21]

The British joked at the time that the Bedu could smell gold on the wind, for the tribesmen were obsessed by the metal. Go to the Hijaz today, and you will find pits in front of most of the abandoned railway stations, dug by the Bedu in search of hoarded Turkish treasure. At Petra, too, the stone urn that tops the front of the famous treasury is pockmarked by the bullets of treasure hunters who were sure it would spill gold coins if only they could smash it. The British played on this fixation and bought their alliance with the Bedu. When Herbert Garland asked one of them whether the tribesmen at one encampment he had visited were for the sharif, "No," he was told: "Not for the Sharif; for British gold."[22]

Given their precarious existence, the Bedu were understandably determined to milk the willingness of both sides to pay them for as long as possible. One sheikh told the Turks that the Arabs commanded considerably more support than they did, apparently to prolong the conflict, in which the Turks were paying him as an informant.[23] As a result, the Turks believed that substantial numbers of British, Egyptian, and Algerian troops had already landed at Rabigh. They certainly knew from spies that Feisal had a British adviser.[24] They may also have thought that their enemy was well fortified since, in a moment of desperation, Wingate had deliberately telegraphed a report saying that he had sent barbed wire to Rabigh *en clair* in the hope that the Turks might intercept it.[25]

The Bedu also encouraged the British to believe that the forces ranged against them were of a higher caliber than they really were, and this fed their jumpy assessment of how badly the campaign was going. In fact, the advancing Turkish force—a camel corps—which was so feared by Feisal and Lawrence, was "short of food and money," in Ali Haidar's opinion, and was eventually forced to turn back because of malnutrition and disease.[26] Late in December, Fakhri toured his frontline troops at Hamra and in Wadi Yanbu. Concerned by their condition and their vulnerability to bombing by British seaplanes, which had now begun operating from off Yanbu, on 23 December he ordered his men to withdraw to positions around Medina.[27] Starved of the resources he would have needed to recapture Mecca, Fakhri had finally given up trying to do so. Out of a mixture of necessity and religious zeal, for the rest of the war he would focus his energies on defending Medina.

It was not immediately clear that Turkish orders had changed, partly because the Turks who had been in Wadi Yanbu were ordered south, in what appeared to the British to be a slow and systematic move toward Rabigh. In a meeting with Lawrence and Wilson on 27 December to discuss the emergency measures needed to defend Rabigh, Feisal raised the possibility of attacking Wajh, a small port 180 miles north of Yanbu. Wajh would be an ideal base for raids on the Hijaz Railway—the Turks' supply line—which would in turn reduce the pressure on Rabigh. The British had considered, and then shelved, the same idea three months earlier, because they deemed the situation at Rabigh too uncertain to risk a leap up the coast.

Feisal, however, had heard that his brother Abdullah had now reached Wadi Ais, an inland valley eighty miles north of Yanbu, which ran toward the railway. With his brother in a position where he could directly threaten Medina, Feisal decided that it was time to take the risk of moving on Wajh. Wilson, unexpectedly, was willing to help him. He offered to mass as much naval support off Rabigh as possible to discourage a Turkish advance while Feisal marched northward. It would take some time to organize the tribesmen's march, and surprise would be an advantage, so the three men decided to attack Wajh on the day after the next moonless night—at dawn on 23 January.

The British decision to advance on Wajh completed the reversal in fortunes that had begun when the Turks switched to the defensive. It was also a godsend to Lawrence. Not only did it promise to break the deadlock in the southern Hijaz, which had so far thwarted his hopes of using the tribesmen to deny the French Syria, but it also extended his own role in the Hijaz. "The situation is so interesting that I think I will fail to come back," he wrote to a colleague stuck in Cairo on 27 December. "I want to rub off my British habits and go off with Feisal for a bit. Amusing job, and all new country."[28]

That same afternoon Feisal and Lawrence began to plan an overland march designed to demonstrate their strength to the country through which they would pass en route to Wajh. Feisal then left the coast for Wadi Ais, where he hoped to meet his brother Abdullah. Abdullah, who had been out of touch for several weeks, had delayed leaving Mecca and taken the inland road to Medina because he was worried that his mainly Utaybah tribesmen would clash with his brother Ali's Harb contingent.[29] Feisal now hoped to inform his brother of his plans.

On 3 January, Lawrence set off with a small party of Harb tribesmen toward Hamra to establish whether the Turks had evacuated Wadi Safra, the valley down which ran the road from Medina to Rabigh. Having climbed the dangerously rotten strata of Jabal Dhifran, a mountain overlooking the road toward Hamra, they saw the following morning Turkish tents far below them. A few potshots at the campsite raised the Turkish garrison; seeing he was outnumbered, Lawrence led the tribesmen away down into the valley back to Yanbu, where they surprised two Turkish soldiers. They were "much unbuttoned, disturbed at their first morning duty," Lawrence sniggered later.[30] It was his first encounter with the enemy in the Hijaz, and he was heartened by it: "They were the most ragged men I have ever seen, bar a British tramp and surrendered at once."[31] Their physical condition and, under interrogation, description of the sickness afflicting the Ottoman forces clearly persuaded Lawrence that his plans to head north could now be resurrected. On 5 January he asked the Arab Bureau for four maps covering Syria and Mesopotamia.[32] It was a significant request.

⁓⁂⁓

On 5 January, Wilson received a telephone call from one of Husein's officials, suggesting that the sharif would be willing to accept troops if Wingate advised that course of action. He reported the approach to Wingate, who seized on the news. Wingate had been busy trying to bully Husein into accepting troops since being installed as the high commissioner in Cairo. He informed the Foreign Office the following day that he had received "a formal application" for help from Husein, and that he would now send troops to Rabigh.[33]

In Cairo, General Murray was surprised by this unexpected development. "I need hardly say what a blow your letter and the Sharif's telegram are to me," he wrote to Wingate the same day, openly accusing him of making Husein feel "more or less obliged to accept this assistance."[34] In the eastern Sinai Desert, his forces—already understrength in his opinion—were on the point of launching an attack designed to drive the Turks back into Palestine, where they could no longer threaten the Suez Canal. Redeploying troops to the Hijaz now would, Murray insisted, "seriously hamper my operations if not entirely bring them to a standstill." Wingate pressed on regardless. Orders were drafted for the "General Officer Commanding, Rabigh," instructing him "that the Sharif is to be maintained and Mecca secured at all costs."[35] But they were never issued, largely owing to Wilson's unexpected intervention.

Wilson increasingly took the view that Wingate's efforts to pressure the sharif into accepting troops were misguided. When he heard what Wingate had told the Foreign Office, he contacted the Arab Bureau. "I consider it most dangerous to send British troops to Hijaz on strength of a telephone message from an Arab Government official which the Sharif can easily repudiate," he ventured: "I much regret this decision."[36] If troops were to be sent, Wilson argued, Husein should be asked how much time he needed to pave the way for their arrival.

Wingate tried to suppress Wilson's opinion, but in the Arab Bureau Hogarth, who also vehemently opposed sending troops, ensured that

Wilson's views were transmitted to London, exposing the flimsiness of
Wingate's assertion that the sharif had asked for troops. At the India
Office a senior adviser was highly critical of Wingate. "HMG have not
been too well served by Sir Reginald Wingate in this most important
matter," he commented, explaining, for the record, that "but for the
fact that Sir Archibald Murray was sufficiently obstinate not to move
without confirmation from the War Office, HMG would not have
known that this 'formal application' was nothing more than a telephone
message in which the whole responsibility was thrown on us. Knowing
it, the War Cabinet declined to act."[37]

Already bruised by this episode, Wingate was then forced to admit
on 12 January that Wilson had just received a further letter from the
sharif, "to the effect that he does not desire us to land British troops in
the Hijaz at present."[38]

Murray now took full advantage of the fact that Wingate had over-
stretched himself. "Things seem to be going so well in the Hijaz," he
archly wrote to Wingate on 19 January, that he saw no further need to
keep the brigade on standby for Rabigh, when it could more usefully
be employed in his approaching offensive in Sinai.[39] With no troops to
deploy, Wingate was forced to concede. On 24 January he wrote to
Arthur Balfour, the new foreign secretary, to try to draw a line under
the affair. While the Turks' contraction around Medina was good
news, he said, the final removal of the menace of a Turkish advance on
Mecca depended on Britain's ability "to help the Arabs permanently to
destroy the Turkish railway communications with the Hijaz." It was to
this end, through the capture of Wajh, Wingate suggested, that "all our
energies should now be directed."[40] With Wingate no longer stoking
the problem, the debate over whether to send troops to Rabigh was
effectively over.

❦

During the argument over troops, Lawrence had been making preparations for the march up the coast to Wajh, which, Feisal hoped, would
advertise the strength of his support, bringing more tribesmen on to
his side and possibly forcing the surrender of Wajh without a fight. On
17 January he landed at Umm Lajj, nearly a hundred miles up the coast
from Yanbu, with Captain Boyle and Major Charles Vickery to meet

Feisal to finalize tactics. "Ginger" Boyle was the captain of HMS *Fox* and, as commander of the Red Sea patrol, the man who would provide the ships to mount the Wajh attack. Vickery was the first of the small mission of regular officers summoned by Wingate to advise the Arabs on destroying the railway. A professional soldier of sixteen years' experience, he made no effort to hide his disdain for the disorganization of the campaign, which he attributed to the disproportionate role that amateurs like Lawrence and Garland had played in it so far. But the professionals seemed on the point of taking over: the meeting was to be Lawrence's last task before he handed over to the leader of the mission, Colonel Stewart Newcombe, and returned to Cairo. Unlike Newcombe, Lawrence was not an explosives expert. "I wish I had not to go back to Egypt," he had ended a letter to his mother the previous evening. "Any way I have had a change."[41]

Boyle, Vickery, and Lawrence rode to Feisal's camp and arrived in time for lunch. "It was a greasy stew," remembered Boyle, "out of which we helped ourselves to pieces of meat with our fingers. Feisal handed me choice morsels and I understood that this was a special mark of favour to his principal guest, so I felt obliged to eat them."[42] Boyle was aching from his camel ride—"Except as a child at the Zoo, or going to the Pyramids as a tourist, I had never mounted one"—and the reek of sun-warmed human feces on the ground around him did not whet his appetite. Vickery was similarly put off. He "saved the situation by producing a large flask of whisky, a proceeding frowned upon by Lawrence, but laughed at by Feisal, and the contents were very welcome," Boyle wrote in his memoirs.[43] Lawrence, who did not drink, slated Vickery's action as "tactless," given the Muslim company, and put it down to years of living in the Sudan, which "took the fine edge off some Englishmen."[44]

After lunch Feisal suggested that Vickery muster a force of several hundred Bedu on an island off Umm Lajj and from there sail up the coast and wait off Wajh until he arrived from the south. The question was how long his army would take to cover the distance, a journey of one hundred miles.

The coastal plain between Umm Lajj and Wajh, hemmed in to the east by low hills and bounded on the west by the turquoise stripe of the Red Sea, was then, as now, a desiccated, empty place. Its monotony was only broken in places by a few stunted, flat-topped trees, their branches cowed and black as if scorched by the sun and the hot onshore wind. It was doubtful whether a force of almost six thousand men, two to a camel, and a further five thousand on foot, would find enough water along the way to sustain itself. If there was not enough water, the force would have to travel more slowly to survive, missing the date of the attack. But there had been heavy rain the previous night, and Feisal decided to take the risk. As a precaution, Boyle agreed to drop twenty tons of water at a point a short distance south of Wajh, which Feisal's force ought to reach on 22 January, the day before the proposed assault. The British decided to give Brémond no warning of their plans to attack.[45]

Stewart Newcombe's arrival would have spelled the end of Lawrence's time in Arabia. But Newcombe was delayed. As Feisal intended to set out for Wajh early the next day, Lawrence realized to his delight that it would be impossible to complete the handover. Knowing, however, that he had made an enemy of Vickery, he decided to take the opportunity to win Newcombe around to his own way of thinking. He had surveyed the eastern Sinai with Newcombe before the war and wrote to his old colleague that night. "This show is splendid: you cannot imagine greater fun for us, greater fury and vexation for the Turks. We win hands down if we keep the Arabs simple . . . to add to them heavy luxuries will only wreck this show, and guerrilla does it," he gushed, before preempting criticism of his approach.

> Vickery had a funny idea that nothing had yet been done out here. It's not true! May I suggest that by effacing yourself for the first part and making friends with the head men before you start pulling them about, you will find your way very much easier? . . . After all, it's an Arab war, and we are only contributing materials— and the Arabs have the right to go their own way and run things as they please. We are only guests.[46]

The following morning the force, composed mainly of Juhaynah tribesmen, which Feisal had spent a fortnight gathering, set out for Wajh arrayed in two wings, which took turns to sing to one another. Newcombe, who had arrived shortly after they set out, rapidly caught up, but he did not send Lawrence back to the coast, preferring to travel with him for the following week. The Arabs' style of marching was "rather splendid and barbaric," Lawrence had written days earlier, as the force

"Not an army but a world." Feisal, farthest left,
conceived the march to win over further adherents
with a show of strength.

moved from Yanbu. Then, Lawrence rode behind Feisal, dressed in the white wedding clothes and a scarlet headdress he had been given. Next to Lawrence, also in a red headcloth, was Feisal's cousin Sharraf, who was wearing the henna-dyed robe and black cloak typical of the Juhaynah tribe. Behind them were three standard-bearers, each carrying the sharif's crimson banner, drummers, and then the twelve hundred mounted bodyguards. Everyone, remembered Lawrence, was "singing at the tops of their voices a warsong in honour of Feisal and his family."[47]

As Feisal predicted, to march in large numbers marked a profound change for the Bedu, who were more used to raiding in parties that rarely comprised more than a dozen of their kinsmen. "We are no longer Arabs but a nation," observed one of the Juhaynah's leaders, Abdel Kerim, somewhat gloomily, as he looked down from his tent at the hundreds of campfires below him one night during a halt in the march. Awed by what he saw, another tribesman declared, "It is not an army but a world which is moving on Wajh."[48]

9

Wajh

On 21 January 1917, 400 Arab tribesmen boarded the *Hardinge* bound for Wajh. "It is one of the extraordinary offshoots of the universal war, that British men-of-war should be co-operating with Arab hordes!" Admiral Wemyss commented in his diary from the Red Sea the same day. The "Arab hordes," however, were always unpredictable. When, as agreed, the following day the *Hardinge* anchored off the coast just south of Wajh to land the emergency water supply, there was no sign of Feisal's 11,000-strong force of tribesmen. With no moon that night, the British had their best chance of slipping inshore unnoticed by the Turkish garrison, which was rumored to be 800 strong, and Wemyss decided to press on to Wajh regardless to deliver his unruly passengers. As he had little faith in the Arabs' willingness to fight if the Turkish garrison did not surrender first, he had also cobbled together a landing party comprising 200 of the *Hardinge*'s marines and its stokers, led by Vickery.[1] And from off Wajh, the guns of the *Fox* and the *Espiegle* would offer the Arabs further support.

A black night gave way to dawn fog on 23 January. "Our little fleet steamed slowly northward like grey ghosts to take up their fighting positions," remembered Vickery's right-hand man, Norman Bray.[2] Vickery decided to go ahead with a landing on the north side of Wajh, which had been planned on the assumption that Feisal would be approaching simultaneously from the south. Just after seven o'clock that morning the silence was interrupted by the rattle of chains, as the *Hardinge* dropped its anchors, and landing boats packed with Juhaynah tribesmen in their damp and smelly camel-hair cloaks were jerkily lowered into the sea and rowed ashore unseen.

Wajh is a much larger town today than it was in 1917, boasting its own small airport. A few once smart merchants' houses and the old mosque, with its fat, stubby minaret, are all that remain of the little walled port that Wemyss decided to attack that chilly morning in January 1917. Foreigners are unusual here and, judging by the few sharp stares I attracted, not especially welcome. The town council has optimistically dotted the seafront with gaudily painted benches—all empty when I went past in March 2005—which perch on the edge of an odd coral plateau, which hangs over the beach below like a petrified breaking wave.

Scrambling from the beach up the crumbling crest of this plateau ninety years ago, Bray found that the mist had cleared. To the south the tops of some of the whitewashed houses in the town of Wajh, which in 1917 was mostly squeezed between the headwall of the plateau and the shoreline, were visible. "We have often wanted to know how the Arabs fight," he reported afterward: "The result now observed was highly interesting."[3] Many of the Arabs refused to go any farther, but a small group of about a hundred advanced at "a very sharp pace" straight at the Turkish lines outside the town. The town was by now defended only by a small garrison, as most of the Turks, who had heard that the Arabs were coming, had already retreated to the old fort six miles inland. When the Turks began shooting from about one thousand yards away, the Juhaynah took no notice: "They appeared," Bray observed incredulously, "to be out for a constitutional." The Arabs finally stopped thirty yards from the Turks and began shooting back. "When the Turks fell they showed not the least emotion or satisfaction and merely said '*mayit*,'" the Arabic word for "dead." Overrunning the Turkish defenses and leaving their own dead on the plain, the tribesmen disappeared into Wajh.

Bray returned to the shore to see what the *Hardinge* could do to help the tribesmen. But the distance from the ships to the shore was so short that shells fired from the British ships simply ricocheted screaming off the rocks before or behind the town to detonate in the hills beyond. The naval party landed, but appeared to him to be at sea on land.

"What would you advise us to do?" its leader asked Bray.

"Well, you are commanding here and not I," Bray retorted.

"Yes, yes, I know. But what would you do if you were I?"[4]

Following the Arabs into Wajh, Bray found mayhem. "The dead were still lying about, the houses had been ransacked from roof to floor, papers everywhere, boxes and cupboards cut open and even the mattresses cut open to find hidden treasure."[5] The cotton stuffing of the mattresses was blowing down the streets. The Arabs had moved from house to house, shooting and looting, "eating their way into the bowels of the town."[6] By the end of that day, only a few Turks continued to hold out in a few houses and the mosque at the southern end of Wajh. Dealing with this opposition would take the British a second day, for there was still no sign of Feisal and his men.

The following morning, 24 January, the Arabs sent one of their Turkish prisoners with a white flag to offer his comrades the chance to surrender. But the Turks refused the offer. Their resistance ended only when, from out at sea in the *Fox*, Boyle decided to shell the mosque: "A huge gaping hole was blown in the wall, and fifteen very bewildered and very dusty and begrimed men staggered out without their weapons, in token of surrender."[7] The *Espiegle*, in the meantime, was trying to hit the old fort to crush any chance of a Turkish counterattack. With its third shell it scored a direct hit, forcing the Turks inside to flee into the hills. By midafternoon on the second day, the British were in control of Wajh. Almost twenty Juhaynah tribesmen had been killed, and the British had lost one man. Stewart, the observer in one of the seaplanes directing the naval bombardment, was leaning forward in his cockpit to send a radio message when he was hit by a bullet and killed. He was buried at sea that evening.

Feisal arrived the following day with his force of more than ten thousand tribesmen. Progress up the gravel plain beside the sea had been slow, and he had reached Habban two days later than planned, on 24 January, by which time the attack on Wajh was almost over. Stung by his failure, Feisal immediately dispatched men to participate in the mopping-up operation, but he had arrived too late.

Over and above the questions it raised about Feisal's qualities as a leader and his own powers of influence, the delay had other consequences that were serious, Lawrence realized when he arrived in Wajh. The townspeople, who had stayed despite Feisal's warning a week earlier that he was coming, were furious at the damage the Bedu and the British had done to their town. All their dhows, the sailing boats vital for the trade they maintained with Egypt, had been destroyed in the bombardment, which had also "punched large holes in all walls," Lawrence noted.[8]

Moreover, although the Arabs' almost twenty killed was a negligible loss as far as either Vickery or Bray—who had both seen action in France—were concerned, in Lawrence's opinion they were unnecessary casualties, who need not have died had Feisal's men arrived in time and forced the Turks by weight of numbers to surrender faster. Instead, he feared, their deaths might easily upset Arab morale. "Our rebels were not materials, like soldiers, but friends of ours, trusting in our leadership," he later wrote. "We were not in command nationally, but by invitation; and our men were volunteers, individuals, local men, relatives, so that a death was a personal sorrow to many in the army."[9]

On 27 January, having spent two days supervising the offloading of stores in Wajh, Lawrence left for Cairo, now much more confident that he would be back shortly. On the march north to Wajh he must have told Feisal of his fear that he would not return to the Hijaz. The rapport he had struck up with Husein's young son—"We are on the best of terms," he told his mother—now paid off, for Feisal rapidly wrote to his father about his concern "that Lawrence should not return [to] Cairo as he has given such very great assistance."[10]

Crucially, Feisal's endorsement protected Lawrence against the scathing criticism of the Arabs' operation that Vickery then predictably made. "Although it only embarked on a four days' march, due north, parallel to the coast line, and within twenty miles of it, a great part of Feisal's army lost its way and arrived at the rendezvous two days late," Vickery commented.[11] His second in command, Bray—piqued in later life that he had never basked in the glory Lawrence had enjoyed—would write how "the excuse was 'lack of water,' but there was nothing to have prevented five hundred men being pushed on ahead to Wajh." This failure, he believed, "was a reflection, both on Feisal's leadership and still more on his British advisers."[12] The real reason Lawrence did not admit until after the war. The day after he set out for Wajh, Feisal received news of his brother Abdullah's successful ambush of the Turks. The Arabs had stopped for some impromptu, exuberant celebrations for this coup and were late to Wajh in consequence.

The capture of the port of Wajh finally tipped the balance fully in the Arabs' favor. It forced the Turks wholly onto the defensive, for their tenuous supply line was suddenly vulnerable. From the port it would be possible to raid a 250-mile stretch of the Hijaz Railway, from Tabuk in the north to Abu an Naam in the south. Although there was a sizable Turkish garrison at Al Ula and Madain Salih about halfway down this stretch, the railway either side was lonely, studded with occasional stations that were vulnerable to attack. And being that much farther from Medina, the region east of Wajh was also a marginally less sensitive area into which British officers might now venture. Moreover, Wajh was easier for the British to supply, for the port was almost two hundred miles closer than Yanbu to Suez. And finally, as news of Feisal's arrival in Wajh traveled northward by word of mouth, Lawrence's hope of bringing the tribes together to "biff the French out of all hope of Syria" silently evolved from wild theory into a distinct possibility.

On his return to Cairo, Lawrence spent several days helping to correct the draft of the *Handbook of Hejaz*—the Arab Bureau's embryonic guidebook to the region—and furiously writing up his impressions of the tribal situation and the attack on Wajh. In meetings with Hogarth, Storrs, and Wingate, he stressed the dividend that Feisal's march was paying: news of the revolt and recognition of Feisal's strength were beginning to spread far to the north into Syria. Tewfiq Majali, a member of the family implicated in a violent uprising against Ottoman rule in the southern Syrian town of Karak in 1910, was one of those who now made contact. The same day that Feisal arrived in Wajh, leaders of the Bali tribe came south to offer him their allegiance. Members of the Aida, Fuqarah, and Wuld Suleiman tribes from east of the Hijaz Railway would also quickly join him in Wajh.[13] All three were satellite clans of the Aniza, the dominant tribe in northern Arabia. Their arrival raised hopes that Nuri Shaalan, the leading sheikh of the largest Aniza subtribe, the Rwala, might also join the revolt. In his seventies, Shaalan was, Lawrence himself admitted, "not a very attractive person," who had killed two of his brothers to seize control of his tribe.[14] He had, however, been imprisoned by the Turks before the war, and one of his close friends had been hanged in the May 1916 executions that had accelerated Husein's decision to revolt, and was thought by Lawrence to be "worth buying."[15] But widespread famine in Syria meant that when Feisal approached Shaalan late in 1916, the elderly chieftain had explained that he depended on Turkish goodwill for grain, which was in short supply because of the famine. "Nothing prevents us from joining you but the lack of food and arms" was Shaalan's tantalizing reply.[16]

Clayton and Lawrence briefly considered flying supplies to Nuri Shaalan's home at Jawf, 320 miles northeast of Wajh. They were encouraged by the local commander of the Royal Flying Corps, who saw no reason why this wild scheme could not succeed, "providing . . . misfortune, such as an engine failure, does not interfere," but Jawf was too remote, and the plan was eventually abandoned.[17] Clayton and Lawrence knew that Feisal's revolt would dramatically expand in scope if Shaalan could be persuaded to support Feisal, because the Aniza were camel breeders who ranged widely between the northern Hijaz, Syria, and Mesopotamia and enjoyed correspondingly far-reaching influence. The Turks shared this view of Shaalan's importance. Their candidate to replace Husein, Sharif Ali Haidar, had given the sheikh a gold watch when he met him en route for Medina the previous summer. Jemal had then awarded him a medal for loyalty and advanced his son part of a large reward for capturing Feisal dead or alive.[18]

On 3 February, Lawrence met Brémond, who was also in Cairo. The bearlike Brémond suggested to Lawrence that the British join the French in an attack on Aqaba, followed by an attempt to seize the railway near Maan. Lawrence, who had visited the port before the war, knew that the beach was surrounded by several ranks of rising cliffs that provided an almost unassailable position from which the Turks could mow down any troops landing on the beach below. Brémond's scheme ran the risk of degenerating into a second Gallipoli, the costly landings in the Dardanelles in 1915 from which the British had been forced to withdraw in a notorious defeat.

Lawrence was sure that Brémond's true agenda was to confine the Arabs' revolt to the Hijaz. If European troops were landed at the northern end of the Hijaz, there would be no justification for the Arabs heading beyond them northward into Syria, which the French wanted to rule uncontested after the war. So he told Brémond he opposed the plan. When Brémond announced that he would put the idea to Feisal anyway, Lawrence decided to get to Feisal first; he did not trust Feisal to refuse Brémond's offer. In a candid admission later of how he liked his relationship with Feisal to work, Lawrence wrote, "Information had better come to me for him, since I usually like to make up my mind before he does."[19]

At the Arab Bureau, Lawrence's mentor David Hogarth watched bemused as his former student hurriedly departed for Wajh the following day. "I've just seen TEL off again to his wilds and I'm afraid that this time it may be for long enough. But don't tell his mother," he warned his wife, Laura, who lived half a mile from Lawrence's parents in Oxford. "It is a queer venture he has gone off upon and I'm sure no Insurance Co. would accept a policy on his life. But if anyone will, he'll come through."[20]

Lawrence took Feisal into his confidence on his return to Wajh. To spike Brémond's impending visit he told Feisal about the French officer's anti-Arab motives and revealed the gist of the Sykes-Picot agreement for the first time. It is not clear exactly how much Lawrence knew about the agreement—he had been a junior officer tasked with tracking Ottoman army units' movements and had been away in Basra when its terms were first transmitted to Cairo in April 1916—but he seems to have known of its existence and to have guessed correctly that McMahon's vagueness over the future of northern Syria and the French sensitivities Sykes had been instructed to mollify were connected. He advised Feisal that they must develop plans to spread the revolt far to the north to foil French ambitions in Syria. Feisal had to reach Damascus before the end of the war, Lawrence believed, because only the Arabs' right by conquest would overturn the historic French claim to Syria. "One night we all swore not [to] go [to] Mecca till after we had seen Damascus. Great fun when I insisted on taking the oath too," Lawrence jotted shortly afterward in his notebook.[21]

Feisal clearly took Lawrence's advice to heart. His "whole attention is now turned northwards and he considers the actual taking of Medina the work of Abdullah, Ali and Zeid," Pierce Joyce wrote several weeks later.[22] "He cares little about Medina," he reported a week after that, adding that he suspected that Feisal's ambitions stretched as far as Damascus. "I have endeavoured to confine Feisal to local ambitions and Military operations," he added, bemused, "but from somewhere he has developed very wide ideas."[23]

Brémond arrived in Wajh on 18 February to meet Feisal. Although

Lawrence seems to have made himself scarce for the meeting, his influence over Feisal did not go unnoticed. A colleague of Brémond reported that Lawrence "maintains Feisal and his people's natural hostility towards foreign intervention in Arabia" and that Feisal seemed to hold Lawrence's friendship in high regard.[24] Brémond presented Feisal with the first of six machine guns and offered the young sharif a French staff officer to advise him. The gift failed to soften Feisal, who told Brémond that he disapproved of his Aqaba plan, and rejected the need for a military adviser on the grounds that "scientific military knowledge" was not needed in tribal warfare.[25]

Later that day, Feisal told Lawrence what he had said to Brémond. He had claimed that it was his lack of artillery that had driven him to move to Wajh so that he could more easily threaten the railway. "Had he had French guns to reply to the guns which the French had supplied to the Turks, he would have gone straight for Medina," Feisal had teased Brémond, explaining that instead he now planned to use his mobility and growing numbers to defeat the enemy.[26] There was, Lawrence noted exultantly, "really no saying where this protraction of his front would end!"

Drawn by spreading rumors of the British gold on offer, tribesmen continued to arrive in Feisal's camp at Wajh to pledge their support. Lawrence thought that the influx would help bolster morale among the local tribe, the Bali, who were threatening to leave the camp, by creating competition for the money the British were paying Feisal. "The whole country is full of envoys and volunteers, and great sheikhs coming in to swear allegiance," Lawrence wrote at the time.[27] He was particularly pleased that Feisal had heard from Nuri Shaalan's son Nawaf, and the infamous Auda abu Tayi. Auda was a legendary outlaw, with a reputation for savagery fearsome even by the high standards of the Hijaz.[28] Lawrence wanted to use Auda's tribe, the Huwaytat, who had "a resounding name for devilry and reckless courage," to attack the railway near Maan, 275 miles north of Wajh.[29] Both Auda and Nuri Shaalan played significant parts in the plans he was developing.

Having seen Brémond off, Lawrence immediately returned to Cairo. Although he had already made up his mind that Feisal was the most useful—and pliant—of the sharif's sons, his view was not yet widely shared, and he knew that he had still to convince his colleagues.

Clayton, in particular, had always been rather doubtful about Feisal's ultimate loyalties, because of Feisal's close contact with Enver during the negotiations over whether Husein would endorse the jihad. Even Lawrence had been taken aback when, having made sympathetic noises about the Arab nationalists hanged in Syria in 1916, Feisal replied that their punishment as traitors seeking foreign intervention was just. But now, Lawrence was pleased to report, Feisal's position appeared to be hardening. Feisal believed that the divide between the Arabs and the Turks was widening and that a rapprochement with the Turks was now "most improbable," not least because the Arabs' aims now inevitably involved the destruction of the Ottoman Empire, rather than, as some had originally wanted, simply greater autonomy within it.

There was another reason for Lawrence's return to Cairo. With Feisal he had been working on how to use Nuri Shaalan and Auda abu Tayi to push the revolt northward into Syria, and he now wanted to brief Clayton with the ambitious plan they had devised, to raise "all the nomad tribes from the Huwaytat at Jurf ad Darawish north of Maan, to Medina." This involved, Lawrence explained, "combining the Auda abu Tayi, Ibn Jad, Ibn Jazi, and Abu Togeiga Huwaytat; the Bani Atiyah; the Bali; the Moahib; the Fuqarah; the Aida; the Wuld Suleiman and the Juhaynah." This welter of tribal names seems to have been calculated as much to demonstrate his mastery of the complex web of alliances that would be needed as to enlighten his chief.[30] Feisal had received promises of support from most of these tribes, he reported, and other Arabs—from the area to the east of the Dead Sea in present-day Jordan, the Hauran east of Damascus in Syria, and as far north as Lebanon—had also been in touch. But as most of these were settlers who owned land, and were consequently nervous about reprisals by the Ottoman government if they joined the revolt, Feisal had told them to bide their time.

If there had been doubts about his usefulness before, Lawrence's ability to demonstrate his knowledge of what was going on inside Feisal's camp sealed his reputation as indispensable. When a colleague commented, "Lawrence with Feisal is of inestimable value," Clayton agreed. He thought that "if we could find suitable men to act in the same way with Ali and Abdullah it would be invaluable. Such men, however, are extremely difficult to get."[31] He wanted to break the infuriating inertia of Feisal's brothers farther south, and he was cautious about Lawrence's plan because it was a distraction from the capture of Medina, in his view the objective of Britain's support for the Arabs in the Hijaz. "This *is* important," he wrote on Lawrence's report, together with a simple further instruction to save it for later: "File."

10

The First Railway Raids

Amid thunder, lightning, and heavy rain, Herbert Garland set out from Wajh to attack the Hijaz Railway after nightfall on 12 February. While Lawrence had been dealing with Brémond, he had finally received permission from Feisal to venture inland. So now he was headed south-

**Herbert Garland, a prewar
metallurgist, was the first British officer
to raid the railway successfully.**

eastward into Wadi Hamd with a guide named Abdel Kerim and about fifty Juhaynah tribesmen. Little was known about where he was going. The *Handbook of Hejaz*, which Lawrence had been proofreading in Cairo, contained the most up-to-date information on the region. But "South of Wadi Hamd . . . is ill-known to us, and the Wadi Hamd . . . has never been described by any explorer," was all this thin new guidebook had to say.[1]

The British had remarkably little information about the railway either. Among Wingate's papers is an intriguing report on the railway's stations and bridges, dated 1907, illustrated with photographs taken from a moving train, and written by someone who self-effacingly identifies himself only as "G"—probably the *Times*'s correspondent Philip Graves.[2] But "G" had traveled only as far as Madain Salih, the northern gateway to the Hijaz, and the section farther south had not yet been completed in any case. The only Briton known to have traveled the length of the line was Arthur Wavell, an enterprising young army officer who disguised himself as a pilgrim to enter Mecca early in 1909. Wavell shared none of "G"'s reticence when it came to publicity. In his hilarious tale of the escapade, published in 1912, however, he mentioned only in passing that the stations south of Madain Salih were fortified with trenches and barbed wire to protect them against marauding tribesmen disadvantaged by the railway. He was killed fighting the Germans in East Africa—another of the First World War's peripheral "sideshows"—before he could share any further details with the Arab Bureau.[3]

The British officers now based in Wajh had discussed at length what they should attack. It is worth remembering that the British at this time had no previous experience of sabotage deep in hostile territory, and the workaday advice on demolitions in the contemporary *Manual of Field Engineering* appears to have been conceived to cover the British army's retreat rather than to cause havoc far behind enemy lines. Moreover, the Hijaz Railway was a single, narrow-gauge track that ran for over eight hundred miles between Medina and Damascus, an unflashy piece of German engineering that ran through just two tunnels and over two viaducts. But all were too remote from Wajh. The railway's many other bridges—which "G" had carefully catalogued— were expected to be vulnerable, but on closer inspection they turned out to be stubby, massive constructions that were not only very solidly built but, being low to the ground, also relatively easy to repair temporarily with heaps of ballast. The forts that studded the railway every twenty miles seemed unsuitable, since, after Wavell, they were assumed to be well defended, and even today it is possible to see the zigzag lines of trenches around them. That left the locomotives. These had all been imported from Europe before the war and were irreplaceable because the British blockaded the Mediterranean and Red Sea coasts and because the railway from Constantinople through Turkey to Damascus was not yet complete. On his expedition to the railway Garland hoped to mine a train.

The ominous weather that accompanied Garland's departure was appropriate, for his journey would also be very hazardous. Water at that time of year was not as scarce as Garland had expected it to be, and so a conventional desert death from thirst or sunstroke was less likely. But the stagnant pools bloomed with luminous green algae, and their water tasted foul. They also attracted other dangers: scorpions, snakes, and spiders, which the Bedu were deft at flicking into the fire. And all around, all the time, swarmed dozens of flies, generating a constant, low, and inexplicably sinister hum.

The other perennial danger was the vicious tribes that roamed the region. They were "of exceptionally predatory character, low morale, and disunited organization," the *Handbook of Hejaz* advised, adding that "safe conducts given, in all sincerity, by their Sheikhs, have less validity and less local range."⁴ To protect Garland, Lawrence had recommended Abdel Kerim, the cheerful twenty-six-year-old who had led him up Wadi Yanbu two months earlier. A leading Juhaynah and a sharif descended from Muhammad, Abdel Kerim seemed the man most likely to ensure that Garland would return safely in one piece to Wajh. But the deference the young tribesman's ancestry attracted, which was Garland's main insurance policy, had an unexpected drawback. Next time, Garland made a mental note, he would take a less distinguished guide, because it was slow work riding with a "Sharif who finds his chief pleasure in dismounting to be kissed by passing kinsmen."⁵

Garland was left in no doubt about the basis for the loyalty of the Juhaynah accompanying Abdel Kerim, who proved disconcertingly fascinated by gold teeth. "It's alright now," one of them told Garland, "we are friends. We realize that the English are good people with much gold, more than the Turks. But if I'd met you in the desert six months ago, I should have cut your head off, and taken it to Mecca as a reward."[6] This was no idle threat. Nine months earlier, on his first trip to the Hijaz, Ronald Storrs had politely declined the offer—in exchange for just one sovereign—of the severed heads of all seven of the German sailors who had been murdered by the Bedu just days earlier. "Knowing as we did that few professing Christians had penetrated the Hijaz, except in a subterranean sense, those of us who set out for the interior, in the early days of the Revolt, did so with some trepidation," Garland later sardonically explained.[7]

The Juhaynah traveled slowly. The year before had been the driest in the region since 1895, but heavy winter rains had now revived the rocky hills.[8] A sparse fur of pale green and the single, pearly grass stalks shooting up here and there through the stones may have seemed unimpressive to Garland, but looked verdant to the Bedu, who were determined to let their camels roam to graze. Garland begged Abdel Kerim to quicken the pace: "I cajoled, urged, pleaded . . . but all my efforts to get him to increase our rate of progress, which was about 10 miles a day, were quite unavailing."[9] The Juhaynah refused to push their camels faster than their natural jaunty lope.

Though the wadi appeared empty, its sandy base was plaited by animal tracks, and the Bedu frequently diverted to follow marks left by gazelles, hyenas, wolves, jackals, or the occasional leopard. Even today the Bedu retain astonishing abilities as huntsmen. In southern Jordan I watched my Bedu guide Attayak Ali, who was driving our jeep, stamp on the brakes and leap from the cab to pounce on a live chikor partridge he had spotted by the wayside. In the Hijaz in 1917 both partridge and sand grouse made "a valuable addition to the stock pot," in the words of another British officer.[10] Desert hare tastes very good as well.

Constantly at the mercy of the elements, the Bedu were a careworn people, Garland felt, who would eat ravenously, not out of greed but from uncertainty. Once he watched a tribesman eat an entire sheep in a single sitting, using his right hand—the left, being unclean, is never used for eating—to roll the rice boiled inside the carcass into a ball, which he then tossed into his mouth. Animals were killed to be eaten only at times of celebration; normally, the tribesmen lived on rice and dates, buttermilk, cheese, and *semn*, a flour milled from the red seed of a plant that flowered intermittently in the desert. Bread was baked hard in the ash of the dying fire. "One was always hungry," another officer remembered, years later.[11] When finally the embers died, and the fireside talk of past feuds and raids trailed off, each man in Garland's party would sleep in the lee of his kneeling camel for protection from the bitter desert wind. "The animal spends the night chewing," Garland discovered: "A camel's head, with its drooping bottom lip, its ill-proportioned ears, and its shaggy eyebrows, is never a thing of beauty, but seen by moonlight when one is only half awake it seems like an animated gargoyle."[12]

As they neared the railway, Garland and Abdel Kerim argued over tactics. Garland wanted to lay a mine beneath the track and stay close on a nearby hill to see whether it worked. Not wanting to be caught by the Turkish patrols that guarded the line, Abdel Kerim flatly refused. He wanted to plant the mine and be away as fast as possible. When, on the night of 20 February, they finally reached the stony, blasted valley through which the railway ran, Garland won, though not through force of argument. As he explained afterward to his envious colleagues, "The approach of the train five minutes after starting work settled the matter."[13]

༄

Trains on the Hijaz Railway were not supposed to run at night.

When, through the darkness, he heard the shriek of a whistle followed by the squeal of metal wheels biting the railway track, Herbert Garland, who was kneeling beside the rails, jerked upright with surprise.[14] He hesitated for a moment. Then he scrabbled for the five-pound cartons of dynamite on the ground beside him. At a pinch, he could squeeze three of them into the hollow he had partially excavated under the rail.

From one of the pockets of the khaki jacket he wore under his black cloak, Garland pulled the action of an old Martini Henry rifle. Its barrel had been sawn off and the trigger guard removed so that all that was left was an oblong of brown steel from which the trigger protruded, exposed. This he loaded with a thick, old-fashioned bullet the size of his thumb, fished from another pocket. Swiveling the mechanism so that the trigger was uppermost, he carefully wedged it into the hole, bullet pointing into the explosive, trigger brushing the rail above. The lights of the engine were now clearly visible, two hundred yards away,

Toweira Station on the Hijaz Railway.
Herbert Garland's attack on 20 February 1917 took place nearby.

coming toward him at—he guessed—twenty-five miles per hour, which left him fifteen seconds.

He got up and ran. "I wished I had devoted more time to physical training in my youth," Garland, who had a weak heart, recalled after the war.[15] His Arab robe swirled around his legs, as if determined to trip him up. Beneath his bare feet the stony ground felt like "carving knives, bayonets and tin tacks."

As the locomotive's front wheels passed over the mine, nothing happened.

But, a split second later, as the heavier driving wheels flexed the track, they crushed the hidden trigger below. The searing yellow explosion tossed the engine from the track, followed a millisecond later by its deafening boom, which rocked the desert. Through the darkness came the "clanking, whirling, rushing" noise of the stricken train, the shouts and screams of those inside it as it corkscrewed off the stony embankment, and the lethal patter of debris returning to earth.[16]

The flash had momentarily revealed Garland's silhouette, Arab robes flapping, as he sprinted away from the railway past the woody plants that could endure this wilderness. On a low hill overlooking the track, he stopped running and, swearing vehemently between gasps for breath, turned to survey his handiwork by the sliver of light from the waning moon. Satisfied, he turned and headed back toward the group of chattering Arabs whose cigarettes glowed in the blackness. It was 20 February 1917, "the first time that the Turks have had a train wrecked," he reported later, and the first ever act of sabotage committed by the British army behind enemy lines.[17]

Six days later Garland was back in Wajh. He was exasperated by the length of time the raid had taken. In a damning report he described his guide Abdel Kerim as "absolutely incapable of action, criminally haphazard and careless . . . responsible for all the delays of the party and none of its success."[18] Unlike Lawrence, Garland did not relish the challenge, or the theater, of fitting in with the Arabs and going at their pace. Most especially, he hated the Arab clothing Lawrence recommended he wear to gain acceptance and to avoid standing out. It was "most annoying and encumbering," he said, having found that the slightest breeze caused the ends of his head scarf to flick the cigarettes out of his mouth.[19]

Garland's colleagues, by contrast, were delighted. "Best congratulations on your successful raid," wrote Joyce from Rabigh, "such a brilliant success."[20] In a sign that he recognized that the balance had finally

An abandoned railway car near Toweira. All the rolling
stock had been imported from abroad and was irreplaceable in
wartime. This made it a tempting target for the British.

shifted in the Arabs' favor, days earlier Joyce had ordered more foot-balls for his men. In Jeddah the French observed that the hard-pressed staff of the British agency found time to practice their golf.[21]

Reports that a train had been attacked also had a dramatic effect in Medina. The atmosphere there was already panicky following an explosion days earlier, possibly due to sabotage, which destroyed one of the city's barracks. The families of government officials were being evacuated to Syria by the time Garland was approaching the railway. Though Garland believed he had hit a train full of troops, it may in fact have been one of these trains, crowded with women and children, that he had mined in the darkness on 20 February. Small wonder, then, that crucifixion was rumored to be the punishment for any British officer caught by the Turks.[22]

As Medina was turned to a war footing, the Holy Mosque was com-mandeered as a store for ammunition and military equipment. Within the city a shortage of supplies and requisitioning by the Ottoman gar-rison drove up prices. Traders in the city's souk stopped accepting the paper notes the soldiers were paid in, and demanded hard currency instead. "An occasional train with a meagre quantity of supplies would arrive from Damascus and bring slight relief to the famished garrison," recalled Ali Haidar, whose hopes of replacing Sharif Husein as emir had been frustrated. "The military situation stagnated, and a general feeling of uncertainty pervaded all."[23]

At the end of February, Fakhri received orders from the governor of Syria, Jemal Pasha, to evacuate the city immediately. "The news hor-rified me," Haidar recollected. "I sent a strongly-worded telegram to Jemal in which I said that the very idea of deserting the Holy Tomb was utterly shameful, and that it should be protected to the last man, if nec-essary."[24] Although he forced Jemal to back down, he soon received a telegram recalling him to Syria. Early in March he bid farewell to Fakhri. "The protection of this Tomb is in the hands of God, but you are His instrument," Haidar told the beleaguered general. "I leave it in your care. Be worthy of the trust."[25] Having locked his own belongings in a mosque, Haidar left for Damascus. He would spend the rest of the war reunited with his family in an isolated palace in the Lebanese hills.

The British intercepted the radio message ordering Fakhri to with-draw but not its cancellation, and Wingate first heard the news that the Turks had been ordered to pull out of Medina on 5 March. As far as he

Stewart Newcombe in the Hijaz in 1917. Newcombe had first encountered Lawrence when both men worked together on a survey in the Sinai Desert before the war. Although they admired one another, they fell out over tactics during the Hijaz guerrilla war.

was concerned, the timing could not have been worse. On the eastern edge of the Sinai Desert, the British were preparing to attack the small town of Gaza at the end of the month. But their force had just been depleted by the withdrawal of seventeen thousand men—one of their four infantry divisions—to France. Alarmed that news of the British attack might hurry Fakhri's withdrawal north to help defend Gaza, Wingate wired an order to Jeddah for Lawrence and Newcombe the following day. They were to keep up the pressure on the railway and to cut the telegraph wire to Medina, which followed the railway track, as far to the north as possible.[26]

By the time that Wingate's demand arrived, Newcombe had already reached the railway at Dar al Hamra, a station 110 miles northeast of Wajh. A tall man whose hawkish stare radiated determination, Newcombe had a reputation for recklessness: "He runs his head into wasps' nests," Hogarth believed.[27] But he was also rather dashing. In a satchel he always carried were two packets, tied with ribbons, of letters from two girls he had met while fighting in France.[28] Having spent two days watching the line, and having decided that demolitions farther south had clearly been ineffective, since trains were running in both directions more or less daily, Newcombe opted for a three-pronged attack on the station.[29] His guide, the young and well-respected Sharif Nasir, hoped that the attack would help persuade the numerous Arabs the Ottomans employed on the railway to desert. The Turks repelled the Arabs' direct assault on the station on 3 March, but demolitions on each side of the station destroyed at least a mile of track and isolated one of the working parties tasked with checking the line each day. Reports that the Turks did not trust their mostly Arab railway workmen proved correct. The captives from this raid, reported Newcombe, were "8 most delighted prisoners."[30]

Wingate's demand was music to Lawrence's ears. All the while Newcombe and Garland had been inland trying to destroy the railway, Lawrence had been stuck in Wajh, charged with supervising the offloading of cars and with erecting a radio mast, both jobs he loathed. "Did 369 things in all today," he wrote sarcastically on 5 March, before jealously recording the news that Abdullah's men had blown up a section of the long bridge at Abu an Naam on the railway seventy miles northwest of Medina.[31] Wingate's demand for urgent railway demolitions gave him the excuse he needed to escape. In a letter to Wilson he outlined a plan—"spur of the moment," he admitted—in which he would attack the stations where water was stored and destroy as many rails as possible. The volume of water the Turks would then need to transport to run repair trains to fix the line would paralyze their efforts to leave Medina en masse. "If only we can hold them up for ten days," he hoped.[32]

The following night, Lawrence set out southeastward for Abdullah's camp in Wadi Ais with a disparate group of local Bedu, a few Ageyl,° and a Moroccan named Hamed. But he was succumbing to dysentery, and his journey quickly assumed a nightmarish quality. At the end of the second day, in a remote valley north of Wadi Ais, Lawrence was lying down recovering from an agonizing day's riding, when suddenly there was a shot. That was not unusual in itself, since the Bedu frequently fired into the air—but then Suleiman, an Utaybah with the party, took Lawrence to the other side of the wadi where one of the Ageyl was lying dead, shot at close range in the forehead. A month earlier fighting between the Ageyl and the tribesmen in the camp at Wajh had left two

---

° Young townsmen from the Qasim area of central Arabia who made a living out of desert trade, from breeding and selling camels to escorting caravans across the desert. Often they had fled the religious strictures imposed by the Wahhabi Saudis.

dead, and in Arabia a dead man's kinsmen avenged his murder by taking blood or money from the killers. Lawrence immediately suspected
Suleiman of a revenge killing until another tribesman vouched that he
had been collecting wood with Suleiman when the shooting happened.

The only person missing was the Moroccan Hamed. It was Lawrence
who found him, collecting his belongings in an apparent bid to escape.
Covering him with his pistol, Lawrence shouted for the other Arabs,
who clustered around the pair. Hamed admitted shooting the Ageyli
following an argument, leaving Lawrence with a terrible dilemma. Tensions in Feisal's camp at Wajh between the different tribes, which were
united only in their interest in the gold on offer, were running high. To
do nothing ran the risk of a blood feud's escalating between the Ageyl
and the Moroccans once they were back at Wajh, with potentially cat-
astrophic consequences for order in the camp. The alternative, which
would prevent a feud, was for Lawrence as a foreigner to kill Hamed.
Shooing the Moroccan into a dank gully in the side of the wadi,
Lawrence gingerly shot him once, twice, a third time before he finally
stopped moving. In his notes he drew a rough map, marking the gully
with a heavily incised > and the word "Deathcrack" and a terse label:

CAMPED HERE.

AWFUL NIGHT.

SHOT.[33]

Lawrence's physical condition continued to deteriorate over the next
three days. The Hijaz was forged by volcanic activity, and riding across
the crazed pavement of disintegrating, brown-black lava field was desperately painful. His boils, aggravated by the bumpy ride, worsened.
"This halt is wonderful," he wrote during one stop: "Am lying under a
low thin thorn tree with tiny buds of leaves sprouting out at the bases
of its plentiful thorns. . . . The air round us is full of the humming of
insects and lively with flies. Heat and a faint cool wind."[34] Back on his
camel the torture resumed: he would afterward describe how "puffs of
feverish wind pressed like scorching hands against our faces," cracking
his lips and drying out his throat until he was hoarse.[35] After five terrible days, on 15 March he arrived at Abdullah's camp, a cluster of yellow tents that French soldiers who had already visited had privately
dubbed "the Camp of the Cloth of Gold," owing to their similarity to
knights' pavilions and the lavish lifestyle Abdullah had adopted.[36] Once

a tent had been pitched for him next to Abdullah's, Lawrence crawled inside to lie down.

Lawrence spent most of the next ten days in the tent. Afterward he suggested that during this time it dawned on him that, using guerrilla tactics, it would be far more economical to tie the Turkish garrison down in Medina than to try to capture the city. "The Turk was harmless there. In prison in Egypt he would cost us food and guards," he later wrote. But as I sat and read his wartime diary in the British Library in London, this feverish revelation seemed unlikely. Not only had he already developed many of these ideas but, as consecutive entries in his diary—written feebly in pencil—show, he was very ill. "Fever bad," he wrote on 17 March. "Fever better; boil worse" two days after that. In the entry for Friday, 23 March, after a week in and around his tent, his diary reads, "Better—decided start on Sunday." But on Saturday he relapsed: "Still hope to start tomorrow; am beastly ill, really." And the following day, there is the plaintive "In Wadi Ais: was unable to get off."[37] His later depiction of these days as valuable thinking time masked a simple truth: the illness stopped him from carrying out his orders to attack the railway.

While Lawrence was languishing in Abdullah's camp, Newcombe returned to Wajh, discovered Wingate's order, and turned immediately back toward the railway. On his return to the line, Newcombe was dismayed to find that the Turks had unearthed all five mines his party had laid on his previous expedition and had, in just four days, repaired what damage he had done to the track. The unexpected speed of these repairs meant that the British would have to cut the line every two to three days to keep it out of action, Newcombe calculated. This was a rate that he knew it would be impossible to maintain, particularly as the tribesmen's attention had been diverted by a new reward that Feisal was offering. Worried that the Bedu would kill the Arabs who had been conscripted by the Turks to work along the railway, and whose loyalty to the Ottoman cause was known to be doubtful, Feisal had decided to pay a sovereign for every prisoner brought back to Wajh alive. Designed though this bonus was to avoid alienating potential Arab supporters, it proved to be an unwelcome distraction from the job in hand. Even Newcombe's guide, Mirzuq, who as a camel merchant by trade should have had a strong vested interest in destroying the track, preferred the thought of the quick profit to be made from taking captives.

**Sharif Abdullah. In his youth he and his brothers
had been sent by their father to live with the Bedu,
to maintain strong links with the tribesmen.**

Mirzuq's leadership depressed Newcombe. "His method is to hear
everyone's views," the impatient veteran soldier complained to Wilson:
"Bedouin talking all day, wanting to capture prisoners, Ageyl wanting
to destroy the line by night and so avoid the dreaded aeroplane and
Bisha [tribesmen] more or less ready to do as they are told, if some
bakhshish° is forthcoming. I manage occasionally to get a word in to
make Mirzuq keep to the point, i.e. prevent trains running."[38]

Lawrence did not feel welcome in Abdullah's camp. "Who is this
'red' newcomer and what does he want?" one tribesman asked Abdullah.[39] "I did not like his intervention as I was suspicious of his influence
among the tribes," Abdullah later recalled of Lawrence. Although he
tried to explain Lawrence's role as an adviser to his followers, he
observed that "the general dislike of Lawrence's presence was quite

---

° Literally meaning "gift," *bakhshish* can be alms given to the poor or, as in this case, a
payment designed to change the behavior of the recipient, especially from inertia into action.

clear," and, unlike his pliable younger brother Feisal, he made no great effort to change this by backing Lawrence up.[40]

Once he had recovered, Lawrence did not stay long with Abdullah. On 26 March he set off down Wadi Ais toward the railway with a small party of Utaybah tribesmen. Sharif Shakir, a young man of about the same age as Lawrence, who—like many Bedu—plaited his black hair into six pigtails kept glossy with frequent applications of camel urine, would follow with a larger group of three hundred Bedu raiders.[41] By the twenty-eighth, Lawrence's scouts were lying on a hill west of Abu an Naam station, "like lizards in the long grass."[42] It was Lawrence's first sight of the railway: through his binoculars he could see a long bridge of nineteen squat arches guarded by a small outpost on a dark knoll, and to the south, the water tower and two station buildings of Abu an Naam itself, all built of lead-gray local basalt. Slightly nearer in the foreground stood a small, nondescript building, which as I discovered in 2005 is in fact a mosque, surrounded by white tents sleeping about three hundred soldiers in all. Although once Shakir arrived the Arabs had as many tribesmen, it was a reflection of their unreliability that Lawrence decided there were too many Turks to dare a direct attack of the sort he had suggested to Wilson before setting out.

Lawrence opted instead to mine the track on either side of the station that night and, at dawn the following day, to bombard the station with the field gun the raiders had brought with them. Under cover of darkness he headed south to lay a mine. Having done so, he left some tribesmen with a machine gun in some nearby bushes to mow down any escaping passengers and, a little farther down the line, shinned up a telegraph pole to cut the wires. The recoil of the pole when he cut the third and final wire was so great that he was shaken off, landing in a heap on a tribesman named Mohamed who tried to break his fall. They had only an hour's sleep before dawn; Mohamed got his revenge when he bellowed the call to prayer in Lawrence's ear.

The artillery attack was a spectacular success. Shells hit both the station buildings and pierced the tank crowning the water tower. A further hit on a freight car in a siding started a fierce fire; its locomotive uncoupled and started south to escape. "We watched her hungrily as she approached our mine,"[43] Lawrence recalled, before there was a puff of dust, a loud bang, and the engine came to a standstill. But there was no machine-gun fire: the Bedu gunners had given up and disappeared. The drivers were able to jack the locomotive back onto the track and head onward, albeit at a snail's pace. Suddenly hidden from the view of the Turks in the station by the thick black smoke that had begun to boil from the burning car, the tribesmen disregarded Lawrence's caution. While he watched from a distance, they advanced toward the station, shooting some Turkish soldiers who tried to surrender. The bombardment had caused the Turks seventy casualties, he estimated, and the Arabs took a further thirty prisoners. Traffic was held up for three days.

Sharif Shakir led the celebrations in Abdullah's camp when he returned with Lawrence. From the darkness outside the circle of tribesmen squatting around the fire, Lawrence watched as, in the center, Shakir sang, raising his hands and throwing back his head at the end of each phrase, while the tribesmen beat time with their hands.

Disappointed by the mine that had merely hobbled the engine at Abu an Naam, Lawrence set out again from Abdullah's camp on 3 April for the railway with Dakhilallah, a sheikh with "the manner and appearance of a toad," who nevertheless commanded respect among the Juhaynah as a judge.[44] This time Lawrence headed toward Mudarraj station, thirty-five miles north of Abu an Naam. Furious, dark-blue clouds hid the summits of the mountains, and the following day the party was engulfed by a dust spout, and then torrential rain, which turned the dust that had covered the men to mud and made the narrow mountain paths so treacherous that one tribesman slipped to his death.

I stopped at Mudarraj in March 2005. It, like most of the stations, is built to a standard pattern, a two-story building about twenty yards square, topped by two taller watchtowers at the back. A narrow gateway facing the railway opens into a small courtyard around which the soldiers who guarded the railway had very basic accommodation, illuminated only by a few small windows and gun slits. Climbing the steps in this courtyard takes you onto the flat roof, and a further set of iron rungs leads to the top of each tower. It was midday and painfully hot, but from there I could see across a wide natural amphitheater dotted with acacia trees, and to the south a bleak pass that was the railway's route through the rugged hills that defined the horizon.

On the evening of 4 April 1917, after the bugler at Mudarraj had summoned his colleagues back to the station for dinner, Lawrence laid a mine under the track where it crossed the pass just to the south of the

**A typical Hijaz railway station. Blockhouses like these were home
to up to forty men, including soldiers and railway workmen.**

station. Meanwhile, the tribesmen trampled on the surrounding sand until it looked "as though a school of elephant had danced on it," before they all retreated up the rough hillside to wait among the crags.[45] From this position the following morning, Lawrence watched as a Turkish patrol scoured the track and the sand on each side for signs of tampering. But although the Turks could see the raiders' footprints, they failed to find the mine. Then, to Lawrence's horror, from the south appeared a train crowded with women and children: evacuees from Medina. The train reached the top of the pass and began to accelerate downhill toward Mudarraj. Then it passed over the point where Lawrence had set the mine.

Nothing happened.

Lawrence's immediate relief rapidly turned to irritation. Not only had his mine failed again, but behind him the Juhaynah had surged to the edge of the outcrop to watch. From Mudarraj station below, the Turks spotted the tribesmen on the skyline and began shooting, though ineffectively owing to the long range. Now worried that the Turks might cut off their line of retreat to Wadi Ais, Lawrence sent the heavy German machine gun he had brought with him away, and returned toward the rails with Dakhilallah. Once it was dark, he began an uneasy hunt for the primed trigger. After some nervous scrabbling among the ballast, he finally found it, reset it, and left for the south. He paused along the way to demolish a bridge and cut about two hundred rails by means of guncotton charges, before heading for safety as fast as possible. A distant boom the following day suggested that the mine had finally worked. Lawrence headed back to Abdullah's camp and from there returned to Wajh. His mission had hardly been the success he had hoped for, and his and his colleagues' frustrations were about to boil over.

11

Differences over Tactics

By April 1917 the port of Wajh had become the center of British operations. The airplanes and pilots of the small Royal Flying Corps detachment had arrived from Yanbu in mid-March. Six days later the flight's
leader, Major Ross, set out up Wadi Hamd with four spare tires
strapped to the side of his car to hunt for a forward airstrip that would
give his biplanes the range to reconnoiter and bomb the railway, one
hundred miles away. Joyce had just arrived from Rabigh and now took
charge of British operations at the port. Soldiers in shorts and pith hel-
mets unloaded stores at the quayside, armored Rolls-Royce cars had
been landed, and two British armorers, brought in to service the tribesmen's—frequently antique—rifles and weapons, had succeeded in
training thirty Arabs in machine-gunning, entirely by mime.

Lawrence reappeared in Wajh on 14 April after thirty-four days
away. In his absence Joyce had been trying to persuade Feisal to go up
toward the railway to boost the tribesmen's morale, but Feisal had
refused. Since Lawrence's chief skill was in steering Feisal, Joyce was
annoyed that he had been gone so long. Lawrence exacerbated the friction in the British camp when he proceeded to criticize British tactics:
"The blowing up of culverts is waste of time and explosive," he argued,
and although he admitted that the mines terrified the Turks, he was
disappointed that they were "not set off till the driving wheels pass over
them . . . and the damage thus tends to be too far back."[1] He felt that,
instead, the Arabs should fight a war that made the most of their mobility and unpredictability, targeting the railway, but not the Turks them-

selves. "We might be a vapour, blowing where we listed," he later said of his philosophy, as hard for the Turks to beat as "eating soup with a knife."[2] He argued that "a constant series of petty destructions" was the best way to keep the railway out of action.

When Newcombe returned to Wajh, having spent most of the previous two months attacking the railway to the northeast, he was not impressed by Lawrence's advice, based as it was on ten days' experience. Taking a sideswipe at the style of his subordinate's reports—"It does not help us to win the war merely to collect scraps of information about Bedouins, unless we also hurt the Turk. But hurting the Turk seems too risky for most Arabs"—he argued that a different approach was needed to obtain a decisive result.[3] "Either all of us are wasting our time here, instead of getting on with the war, or an entirely new line must be taken, of making camel corps and training Bisha [a loyal tribe]" to execute attacks on a much greater scale.

Newcombe had been joined by another young engineer, Henry Hornby, at the beginning of April, and Lawrence criticized his and Newcombe's handling of the Arabs. "Hornby spoke little Arabic; and Newcombe not enough to persuade, though enough to give orders; but orders were not in place inland." Newcombe had been shot at by his own tribesmen on his last raid. The tribesmen's extreme reaction, Lawrence believed, had been prompted "out of disgust at his hardness, always wanting to ride when they wanted to stop and eat. Also hard on water and food." His own conclusion from Newcombe's troubles was blunt: "Mem: Don't attempt too much."[4]

Unlike Newcombe, who arrived in the Hijaz under the impression he was to lead the band of British military advisers *and* the Arab tribes, Lawrence always knew that he was an adviser, not a leader. His role was to steer, and not command.[5] He knew that there was no way of changing the Bedu's unique style of fighting. The difficulty of surviving in the Hijaz meant that, for the sake of their families, the tribesmen would always rather flee and live to fight another day unless their honor within the tribe was at stake. To force them to stand and fight, as Newcombe wished he could, would lead to casualties that would break the tribesmen's brittle morale, because, in Lawrence's words, "An individual death was like a pebble dropped in water. Each might make only a brief hole, but rings of sorrow widened out from them. We could not afford casualties."[6]

While his colleagues were increasingly frustrated by the tribesmen's behavior, Lawrence took a perverse satisfaction in finding virtue where his colleagues saw only vice. "The Harith are not a large clan," he wrote of one set of arrivals to Wajh, "but have been robbers for generations, and so capable men of action."[7] It was this acceptance of the Bedu's way of life and his realization that their inability to strike a decisive blow was a blessing in disguise that determined Lawrence's support for guerrilla tactics.

Two important men had also arrived while Lawrence had been train-wrecking inland. The day after his return, Lawrence was sitting in Feisal's tent catching up on news when there was a call from outside the tent, and Feisal, he remembered, turned to him "with shining eyes, trying to be calm, and said, 'Auda is here.'"[8] Auda abu Tayi was the man whom Lawrence had wanted to meet since February. With him was Nuri Shaalan's nephew.

Auda abu Tayi was infamous. A traveler in the region a few years earlier incredulously recorded how Auda was reputed to have "cut the heart from a wounded enemy and bit at it," but in fact, as Richard Burton discovered when he passed through the Hijaz in 1853, the custom of trying a dead rival's gore had once been widespread, and Auda's continuing attachment to the practice simply marked him out as a tradi-

Auda abu Tayi. The arrival
of this fearsome outlaw in Wajh
in April 1917 enabled Feisal
and Lawrence to realize their
hopes of moving northward
into Syria.

tionalist.[9] So it was not surprising that Auda had taken an instant dislike to the Ottoman tax men who appeared in the region following the construction of the Hijaz Railway. In 1908 he had fallen out with the Ottomans over payment of tax. After Auda shot dead two officials sent to bring him to Maan, a warrant was issued for his arrest.[10] Since then he had become an outlaw, "a tall, strong figure, with a haggard face, passionate and tragic," who had married twenty-eight times and been wounded thirteen times and who dramatically rushed out of Feisal's tent to smash his false teeth with a stone when he realized they were Turkish made.[11] In one contemporary photograph Auda, wearing a European suit jacket over a patterned Arab robe, stares unnervingly straight at the camera. He instantly mesmerized Lawrence.

The plan that Feisal then put to Lawrence bore the hallmarks of Auda's overpowering influence. It developed the northward advance that Lawrence had already suggested but in a way that bolstered Auda's prestige by strongly benefiting his tribe, the Huwaytat. Leaving Feisal behind in Wajh, Lawrence would ride northeast with Auda far beyond the railway into northern Arabia to buy one thousand camels and arrange food and forage at Jafr, thirty-five miles northeast of Maan, for a force of about six hundred regular troops led by Feisal, who would follow late in June. The decision to search for food and transport in this area was designed mainly to reward the Huwaytat, who roamed the area between Maan and Aqaba, and who were undoubtedly affected by the famine in Syria at that time.[12] While Lawrence and Auda were dealing with the logistics, the British would move arms, ammunition, explosives, and food from Wajh to a midway point just southwest of Tabuk. By means of the camels Lawrence would acquire, these supplies would then be shuttled up to Jafr, an operation that Feisal hoped to complete by 10 July.

With the support of the Huwaytat, the operation had two further objectives. The first was to incite the Druses to the north to revolt. From Jafr the entire force would then head north to Azraq. Here there was a tumbledown castle hidden in a remote oasis fifty miles east of Amman. Azraq was an infamous hideout for outlaws, in which Nuri Shaalan could frequently be found and which would play a central role as the base for Arab operations later in the war. From Azraq, Feisal would try to stir up the Druses nearby and launch operations against the railway.[13] A small and esoteric Islamic sect that farmed the fertile area around Damascus, the Druses had revolted against the Turks twice in recent memory, in 1895 and 1910. Both uprisings had been violently suppressed by the Turks. Feisal calculated that it would not be difficult to stoke up Druse feeling again. The other objective of the plan was to capture Aqaba. Auda had first asked the British to capture the port that February; he now hoped that by causing trouble around Maan he could force the Turks in Aqaba into surrender himself. This landward approach to Aqaba solved the major problem Lawrence could see with a seaborne attack on Aqaba. The occupation of Aqaba, which Feisal planned to achieve by a landing of tribesmen late in July, would open the port as a route for supplies to ensure that the Huwaytat could not be starved by the Turks. Hopes that Aqaba would be easily overthrown were raised on 20 April when, in an opportunistic raid on the port, a British landing party snatched nine Ottoman soldiers. Of the nine, six were Arabs who wanted to join Feisal.[14]

The main obstacle to this plan was Lawrence's own chief, Clayton. Reviewing Feisal's intentions, Clayton noted that the scheme "must not be allowed to interfere with the business which is already in hand, viz, the defeat of the Turks at Medina, Al Ula and Madain Salih, which should be cleared up in order to make the Northern move fully effective."[15] It was only later that Clayton revealed his true objections to the plan. In his opinion Aqaba would be critical to Britain's future defense of Egypt, and he feared that its occupation by the Huwaytat tribesmen "might well result in the Arabs claiming that place hereafter."[16] And that was one of the reasons why the scheme appealed to Lawrence.

Lawrence feared that Clayton's determination to capture Medina would instead pass the initiative to Abdullah, who was closest to the holy city. He knew that he was competing with Abdullah for scarce British resources. While he wanted British support to extend the uprising northward into Syria, Abdullah was stockpiling the gold and weapons he had been given to strengthen his father's position in Arabia to the south. He worried that, if the British decided to transfer their allegiance to Feisal's older brother, Abdullah would then have the resources to capture Medina when it suited him.

Feisal had warned Lawrence early that year that, though his older brother was "inclined to be lazy," he was "quick when he does move."[17] Abdullah's timetable, whatever it was, did not suit Lawrence. For if Abdullah succeeded quickly, British backing for the uprising would evaporate. But if this consequence dawned on Abdullah—as seems to have been the case—so that he took his time instead, he would deny Feisal the gold and guns that Lawrence needed to fulfill his private ambition to biff the French out of all hope of Syria.

To keep his hope alive, Lawrence urgently had to counter Clayton's skepticism about a northward move. For if the Arabs could enter Aqaba before Medina was taken, they would not only establish a foothold in Syria but, if the British army captured Gaza, could also play a useful part in the British advance that would ensure that their funding did not dry up. Moving the Arabs' center of operations to Aqaba would irreversibly turn their horizons northward and ensure there was no premature ending to the revolt. But he could hardly argue the danger of the Arabs' premature success. Instead, to win his colleagues over, he had to dwell on the possibility of their failure. To undermine their faith in Abdullah's ability to capture Medina, Lawrence turned to his favorite weapon, the venomous report.

In a letter to his chief, Colonel Wilson, on 16 April Lawrence suppressed his opinion when he was with Abdullah that, compared with Feisal's camp, "things here are more businesslike" and accused Abdullah of being complacent, lazy, profligate, and incompetent.[18] "He considers the Arab position as assured with both Syria and Iraq irrevocably pledged to the Arabs by Great Britain's signed agreements, and for himself looks particularly to the Yemen," Lawrence observed, in a tone suggesting that Abdullah's assurance was ill founded.[19] Abdullah spent his day "reading the Arabic newspapers, in eating, in sleeping and especially in jesting." It was the time Abdullah allocated daily to this last activity, of which the camp's muezzin* was normally the butt, that particularly riled Lawrence, who wrote while he was in Wadi Ais that he was "not in the mood" for all the jollity.[20] The day before he had arrived, Lawrence reported, Abdullah had apparently shot a coffee pot balanced on the muezzin's head three times from twenty yards, in exchange for £30. Abdullah's tribesmen, meanwhile, had gone two months unpaid, "simply through *laisser faire*, for the gold was present in the camp to pay them up in full." Abdullah, Lawrence concluded, was "incapable as a military commander and unfit to be trusted alone, with important commissions of an active sort."

* The man responsible for proclaiming the call to prayer.

Lawrence did turn briefly to the consequences if Abdullah did succeed, and in fact it was this argument that seems to have carried most weight. He told Wilson that Abdullah had thought through how he would impose his father's authority on the other major Arabian sheikhs following the capture of Medina. As Lawrence told Wilson, "This sounds a large operation, but Abdullah is convinced of its practicability, and has even worked out the details of his actions." This observation struck a raw nerve, for Wilson was already concerned that if Abdullah captured Medina he would then turn on his Arab rivals, including Britain's other ally, Ibn Saud, and chaos would ensue. In May, Wilson recommended to Wingate that Feisal be encouraged to begin operations as far north up the Hijaz Railway as possible. In Cairo, Wingate instructed a reluctant Clayton to investigate how best to support Feisal's move northward. Clayton remained reluctant—"The venture is in the nature of a gamble," he believed, but he had no choice except to follow Wingate's order.[21]

Lawrence had successfully undermined Abdullah, but he had been helped by a combination of events far beyond the Hijaz—a revolution in the Russian capital, Petrograd, and a change of policy in London—well outside his control. On 15 March, after large-scale strikes and then a mutiny in Petrograd had thrust a spanner in the works of Russia's industrial machine, the tsar, Nicholas II, abdicated. Britain and France cast around for ways to keep their ally in the war because, if the Russians sued for peace, the German and Ottoman troops ranged against them could then be redeployed to other fronts, increasing the pressure on the Allies. In the Middle East the Turks would be able to move troops from the Caucasus front south to fight in Palestine, where General Murray was trying to capture Gaza, and in Mesopotamia, where British forces under General Stanley Maude had only just occupied Baghdad. Russia's collapse also made it more likely that the Ottoman Empire would survive the war intact, and this raised the worrying possibility that the Arabs would seek to make peace with the Turks: the very outcome the Arab revolt had been designed by Britain to prevent.

Finally, in London, Prime Minister David Lloyd George worried that British workers might follow the Russians' example. He urgently wanted a victory to revive public morale and fend off the possibility of labor unrest, which might paralyze Britain like Russia. Deeply anti-Turkish, Lloyd George had for some time nursed an interest in a British offensive into Syria that, as prime minister, he was now in a strong position to pursue. Rather than treating the capture of Gaza as the final move in the existing policy of a belligerent defense of Egypt, he envisaged the capture of the seaside village as the first stage of a push into Palestine.[22] Was there a more resonant target than Jerusalem, last in Christian hands in 1187, to reflect the rightness of Britain's cause?

Wingate's decision to endorse Feisal's aspirations reflected all three factors. By encouraging the Arabs to advance northward between their two fronts, the British hoped not only to divert some of the Ottomans' spare resources but also to stop the Arabs' wavering. It reflected, too, a realization that, if the British did advance beyond Gaza, the Arabs might be useful to them militarily. This had already occurred to General Murray, who increasingly viewed his and the Arabs' fortunes as positively interlinked. "If I can gain a further success against the troops in front of me," he had told Robertson before attacking Gaza, "it will immensely help the Arab Movement, and I *may* yet see them in force in the neighbourhood of Maan—an additional security to southern Sinai."[23]

The capture of Baghdad, the fall of the tsar, and the possibility of an offensive into Palestine also raised questions about the validity of the Sykes-Picot agreement that would need to be addressed. Although, after he entered Baghdad, General Maude announced that the British came not "as conquerors or enemies, but as liberators," the Indian army's involvement in the capture of that city triggered an argument between London and Delhi over just how liberating British rule in Mesopotamia after the war would be. Yet whatever the outcome of this debate, it was a domestic matter Britain intended to decide without reference to the French, or anyone else. If, as the third signatory to the agreement, Russia withdrew from the war—a possibility that looked increasingly likely—then the Sykes-Picot agreement would arguably be void. And if Britain advanced into Palestine, conquest would supersede the treaty's theoretical placement of Palestine under international control, just as the capture of Baghdad already raised the question of the status of Mesopotamia. That spring, a committee chaired by the former viceroy and arch-imperialist member of the War Cabinet, Lord

Curzon, provided some simple answers to two of the three issues. It decided that it would be in Britain's best interests to control both Mesopotamia and Palestine after the war.

On 3 April the British prime minister, David Lloyd George, called Mark Sykes in to see him. Sykes was about to leave for Cairo, having been appointed chief political officer to the Egyptian Expeditionary Force in anticipation that a second assault on Gaza (the first had failed) would open questions about the treaty he had negotiated with François Georges-Picot that he was the obvious candidate to consider. Lloyd George was also keen to take advantage of the Russians' disarray and told Sykes to do his best to add Palestine—which the Russians had insisted should be internationally administered—to the British sphere of influence. Sykes told him how he hoped to develop relations with the various tribes in Palestine "and, if possible, to raise an Arab rebellion further north in the region of Jabal Druse with a view to attacks on the Turkish lines of communication, particularly against the railway between Aleppo and Damascus."[24]

Lloyd George, who clearly did not share Cairo's calculation of the Arabs' usefulness, was alarmed by Sykes's plans. He told Sykes that it was vital not to commit the British government to any agreement with the tribes that would be prejudicial to British interests and might upset the French. He had also had breakfast that morning with the leading British Zionist and scientist Chaim Weizmann. Many Jews in Britain, Weizmann had told him, knew Palestine well and might usefully be employed in the theater. Knowing how important Weizmann's scientific expertise had been to the British war effort, Lloyd George was easily persuaded. With the conversation fresh in his mind, he suggested to Sykes that the Jews "might be able to render us more assistance than the Arabs" and warned him of the "importance of not prejudicing the Zionist movement and the possibility of its development under British auspices."[25] Before Sykes left, Lloyd George repeated his initial warning. There should be no "political pledges to the Arab, and particularly none in regard to Palestine." This demand effectively hobbled Sykes, but he set out for Egypt nevertheless.

By the time Sykes reached Egypt, the second attack on Gaza had failed, just as the first had done. He continued on to Jeddah and there met Husein for the first time on 5 May. In a cartoon he drew of their three-hour meeting, he depicted himself in his army uniform with sweat dripping off his brow while Husein sat cross-legged on a divan looking at him enigmatically. Behind the pair, a thermometer registered 120 degrees Fahrenheit. Sykes had passed Husein a message from King George V, welcoming Husein's efforts in the "cause of Arab peoples whose ultimate enfranchisement from persecution will mark an epoch in development of civilization and prosperity in Asia."[26] Guff like this failed to impress the sharif, who replied that unless Arab independence was assured "he feared that posterity would charge him with assisting in the overthrow of the last Islamic power without setting up another in its place" and that if France annexed Syria he would be open to the charge of breaking faith with the Muslims of Syria "by having led them into a rebellion against [the] Turk in order to hand them over to [a] Christian power."[27] Sykes tried to reassure Husein about French ambitions in Syria by telling him that the treaty he had agreed with Picot contained a commitment to create an Arab confederation.[28] And afterward he claimed that he had persuaded Husein "to admit at last, but only after lengthy argument, that it was essential to Arab development in Syria" to accept overarching French influence there.[29]

It was an unconvincing argument, and Sykes himself was not convinced. British disquiet about French activities in the Hijaz had been growing since the beginning of the year. In January, according to Lawrence, Brémond had told Feisal that the Allies' wartime alliance was "only temporary" and that "between England and France, England and Russia, lay such deep and rooted seeds of discord that no permanent friendship could be looked for."[30] The French officer also seemed to have suggested to Abdullah that "the English were surrounding the new Arabic kingdom on all sides, quoting Aden, Baghdad, and Gaza as instances."[31] Sykes realized that Brémond's continuing presence in Jeddah was doing little to help his cause. "I am convinced that the sooner the French military mission is removed from Hijaz the better," he told Wingate in a telegram that evening. "The French officers are without exception anti-Arab. . . . Their line is to crab British operations to the Arabs, throw cold water on all Arab actions to the British, and make light of the King to both," he railed, before attacking "the deliberately perverse attitude and policy followed by Colonel Brémond and his staff."[32] Days later, the British ambassador in Paris complained to the French government about Brémond's conduct.[33]

In Cairo, Clayton was skeptical as well. He did not trust Sykes's version of his discussions with Husein and warned that the sharif was likely to go back on his word once Sykes had left. He also reacted with surprise to Husein's response. The British, he said, had assured Husein that Arabia would be formed of "a series of more or less independent states or confederations which would be loosely bound into an Arab federation." Now, he claimed, "the Sharif has perverted these assurances into a support of himself as supreme ruler."[34] While it was true that the British had never explicitly committed themselves to supporting Husein except against the Ottomans, it was hardly surprising that Husein was under the impression that he could count on the British to endorse his claim to the political leadership of the Muslim world, given the encouraging message sent to him at the beginning of the war by Lord Kitchener that "it may be that an Arab of true race will assume the Caliphate at Mecca." But it was not only Husein who was surprised by the extent of French influence that Sykes now admitted over the area which he claimed. So too was T. E. Lawrence.

12

Fighting for Us on a Lie

It is still possible to visit the old pilgrim caravanserai of Qalaat Zorayb, which stands in a secluded valley a little way inland from Wajh, as long as you don't mind crawling under the wire fence that the Saudi Department for Antiquities has recently erected around the site. The *qalaat* is an elegant building, a hundred yards square with high walls that meet at neat round towers, built from a warm, smooth stone that contrasts with the rough hills around. It was from here that Lawrence set out on 10 May 1917 on the first leg of his mission with Auda to secure food and camels for Feisal's planned march north. Over the back of his camel sagged a 45-pound sack of flour, which had to last him six weeks, and in his saddlebag he carried £1,000 in gold, which Feisal had given to him the day before as a reserve in addition to the £22,000 the baggage camels were carrying.

Three days earlier Lawrence had met Sykes for the first time. Besides the briefest entry in his diary, there is no record of their meeting, but it seems probable that because of his key role with Feisal, he was now told the full details of the Sykes-Picot treaty by Sykes himself. These secret provisions had stunning implications, which he would thrash out in the lonely weeks ahead.

"We thought you had been generous to the Arabs," he later wrote accusingly to Sykes, although the letter was never sent, "and were told unofficially that the need of bolstering up French courage and determination in the war made it necessary to surrender to her part of our own birthright."[1] He went on to express his disillusionment at what had followed after the revolt began. "What had been a generous attempt to revive an Arab state in Syria under the aegis of France and England, became the sphere which the Sharif might obtain if he succeeded. You observe that we gave him no reward for his efforts on our side. He might take—what we had already given," he said, in a reference to the way in which the Sykes-Picot agreement overturned the commitment made by McMahon.

Up until this time Lawrence had been working on the assumption that it was in both the British and the Arab interest that the French were denied Syria. His discovery that Sykes had already offered Syria to the French knocked him sideways: Sykes had effectively pitted Britain and France together, against the Arabs. As Lawrence turned this apparent fait accompli over in his mind, he became only more determined that the Arabs should reach Damascus first. If Husein's forces could reach the city before either the British or the French, his claim to the surrounding area that Sykes had conceded to the French would be much stronger. What he heard from Sykes spurred Lawrence into action: it may even be that the meeting was the catalyst for the decision to depart northward almost immediately.

Feisal had chosen Sharif Nasir to lead the little expedition northward. The twenty-seven-year-old Nasir had apparently fired the first shot of the abortive uprising in Medina the previous June and had distinguished himself as a loyal supporter of Feisal. The brother of the emir of Medina and a descendant of the Prophet, he had already raided the railway with Newcombe and would establish a reputation for being capable, honest, and hardworking. Importantly for this mission, his character and his ancestry ensured that he commanded widespread respect not least because, unusually in the Hijaz, he was a Shia Muslim. Nesib al Bakri, a member of one of Damascus's leading families and an Arab nationalist whose help would be needed to spread the revolt northward, also joined them. Lawrence took two servants, whose stories reflected the origins and aims of the revolt. One, named Gasim, was a tax exile from the Maan district who, like Auda, was wanted for killing an Ottoman official. The other was Mohammed, a villager from the Hauran, where Feisal wanted to incite revolt. To protect them on the journey came seventeen Ageyl, the young townsmen from central Arabia, whose camels were slung with red and blue woolen saddle bags with scarlet tassels that reached the animals' knees. They were "nice fellows, large-eyed, cheery, a bit educated, catholic, intelligent, good companions on the road," said Lawrence.[2] They had a talent for telling long verse stories about war, love, travel, and magic. "Needless to say," commented another British officer, "the love stories were unexpurgated."[3]

Days of incessant, roasting sunshine had replaced the variable weather of springtime in the Hijaz. Heat pulsed off the ground in nauseating waves, and flies buzzed in the stagnant air. Lawrence quickly suffered a rapid and debilitating relapse of his fever. "Tired and sorry," he wrote in his diary after a day in the saddle, "v. sick," the following day, and "pain and agony today" the day after that.[4] The party stopped for two days to let Lawrence's fever pass, before heading on to Abu Raqah, a valley of variegated sandstone that glowed pink at dawn and dusk. There Lawrence persuaded a local Bedu to part with his two servants, Ali and Othman. "Othman soft-looking. Ali fine fellow. Both apparently plucky, and Mohammed and Gasim are so useless that I must have extra men."[5] Ali and Othman appeared inseparable. "They were an instance of the eastern boy and boy affection which the segregation of women made inevitable," he would write after the war. Their love was not sexual, he believed, but a "manly love of a depth and force beyond our flesh-steeped conceit." Lawrence took them on "mainly because they looked so young and clean."[6] On 17 May, the day after Lawrence hired Ali and Othman, the Arabs' party headed on toward the railway.

ჯა

After his first, stilted meeting with Husein, Sykes returned to Cairo to discuss the administration of Syria with Picot and put an idea to him. He argued that the administration of Mesopotamia should be placed in Arab hands and suggested to Picot that France might match this stance in Syria. In doing so, Sykes was responding to a change in the political weather.

The previous month the United States had joined the war against Germany. But when the American president, Woodrow Wilson, announced his government's decision, he launched a much more general attack on the conduct of European foreign policy that had led to war. He attacked the "little groups of ambitious men who were accustomed to use their fellow men as pawns and tools" and declared, "We have no selfish ends to serve. We desire no conquest, no dominion." The United States, Wilson concluded, would "fight for the things which we have always carried nearest our hearts—for democracy, for the right of those who submit to authority to have a voice in their own governments, for the rights and liberties of small nations."[7] Rhetoric of this kind made Sykes feel decidedly uncomfortable. Unsurprisingly, when Wilson's foreign-policy adviser, Edward House, found out about the Sykes-Picot treaty, he was blunt. "It is all bad, and I told Balfour so," he wrote.[8] Sykes sensed a hostile turn in the mood toward British and French imperialist war aims and began to change his tune.

On 18 May, Sykes returned to Jeddah with Picot and Feisal, whom he had picked up from Wajh on his way south. This time he intended to make Husein realize "the inevitable fact of French influence in Syria" by giving him full details of the Sykes-Picot agreement. In the clearest indication that the message Sykes was about to give conflicted with what McMahon had led the sharif to believe, the Foreign Office agreed that Sykes could sugar the bitter pill by telling Husein that the British government would increase his monthly subsidy by £75,000 to £200,000 with immediate effect. In an indication that Britain's priorities were changing, Husein was promised a bonus of just £125,000 if Medina were captured.[9]

Sykes and Picot went ashore in separate launches for a lunchtime meeting with Sharif Husein. Sykes showed Husein a prototype Arab flag, which comprised three horizontal stripes representing the Arab dynasties— "Abbasid black, Omayad white, Alid green," Sykes explained—unified by a red triangle on the hoist side, representing the sharif.[10] Husein preferred scarlet to the dark red Sykes proposed, but otherwise approved Sykes's design, which again strongly suggested that Britain saw him as the dominant force among the Arabs, including Britain's other ally, Ibn Saud.

It was the first time Husein had met Picot, and the conversation rapidly turned to the status of coastal Syria, over which McMahon and the sharif had disagreed. Picot explained that France would recognize the principle of an autonomous Arab government in its sphere of influence, but that a French "adviser" would possibly reside at Damascus. In the "Blue" area on the Syrian coast, which came under French control, a Franco-Arab administration would be formed, where French and Arab flags would be flown. The French, Sykes added, had not ruled out the principle of fusing the government of the "Blue" area with that of the adjacent Arab state under French influence, though whether this would result in French annexation or Arab independence he did not specify. Husein did not like what he heard, frequently calling breaks for prayers, which Sykes suspected were simply designed to give him time to consult his advisers without either Sykes or Picot in earshot. "The interview closed most inconclusively, and was adjourned until the following morning, M. Picot being rather unfavourably impressed by the King," Sykes told Wingate.[11] The chess-playing Admiral Wemyss, who was also present, described how the discussion started badly, and "at one moment [it] looked as though conversations would be broken off without any result," before it was agreed that Husein should come aboard Sykes's ship, HMS *Northbrook*, the following day.[12]

Overnight Sykes worked on Picot and Husein—who he thought was "straight, rather crabbed in mind (through theological training) healthy, courageous, and fussy."[13] Having persuaded Picot to accept his proposal that Syria and Mesopotamia should be governed similarly, he then put the idea to Husein, suggesting that his acceptance of the formula would break the impasse.[14] Husein, who realized that the increased British subsidy depended on his answer, eventually agreed.

Aboard the *Northbrook* the following day, "matters took a decidedly more favourable turn," reported Wemyss afterward, because "the King verbally agreed to cooperate with the French in their sphere on the understanding that the French policy towards the Arabs should be similar to the British policy in the British sphere."[15] Husein's and Picot's apparent agreement "greatly improved the atmosphere," according to Sykes, who was pleased with the devious solution he had brokered.[16]

Husein was delighted. During his correspondence with McMahon, he had proposed that the British lease Mesopotamia from him for a set period prior to handover. He envisaged, as he later explained to Lawrence, that Britain's "temporary occupation of the country for strategical and political reasons" would be accompanied by the payment of an annual grant to compensate him and the purchase of "concessions in the way of public works."[17] Not wanting to upset Husein, McMahon had never dismissed this idea outright, arguing disingenuously that the issue required "fuller and more detailed consideration than the present situation and the speed with which these negotiations are being conducted permit."[18] Under the impression that his leaseback scheme remained viable, Husein now optimistically interpreted Picot's agreement as a commitment to extend it to include Syria.

Picot, however, knew nothing of this leaseback scheme. He simply believed that British plans for Baghdad would actually involve annexation, just as France intended in Syria, and was happy to accept Sykes's formula on that basis. He must have left the meeting puzzled by Husein's enthusiastic acceptance of annexation. What is not clear is whether Sykes introduced the formula simply because he knew that it had an agreeable—but in fact opposite—meaning for each party, or whether, motivated by his recognition that annexation was "quite contrary to the spirit of the time," he thought he could draw Picot into an agreement that would ultimately benefit the Arabs when Britain accepted the need for Arab self-government in Mesopotamia, for which he was now arguing.

The oral agreement—for nothing was signed by the three men—was a temporary palliative that became the source of increasing embarrassment as it grew clear that, contrary to what Sykes had suggested to Husein, Britain had no plans to allow Arab self-government in Mesopotamia. "We have to bear in mind that unfortunate formula which the King of the Hijaz was induced to agree to at the meeting between him and Mark and Picot," Clayton reflected nearly a year later. "That embarrassing formula . . . places us in an awkward position."[19]

After the meeting Feisal grasped Sykes by the hand and took him to one side. "We are ready to cooperate with France in Syria to the fullest extent and with Great Britain in Mesopotamia," he said quietly, "but we do ask that Great Britain will help us with Ibn Saud and the Idrisi,* without in any way infringing on their independence, rights, or liberties—we beg that Great Britain will endeavour to induce them to recognize the King's position as leader of the Arab movement."[20] The following day Sykes sent a telegram to Percy Cox, the political officer with British forces in Baghdad, to ask whether he could persuade Ibn

---

*Muhammad al-Idrisi, ruler of Asir, the mountainous region immediately south of the Hijaz. Like Ibn Saud, he had entered into a treaty with the British in 1915.

Saud to tell the sharif "that he regarded him as a titular leader of the Arab cause without in any way committing his independence or local position."[21] Not wanting to annoy Ibn Saud, Cox refused to act.

❧

Over 600 miles north of Jeddah, early in the evening of 19 May, Sharif Nasir, Lawrence, and Auda abu Tayi crossed the railway. Lawrence paused briefly for twenty minutes to blow the track with guncotton and cut the telegraph wire, which he then tied to the saddles of the camels, before shooing them on, to pull down the telegraph poles behind them. Then the party headed east, crossing the watershed between the Hijaz and Wadi Sirhan, still 150 miles away to the northeast, early the following morning. They now faced the worst part of their journey to Wadi Sirhan, where they hoped to find the Huwaytat. Between the Hijaz Railway and the wadi lies an enormous empty plain, scored by the sand and devoid of life, then known to the Bedu as Al Houl—"the Terror." "This is a grey country, utterly without trees or shrubs, or any grazing—whence its name," Lawrence observed.[22] The only noise was the "hollow tapping and cracking of rock slabs" as the camels trod on them, and the sound of the sand "creeping round the ridges and along between the rocks."[23] Hot gusts blasted them with sand. "This wind is killing me," Lawrence jotted.[24] He was carrying a sheaf of blank army telegraph forms, writing copious notes on the plain reverse side. The other, boxed side was a testing ground for odd phrases he might use in his book: "*Harra* drinks starlight" was one musing on the blackness of the weathered lava flows they had to cross; "deadness of this open country without wind," "the incredible slowness of the moon," "Auda's wonderful echoed singing," others.

To pass the time, Auda began to describe the complex politics of the fractured Huwaytat tribe, telling Lawrence for the first time that he had seized the leadership of the tribe from his rival Ibn Jazi, who had in turn killed his own son, Annad. In the course of the tribal feud that followed his coup, Auda had killed seventy-five men since 1899, when, Lawrence noted, "he began to keep tally."[25] He did not bother to keep count of the Turks he had murdered. It was a relief when they finally reached Fajr well, halfway to Wadi Sirhan, on 21 May. There they watered the camels before camping half a mile away to avoid raiders who might pass by the well in the night for, as Lawrence later wrote, "in the hours of darkness there were no friends in Arabia."[26]

Continuing northeastward, the following day's route took them across vast mudflats. These pans of dazzling white mud were "purgatory. Sun reflects from them like mirrors."[27] The answer seemed to be "Ride eyes shut," but the light was blinding even then.* The heat pumped off the blazing ground, and Lawrence found himself occasionally blacking out—a brief release before more torture.

The twenty-fourth of May was Empire Day. While, in the neat, verdant gardens of the residency in Cairo, Wingate held a tea party for a thousand convalescing soldiers wounded in the two failed attempts to capture Gaza, Lawrence hoped to escape the endless mudflats and reach Wadi Sirhan, where he expected to find the Huwaytat and sufficient meat and grazing to meet the needs of Feisal's force. At Auda's insistence they started in the middle of the night. Dawn revealed a level plain of stones sunburned to the color of congealed blood over which the mirage shimmered into a dirty, pale blue sky. Suddenly, however, they scared two ostriches and stopped to cook, over a fire of shredded blasting gelatine, the two enormous eggs the birds abandoned. One of the two was rotten.

Straining to see further signs of life ahead, Lawrence suddenly realized that he had lost Gasim, one of his two "useless" servants. "This was a dreadful business," he recalled.[28] There was no chance that Gasim would catch up. Lawrence believed that, by desert law, he was responsible for his servant. He, more than any of the other British officers, tried to understand and fit in with the Bedu. "Get to know their families, clans and tribes, friends and enemies, wells, hills and roads," he advised his colleagues afterward: "If you wear Arab things at all, go the whole way. Leave your English friends and customs on the coast, and fall back on Arab habits entirely."[29] Exactly why he was so well suited to this life of pretense is an interesting question, to which the answer may be rooted in Lawrence's past, for he was illegitimate. His father had been a well-heeled and married Irish landowner who had run off with his daughters' governess, Miss Sarah Lawrence. The couple

---

*Sunglasses did exist in 1917, but their use was confined to mountaineers, polar explorers, and the mentally ill. There is no evidence that any British officer in the Hijaz owned a pair. In summer the British found it too hot to wear a head scarf across their faces to protect themselves from the glare.

moved to England, where they lived an unobtrusive life together under
Sarah's surname, but the realization that his name was an arbitrary tag
and the stigma that it hid stayed with Lawrence all his life.

Lawrence had lived by the Bedu code for months, and now he might
have to die by it, for by its terms he would have to turn around and try
to find Gasim. He had been carefully tracking the party's course since
they left Wajh, so now he twisted his compass through 180 degrees,
turned his camel, and began to retrace his steps. The only signs of
human habitation were strange threshing pits scraped in the ground six
years earlier, when there had last been a good harvest of *semn*, a red
seed that could be milled into flour. Filled with drifting sand, the pits
looked like "grey eyes in the black stony surface."[30]

After an hour and a half's riding, through the wobbling mirage
Lawrence saw a black blob. It was Gasim, nearly blinded and mad from
the sun. He was "standing there with his arms held out to me, and his
black mouth gaping open."[31] Lawrence gave him some water, hoisted
him onto his camel behind him, and turned to hurry back toward the
caravan. Another hour's riding passed. Then in front of them another
black bubble appeared, "lunging and swaying in the mirage ahead."
Auda emerged. He had turned back in search of Lawrence and was
angry that Lawrence had gone back for Gasim, whom Nasir and he
deemed worthless. "Wasted two hours and a half looking for Gasim,"
Lawrence recorded that night, wishing perhaps that Auda had seemed
slightly more impressed by his decision to impose the obligation upon
himself.[32] Had he shirked the duty, he later wrote, Auda and Nasir
would have understood, "because I was a foreigner: but that was precisely the plea I did not dare set up while I yet presumed to help these
Arabs in their own revolt."[33]

That evening the party reached the edge of Wadi Sirhan. Having
run out of water, they had no way to turn the flour they had carried
with them into bread. Lawrence was forced to sleep the night on his
stomach to ward off the cramp of hunger. Early the following morning
they finally reached water. But there was no sign of any of the Huwaytat. Lawrence instantly disliked the wadi. The abundant tamarisk
bushes were too tough for the camels to eat, yet too green to be used
as firewood. The wiry *dum* palms yielded only bitter, inedible dates.
He summed it up in two words: "Pretty barren."[34]

It was also a dangerous place to halt. The brackish water holes attracted poisonous snakes, which would swim in the water after dark and festoon themselves in the bushes by day. The Bedu had a treatment for snakebite: they would bind the affected part "with a snakeskin plaster, and read chapters of the Koran to the sufferer until he died," Lawrence recalled.[35] The availability of water also attracted other raiding parties, who had no shortage of hiding places in the thicket that grew in the wadi's flint-and-gravel bed. One night, when Lawrence's party was having coffee around the fire, there was a shot. The Ageyli pouring the coffee, who had just stood up from serving Lawrence, fell fatally wounded into the circle "with a screech." As one of Auda's tribesmen scuffed sand into the fire to extinguish its flames, the others rolled down behind the bushes and started firing back in the direction of the dunes from where the shots had come. For a few minutes the darkness bristled with yellow muzzle flashes, before the invisible assailants stopped shooting. Then the silence was broken only by the moans of the dying man.

Persevering northward down Wadi Sirhan, they reached on 27 May the first Huwaytat tents and relative safety. At lunch and dinner for the next three days Nasir, Auda, and Lawrence were invited to feast. Each meal followed an increasingly wearying formula. The diners sat down while, from one end of the tent, "urgent whispered cooking directions wafted through the dividing curtain, with a powerful smell of boiled fat and drifts of tasty meat-smoke."[36] After a lengthy wait two men staggered out from behind the curtain, carrying a deep copper tray, piled with rice, which was topped with pieces of sheep and crowned by the sheep's boiled head, buried in rice to its ears, "jaws opened to breaking-point and yawning upwards showing the open throat, the tongue sticking to the teeth and the prickly hair of the nostrils."[37] Heaving the dish into the center of the diners, the men ladled over it the remains of the cooking juices: intestines, fat, muscle, meat, and skin, swimming in grease. The feasters watched intently, "muttering satisfactions when a very juicy scrap plopped out."[38] Once the host had reached into the cauldron, found the liver of the sheep, and placed it on top of the pile, there was a chorus of *"Bismillah al Rahman al Rahim,"*[*] and each man could finally delve into the scalding pile of rice with his

---

[*] An Arabic prayer that might be translated rather prosaically as "To the glory of God the creator and sustainer of all."

right hand to knead a ball of rice, meat, and offal, which he then tossed into his mouth. The experience rapidly paled. "Have feasted noon and sunset since evening of May 27 and am very tired of it," Lawrence wrote three days later, depressed that feasting had eclipsed the hunt for supplies that the party was supposed to be undertaking.[39]

Auda, in the meantime, had set off to meet Nuri Shaalan, taking with him a further £6,000 in gold to try to win the backing of the powerful old sheikh. On 2 June the party regrouped at Nabk, 120 miles north-west down the snake-infested wadi. There Auda reported that Nuri had again been sympathetic, but he remained unwilling to back Feisal openly, for fear of Turkish reprisal. This was a blow. Farther headway north depended on Shaalan's support, which Feisal had hoped to secure by approaching the old sheikh overland—addressing Shaalan's fears that if he backed the Arabs the Turks could cut his food supply off.

Lawrence by now was utterly dejected. His mission to find food for Feisal's men, who would be about to set out, was impossible in the disappointing wastes of Wadi Sirhan. And he was disgusted by the concessions that Sykes had made to the French. But there was still a glimmer of a chance that, if only he could help the Arabs win Syria, he could frustrate French ambitions. At the full moon on 5 June, he wrote in his diary, "Can't stand another day here. Will ride N[orth] and chuck it."[40] On one of the telegram sheets he composed a farewell note to his boss: "Clayton: I've decided to go off alone to Damascus hoping to get killed on the way. For all sakes try and clear this show up before it goes further. We are getting them to fight for us on a lie and I can't stand it."[41]

13

Stalemate in the Hijaz

Now that Lawrence was out of their way, his colleagues redoubled their efforts to force the Turks in Medina to surrender. They were supported from Cairo by Clayton, who continued to insist that "the fall of Medina, or even a striking success against the Hijaz railway in the neighbourhood of Al Ula or elsewhere would greatly strengthen his [Feisal's] position." He believed that "it would appear the wiser course to delay the northern move until his position is more assured and until the situation has developed further."[1] And so, in the Hijaz, plans were put in place for a spectacular raid on the railway, designed to throttle the slender supply line on which Fakhri's army depended.

Support for a large-scale raid reflected the British officers' frustration at the indecisiveness of their tactics so far. "Someone in authority had formed the opinion that we possessed more dynamite than the Turks did rails," Garland afterward recalled.[2] He disagreed, believing that the British "efforts were but little worry to the Turks. They had an inexhaustible stock of spare rails." The Turks also showed an uncanny ability to locate mines the British officers had buried. Hornby and Newcombe toyed with trying to fix explosives under one of the bridges, where they would not be noticed, "to be let off either by shooting or by the engine cutting a string to drop a weight," but this idea proved as unworkable as it was ingenious.[3] In the end Newcombe resorted to laying mines in broad daylight after the search parties had passed by.

Garland wondered whether more devious methods might drive the Turks to distraction. He advocated cutting the track at the same point

Turkish repairs to the railway line. Despite the frequent
demolitions, Turkish repair gangs were able to keep
the railway working until April 1918.

two nights running, blowing up alternate rails to maximize the length
of line that needed repair, and bashing the heads of the screws holding
the rails together with a hammer, to make it harder to remove the damaged sections. He also suggested destroying curved sections of track,
which had to be specially manufactured, wherever possible and deto-
nating the charges just before dawn to limit the hours of darkness when
the Turks could replace the broken rails with less danger of being shot
at by the Bedu.[4]

It was not just that the Hijaz Railway and its timetable were proving
unexpectedly resilient. Newcombe, Hornby, and Garland were all discovering that the Bedu were remarkably intractable. That May, Hornby
reported "a pretty strenuous and exasperating seven days" to Newcombe, in which his Ageyl dynamiters had managed to waste most of
their explosive: "How you stuck it for so long, beats me!"[5] Garland was
more philosophical: "I am not sure that the taking of Bedouin parties is
a white man's job. They always leave you in the lurch."[6] Newcombe
moaned about his inability as an adviser to enforce any discipline: "A
man has but to refuse to do a thing and he is petted and patted and given

bakhshish. I am not allowed to punish anyone and cannot send a man back or take away his rifle. Everyone knows this; hence the trouble."[7]

Problems with the Bedu made the British officers sympathetic to plans to create an Arab legion. This unit, which would consist of trained Arab troops, had been dreamed up by Sykes on his way out to Egypt earlier that spring. It was designed to reinforce the existing small army of ex-Ottoman Arab soldiers already fighting for Husein in the Hijaz alongside the tribesmen. In Cairo, Clayton had by now formed an idea of the officer who might lead this force to strike the railway.

Jafar Pasha al Askari was a former Ottoman army officer who had fought one irregular conflict during the war already. Early in 1915 he had been sent to assist the Senussi, a fanatical sect who lived in the Libyan desert, in an uprising against the British. Captured by the British in February 1916, he was sent to Cairo as a prisoner of war. A burly Iraqi who "closely resembled the statues of the human-headed bulls that are found in the ruined palaces of ancient Assyria," Jafar had tried to break out of the citadel in Cairo, where he was being held, to rejoin the Senussi's campaign.[8] Having filed his way through the bars of a window, he had begun to descend the prison's fifty-foot curtain wall when his "rope" of knotted blankets broke under his considerable weight. While his ankle healed from the fall, Jafar was shown a copy of a newspaper that described the hangings carried out by the Ottomans in Beirut and Damascus that May. One of his friends was among those executed. "I made up my mind there and then to seek revenge, and to make every effort to join the Sharif of Mecca at the earliest possible opportunity," he explained in his memoirs.[9] His interest in doing so quickly came to the notice of Clayton in Cairo. Clayton had summoned him early in the summer of 1917, explained that Feisal needed a commander for his regular troops, and sent him to the Hijaz.

Early in June, after a short rest in Cairo, Newcombe began to make detailed plans for an ambitious raid in which he hoped to destroy ten thousand rails—or nearly 60 miles of railway if Garland's idea of destroying every other rail was followed. He intended to isolate the major Turkish depot at Al Ula, a mud-brick town in a dramatic, red sandstone valley 180 miles north of Medina, and then occupy the line for a fortnight, stopping trains from running in either direction and so forcing the smaller stations to surrender for lack of food and water.

The base for these operations would be at Jaydah, a wadi high in the mountains halfway between Wajh and Al Ula. Aerial reconnaissance on 30 May had established Jaydah's exact location, and days later, Royal Flying Corps pilots set out by car to take a closer look. They returned to Wajh having discovered a possible landing ground in the 3,000-foot-high valley and, as one of them put it, "water in abundance (for the Hijaz)."[10] Plentiful water made Jaydah an attractive location to spend the summer, but a risky place from which to launch bombing raids, since the heat and the altitude made it harder for the heavily laden biplanes to take off. Nevertheless, detailed aerial photographs of Al Ula for Newcombe's raid were finally taken on 17 June.

Newcombe and Hornby joined the biplanes at Jaydah toward the end of June, followed by a detachment of Indian machine gunners, and camel-mounted Egyptian soldiers, and Arab volunteers. Joyce and Feisal arrived at the end of June; by then, however, Newcombe had received copies of the aerial photographs taken a fortnight earlier. Having called the officers together, he explained that the photographs showed that both Al Ula and the station immediately to the south were too heavily defended for them to risk a direct assault. Besides, the Arabs were also reluctant to fight because Ramadan had begun. Newcombe's grand plan was reluctantly abandoned. Instead, "all energies have to be concentrated on line smashing," Joyce reported.[11]

A week later Newcombe launched two attacks on the railway north

Sahl al Matran station in the Hijaz.

and south of Al Ula. After dark on 6 July a party of Egyptians and Harith tribesmen—Lawrence's "robbers for generations"—trekked forty miles south of Al Ula before picking Sahl al Matran, a honey-pink fort on a gray plain fenced in by jagged mountains, as their target. "We crept up to the tracks at the dead of a very dark night," recalled Jafar Pasha, the burly Iraqi who was also there.[12] Near the station the party laid over five hundred charges—one to each rail—which they detonated at two in the morning. "The noise of the dynamite going was something grand and it is always satisfactory finding one is breaking things," reported an excited Joyce, who was more usually burdened with administrative chores like that, a few weeks earlier, which had required him to guess the average shoe size of arriving Arab volunteers, so that a selection of appropriately sized boots could be dispatched from Suez to Wajh.[13]

From inside Sahl al Matran, three signal rockets shot into the warm night sky to warn the stations on either side that they were under attack. "When the dynamite went off in a series of terrifying explosions I could see the silhouettes of a horde of Turkish soldiers coming towards us," Jafar remembered.[14] This counterattack caused some panic among the Arabs: Newcombe and Joyce decided to depart rapidly. Only at dawn did Newcombe realize that several of his Egyptian soldiers were missing, but there was no time to go back. "It was a great pity . . . but we were thirty miles from water and dared not stay," Joyce explained to Wilson.[15] A few miles north of Al Ula, the same night Hornby supervised the destruction of three hundred more rails. On 8 and 10 July, Hornby continued to destroy rails nightly, even after a guncotton charge exploded in his face, rupturing his inner ear and leaving him permanently slightly deaf.[16] "Arabs told me . . . that Hornby would worry the metals [the rails] with his teeth when guncotton failed," Lawrence later joked, of Hornby's tenacity.[17]

On 11 July three British biplanes left Jaydah to bomb Al Ula. One clipped a bush while taking off and crash-landed, but the other two successfully reached the target. The raid was repeated the following day. A further sortie on 16 July hit the water tower at Al Ula station. "Unfortunately we now found ourselves short of petrol," explained one of the pilots, Thomas Henderson, "as many tins had been lost or damaged in transport and several had burst with the heat of the sun, which was intense."[18] Alternately roasted in the sun and drenched by dew at night, the biplanes also suffered from the sand devils that scoured Jay-dah daily. At first sight of these whirling dust spouts "everyone would stand to and hang on to the machines," Henderson remembered. "The tents went down every time. Sometimes they went up. Afterwards all was chaos and the noise of the sandstorm was only equalled by the expressions of discontent by the RFC personnel and the wailings of the Arabs."[19]

Following the attack on Sahl al Matran, Newcombe, Joyce, and Jafar Pasha went south to see Abdullah, who was still based in Wadi Ais. Newcombe, finally reconciled to the fact that finishing the campaign through a single, large-scale raid was unachievable, now told Abdullah that "the easiest and best way to cut the railway was in small lots, but frequently; that this achieved better results than all going in one day and doing 6,000 rails at a time."[20] It was, he said, "much better to do what we can at once and cut line now, when it will be much easier to make big operations on a line already cut."

Soaring daytime temperatures seemed likely to scotch plans for further raids—big or small—against the line, however. "The heat is grilling us all . . . I have experienced nothing to equal it," Joyce told Wilson: "the hot wind off the rocks is like the wrath of a furnace."[21] Even Jafar, who had served before the war in central Arabia, said that he had never experienced anything like it. In his memoirs he admitted being "overwhelmed by anxiety that we would all die if we stayed here much longer."[22]

Yet Newcombe refused to be defeated by the heat. Late in July he set out in search of the old pilgrim caravanserai at Zumrud, which was close to the railway about fifty miles south of Al Ula and rumored to have fresh water. Before dawn on 26 July he found the grim little fortress, standing in a gravel wadi two miles west of the railway. Though in a decrepit state today, it was in 1917 a perfect base for raiding, but its supply of water meant that the Turks would not concede it without a fight. Four days later W. A. Davenport, the latest recruit to the campaign, received an anxious message from Newcombe in the caravanserai, saying that he was under attack. When Davenport arrived, Newcombe sent him with his party of Egyptians into the hills immediately to the north, while he headed south. It was an uneasy night. The "Turks were very jumpy and kept up bursts of excited fire at intervals," Davenport reported, but Jafar Pasha arrived the following day with a relief force, which diverted the Turks and freed Newcombe to return to the railway.[23]

Newcombe's strike on the railway south of Zumrud was almost a disaster. After dynamiting nearly five miles of track with Davenport—a significant achievement in itself—he went south to demolish a further section. It proved an unwise move. Newcombe and Davenport had already alerted the Turks to their presence in the area by seizing the only water supply and then attacking the railway. So it was hardly surprising when the Turks appeared in force. The two British officers were lucky to escape after a three-hour rearguard action in which Newcombe lost his satchel and, with it, his maps, reports, and, of course, his prized billets-doux. Jafar remembered, "After that, when we wanted to pull his leg . . . we would bring up the loss of his beloved and irreplaceable pouch."[24]

Although his colleagues joked about it, Newcombe's near-miss was a reflection that he had finally pushed himself too hard. Shortly afterward he returned to Egypt. He was "ill; (nerves mostly)," Lawrence commented in a letter home.[25] Newcombe would not fight in the Arabs' campaign again, and the Turks would hold out in Medina until after the war was over. His and his colleagues' efforts that hot summer marked the zenith of the war in the Hijaz for, far to the north, Lawrence and his Arab companions Nasir and Auda had far exceeded anyone's expectations. What they had done would turn the revolt away from Medina and focus it firmly to the north.

14

Triumph at Aqaba

After making up his mind to leave behind the gluttony in Wadi Sirhan and "chuck it," Lawrence had on 5 June set out on one of the most daring, behind-the-lines missions ever made, deep into Turkish-held Syria. Three days later he reached Ayn al Barida, a spring 130 miles northeast of Damascus. There he met a sheikh from a branch of the Aniza tribe named Dhami. Dhami proved friendly and led Lawrence westward, around the head of the Anti-Lebanon mountains in a hundred-mile journey that enabled him to demolish a small railway bridge at Ras Baalbek—sixty miles northeast of Beirut in the Bekaa valley in modern Lebanon—on 10 June. The impact of this action, which seems to have spurred the local Metawala* tribesmen into open revolt, excited Lawrence: "The noise of dynamite explosions we find everywhere the most effective propagandist measure possible."[1]

From Ras Baalbek, Lawrence rode southward, passing tantalizingly close to Damascus. Nearby he met Ali Riza al Rikabi, an Arab nationalist who had kept his true leanings so secret that he had been entrusted with the defense of the city by the Turks. Rikabi, however, was not encouraging. He told Lawrence that without outside assistance he was in no position to help Feisal. Departing southeast, Lawrence then passed by Salkhad, a castle built on an old volcano in the Jabal Druse,

---

*The Metawala were Shia Muslims who came from the area now in southern Lebanon that is Hizbullah's stronghold. According to Gertrude Bell, they were "an unorthodox sect of Islam" that had "a very special reputation for fanaticism and ignorance"; *The Desert and the Sown* (New York, 1907), p. 160.

where he met the leader of the rebellious Druse sect Hussein al Atrash. Atrash seemed willing to revolt, as long as Feisal met a number of conditions, which, though Lawrence did not specify them, would seem likely to have included the provision of food and arms. Accompanied by Atrash, Lawrence headed south to the tumbledown castle at Azraq, where he finally met Nuri Shaalan, the intimidating warlord on whose approval the Arabs' northern plans would rest. An old man with a bitter smile, who dyed his hair and beard "a dead black" and whose eyes seemed to glint red in the sunlight, Shaalan, however, remained wary.[2] He would not revolt unless the Druses did, he told Lawrence, although he admitted that "he would certainly be involved sooner or later" and was determined to back Feisal ultimately. "He is willing now to compromise himself to any extent, short of open hostilities pending the collection of his year's food supply" from the Turks, Lawrence wrote in his notes.[3] Having encouraged Shaalan to tell the Turks where the Arabs were, to allay any suspicions about his loyalty, Lawrence left. He arrived back at the mouth of Wadi Sirhan on 18 June.

Lawrence returned to a debate about what the Arabs should do next. In his absence the young expedition leader, Sharif Nasir, had mustered a force of just 560 Huwaytat tribesmen. He said, nevertheless, that he was ready to head west toward Maan, where his aim was to frighten the local Turkish forces enough to achieve the recall of their 300-strong garrison at Aqaba, at the head of the Red Sea. But Nesib al Bakri, the Damascene who had accompanied the party, advocated heading to his home city to incite revolt among the nationalists there. Lawrence disagreed. From his prewar experience and his reconnaissance, he suspected that the nomadic tribesmen, whose reputation for violence went before them, would encounter fear rather than friendship in the cultivated settlements of Syria. Nor did he see Syrians reacting en masse to a call to arms, as Sharif Husein had promised they would before the revolt began. In an article published in the *Arab Bulletin* earlier that year, he had warned, "Syria and Syrian are foreign words. Unless he has learnt English or French, the inhabitant of these parts has no word to describe all his country. . . . This verbal poverty indicates a political condition. There is no national feeling."[4] Lawrence worried that precipitate action of the sort that Bakri now suggested would meet with a weak response. The Turks would deal savagely with any troublemakers, terrorizing the remaining population into acquiescence. Bakri, however, ignored him and decided he would set out for Damascus.

With Bakri gone, Nasir and Lawrence, Auda and the Huwaytat left Wadi Sirhan in the direction of Maan, intending to stop about halfway at the remote well at Bair. But when they reached Bair, on 19 June, they discovered that three out of the four wells had been recently dynamited; the fourth would not supply enough water daily for the five hundred camels in the party. As the only man with any knowledge of explosives, Lawrence was obliged to climb down into the least damaged of the wells. There, having extracted some unexploded charges, he was able to establish that the well was not completely blocked at the bottom. It was a "nasty job for all well lining was loose," he wrote.[5] Realizing the Turks had worked out where he was, Nasir decided to stop while the next wells, forty miles farther southwest at Jafr, were cautiously reconnoitered. While the remaining tribesmen waited, buoyed by the effect he had had at Ras Baalbek, Lawrence turned his attention northward once again.

With Auda's young nephew, Zaal, and one hundred Huwaytat, Lawrence rode north to Jizah, just south of the modern Jordanian capital, Amman. There he met another Arab dissident, Fawaz ibn Faiz, a leading sheikh of the Bani Sakhr tribe,* before crossing the Hijaz Railway and heading northwest to Um Keis, a village in the strategically important Yarmuk valley, down which ran the railway from Syria into Palestine: the main supply route for all the Turkish troops in Palestine. From there the party returned to Minifir, a point on the Hijaz Railway halfway between Dara and Amman. There Lawrence spent some time observing the railway, before demolishing a curved section of the track and leaving a Garland mine, which apparently wrecked the train that later came down to repair the damage. Turning south, the Arabs paused to launch a surprise attack on Atwi station one morning. Lawrence would later vividly recall how Zaal had carefully taken aim at the easiest target among the group of officials sitting in the shade outside the ticket office. When he squeezed the trigger, "the fattest man bowed slowly in his chair and sank to the ground under the frozen

---

* The Bani Sakhr were the dominant tribe in the upland region immediately east of the Dead Sea. Lawrence had identified Fawaz ibn Faiz as the "biggest man" of the tribe by October 1915.

stare of his fellows."[6] After killing the four members of a returning Turkish patrol in the ensuing chaos, the tribesmen drove the station's herd of sheep away before butchering them and feasting lavishly. Then they rode through the night back to Bair.

No sooner had Lawrence reached Bair than Sharif Nasir and Auda wanted to set out for Aqaba, which was now their goal. Aqaba was attractive for a simple reason: the port would provide a natural base closer to Suez than Wajh, to which British explosives, ammunition, and gold could be shipped to foment unrest farther north in Syria. Unlike Wajh, moreover, Aqaba lay outside the Hijaz, and there would be no religious objections to British soldiers' being there. Although Aqaba could easily be defended against an attack from out at sea, the port was vulnerable from the landward side through Wadi Itm, a shattered chasm of red and black rock, and it was down here that Auda now intended to go.

The Arabs started southwest from Bair, reaching the shining mud-flats of the Jafr plain on 30 June. They stopped at Jafr, a clump of dirty-green palms flickering in the silty mirage. Nasir and the majority of the Arab force waited while parties of Huwaytat tribesmen launched two diversionary attacks north and south of Maan. Alarmed by the sudden appearance of the Arabs, the Turks sent troops to reinforce Abu al Assal, a well on the pass over the Batra ridge and the key to Aqaba.

Once Nasir had heard that the Huwaytat had attacked Fuweilah, he decided to cross the railway twenty miles south of Maan and ascend the Jabal al Batra ridge to attack the Turks at Abu al Assal. He, Auda, Lawrence, and the remaining tribesmen, mounted on a mixture of camels and horses, headed south across the flat gray plain toward the Hijaz Railway. They wrecked the station of Ghadir al Hajj and then found one of the stocky bridges that had so far defied the demolition teams in the Hijaz. It was the first time Lawrence had seen one of these bridges close up, but the drainage hole that emerged from the span-drel between each arch invited an idea. Lawrence plugged this fist-sized outlet with several pounds of explosive, which, when fired, "brought down the arch, shattered the pier and stripped the side walls, in no more than six minutes' work."[7] Hoping that the explosions would draw the Turks' attention southward, the Arab party now hurried away west, climbing the Jabal al Batra ridge in the dark. To the south the Quwayrah plain glowed green and gold in the dawn light, and angular mountains in the distance marked the head of Wadi Itm, the gorge leading down to Aqaba.

The Arabs found the Turks at Abu al Assal. Evidently the Turks were not expecting to be attacked, for they had clustered around the well there and failed to secure the surrounding high ground. It proved to be a fatal mistake, which gave the Arabs the advantage. Having surrounded the Turkish outpost early on 2 July, Auda's men began to snipe at the soldiers below. "Our rifles grew so hot with the sun and the shooting that they seared our hands," Lawrence later remembered: "It was terribly hot—hotter than ever before I had felt it in Arabia and the anxiety and constant moving made it hard for us."[8]

Although the Turks were trapped, the Arabs' attack stalled in the withering heat, and they were running out of daylight. Lawrence paused for a rest in the safety of a hollow behind the ridge, where he was joined by Nasir and then Auda. When Auda accused him of slacking, Lawrence angrily replied that his tribesmen were no use: "they shoot a lot and hit a little."[9] This accusation enraged Auda, who turned and ran back up the hill, shouting at his men to gather around him. Lawrence, who had followed Auda back to the crest of the ridge, wondered whether he had done the wrong thing. Suddenly there were yells: Lawrence crawled forward to the edge of the ridge, to see, led by Auda, "our fifty horsemen coming down the last slope into the main valley like a run-away, at full gallop, shooting from the saddle."[10]

Sharif Nasir now saw an opportunity. "Come on," he shouted at Lawrence, and they mounted their camels and led the remaining tribesmen in a headlong dash down the hill into Abu al Assal. The Turks, who were transfixed by Auda's charge, did not see them until it was too late. They "fired a few shots, but mostly only shrieked and turned to run," recalled Lawrence, who, bouncing along on his galloping camel, was shooting back with his pistol.[11] Suddenly his camel tripped and fell. "I was torn completely from the saddle, and went sailing grandly through the air for a great distance, and landed with a crash which seemed to drive all the power and feeling out of me."[12] When he came around, Lawrence found that he had shot the beast in the back of its head.

Auda appeared. His horse had been killed under him, his binoculars were shattered, and his holster and scabbard holed. Six bullets had hit his equipment in total, but none had touched him, an escape that he attributed to his purchase years earlier of a miniature Quran, for which Lawrence privately thought he had vastly overpaid. In all, the Arabs had suffered two deaths and one man was seriously wounded. Three hundred dead and dying Turks lay in the scorching hollow around the well, of a force which that morning had numbered five hundred.

From a prisoner Lawrence learned that it would probably have been easy to capture Maan, but to do so at this point would have been a diversion from the opportunity that now existed to secure the surrender of Aqaba. In his diary Lawrence recorded that he slept after the battle, which had lasted throughout the afternoon. But in *Seven Pillars of Wisdom* he described spending much of the night neatly arranging the naked bodies of the dead in line—the tribesmen always stripped their victims and wore their clothes as trophies—under the light of the waxing moon, before helping Auda to write letters to the Turkish outposts down to Aqaba, threatening them with a similar fate unless they capitulated quickly.

The letters had some effect. On their way down to Aqaba, the Arabs encountered three more Turkish outposts, all of which surrendered quickly. Quwayrah, a tiny telegraph station, fell without a shot being fired. In 2004 I followed the Arabs' route down through the deep cleft of Wadi Itm to the sea. "There are dark red rocks with banded black stripes pressed between them. It is a very uninviting landscape. The rock is shattered by forces unknown and there is a great sense of moving into the unknowable," I wrote in my diary at the time.

On 4 July the Arabs surrounded the next Turkish outpost, halfway down the wadi. An attack that coincided with the lunar eclipse that night, which gave the moon a copper color, persuaded the already terrified Turks to surrender. Finally the Arabs found the three hundred Turks of Aqaba's garrison entrenched at Wadi Itm's mouth. Though their defenses pointed out toward the sea, the Turks proved reluctant to give in, but, Lawrence recollected, when Nasir explained that in battle he might not be able to stop a massacre, the Turkish officer agreed to surrender at dawn the following day. "We mounted our camels," Lawrence recalled, "and raced through a driving sand-storm down to Aqaba, only four miles further, and splashed into the sea, on July the sixth, just two months after our setting out from Wajh."[13]

Lawrence paused only briefly in the port, shattered by frequent off-

**Wadi Itm, 5 July 1917. The tribesmen surprised
Aqaba's garrison by approaching from inland
down this narrow, red valley.**

shore bombardment by the British. The dates in the palms were still
green and unripe and, short of fishing by means of dynamite or killing
their own camels, there was no other available food. His diary chroni-
cles a rapid turnaround, but also the fact that his arrival was expected,
for by now British warships were monitoring the port closely: "Entered
Aqaba 10am. Read letter from Newcombe. Left in afternoon."[14] With
a select band of tribesmen, he immediately set out westward across
Sinai on the 150-mile trek to Suez to raise food and help, and to break
the news of the Arabs' momentous achievement himself.

15

The Impact of Aqaba

In Cairo, Bertie Clayton spent the morning of 10 July putting the finishing touches to a memorandum that summarized the difficulty of supporting Feisal's imminent move northward. He remained concerned about how Feisal would be supplied with food, money, weapons, and ammunition, which had fueled the revolt for over a year. Supply via Aqaba, Clayton said, involved "insuperable difficulties at present" partly because "the section between Aqaba and Maan is in Turkish hands."[1]

With the memo dispatched, and after a brief lunch, Clayton was back at his desk in the Savoy Hotel when he became aware that an Arab had walked into his office. "*Mush fadi*," he said, without looking up: telling whoever it was to leave him be.

The Arab replied in Oxford English: Clayton's head shot up.

"I . . . got a very hearty welcome," Lawrence later recalled.[2] He had crossed the Sinai by camel in just over three days. He gave Clayton his report of his journey northward straightaway and presented him with a long list of supplies that were urgently needed in Aqaba, including a request for six thousand cigarettes.[3] That afternoon Clayton withdrew £16,000 in gold to cover the promises Sharif Nasir had made to buy tribal support and dispatched the money by train to Suez for immediate shipment to Aqaba. Then the two men sat down to talk.

Wingate was delighted by Lawrence's sudden appearance and his news of triumph too. That night he telegraphed the chief of the Imperial General Staff, Sir William Robertson, with the news that "Captain

Lawrence arrived Cairo today by land from Aqaba. Turkish posts between Tafilah, Maan and Aqaba in Arab hands. Total Turkish losses 700 killed, 600 prisoners including 20 officers."[4]

For the time being, however, Lawrence's exploits were kept a secret. It was only two weeks later that the *Arab Bulletin* archly reported that the explanation for recent disturbances in the Maan area that it had already reported "has reached us in the person of Captain Lawrence." It did not mention that he had reached Aqaba or that the port was now in Arab hands.[5] There was a good reason for the secrecy. As Wingate immediately recognized, and warned London when he heard where Lawrence had been, "for political reasons it is very important that nothing should be known publicly as to Lawrence's Syrian reconnaissance."[6] First, there was the danger that if news of Lawrence's travels was leaked, it would spark a witch hunt in Syria by the Turks for anyone who had helped him.[7] Then there was the worry that the French would be outraged that Lawrence had been fomenting rebellion among the Arabs at Ras Baalbek, which lay inside the zone allocated to them by the Sykes-Picot agreement, and might seek to frustrate the Arabs' Syrian ambitions by leaking details of Lawrence's trip. Although the French knew about a "little revolt" that had followed Lawrence's raid there, they had no idea that Lawrence was involved, and they remained under the impression for several months that Lawrence's journey to Aqaba had taken him no farther north than Tafilah, in the south of modern Jordan and safely inside the zone allocated to the British.[8]

Lawrence afterward reveled in the mystery that surrounded his two forays northward into Syria. Evasively he described his subsequent report on the missions as "part of the truth." In the earliest surviving draft of *Seven Pillars of Wisdom*, he would gloss over his first ride as "long and dangerous, no part of the machinery of the revolt, as barren of consequence as it was unworthy in motive," but could not resist a fleeting reference ten pages later to his "long trip round Baalbek and Damascus and the Hauran."[9] Quizzed by his biographer Robert Graves, he suggested some tantalizing text that Graves might use, which would encourage Graves's readers to believe that Lawrence had achieved all he claimed.[10] Graves, though slightly skeptical, used Lawrence's suggested words in full.

Lawrence's coyness, the scale of his achievement, and the claims by some Arabs, including Nesib al Bakri, that Lawrence never set out north on his own encouraged a debate over whether in fact he invented these exploits. Yet recently unearthed British and French intelligence reports, which both refer to trouble in the Ras Baalbek area, separately corroborate the most audacious episode in Lawrence's story.[11] So, too, perhaps, does the untimely death of Fawaz ibn Faiz, possibly poisoned by the Turks, within weeks of his meeting Lawrence.[12]

Partly because of the need for secrecy, it took weeks for the true significance of Lawrence's achievement to sink in. Writing after the war, the military historian Basil Liddell Hart summarized its dividends. There were the strategic effects of blocking a Turkish raid through the Sinai Desert on either the Suez Canal or the supply line to the British army outside Gaza; it opened the way for the Arabs to support a British advance into Palestine. But to Liddell Hart, who had served on the western front, it was the expedition's tactical outcome that was so extraordinary. "By the World War standards of 'killing Germans' or 'killing Turks,' it was an unrivalled achievement," he wrote in 1934.[13] "The British forces in trying unsuccessfully to capture Gaza in March and April had only succeeded in killing or capturing 1,700 Turks at a permanent cost to themselves of 3,000 men. In other words, they had sacrificed roughly two men to 'kill' one Turk, the same number that the Arabs sacrificed to 'kill' twelve hundred Turks. As an object lesson in the abstract principle of economy of force the Aqaba operation was remarkable." Moreover, it had been attained "by the detachment of merely one unwanted officer from the forces in Egypt." Wingate recommended Lawrence for a Victoria Cross, Britain's highest decoration for bravery, but, seemingly because there was no witness to his actions, Lawrence was promoted to the rank of major and made a CB—a Companion of the Order of the Bath and one of Britain's greatest honors—instead. "He ought of course to have a VC," commented another intelligence officer in a letter that gives a flavor of the mood: "still a CB is almost unheard of for a major. However there is nothing they could give him which would be too great."[14]

Wingate himself was now determined to revise the Sykes-Picot agreement. At the beginning of July he approached the Foreign Office, arguing that the British zone of influence delineated in the treaty should be extended southward to encompass the whole of Arabia. "Anything less than this jeopardizes our whole position in the East," he claimed. This one-sided alteration to the Sykes-Picot agreement was justified, he said, on the grounds that while Britain had helped the sharif and captured a chunk of Mesopotamia, the French had done next to nothing.[15] Wingate had already dispatched Hogarth to London to press for the existing treaty to be torn up.

Hogarth's return to London was badly timed, however. Although widespread dislike of the Sykes-Picot agreement favored him, events in France, Russia, and Turkey did not. During June the French army had been shaken by a serious mutiny. The British government was unwilling to do anything that might undermine its ally further. The government also, curiously, remained hopeful that, even under the Bolsheviks, Russia might yet remain in the war. And finally, following rumors that the Turkish high command had fallen out with its German advisers, the British had entered secret talks with the Turkish minister for war, Enver Pasha, to try to secure the Ottomans' exit from the conflict in return for a very large bribe. This combination of fear, hope, and work in progress meant that there was little appetite for reopening the treaty.

Yet Hogarth's proposal still made Mark Sykes livid. "Hogarth arrived and played hell by writing an anti-French anti-Agreement memorandum. Pouring cold water on the Arab movement and going in for Gnome-Imperialism and a British Mecca," Sykes wrote to Clayton.[16] Against Sykes's fierce opposition, Hogarth made no headway. "I doubt if my note has effected anything except the embitterment of Mark Sykes," he concluded dolefully.[17]

Sykes was beginning to realize that Hogarth was not his only adversary. Although he told Clayton through gritted teeth, "Lawrence's move is splendid and I want him knighted," in a bitter, defensive letter to the foreign secretary, Arthur Balfour, he complained of being faced with "the prejudices of the past both British and French, the mutual suspicions and susceptibilities of out-of-date minds," which manifested themselves in the "anti-British policy of Brémond [and] the anti-French attitude of Lawrence and Newcombe."[18] It was Lawrence who was the most ardent opponent of his cherished Middle Eastern plans.

Hogarth told Clayton to warn Lawrence "not to justify Mark's idea of him," but he was confident that the allegation would not stick: "The W[ar] O[ffice] is optimistic about Arabia and Syria," Hogarth said, "and much bucked by TEL's report and scheme."[19]

Lawrence had originally devised his scheme, for the next stage of the Arabs' revolt, on the back of a sheet of telegraph paper. In the final version, after Clayton had encouraged him to be more cautious about the chances of success, he envisaged a roughly coordinated attack by up to seven different Arab forces, which he believed could be arranged by the end of August if they were given the necessary assistance.[20] A southern force would seize the fertile, grain-producing upland areas east and southeast of the Dead Sea as soon as possible. Four other forces, based at the wells in the desert east of the Hijaz Railway, would stage simultaneous attacks along a 350-mile stretch of track between Maan, in the south of modern Jordan, and Hama, 100 miles north of Damascus in present-day Syria. Then, from the Hauran, six thousand Druses would once again rebel, descending westward on Dara, the vulnerable ganglion of the Syrian railway network that connected Palestine, southern Syria, and the Hijaz to Damascus. At the same time Lawrence advocated attacking the railway west of Dara, where it descended the Yarmuk valley, to cut the Turks in Palestine off from Syria. He hoped that the Druses might follow up success at Dara with the occupation of Damascus, but his final proposal was less assured than his original draft, in which he anticipated the early occupation of the city. His tactics relied on tribesmen and the Druses, but he hoped that their concerted action would precipitate unrest throughout the settled, agricultural belt east of the Jordan.

If the uprisings Lawrence envisaged were successful, Turkish rule in Syria would be short-lived. But if they failed, the consequences were likely to be terrible. The Turks had crushed an uprising in Karak—a hilltop town in southern Jordan—seven years earlier by hanging eight members of the town's two leading families in the market square, and Clayton and Lawrence both knew that local fears of Turkish recrimination stood in the way of their plan's succeeding. To back Lawrence up, Clayton now began to push for a British invasion of Palestine to keep the Turkish army busy. A revolt in Syria, he said, was "entirely contingent on a decision to undertake major operations in Palestine with which the movement of the Arabs must synchronize. . . . Unless operations of such magnitude as to occupy the whole of the Turkish Army in Palestine were undertaken the proposed Arab operations must be abandoned."[21]

On 12 July, General Sir Edmund Allenby, the new commander in chief of the British forces in Egypt, called Lawrence in to see him. He had been sent out to Egypt to replace Archibald Murray following the failure of Murray's second attempt to take Gaza in April. Allenby's was not an enviable position. Before leaving London, he had come under significant pressure from the prime minister to take "Jerusalem by Christmas," but the War Cabinet was split on this strategy. Robertson continued to argue forcefully against any distraction from the western front and repeatedly warned Allenby privately that he could not expect to receive further troops to meet his needs. The combination of political pressure and Robertson's opposition had pushed Murray to try to capture Gaza with too few troops and had undone him. Allenby realized he needed to tread carefully to avoid falling into exactly the same trap.

Lawrence must have approached the meeting with some trepidation, for Allenby was a man with an infamously filthy temper, known to his men as "The Bull." Being told off by him, Ronald Storrs recalled, was like being blown from the muzzle of a gun. But, a fortnight into his new job, uncertain of the bewildering array of tribal allegiances, but ready to listen to advice, Allenby sat almost silently as Lawrence explained his plan. Lawrence was effectively asking him to support the Bedu by committing himself to an invasion of Palestine, an offensive for which so far there was inadequate support from London. It was perhaps just as well that he did not know that, three days earlier, Allenby had written to his wife, "The Bedouin are not very friendly to strangers, British or Turk; and we don't allow them near us," he explained, adding, "Of course, they are Turkish in sympathy as a rule."[22]

"At the end," Lawrence later recollected, Allenby "put up his chin and said quite directly, 'Well, I will do for you what I can.'"[23]

Allenby's guarded response concealed the fact that the new commander was greatly impressed by what he had just heard. He also realized that the excitement generated in London by Lawrence's journey could reinforce his own request for two more divisions of men, which he transmitted to London the same day, and which was rapidly approved.[24] He wrote to Robertson four days later, warmly reporting Lawrence's ideas. "Even the partial success of Lawrence's scheme would seriously disorganize Turkish railway communications south of Aleppo, whilst its complete success would destroy effectively his only main artery of communication," he explained.[25] Besides the possibility of causing havoc behind Turkish lines, Allenby also welcomed the security the Arabs could bring to his eastern flank, because he worried that the Turks might counterattack from the Maan area as he advanced northward. But he did not fully endorse Lawrence's strategy straightaway.

Fulsome praise of Lawrence for the capture of Aqaba from both Wingate and Robertson—who must have rather liked Lawrence's economical approach to warfare—made it possible for Allenby to go further. With the backing of the high commissioner for the scheme and an enthusiastic endorsement from the War Office, Allenby sent another telegram to Robertson on 19 July, this time making his support explicit and using Lawrence's success to justify his own intentions. "The advantages offered by Arab co-operation on lines proposed by Captain Lawrence are, in my opinion, of such importance that no effort should be spared to reap full benefit therefrom."[26] If the Arabs' operations were successful, he said, "such a movement, in conjunction with offensive operations in Palestine, may cause a collapse of the Turkish campaigns in the Hijaz and in Syria and produce far-reaching results, both political as well as military." He warned Robertson, however, that "the scheme proposed by Captain Lawrence can only be realized in conjunction with the prosecution of offensive operations by me in this theatre." He intended to be ready to advance northward into Palestine by mid-September, a date fixed by the fact that action was needed before the tribesmen headed deep into the desert during the winter to graze their livestock. To coordinate the tribesmen to the east of the Jordan valley with the British army to the west, Allenby proposed bringing Feisal and Lawrence under his command. Deliberately perhaps, one consequence of this arrangement was to undermine the Sykes-Picot agreement's attempt to lock the Arabs out by drawing them formally into the British plans to invade Palestine. Now that the Arabs were formally an ally, Clayton warned Sykes, "My own advice to the French would be to encourage and back Feisal and the northern Arab movement as much as possible."[27] With American criticisms of annexation already ringing in his ears, Sykes agreed with Clayton. "I am going to slam into Paris to make the French play up to the Arab cause as their only hope," he replied, adding very optimistically, "Colonialism is madness and I believe Picot and I can prove it to them."[28]

Expecting Sharif Husein to be suspicious of Allenby's subordination of Feisal, Lawrence volunteered to go to Jeddah to reassure him. On his voyage southward he stopped at Wajh and was flown inland the same day to meet Feisal, who was up at Jaydah supporting Newcombe's abortive attempt to smash the railway. The situation in the wadi was chaotic. A sandstorm had hit the camp earlier that day, badly damaging two of the airplanes and preventing further air raids. Lawrence spent the night there, describing his two-month-long journey to Feisal and making preparations to move the British and Arab operations at Wajh north to Aqaba. He left for Jeddah the following morning, with letters from Feisal to Husein to allay any fears his father might have about the new command structure set out by Allenby.

Husein came down to Jeddah to meet Lawrence on 28 July, and approved Feisal as his military representative in the north.[29] Most of the meeting he devoted to his concerns about the postwar settlement of Syria. He told Lawrence that he would refuse to accept French annexation of Beirut and Lebanon, but explained how delighted he was to have "trapped" Picot into admitting that Syria should be governed along similar lines to Mesopotamia, where he expected the British to honor his leaseback scheme. Husein devoted much of a second meeting the following day to a description of the threat posed to him by Wahhabism, the austere version of Islam espoused by Ibn Saud.

Husein's agreement with the command arrangements that Lawrence explained to him meant that Allenby could confirm early that August that he would now control all operations north and west of a line between Aqaba and Maan.[30] The British commander also received a letter from Robertson, who was worrying that the Russian collapse would allow the Germans to concentrate their forces on the western front. "With Russia practically out of the war we have got to consider the necessity for economizing shipping and men and also for being strong on the West front," he told Allenby, grumbling, "Extensive operations in distant theatres mean a great strain upon shipping."[31] But even he was also forced to admit that, whatever his own reservations over an advance into Palestine, "the Prime Minister is very much in favour of it and eventually the Government may decide to do it." A further sentence in the letter was pregnant with possibility: "Lawrence's scheme seems to be a good one and I hope we shall be able to take advantage of it."

16

Impolitic Truths

The orders that Allenby received from the War Cabinet on 11 August 1917 marked a crucial sea change in the purpose of Britain's support for the Arabs. Previously Britain had backed the Arabs in a defensive political move designed to ruin the coherence of the Ottomans' call for jihad. Now British support rested on the understanding that the Arabs would help them achieve an aggressive, military objective.

The War Cabinet ordered Allenby to take advantage of the capture of Aqaba and attack the Turks, "since a good success achieved against them will tend to strengthen the morale and staying power of this country during a season when important successes in Europe may not be feasible."[1] Rightly worried that the Russian collapse would shortly liberate thousands of Ottoman soldiers to fight on the Palestine and Mesopotamian fronts, the War Cabinet's orders revealed a heavy reliance on Lawrence's belief that he could mobilize thousands of tribesmen in Syria to paralyze the Ottoman rail network that September. On this assumption the War Cabinet advised Allenby to press the Turks soon, to draw them into Palestine rather than Mesopotamia. Lawrence's Arabs would swing into action behind the Turks, bottling them up in Palestine by destroying the slender railway link that connected Palestine with Syria. It was a clever plan, in theory.

Robertson remained skeptical. While he liked Lawrence's scheme because it was so economical, in a letter to a colleague he privately admitted he was "a bit doubtful" about Allenby's plans, though he thought they were worth trying. To those politicians who were "dying to go to

Jerusalem and Damascus, and other places," however, Robertson remained an implacable opponent.[2] His opposition explains why the cabinet's orders set Allenby no geographical objective, nor, more alarmingly, did they explicitly promise him enough troops to continue beyond Jerusalem, or even to maintain his position if he reached the holy city. Robertson also wrote a private letter to Allenby, designed to undermine his faith in the orders, which he said "simply amount to doing the best you can with what you have got." He also warned Allenby not to get into "a position from which you can neither advance nor go back and which might involve us in commitments which we could not properly meet having regard to other places and to our resources."[3]

Robertson's caveats made the Arab support Lawrence had promised all the more important, for the Arabs would be protecting Allenby's right flank as he advanced eastward into Palestine. So Allenby was relieved to hear from Lawrence that the situation in Aqaba was good. Lawrence had passed through the port on his return from seeing Husein in Jeddah, and told Allenby on his return to Egypt that all was well there and that, contrary to his earlier fears, the tribesmen would not disappear into the desert to graze their camels at the first sign of the winter rains.

In fact, Lawrence was simply buying time to cover up the possibility of Arab treachery. Down at Jeddah he had received intelligence that suggested that Auda had contacted the Turks in Maan, offering his services if the Turks treated him as well as they had Nuri Shaalan. He raced to Aqaba and rode back up Wadi Itm to Quwayrah, where the Huwaytat were based. There Lawrence challenged Auda and his deputy, Mohammed al Dheilan, about the letters he revealed he knew they had sent to Maan. According to Auda, Mohammed had borrowed his seal to write to the governor of Maan, offering to swap sides. The Ottomans replied enthusiastically, promising a reward if he did. When Auda found out, he robbed the Turkish messenger who had come bearing an advance. Lawrence was clearly unconvinced by this story. Although he wired Wilson to say that the situation was "satisfactory" and although he then told Allenby all was well, he later admitted that his claim that there was "no spirit of treachery abroad . . . may have been hardly true, but the deception was mine, and I regularly reduced impolitic truth in my communications."[4] Lawrence had no qualms about lying to his superiors when it was expedient for him to do so.

Trusting Lawrence's assurance, Allenby told Robertson that Lawrence would "organize a movement, on a large scale, between Aqaba and the Dead Sea" and that "now the Arabs are in, he can keep them in, and an early start in September by my troops is not now a necessity."[5] This was a good excuse for Allenby, because his troops' special training and the supply arrangements needed to sustain them in a rapid advance through waterless country were taking longer than expected to complete.

Arab reinforcements began arriving in Aqaba late in August. On 18 August, Jafar Pasha arrived with 800 men. A further 300 disembarked two days later, and Feisal arrived on 23 August with 500 more. These were mostly the Iraqi and Syrian former Ottoman soldiers and some Meccans who had volunteered to fight for Husein. They left behind most of the tribesmen who had fought with them in the Hijaz, as they refused to fight so far from home. Pierce Joyce also arrived in Aqaba late in the month to take charge of running the Arabs' base and overall operations, and British soldiers arrived to build a road up Wadi Itm that would improve communications with the Arabs' forward base at Quwayrah. Joining them shortly to start demolitions on the railway was Hornby, but not Newcombe. Following his narrow escape from the Turks, Lawrence advised Wilson that Feisal would not need Newcombe's services in the northern campaign. Of the British officers in the Hijaz, only Garland and Davenport remained. They would continue to wage their lonely war against the railway in the south until the end of 1918.

Aqaba today is a hot and sprawling town with roads blotched black with oil from the lorries that ferry cargo in and out from this, Jordan's only port. Down-at-heel hotels advertise diving courses in the Red Sea, which laps invitingly against the palm-shaded shore. But in 1917 it was a backwater of about a hundred mud houses screened from the sea by a belt of palm trees, and a square fort that the British had already ruined by naval bombardment and that today is the only recognizable relic of that time. The sandy shoreline ran back from the sea to end at the base of the gigantic cliff wall that separated Aqaba from the hinterland. There was no grazing or, besides the slowly ripening dates, any local source of food: the port would be entirely dependent on the Royal Navy for supplies from Egypt.

Although Aqaba was protected by a British warship, HMS *Humber*, which was moored offshore like a seaborne goalkeeper, Joyce felt vulnerable. There were two routes from Aqaba to Maan, where up to four thousand Turkish troops were based. One—still impassable to motor vehicles—followed Wadi Itm; the other, easier road went north up Wadi Araba then east over the 3,000-foot-high ridge and down toward Ain Dilagha and Maan. The British urgently needed to build a road up Wadi Itm to supply the tribesmen on the Quwayrah plain. But while Wadi Itm reverberated with the crack of exploding dynamite as British soldiers hurriedly cleared a road up the narrow valley, the Turks were reported to be gathering in numbers at Ain Dilagha to retake Aqaba via the easier road. They had also retaken Abu al Assal, the well at the head of the pass between Aqaba and Maan where they had been massacred by the Arabs that summer.[6]

This report of Turkish activity seems to have galvanized Lawrence, who had been taking a few days off in Cairo. With a promise of support from the Royal Flying Corps, he immediately returned to Aqaba and headed northwest to the edge of the Sinai to set up a rudimentary airstrip stocked with fuel and bombs for British aircraft flying from Egypt. The aircraft—new biplanes to replace those damaged in the sandstorms at Jaydah—flew to this airstrip on 26 August and flew on to bomb Maan, a station farther south, and the advance Turkish camps at Fuweilah and Abu al Assal over the next three days.

Back in Aqaba, Lawrence found that another officer from the Arab Bureau, MacIndoe, was planning to write a critical report on the situation there. Having seen the report, he worried that it could erode Allenby's trust in the Arabs' operations. On 26 August—the day before MacIndoe dispatched his conclusions—Lawrence wrote to Clayton to explain that the point of Jafar's force was "not so much to engage Turkish forces on equal terms, as to stiffen the Beduin resistance, by providing the comfortable spectacle of a trained reserve."[7] The Turkish commander, he argued, would not dare to attack Aqaba with fewer than two thousand men, the number under Jafar Pasha's command, whose "quality, so long as it is not proved bad by premature action, has of necessity to be estimated by the Turks as good."

Fortunately the Turks did not come, because the Arabs were disorganized. "Most troublesome were the volunteers from the Hijaz and Yemen," their commander Jafar Pasha wrote afterward. "They were unaccustomed to obeying orders and wearing army uniforms."[8] In particular, they "seemed to be allergic" to wearing trousers. "One day, with his trousers over one shoulder, one of them fell to his knees before . . . Feisal. Pointing a finger at the offending legwear he cried: 'My Lord, I will withstand eternal hellfire but I shall never stand these!'" Feisal burst out laughing and asked Jafar not to insist that the men wear uniform. Jafar came up with an alternative, like a kilt, to keep the volunteers happy.

Amid scenes like these, Lawrence's fears were justified, for MacIndoe's report, in which he described Jafar Pasha's men as "so-called Regular Troops" whose "one desire . . . is to be left alone to eat and sleep," turned out to be sufficiently damning to encourage Clayton to come to Aqaba to see for himself.[9] Once he had arrived, however, Clayton endorsed Lawrence's opinion. Joyce, as the man who would have to organize the impromptu defense of Aqaba if the Turks broke through, drew no consolation from his own belief that Jafar Pasha's men were divided into Syrian and Iraqi factions and "in reality more of a bluff than an effective fighting force."[10] He wanted reinforcements from the Imperial Camel Corps, which consisted entirely of white British, Australian, and New Zealander soldiers, of Allenby's army, to come to Aqaba. Lawrence disagreed. "One squabble between a trooper and an Arab, or an incident with Beduin women, would bring on general hostilities," he wrote, in a robust rebuttal of the idea.[11]

While he was in Aqaba, Clayton showed Lawrence a blustering letter he had received from Sykes, in which the Tory member of Parliament vehemently attacked what he described as the "Foreign Office pro-Turk gang," who had been trying to negotiate a separate peace with the Ottomans over that summer, and told Clayton to stamp on rivalry toward the French among his officers. On this subject Sykes had a blunt message for Lawrence. "Tell him now that he is a great man he must behave as such and be broad in his views. Ten years' tutelage under the *Entente** and the Arabs will be a nation. Complete independence means Persia, poverty and chaos. Let him consider this, as he hopes for the people he is fighting for."[12]

Lawrence was not in the mood to take high-minded advice from

---

* Sykes was referring to the Entente Cordiale of 1904. This agreement between Britain and France was designed to reflect a new era of friendly relations between the two countries. It lent its name to the two countries' alliance with one another and with Russia in wartime.

Sykes, and he wrote a long and penetrating reply in which he attacked Sykes for his concessions to the French and asked him to clarify British policy toward the Zionists, whose confident plans to buy up Palestine had alarmed him when he had last visited Cairo. He warned Sykes, too, that Husein's title to the regions that his forces captured would be "a fairly strong one—that of conquest by the means of the local inhabitants—and what are the two powers going to say about it?" The letter ended,

> You know I'm strongly pro-British, and also pro-Arab. France takes third place with me: but I quite recognize that we may have to sell our small friends to pay for our big friends, or sell our future security in the Near East to pay for our present victory in Flanders. If you will tell me once more what we have to give the Jews, and what we have to give the French, I'll do everything I can to make it easy for us. . . . We are in rather a hole: please tell me what, in your opinion, are the actual means by which we will find a way out.[13]

Lawrence finished the letter and attached it to a covering note to Clayton, asking him to forward the letter to Sykes. In this he admitted his reasons for writing to Sykes: "Some of it is really thirst for information, and other is only a wish to stick pins in him."[14]

Lawrence then headed up Wadi Itm to raid the railway. With him went the two instructors drafted in to train the Bedu, Sergeant Yells and Corporal Brook, whom Lawrence christened "Lewis" and "Stokes" in line with their respective fields of expertise: the Lewis machine gun and the Stokes mortar. They were joined by the crack Bedu shot Zaal and tribesmen from the Huwaytat and Bani Atiyah tribes, who lived in the area east of Aqaba where Lawrence now planned to operate. His target was Mudawwarah, a remote station about halfway between Maan and Tabuk, which was the only source of water between the two towns. Lawrence's plan was to destroy the water tower at the station, creating a waterless stretch of track of almost 150 miles along which the Turks would have great difficulty running any trains. The other advantage of destroying the line at this point was that it would enable the British to wind up operations in Wajh and concentrate their stretched resources on supplying Aqaba.

He also took a new electric, ACME-type detonator, which he hoped would enable him to mine a train more effectively than the pressure mines devised by Garland. The raid, believed Clayton, would be the first litmus test of Lawrence's plan.

Tribal trouble among the Huwaytat at Quwayrah and a shortage of camels both delayed Lawrence, who finally set out on 16 September from Wadi Ramm, a cluster of mighty sandstone buttresses that tower a thousand feet over boulevards of pink-orange sand, which made one set of British visitors feel "like gnats in size."[15] In September 2004 I followed Lawrence's route by four-wheel drive, plowing through the sands of Wadi Ramm into a bumpy landscape of low, decapitated hills rising out of the sand, rendered very desolate in places by a thin layer of stones weathered to the color of pencil lead by the sun. My guide, Attayak Ali, said that his grandfather had followed Lawrence down to Aqaba in 1917. We drove the fifty miles to Mudawwarah in just a day, racing across the stony flats, then slewing through the sand dunes drunkenly, with a hot breeze in our faces and a long trail of yellowy-gray dust in our wake.

For Lawrence it was a much more awkward journey. The sheikh accompanying him went blind, and he was left with the task of trying to unite the disparate elements of the raiding party, which he described as like "a broken necklace."[16] Consequently, he complained, he had "more preoccupation with questions of supply, transport, tribal pay, disputes, division of spoil, feuds, march order, and the like, than with the explosive work."[17]

Toward evening the following day Lawrence stopped at a well in the hills about three miles west of Mudawwarah station. Its water was a disappointment, "for over its face was a thick mantle of green slime, from which swelled curious bladder-like islands of floating fatty stuff." The Bedu explained that months earlier the Turks had thrown dead camels into the pool to deny them water. The foul taste these left, they reassured Lawrence, had now grown faint. "It might have been fainter for my taste," Lawrence would later recall, "but it was all the drink we could get in the neighbourhood, unless we took Mudawwarah station, so we . . . filled our water-skins at once."[18]

When I followed in Lawrence's footsteps in 2004, I found that the station—two single-story whitewashed buildings and a wind pump, but missing the water tower that stood there ninety years ago—is today occupied by the Jordanian police, and as I arrived, a miscreant was being led inside, his arms firmly handcuffed behind his back. After shaking many hands, I was quickly installed on a cushion under an awning outside—decorated with a photograph of Jordan's late king, Hussein, the grandson of Abdullah—with a hot glass of tea in my hand.

Lawrence's intelligence was absolutely right. The Jordanians have tapped the water beneath Mudawwarah so that the surrounding area now sprouts circular green fields, which, from the air, look like verdant, alien crop circles. All that remains of the railway are its corrugated-iron ties, which serve today as simple fencing. From the police station, three hundred yards away to the west, I could see a dark hill that rises steeply out of the dusty plain. It must have been from there that, on the night of 17 September 1917, Lawrence, Zaal, Yells, and Brook looked down on the station behind me, which was blazing yellow light from within. Lawrence thought that the range was too long for them to use the mortar, and he and Zaal crawled in closer to estimate the Turks' numbers. Deciding that the garrison was perhaps three hundred strong and therefore twice the size of the raiding party, which was in any case "not a happy family," Lawrence ruled out a direct assault.[19]

The next day the raiders followed the railway south until they found a perfect site to bury the mine: a bridge on a bend overlooked by a hill close by. This hill, from which the track and the bridge looked like a toothy smile, was a near-perfect site for the mortar and the two machine guns. Leaving Yells and Brook on this spur behind him, Lawrence descended to the bridge, where he excavated some ballast and buried a sandbag packed with fifty pounds of gelatine under the rails. It was an enormous mine, three times the size of the one placed by Garland that February on the first successful British raid.

Lawrence worked alone. This part of the line is sandy, and he wanted to keep the number of footprints near the track to a minimum. Inserting an electric detonator into the now hidden bag of sun-warmed explosive, Lawrence attached the wires and ran out the coil away from the track. It had already taken him two hours to lay the mine, and would require nearly four more to bury the wires under sand, which Lawrence tried to sculpt convincingly with a sandbag and wafts of his cloak.

No amount of artistry, however, would keep the tribesmen quiet and out of sight for such a long period of time, and early the following morning shooting broke out from the station immediately to the south, from where the Turks had spotted the Bedu on the horizon. Some Turkish soldiers emerged from the station, but Lawrence managed to divert them by sending some tribesmen to shoot at them before disappearing into the hills. There was further danger when another party of one hundred Turks appeared from Mudawwarah to the north. Lawrence was on the point of calling for a retreat when from the south a train was spotted. When he saw that there were two locomotives tugging ten freight cars slowly up the line toward him, Lawrence decided to wait and detonate the mine under the second engine, hoping that the explosion would also pitch the front locomotive off the track and over the side of the bridge into the wadi below. Just after the front locomotive reached the bridge, Lawrence gave the order to press the plunger.

> There followed a terrific roar and the line vanished from sight behind a spouting column of black dust and smoke a hundred feet high and wide. Out of the darkness came shattering crashes and long, loud metallic clangings of ripped steel, with many lumps of iron and plate; while one entire wheel of a locomotive whirled up suddenly black out of the cloud against the sky, and sailed musically over our heads to fall slowly and heavily into the desert behind.[20]

For a moment there was silence, and a gray haze bearing the metallic tang of burned explosive drifted toward the Arabs.

As fire from Yells's machine gun erupted overhead, Lawrence went back up the hill to join him and Brook. "In the midst of the affray, with a complete disregard of flying bullets, he strolled over to see how we were faring: his bearing made us feel that the whole thing was a picnic," Brook would remember years later.[21] The Turks who had survived the explosion took cover on the far side of the railway embankment and were shooting back from between the wheels of the cars at the Arabs, who, seemingly oblivious to the gun battle and united in pursuit of loot, were running toward the train. Brook fired two mortar bombs, which dropped in the area beyond the track, killing twelve Turks and forcing the rest to flee. No longer hidden behind the cars, the Turks were exposed to further devastating machine-gun fire.

Within ten minutes it was all over. "All but 20" of the Turks were dead, according to Lawrence, who ran forward to inspect the dreadful wreckage. The first arch of the bridge had vanished, and into the void had fallen the first car of the train. Lawrence peered inside. It had been "filled with sick. The smash had killed all but three or four, and had rolled dead and dying into a bleeding heap against the splintered end. One of those yet alive half-deliriously called out to me something which contained the word typhus. So I wedged shut the door, and left them there, alone."[22] Nothing but "a blanched pile of smoking iron" remained of the second engine, under which the mine had exploded. Seeing that the first locomotive, still teetering on the bridge, was not beyond repair, Lawrence tried to break its boiler with a slab of gun-cotton. He had almost forgotten the Turks who were closing on them from each station on either side. Surrounded by hysterical women who had been traveling at the rear of the train, the Arabs piled their camels high with loot from the train, and fled west back toward Wadi Ramm. Having set the charge, Lawrence grabbed a blood-red Afghan prayer rug as a trophy of the ambush and hurried after them. In the British army looting was an offense, but Lawrence knew better than to deny the Bedu the spoils of victory. The raid had been a success, although not on the scale that he had originally hoped.

Back in Aqaba afterward Lawrence wrote two letters describing what had happened. In the first, to his friend Edward Leeds, a shy archaeologist who worked in Oxford, he briefly explained how, during "the last stunt," he had "potted a train with two engines (oh the gods were kind) and killed superior numbers." But doubts had set in: "I'm not going to last out this game much longer," he confided to Leeds, describing his "nerves going and temper wearing thin, and one wants an unlimited account of both."[23] And beneath the bravado, he was shocked by the devastation he had caused.

> I hope that when the nightmare ends I will wake up and become alive again. This killing and killing of Turks is horrible. When you charge in at the finish and find them all over the place in bits, and still alive many of them, and know that you have done hundreds in the same way before and must do hundreds more if you can.

A day later he wrote to Frank Stirling in Cairo. His tone, to a fellow intelligence officer, was rather less soul-searching, and Stirling, who would later title his own memoirs *Safety Last*, received a *Boy's Own* abridgement of events a week earlier. Branding the ambush as "the hold up of a train," he explained how the mine had "gutted" the locomotive and "rather jumbled up the trucks," and Turkish resistance had been crushed by "two beautiful shots" from the mortar. "I hope this sounds the fun it is. . . . It's the most amateurishly Buffalo-Billy sort of performance, and the only people who do it well are the Beduin. Only you will think it heaven, because there aren't any returns, or orders, or superiors, or inferiors; no doctors, no accounts, no meals, and no drinks."[24]

The intoxicating elation of simply surviving these ambushes, glimpsed in both letters, was a short-lived elixir. The long-term psychological impact of what he had seen would haunt him for the rest of his life. In a later letter to another friend, Lawrence shed some light on the contradiction: "We ride like lunatics," he wrote, "and with our Beduins pounce on unsuspecting Turks and destroy them in heaps: and it is all very gory and nasty after we close grip. I love the preparation and the journey, and loathe the physical fighting."[25]

When Hogarth met Lawrence a fortnight after the raid, for the first time since February, he noticed a distinct change in his former student. Lawrence was, he wrote to his wife, "rather run down but very hard and his reputation has become overpowering."[26] It was not just Lawrence's nearly single-handed capture of Aqaba that contributed to his renown. Following the rushed retreat from the Mudawwarah attack, in which Yells and Brook both lost pieces of their kit, Lawrence wrote to Clayton, requesting that the items lost be replaced without charge to either man. "He was ever thoughtful of us," Brook remembered afterward.[27]

Joyce believed that the great weakness of the British was having no one else with nearly the same expertise as Lawrence: "We can all perhaps help a bit having gained some knowledge, but it is his intimate and extensive knowledge of the history and the tribes and the language that really counts."[28] From Cairo the Conservative politician George Lloyd,* who was working for the Arab Bureau, observed how Lawrence had "done wonderfully good work and will some day be able to write a

---

*Not to be confused with the British prime minister and Liberal MP, David Lloyd George.

unique book. Generally the kind of men capable of these adventures lack the pen and the wit to record them adequately. Luckily Lawrence is specially gifted in both."[29] Lawrence knew it too. Responding to a generous letter of congratulation from Wilson, who was sore that his own efforts had not been recognized at all, Lawrence promised he would recognize Wilson's contribution, "if ever I get my book on it out."[30]

17

Difficult Times

Clayton read Lawrence's barbed letter to Sykes and decided not to forward it. In a reply to Lawrence dated 20 September, he argued that the Sykes-Picot agreement was "in considerable disfavour in most quarters" and "now almost a lifeless monument."[1] But the real reason why Clayton did not want to pass the letter on had nothing to do with the potential life span of the treaty. It was because he did not want to make a powerful enemy. He had only just reassured Sykes that the Arab Bureau was not a breeding ground for Francophobia, and Lawrence's letter only undermined this claim. "I am somewhat apprehensive lest your letter to Mark may raise him to activity," he explained. Although he believed that the imminent British advance into Palestine would destroy the agreement altogether, Clayton did not want to draw unwelcome attention from a politician who might easily ruin them both. And with the British offensive still a month away, he warned Lawrence not to take precipitate action: "I want to ensure that . . . nothing is done which will bring down upon Syria a storm which we cannot avert and for which we shall inevitably have to bear the blame."

Lawrence must have received Clayton's letter after he had returned to Aqaba from the Mudawwarah raid. The situation he found on his return to the port was bleak. German aircraft based at Maan had begun bombing the port, and though Joyce laughed off the danger—"Fritz comes over most mornings but he is a dam[n] bad shot so far thank God!"—the Arabs had suffered casualties.[2] Feisal, who was suffering from an ear infection, was "rather despondent and thinks he is being let down by the British Government," Joyce reported. Chief among the problems for which Feisal blamed the British was a shortage of food and money, which had already caused some of the Huwaytat tribesmen defending the plain above Aqaba to surrender to the Turks. As problems with supplying the Arab forces at the port arose, the next six weeks were to prove difficult times.

Problems with supplies came as no surprise to Lawrence, who had warned Clayton a month earlier that paying and feeding all the local Bedu who were now flocking to Aqaba to join Feisal would be very difficult. "It seems . . . as if we had underrated the local requirements," he wrote, as hundreds of men began to appear daily to pledge their allegiance.[3] By the end of August, Lawrence estimated that ten thousand Huwaytat Bedu had arrived, and he expected two thousand tribesmen more to appear imminently. Contrary to what Lawrence would later claim, ideological commitment to Feisal's cause was rarely the reason for their appearance: news of free food traveled fast at a time when famine afflicting Syria may have killed as many as half a million people.[4] The arrival of so many tribesmen, often with their families, as well as refugees from Syria all at once strained food and also financial resources. On 18 September, Joyce advised Clayton that the anticipated expenditure of £50,000 a month for buying the tribesmen's support was inadequate. He calculated that a sum of up to £80,000 was needed.[5]

Although it was impossible to predict how many tribesmen would arrive each day, Feisal was also buying their support too fast with the gold supplied to him by Britain. When a further shipment of gold arrived days later, Joyce decided to ration it out in an effort to slow down Feisal's spending. "Lawrence and I did a dreadful thing and only gave him £10,000 instead of £50,000," Joyce confessed to Clayton:

> The other £40,000 remains on the *Humber* to be given to him as occasion arises. We have now been through so many of these critical moments when we have been told success or failure depends on a few thousands that we know the absolute necessity of a certain amount at short call and therefore dared to keep back the above amount. We hope you won't give us away to the police![6]

High and unpredictable demand was not the only problem, however. Admiral Wemyss, who had done so much to help the revolt in its early stages, had been recalled in July to London, and his replacement, in Lawrence's words, "did all he could to be obstructive."[7] Three of the ships that had previously run supplies to Wajh were withdrawn for other duties. Since Lawrence had failed to smash the railway at Mudawwarah, the remaining ships still had to supply both Aqaba and Wajh. As a result, deliveries of food to Aqaba became unpredictable, and shortages persisted through September. By 1 October the captain of the *Humber* reported that, because of the absence of animal fodder, the horses, mules, and camels at Aqaba had had no food for four days. An attempt, he said, was being made "to get them to eat rice, but they are all looking very poor."[8]

Feisal was badly affected by the problems. He was frightened that the Turks might attack at any time, in which case "he would not have a single transport animal fit to carry supplies and ammunition to his troops," and he was frustrated by the lack of progress since the capture of Aqaba almost three months earlier.[9] If the British had not been so "completely disorganized," he complained, "he would now have been on the *offensive* and not the *defensive* and . . . the whole of the Arab tribes of the interior would be on his side," the *Humber*'s captain reported. Feisal even threatened suicide. Although the British did not seem to take this threat especially seriously, it confirmed the negative impression of Feisal as "rather weak and wanting in command," which Sykes had formed earlier that year.[10]

"I had a very difficult time with Feisal for a few days. He is not a strong character and much swayed by his surroundings," Joyce reported to Clayton. "However your messages and information did much to reassure him and we got him over the bad days."[11] Clayton had tried to defuse the situation by telling Joyce that he did not expect the Turks to attack, because they were too busy safeguarding their own supplies of food and timber to the north from an expected Arab attack.

Feisal was also depressed by the attitudes of his father, Husein, and his elder brothers, Abdullah and Ali, who, he told Joyce, were "taking no interest in the Syrian movement." He was also under pressure from his father, who was reluctant to let the revolt slip out of his grasp and had made it clear to Feisal that he did not support his move north to Aqaba. When the French paid almost a million francs to Husein that summer, he refused to share any of it with Feisal.[12] Feisal himself played a very minor role in the Arab operations up until the closing stages of the war.

One reason for Husein's frugality was that he was becoming increasingly worried about the challenge to his authority east of Mecca posed by his rival Ibn Saud. The annual pilgrimage to Mecca, the hajj, fell in September that year. The most notable visitor was Ibn Saud's brother, Mohammed, who brought seven thousand armed tribesmen to Mecca with him. While the British necessarily reported that the encounter between the followers of Husein and Ibn Saud—both British allies— went smoothly, Brémond witnessed friction between the Saudi tribesmen and the cosmopolitan populations of Mecca and Jeddah. Ibn Saud's men were "real savages, taking everything they saw if needs be by violence; some even said: monkeys," he claimed.[13]

Abdullah shared his father's concerns about the Saudis. Although, after the war, Abdullah put his own inability to capture Medina down to the fact that his resources were too thinly spread along the railway line, and that the quality of his troops and guns was inferior to those of Feisal, Feisal believed that Abdullah's unwillingness to capture the city stemmed from a fear that if he did so, the monthly British payments to his father would cease, leaving the family without revenue and vulnerable to Ibn Saud. To guarantee ongoing financial support from Britain, Husein and Abdullah were keen to keep the situation at Medina unresolved. There seems to have been some truth in this. The British heard that November that Husein had turned down an offer from Fakhri to leave Medina and withdraw to Syria.[14] And, earlier that summer, Abdullah's elder brother Ali had angrily vetoed a letter one of his Iraqi officers, Ali Jawdat, wanted to send to the Turkish general Fakhri, demanding his surrender. The incident caused a breakdown in relations between Husein's sons and their Iraqi soldiers, and the Iraqis' leader Nuri Said took advantage of a bout of pneumonia that summer to be transferred to work with his brother-in-law and fellow Iraqi Jafar Pasha in Aqaba. Other officers, including Ali Jawdat, followed Nuri Said, and the campaign against the railway in the Hijaz lost momentum. No sooner had Jafar and Feisal gone than, from Abdullah's camp, Davenport reported that "practically all interest in the war" had "ceased."[15]

⁓✲⁓

On 26 September, Allenby informed Robertson in London that he expected to be ready to launch his offensive one month later, on 27 October. He planned to open the attack by bombarding Gaza, hoping to make the Turks believe that again, the main British assault would focus on the town. The bombardment was designed, however, to be a diversionary ruse. Three nights later, at the full moon, Allenby's main force would strike the town of Beersheba, thirty miles inland, to the southeast. His aim was to capture the wells there and expose the Turkish defenses near Gaza, which faced southwest toward the original British position, to a devastating assault from both the front and the side.

Excited by the imminent prospect of Allenby's attack, the War Cabinet discussed the situation in Turkey in its meeting on 5 October. At its conclusion Robertson—as ever, opposed to action in Palestine—was instructed to contact Allenby to explain that the War Cabinet believed that a push to Jerusalem would, "if followed by suitable diplomatic measures, induce her [the Ottoman Empire] to break with her Allies."[16] Asked for his opinion, Allenby disagreed. Having explained that the security of his right flank now depended on the Arabs in the hills east of Wadi Araba, the fault that forms the modern border between southern Jordan and Israel, he told the politicians bluntly that ongoing help from the Arabs "depends on continued belief by them that we shall keep our promises not to conclude any peace which would leave the Arab territories under Turkish domination. Any idea in their minds that we intend separate peace with Turkey with possibility of their being left under Turkish rule would bring them against us and endanger my communication."[17]

Other factors also ruled out further attempts to secure peace with the Ottomans. At the time the German kaiser was visiting Constantinople, and the British feared that he might encourage the Turks to offer the Arabs autonomy and to bribe them into quiescence. This possibility alarmed British officials in Egypt since any deal the Turks did with Arabs would inevitably increase the pressure on the British to offer similar concessions in Egypt, where the political situation was already unstable. At the outbreak of war in 1914 Britain had turned Egypt—then still officially part of the Ottoman Empire, albeit a part that Britain ran—into a protectorate, deposed the Ottoman-appointed ruler, and created a sultan deliberately chosen for his complaisance.

This move had not been entirely successful for, although Clayton dismissed Egyptian calls for self-government as "rot," the fact was that nationalist sentiment was rising by 1917.[18] A secret note circulated that summer warned, "From the immediate entourage of the Sultan down through all the educated classes runs an almost unanimous wish that we may be compelled to withdraw at the end of the war."[19] Then the pliable sultan died in early October, and the British were forced to appoint his brother, who was regarded as less loyal, as his successor. When, a few days after the kaiser's arrival in Turkey, an intelligence report received from Switzerland seemed to confirm that the Ottomans were about to offer autonomy to the Arabs, the Foreign Office abruptly shelved its plans to approach the Turks once Jerusalem was in Allenby's hands, because it would "discourage our friends in the East in general and the Arabs in particular."[20]

⁓✻⁓

On the same day that Allenby informed Robertson that he was nearly ready to attack Gaza, Lawrence set out again for the railway. He was accompanied this time by an Algerian French officer, Captain Rosario Pisani. Pisani, who was described by another British officer as a "brigand disguised unconvincingly as a French officer" and who claimed that he "had a wide variety of lovers anxiously awaiting his appearances on leave," had arrived in Aqaba as the French military's representative.[21] Brémond had warned him that Lawrence was a "focused character," who dreamed of "an English Syria and has some difficulty in giving up this idea," and encouraged Pisani to follow Lawrence around.[22]

Besides Pisani, Lawrence took three Syrian nationalists who had escaped Turkish custody, and a handful of Haurani peasants, whose unruly credentials he was hoping to assess. As well as another electric mine, he took a pressure mine because he did not expect to be able to bury the wire on the stony plain south of Maan where he planned to operate. Pausing under the cliffs at Ramm to explain to the tribesmen how both types of device worked, Lawrence recruited almost a hundred Bedu and headed toward the railway.

Disagreements between the Huwaytat who followed Lawrence made it a difficult journey yet again. "During the six days' trip I had to adjudicate in twelve cases of assault with weapons, four camel thefts, one marriage-settlement, fourteen feuds, two evil eyes and a bewitchment," Lawrence reported in the *Arab Bulletin*.[23] On 3 October he buried the pressure mine south of Shedia station, over the most southerly of three culverts piercing an embankment across a wadi. But no train appeared on the following day, or the day after that.

When, early on 5 October, a water train arrived from the north and passed over the mine, there was no explosion. At midday, when he hoped the Turkish guards were taking a siesta, Lawrence crept forward again and laid an electric mine beside the pressure mine. Then he sent everyone forward toward the culverts. Having laid the mines over the most southerly, Lawrence left a party under the middle bridge with the detonator and positioned the machine guns under the northern bridge, from where they could cut down anyone escaping from a disabled train.[24]

"I asked Major Lawrence for the honour of positioning myself beneath the bridge so that I could blow up the train," Pisani reported afterward.[25] Lawrence, however, refused. Though he told Pisani that he was worried that, in the chaos of an attack, the Bedu might mistake him for a Turk because of his uniform, and shoot him, it seems equally likely that he did not want Pisani to play too central a role in the ambush.

At eight o'clock the following morning a train arrived from the north. From off to one side, Lawrence signaled to the men with the detonator when the locomotive was over the bridge. The explosion was devastating. It "shattered the fire-box of the locomotive (No. 153, Hijaz), burst many of the tubes, threw the l.c. [locomotive] cylinder into the air, cleaned out the cab, warped the frame, bent the two near driving wheels and broke their axles. I consider it past repair," Lawrence dryly reported, like some sort of malevolent train spotter.[26] Twenty passengers traveling in the first car were killed by the blast, the force of which decoupled the rear cars, which began to roll back down the hill. The Bedu snatched some booty, but with the Turks approaching from blockhouses to the north and south, they did not delay for long, hurrying away westward to safety and Wadi Ramm.

This devastating attack, following the ambush at Mudawwarah seventeen days earlier, had a profound effect, Lawrence believed after the war. The locomotives' drivers went on strike, and, for those brave enough still to travel, seats at the rear of the train could be purchased at a premium.[27]

✧

On his return to Aqaba on 9 October, Lawrence found a summons to go to Egypt to see Allenby. Allenby wanted to brief Lawrence on his offensive at the end of the month, but he also wanted Lawrence to clarify his own tactics. Clayton had already warned Lawrence of the danger that, if Lawrence and Allenby each succeeded in pushing the Turks northward, they would actually make their enemy more compact, more easily supplied, and therefore stronger.[28] Lawrence therefore changed his tune. When he met Allenby, he argued that his attacks—against the trains and not the track—were designed to attenuate Turkish resources along the railway without doing so much damage that the Turks took the decision to abandon Medina and consolidate at Maan, where they would present a serious threat to the rear of Allenby's army as it advanced into Palestine. Allenby was satisfied: "Lawrence is doing good work on the Hijaz Railway," he told Robertson on 17 October.[29]

By now the French knew about the true extent of Lawrence's Syrian journey earlier that summer. They were alarmed by the political ramifications. Allenby also told Robertson how he had batted away a French attempt to attach Pisani to all Lawrence's missions north of Aqaba.[30] Allenby justified himself on the grounds that "so far there has been no action by Lawrence in French zone," but this was wrong since Ras Baalbek, where Lawrence had sparked unrest by destroying a bridge, fell inside the region earmarked for future direct French rule in the Sykes-Picot agreement. If Lawrence did enter the French zone in the future, Allenby said that he would inform the French "as fully as military exigencies permit." There was a particular reason for this caveat. Information Allenby had received led him to believe that the number of enemy divisions facing him had more than doubled. He urgently wanted to stop further Ottoman reinforcements from arriving in Palestine and decided that the best way to do this was to disrupt the railway running down the Yarmuk valley, the Turks' vulnerable supply route from Syria into Palestine and also the border of the zone that would come under French influence. Allenby did not want inevitable French objections to obstruct his plans to attack the railway there.

Lawrence believed that the railway that crossed and recrossed the Yarmuk valley over a series of bridges to achieve the gentlest gradient was very vulnerable. When Allenby asked him whether he could attack one of the Yarmuk bridges on 5 November, six days after his offensive was due to begin, Lawrence said he could. He was deeply despondent. His triumph at Aqaba had been followed by anticlimax as the timetable of his optimistic summer plan was ruined by Arab intrigue and problems with supplies. Any chance the Arabs had of reaching Damascus, he felt, now rested on the successful demolition of the railway at Yarmuk, which would leave the way to Damascus clear.

Hogarth briefly saw Lawrence during his visit to Allenby's headquarters. Lawrence was "not well," he told a colleague, "and talks rather hopelessly about the Arab future he once believed in." He was also pessimistic about Lawrence's chances of success. "I doubt if he will manage to get North again. Recent successes have drawn rather too many troops down on to the Maan section of the Railway. Medina probably cannot be starved out, and nothing short of a local mutiny will reduce Fakhri."[31]

Clayton, on the other hand, was altogether more confident. He was delighted that Allenby had vetoed any attempt by the French to follow Lawrence around, and with the Palestine offensive days away he wrote again to Sykes:

> As the situation develops, it becomes more and more evident that the French will never make good their aspirations in Syria unless they take some more active military part in this theatre. It cannot be disguised that they are unpopular with both Arabs and Syrians as a whole—their colonial and financial methods are disliked, and they have never been able to live down the seizure of Picot's papers by the Turks and the consequent execution or ruin of various notables.

A British victory in Palestine and east of the Jordan for the Arabs would, Clayton crowed, "still further weaken the French political position."[32] He could barely hide the note of triumph in his voice.

18

Gaza and Yarmuk: Victory and Failure

"You want to buy gun?"

"No, thank you," I replied, anticipating the reception I might meet at the airport if I tried to export the particular memento of Jordan that I was holding. Then I put the rifle back where I had found it.

Few castles have quite the range of antique firearms that the enthusiastic souvenir seller below the ramparts of Shawbak castle, in southern Jordan, will try to sell to the departing visitor. It was here, midway through October 1917, that Pierce Joyce arrived during a brief raid. On 12 October he had set out north from Aqaba into the hills west of Maan on a foray with Mawlud Mukhlis, another of the Iraqi officers who had joined the Arabs' army. Just as they had been for the Crusaders hundreds of years earlier, the hills were a vital source of grain and wood, which the Arabs had been anxious to seize from the Turks as soon as they arrived in Aqaba. They captured the mighty Crusader castle at Shawbak without difficulty and, from there, went on to destroy part of the light railway that linked the area with the Hijaz Railway to the east. They had also tried to persuade the Arab and Armenian woodcutters who worked there to join them, but without success. As Joyce commented afterward, that failure "demonstrated that the 'tip and run' operations to which they have been accustomed in the Hijaz, will not suffice in Syria."[1] He believed that although the people of Shawbak backed Husein, until they thought that the Arabs would protect them against Turkish retaliation, they could "scarcely be blamed for being somewhat cautious about arousing the anger of their oppressors."

In fact, not wanting to aggravate the population by a heavy-handed approach, the Turks, who rapidly reoccupied the area after the Arab raiders had withdrawn, decided there should be no retribution in Shawbak.[2] Their shortage of fuel forced them instead to concentrate on trying to expel the Arabs from the villages they had occupied in the hills. On 21 October they attacked Wadi Musa, the valley of the ancient city of Petra, in strength. The Turks were routed. "Even though their strength was about double our own," recalled Jafar Pasha, who led the Arabs' defense, "we managed to inflict such a severe defeat on them that we were unable either to bury their dead or move the injured from the battlefield."[3]

The Arabs' victory increased the pressure on the British to speed up the deployment of the Arab legion to hold their gains in the hills, but it was still being trained in Egypt. "There is an awful lot to do," reported the British officer in charge of the legion at the beginning of October: "pay sheets are taking a tremendous lot of doing. Nearly everybody is passing himself off at least a grade higher than that he had in the Turkish Army."[4] He worried constantly that one of his trainees might raise the question "as to what was intended with regard to Syria and Baghdad. In anything I have said I have been most awfully careful to steer clear of such things, but I cannot help feeling that we are not absolutely straight with these people."

Having agreed with Allenby that he would attack a bridge in the Yarmuk valley, Lawrence arrived back in Aqaba on 15 October. He thought he had good news for Feisal because Allenby had promised to increase the flow of supplies to Feisal's army. However, cholera had been diagnosed in the Arab camp at Aqaba the day before, and, worried that the outbreak might spread to Egypt, the British army's medical officers instantly vetoed all traffic to and from the port.

"You can have no idea how this cholera business has upset everything here," Clayton told Joyce. "It is most annoying that this should have happened at this particular time when your operations were coming on and Lawrence was just moving out, and we particularly wanted plenty of intercommunication."[5]

The interruption in supplies infuriated Lawrence, who was on the point of starting north for the Yarmuk valley. Feisal was "touchy at the moment," he said, and he did not want the British to fuel Feisal's uncertainty about the future of Syria by appearing reluctant to help the Arabs.[6] In a letter to Clayton on 24 October, he asked for the immediate dispatch of the Arab legion and some armored cars, regardless of concerns about cholera. Even if the legion's training was unfinished and the armored cars required further maintenance, he said, "something should come down in the *Hardinge*; They will be a great comfort here."[7] On 2 November, Clayton wired the Foreign Office, asking it to approve the dispatch of the legion to Aqaba immediately.

Apprehensive about attacking Yarmuk, Lawrence also complained to Clayton that the equipment he had requested had not arrived. "I asked for nine exploders. Only four have been sent. . . . Also about the cable. I received at first 400 yards thick single cable (doubled this makes 200 yards of line) and after using it wired for 1000 yards light twin cable. You sent 500 yards of the old thick single in reply."[8] This error was to have serious consequences, for Lawrence would need to be dangerously nearby to trigger an electric mine under a train. But he could not afford to wait any longer. Having let off steam to Clayton, that afternoon he left Aqaba for the north.

Lawrence was under no illusion about how dangerous the task ahead was. In case he was killed, he also took an engineer named C. E. Wood, an explosives expert who was recovering from being shot in the head in France. To lead the raid, he picked Ali, a sharif from the Harith tribe. Ali was a headstrong, conceited man with luxuriant black hair, whom Lawrence chose because he had "out-newcombed Newcombe about Al Ula"—a comparison with his British colleague's daredevil exploits in the Hijaz that summer.[9] Finally, he added a handful of Indian machine gunners to his party. There were also two last-minute additions: the MP George Lloyd (from the Arab Bureau, not the prime minister) and another escapee from Turkish incarceration, Abdul Qadir al Jazairi, who had lived in Damascus and who told Lawrence that he could command the support of the Algerian community clustered on the north side of the Yarmuk valley. It was Abdul Qadir's eponymous grandfather who had led resistance to the French in Algeria in the 1840s. Attracted perhaps by this promising ancestry, Lawrence ignored Brémond's warning that the young Abdul Qadir was a traitor.

Lloyd's sudden interest in joining Lawrence seems to have stemmed from rising concerns about Lawrence's health among his colleagues. "I am very anxious about Lawrence," Clayton wrote. "He has taken on a really colossal job and I can see that it is well-nigh weighing him down."[10] He had wanted to pull Lawrence out, but recognized that "the time is not yet, as he is wanted just now." Instead, Clayton sent Lloyd to Aqaba to offer Lawrence some company. He also wanted Lloyd to calm Lawrence down over the Sykes-Picot agreement. Lloyd was the ideal man for this task: as an unashamed imperialist, he too was vehemently opposed to French ambitions in the region.[11] Clayton hoped that Lloyd could persuade Lawrence that the Sykes-Picot agreement was unlikely to pass the test of time.

Lloyd was amazed by the scenery as he and Lawrence set out from Aqaba late on 24 October. The view up Wadi Itm, he recalled, "was magnificent, 400 feet of jagged towering basalt and granite rock on either side of us, and the moon shining in our faces adding to the impression. Sharif Ali rode ahead of us with two or three . . . slaves and looked like some modern Saladin out to meet a crusade."[12]

As he had been instructed, Lloyd quickly raised Clayton's concerns with Lawrence. Rather belatedly, he reminded Lawrence that it was vital that the British confined the Arabs' revolt to its military objective of tying up the Turks and "to risk no breach of faith with the Arabs by raising hopes beyond it." But from there the two men's conversation ranged much further. Lloyd mentioned his own hopes of encouraging a revolt in the town of Karak if Lawrence's attack at Yarmuk succeeded, and they discussed the position of the French depending on how the revolt, and the Palestine offensive, developed.[13]

There were evidently worries back in Cairo that Lawrence identified himself more closely with the Arabs than with the British, for Lloyd also reported that he had had "a conspicuous success in making Lawrence eat a real European breakfast, tea, bully beef, and biscuits. He is only too glad to behave like a Christian—gastronomically at all events—if he is taken the right way."[14] As the time passed, Lawrence increasingly opened up to Lloyd. He showed Lloyd the *Times* clipping in his notebook about his dead brother, Will, and told him about his family and upbringing, his time at Oxford, archaeology in Syria before the war, and Hogarth, with whom Lloyd worked in Cairo. Finally, their conversation soared toward escapism. "Lawrence and I made great plans for a peace tour in Arabia after the war," Lloyd also reported. "We would defy Victorian sentiment and have a retinue of slaves and would have one camel to carry books only . . . and we would talk desert politics all day."

"He was the one fully-taught man with us in Arabia," Lawrence later said of Lloyd, "and in these few days together our minds had ranged abroad."[15] From the rough notes Lloyd made at the time, it is clear that Lawrence also explained his strategy of trying to ensure that the Arabs occupied the French zone before the war's end, and claimed that Feisal would refuse to negotiate. Lawrence's view was that as the sharif was never a party to the Sykes-Picot agreement—indeed, he said, Husein had never even seen it—"agreement at best one between France and England for partition of a country in armed occupation of forces of Sharif of Mecca."[16]

That evening they reached a point a few miles west of the railway, where they stopped to wait until it was dark and they could cross in safety. Lawrence and Lloyd went on ahead and narrowly avoided walking straight into Ghadir al Hajj station. Turning back to prevent the other members of their party from making the same mistake, when they turned toward the railway again, they became lost. Lawrence, who usually used a compass, then evidently tried to impress Lloyd. "For some reason or other," Lloyd recalled afterward, Lawrence was "convinced that if we marched faithfully with our eyes fixed firmly on Orion we should find the railway again." Lloyd—in Lawrence's words—"began to speak bitterly of reaching Baghdad in the morning."[17] Lloyd eventually snapped: "An hour's pursuit of Orion shook Lawrence's faith, and I insisted on a compass, and at midnight we struck the railway." They crossed the track without incident and, after a full day's riding next day, reached Auda at Jafr, the wells marked by a thicket of palms at the edge of an enormous plain of baked white mud. Though worried about the defection to the Turks of two tribes previously allied to him, Auda seemed to have overcome the earlier wobble in his own loyalty. His looks, Lloyd reported, "are much enhanced, as his allegiance to us is much fortified—by the timely gift of a set of false teeth from Cairo made some weeks ago by Lawrence," which finally replaced the set he had smashed in disgust at Wajh that May.[18]

The rest of Lawrence's party arrived in Jafr later the same evening. Although Lloyd wanted to accompany Lawrence farther, Lawrence would not let him. According to Lloyd, Lawrence said that "although he did not pretend he would not like me to come he felt that any additional individual who was not an expert at the actual demolition only added to his own risk."[19] As one of the most strident critics of the Sykes-Picot agreement and a politician, Lloyd was more useful back in Britain, Lawrence suggested.

Later that evening Auda suddenly called for silence. A hush descended as each man strained to hear the threat Auda seemed to have heard. "After a while," Lawrence recalled, he distinguished "a creeping reverberation, a cadence of blows too dull, too wide, too slow easily to find response in our ears. It was like the mutter of a distant, very lowly thunderstorm." Auda turned to look westward, and said, "The English guns."[20] Some 130 miles to the northwest the British bombardment of Gaza had begun.[21] Knowing that Allenby would now be trying to move his attacking force secretly east in preparation for the main attack on Beersheba, on 30 October, Lawrence started north. Before he did so, he discussed the timing of his raid with Lloyd. "I said I thought Nov 5th was traditionally auspicious," remembered Lloyd, thinking of the failed attempt to blow up Parliament on that day in 1605, "and he decided to do it that night if in any way possible."[22]

Following several days' bombardment of Gaza—believed to be the most intensive shelling in the war outside Europe—the British attacked Beersheba in the early hours of 31 October, a misty, moonlit night. The attack caught the Turks completely by surprise. During the fighting Newcombe outflanked Turkish lines with a small force of about a hundred soldiers and Bedu. He succeeded in generating the impression that a much larger British encircling movement was under way, but the perhaps inevitable consequence of this achievement was that he was captured on 2 November by the large Turkish force that had been sent to deal with him. Hogarth was not surprised. "It was mainly his own fault," he wrote to his wife, describing Newcombe as "a wild bird who will beat against the bars."[23] He was on edge. Newcombe's capture only reminded him of Lawrence's equally dangerous mission.

With Beersheba in British hands, Hogarth went up to the front to watch the secondary attack on Gaza, which began late on 1 November. "It was rather terrible both to hear and see," he wrote to his son Billy the following day: "From 11pm to 4am was a continuous roar with the horizon lit up as by summer lightning."[24] The attack was a success. By dawn British forces had captured a crucial position overlooking Gaza's harbor. Gaza itself was evacuated by the Turks overnight on 5 November. In the Beersheba area to the east, however, British forces were faced with serious water shortages and a violent sandstorm that engulfed much of the front. "We could not see the road for a yard ahead and once ran right into a mule column," Hogarth told his son. Given time to regroup, the Turks avoided the British pincer movement from Gaza and Beersheba and withdrew with most of their force intact. The British restored the momentum of their offensive with a cavalry advance. On 13 November they captured Junction station, which linked the Gaza and Jerusalem lines to the railway north toward Dara, and three days later British troops entered Jaffa. At a cost of over six thousand casualties, they were now within striking distance of Jerusalem.

"Lawrence by now must be very near his objective," Joyce had written to Clayton on 4 November: "I hope he is lucky. Fortunately he has got brains as well as dash and the two I trust will pull him through, but one cannot help feeling anxious."[25] Lawrence, in fact, was still over fifty miles from the Yarmuk valley. He had experienced problems at Azraq, the rundown castle east of Amman where he had hoped to enlist the support of the Serahin, the local tribesmen from Wadi Sirhan. But the tribesmen proved reluctant to accompany him as far as the westernmost bridge in the gorge, which had been his original target, as they feared being discovered by the Turkish forces in the area. Lawrence decided instead to approach the valley from the north, through the villages where Abdul Qadir claimed he had support. The Serahin, however, were suspicious of Abdul Qadir, who then disappeared. Brémond had been right to warn that Abdul Qadir was a traitor.

"We were now in deep trouble," Lawrence later wrote. "The Serahin were our last resource, and if they refused to come with us we would be unable to carry out Allenby's project by the appointed time."[26] That night, beside the dying fire, Lawrence made a last-ditch effort to get the tribesmen to follow him. It was only after he had offered to attack the nearest bridge in the Yarmuk valley, at Tell al Shehab, and appealed to their honor that the Serahin agreed to join him.

After a long night march with the Serahin, a few Bani Sakhr who had now joined him, Wood, and the Indian machine gunners, Lawrence

The bridge over the Yarmuk at Tell al Shehab.

reached the eastern end of the Yarmuk gorge early in the night of 7 November. Across the valley the dim glimmer of a fire identified the location of the Turkish guard tent. Having left the Indians at the top of the scarp to machine-gun the tent if the lone sentry on the bridge raised the alarm, Lawrence crept forward with Sharif Ali and the Serahin, who were carrying the bags of explosive, down toward the metal bridge that spanned the black chasm. Discovering that he could not reach its vulnerable lower girders, Lawrence had just turned to tell the Serahin to follow him on when, far above, there was an unmistakable clatter as someone dropped a rifle.

Sixty yards away across the void, the Turkish sentry twitched, looked up, and spotted the Indians, who were in the process of moving to a more shadowy position because the moon had risen. He shouted a challenge and began shooting, yelling at the same time for help. "Instantly all was confusion," Lawrence later recollected.[27] The Bani Sakhr behind him, who had been invisible, immediately returned fire, giving their position away in the process. Before the Indians had had time to riddle the guard tent with bullets, the Turkish guards rushed out and began shooting back at the Bani Sakhr. The Serahin carrying the dynamite panicked because they had been warned that, if hit by a bullet, their burdens would explode, blowing them to smithereens. Awoken by the gunfire, the villagers turned out to defend their property. With volleys of shots blasting into the night sky, the raiders beat a hasty retreat. The raid was a complete failure. "Tell al Shehab is a splendid bridge to destroy, but those Serahin threw away all my explosive when the firing began and so I can do nothing," Lawrence wrote to Joyce. "I am very sick at losing it so stupidly."[28]

The loss of almost all his blasting gelatine left Lawrence with some mines and an inadequate length of electric cable with which to detonate them. He had intended to head north after the Yarmuk raid to attack the railway where it crossed the river Orontes at Hama, a hundred miles north of Damascus, to encourage as widespread a revolt as possible in Syria if the British breakout from Gaza succeeded. With little explosive and no news of what had happened in southern Palestine, Lawrence was unsure what to do next.

"Let's blow up a train," the Harith sheikh Sharif Ali suggested.[29] Lawrence reluctantly agreed. He would have preferred an ambush supported by the Indian machine gunners, but they were exhausted from the cold and hunger. He was forced to send them back to Azraq with Wood to recover, before riding with Ali and the remaining Bani Sakhr on to Minifir, midway between Amman and Dara, where he had mined the track earlier that year. Then he had been gently baked by the June sunshine; now shards of icy rain soaked his clothing as he excavated a space for an electric mine under the rails where the track crossed a bridge. A train had passed just as they arrived at the railway. Another passed before there was time to set up the exploder. The wires would stretch only sixty yards from the track, and Lawrence had no choice but to huddle behind a small bush with the plunger. Now from the south another train appeared, groaning with the weight of its open cars full of soldiers as it struggled up the hill, bound for Palestine. As it passed, he pushed the trigger; but nothing happened. The rain or the ride had broken the detonator, and Lawrence found himself sitting in his white robes in full view of the troop train as it crawled past. "The bush, which had seemed a foot high, shrank smaller than a fig-leaf; and I felt myself the most distinct object in the country-side," he would remember.[30] Though the troops ignored him, the officers stared at Lawrence and pointed. Lawrence waved back, waited for the train to inch by, and then ran.

The following day the Arab watchman Lawrence had posted to the north signaled that a two-engined train was rapidly approaching. Having mended the exploder, Lawrence raced back to the tiny bush and fired the mine as the train passed over it. Too close to the track, "the explosion was terrific," he recalled afterward.

> The ground spouted blackly into my face, and I was sent spinning, to sit up with the shirt torn to my shoulder and the blood dripping from long, ragged scratches on my left arm. Between my knees lay the exploder, crushed under a twisted sheet of sooty iron. When I peered through the dust and steam of the explosion, the whole boiler of the first engine seemed missing. Just in front of me was the scalded and smoking upper half of a man.[31]

Both locomotives and the first two coaches plunged through the hole in the bridge, and behind them the next three or four cars were derailed. A flag flew from one of the rear coaches, which, as Lawrence later discovered, was carrying a Turkish general, Mehmed Jemal Pasha, the commander of the Ottoman army's Eighth Corps, to reinforce Jerusalem. Lawrence had nearly claimed a very significant scalp.

Reeling from the impact, and lacking the support that the Indian machine gunners could have provided, Lawrence came under fire from the surviving Turks. He was rescued by Ali and the Bani Sakhr, but not before seven of the tribesmen had been killed by Turkish fire. Lawrence discovered that a piece of shrapnel had broken his toe and said he had been grazed by five bullets. The Arabs hurried Lawrence, limping, up the wadi and turned only to fire delaying potshots at the Turks. It was a narrow escape.

The following day Ali and Lawrence arrived back at Azraq. Jackals, hyenas, even leopards prowled through the undergrowth. The lakes, which gave the place its name—Azraq means blue in Arabic—resounded with the liquid croaking of thousands of frogs. Overhead, black kites swirled.

Almost none of this survives today. The lakes have shrunk, the wild boar hunted, the trees cut up for firewood, the thickets grazed into dust. Azraq is now a grimy truck stop on the road to western Iraq. But among the grubby flat-roofed houses sporting large and rusty satellite dishes, the castle yet survives.

The southern gate of
Azraq castle: Lawrence's
home in November 1917.

It was here that in November 1917 Lawrence installed himself in the
dark, vaulted room over the southern gate. His first task was to let his
colleagues know that he had failed to demolish the Yarmuk bridge, but
had survived. And so, the following day, 14 November, he wrote to Joyce
to tell him what had happened and suggesting that the British report
the Arab success at Minifir to the press. Lawrence had realized quickly
that press coverage of the Arabs' northernmost achievements would
bolster their claim against the French after the war, and he would write,
a month later, "We must try and enlist on our side a favourable press."[32]
Lawrence also wrote to Hogarth the same day. Finally he wrote to his
mother, telling her about his plans to stay at Azraq for a few days before
heading back to the railway. As Wood was suffering badly with dysentery, Lawrence sent him with the letters back to Aqaba.

Wood arrived in Aqaba on 24 November, bringing the first news of
Lawrence. The following day Joyce paraphrased Wood's muddled
report and transmitted it to Cairo. Wood, he said, had "returned last

night. L[awrence] left at Azraq. Found original objective impossible. On Nov 7th L[awrence] destroyed 1 train with 2 engines. Reported considerable casualties to Turks."[33]

Hogarth was relieved to hear that Lawrence was safe. "I have been on tenterhooks," he told his wife, "as he was on a very dangerous venture, which failed as I feared it must, but without involving him in the worst fate."[34] Three days later he added, "Tell his mother I have news of him up to about the 20th and know where he is now, what doing, whither about to go. So far as I can judge he will be safe; but he won't return to our Ark just yet."[35] Hogarth knew that Lawrence next planned to go north to attack the railway beyond Damascus. The implication in Hogarth's letter is that Lawrence had told him he had not planned to start north until about 20 November. His full report on the destruction of the train near Minifir confirms the reason why. In it he concluded, "Sixty yards of cable is too little for firing heavy charges under locomotives. I had first to survive the rain of boiler plates, and then to run up a steep hill for 400 yards under fire." Unsurprisingly, Lawrence had been unable to take the firing cable with him and reuse it: before he could carry out further demolitions he would have to wait for more to come from Aqaba.[36]

According to his later account in *Seven Pillars of Wisdom*, Lawrence now decided it was time to have a closer look at Dara, the nerve center of the Turks' railway network in Syria. While Wood carried his request for more supplies southward, Lawrence apparently decided to go north to reconnoiter the junction, which was the target of the next stage of the grand plan he had concocted earlier that year. He said he spent a "few days' march" circumnavigating the town with a sheikh, Talal, another outlaw who hailed from Tafas, a village north of Dara, before setting out on an expedition of his own, which can only be described as mad.

19

Dara or Azrak: Where Was Lawrence?
(15–21 November 1917)

Great uncertainty has since surrounded Lawrence's whereabouts from 15 to 21 November 1917. He said he entered Dara late on 20 November, accompanied only by a Haurani peasant. In his account in *Seven Pillars*, he described how, while looking around the town, he was apprehended by a Turkish soldier who seemingly suspected him of being a deserter. "The Bey wants you," the soldier reportedly said, and Lawrence followed him. "There were too many witnesses for either fight or flight," he later explained.[1]

If indeed Lawrence was captured in Dara, none of his colleagues knew for eighteen months, because it was only midway through 1919, while Lawrence was writing *Seven Pillars of Wisdom*, that he abruptly told Stirling,

> I went into Dara in disguise to spy out the defences, was caught, and identified by Hajim Bey, the governor, by virtue of Abdul Qadir's descriptions of me. (I learnt all about his treachery from Hajim's conversation, and from my guards.) Hajim was an ardent paederast and took a fancy to me. So he kept me under guard till night, and then tried to have me. I was unwilling, and prevailed after some difficulty. Hajim sent me to the hospital, and I escaped before dawn, being not as hurt as he thought.[2]

The reason why Lawrence decided to write to Stirling lies in the context of the events that took place immediately after the war. In

Damascus in 1919 Feisal came under pressure from the French to accept the crown of Syria in return for achieving a settlement with the militant Arab nationalists in the city, who included Mohammed Said al Jazairi, the brother of Abdul Qadir. Abdul Qadir himself had been shot dead in Damascus shortly after the end of the war; his brother continued to nurse ambitions to replace Feisal, which Lawrence deeply opposed—not just out of loyalty to his wartime Arab comrade but because he believed that Mohammed Said was completely untrustworthy. This revelation of what had happened to him at Dara was the most graphic, personal illustration he could offer Stirling, by then the deputy chief political officer in Cairo, to warn the British not to press Feisal to accept the French proposal, which would give Mohammed Said al Jazairi greater power.[3] The question is whether the incident ever took place.

Lawrence had a track record of changing the facts when it suited him. He had already portrayed the ambitious Abdullah as lazy and conveniently overlooked Auda's treachery. And by the time he wrote the Dara story in *Seven Pillars of Wisdom*, he changed a key detail. In contrast to his letter, his book said that Hajim did not recognize him, suggesting that Abdul Qadir had not betrayed him. But he expanded on the bones of the story he had given to Stirling. His friends, among whom he circulated the first printed draft of *Seven Pillars* in 1922, must have found the lengthy account disturbing. According to Lawrence, the bey—a great, stubble-haired bully—grabbed him and tried to drag him onto his bed. "When I saw what he wanted," Lawrence wrote, "I twisted round and up again, glad to find myself equal to him in wrestling."[4] The bey tried a new tack, promising that he could make Lawrence his orderly, relieving him from parades and duties, if only he would acquiesce. Lawrence refused. When the bey came close, he said that he had kneed the Turk so hard that he "staggered back to his bed, and sat there, squeezing himself together and groaning with pain."[5]

Gasping for the guards, the bey had Lawrence whipped. According to Lawrence, one soldier began "to lash me across and across with all his might, while I locked my teeth to endure this thing which wrapped itself like flaming wire about my body. At the instant of each stroke a hard white mark like a railway, darkening slowly into crimson, leaped over my skin, and a bead of blood welled up wherever two ridges crossed."[6] Finishing by slashing the whip across Lawrence's groin, two guards pushed him to the floor and pried his legs apart, while the third, astride his back, rode him "like a horse."[7]

Repelled by the sight of his potential "bedfellow streaming with blood and water, striped and fouled from face to heel," Hajim then ordered the soldiers to carry Lawrence away. After they had dressed his wounds, the soldiers locked Lawrence in an outhouse. There he lay until dawn, when, having recovered a little, he discovered that his makeshift prison was insecure. He found some tatty clothes, clambered out through a window, and hobbled away toward Azraq, seventy miles away. It was early on 21 November. Five days later he would be back in Aqaba.

Almost immediately after Lawrence reached Aqaba, he wrote up in his diary where he had been on his return journey. There are some crossings-out—the previous days were evidently a blur—but the writing itself is firm and breezy: quite different from the tiny scrawl of the desperate moments that summer when he was utterly exhausted.[8] There is other evidence to suggest that he was in rude good health. When Hogarth saw Lawrence on 9 December, he described him as "looking fitter and better than when I saw him last."[9] His view is backed by some of the only footage of Lawrence from the campaign, taken two days later during Allenby's formal entry into Jerusalem, which shows him grinning broadly.

This evidence reinforces doubts over whether Lawrence could have completed his return journey so quickly if he sustained the injuries in Dara that he later described. There is no independent corroboration of Lawrence's story, and the relevant page of Lawrence's pocket diary, covering the period 15–21 November, when these events allegedly took place, is missing. It was probably torn out by Lawrence himself and is the only page missing from either of his diaries for 1917 or 1918, both of which he gave in 1926 to his confidante, Charlotte Shaw, telling her to burn them when she had finished reading them. There was no need to hide the matter from Shaw, who had read his account of the assault in the draft of *Seven Pillars of Wisdom*—unless of course the diary contradicted Lawrence's later story.

Charlotte Shaw did not burn the diaries, but instead gave them to the

British Library, where they can be read today. The three entries before the torn-out page are all, as Lawrence spelled them, for "Kasr Azrak."* Below the last of these, on 14 November, there is an additional vague note: "To Hauran," a reference to the fertile region east of Dara, but it is written differently. The first entry following the missing page, on 22 November, is also for "Azrak": the writing is slightly more pinched, but at the same angle as the entries over a week earlier, suggesting that Lawrence may have written all the entries up in one go afterward.

What was written on the diary's missing page? Forensic scientists have developed a technique using electrostatic detection apparatus, or ESDA, to disclose words written on a missing sheet of paper, using static electricity and fine carbon powder to reveal any indentations made by a pen or pencil through that absent page on a surviving sheet of paper below. At the beginning of 2005 the British Library gave me permission to have Lawrence's diary analyzed by ESDA in an attempt to establish what he may have written on the missing page.[10]

A ninety-year-old piece of paper, exposed to extreme heat and humidity, did not make firm results likely, and the three speckled gray transparent films produced by the process looked, unsurprisingly, disappointing. But a close look later revealed that in the space for 18 November—four days *after* Lawrence suggests he set off "To Hauran"—there are the faintest signs of a short, lost word beginning with Lawrence's characteristic capital a, a word that is almost certainly "Azrak." There are other tantalizing signs of handwriting, but none of it is legible.

The rediscovery of this lost word suggests that Lawrence did not leave Azraq for the Hauran when he claimed. The likelihood that Lawrence was still at Azraq on 18 November is corroborated elsewhere. His lengthy description of the days and "slow nights" at Azraq in *Seven Pillars of Wisdom* lends the impression that he spent rather more time at the castle than his diary would suggest, and so do comments in letters to his mother that he was "staying here a few days," on 14 November, and to his parents in December that he "stayed for ten days or so there," which might otherwise be discounted as white lies he told to hide a horrible incident.[11] The suggestion from the ESDA film that he was still at Azraq on the night of the eighteenth dramatically

* *Kasr*: a palace.

shortens the time he had left to do both the reconnaissance around Dara—which he said lasted "a few days"—and visit the town itself, where he said he was arrested on the twentieth, since he cannot have left Azraq before 19 November. Lawrence had only four days to accomplish what he later implied had taken eight.

The discovery also makes it clear that Lawrence added the "To Hauran" note later and raises the question of why he did so. If he tore out the missing page to try to obliterate the memory, which is the other plausible reason why the page is absent, he cannot have needed to remind himself of where he had gone. The only other motive can have been to mislead. So it seems very likely that he tore out the page and added "To Hauran" for the sole purpose of deceiving Charlotte Shaw and to make the diary consistent with what he had told her about his capture at Dara.

Why Lawrence included so much detail about his experience at Dara, including the vivid description of the effects of the whip on his back, which he could not possibly have seen, can be explained, like his letter to Stirling, in the light of what happened after the war. From early in the 1920s Lawrence revealed a masochistic urge to be whipped. One man, John Bruce, whom he paid to administer beatings to the backdrop of Beethoven on the gramophone, Lawrence described to Charlotte Shaw as making him feel like "a squashed door-mat of fossilized bones, between two layers. Good, perhaps, to feel like a prehistoric animal, extinct, and dead and useless: but wounding also."[12]

Lawrence was probably seeking to come to terms with his own sexuality through these beatings. At a time when descriptions of homosexuality were vigorously censored, he wrote openly in *Seven Pillars of Wisdom*—initially for the very small audience of subscribers who supported the book's publication—about the Arabs in the desert who avoided the "raddled meat" of women, preferring "indifferently to slake one another's needs in their own clean bodies."[13] He described how "some began to justify this sterile process, and swore that friends quivering together in the yielding sand, with intimate hot limbs in supreme embrace, found there hidden in the darkness a sensual coefficient of the mental passion which was welding our souls and spirits in one flaming effort."[14]

Lawrence himself was repelled by sexual activity in general, "holding procreation and evacuation alike as inevitable movements of the body."[15] He made fun of the Arabs for their obsession with "our comic reproductive processes not as merely an unhygienic pleasure, but as a main business of life."[16] Partly, this attitude was shaped by inexperience. Even later in life Lawrence admitted that the only sensation that the thought of sex aroused was dread. Describing his refusal after the war to accompany other soldiers to brothels, he admitted to Charlotte Shaw his fear of "seeming a novice in it . . . it's because I wouldn't know what to do, how to carry myself, where to stop. Fear again: fear everywhere."[17]

The Dara story in *Seven Pillars of Wisdom* was a device that gave Lawrence the opportunity to reveal his secret predilections, but also left him with a dilemma, as he explained to Shaw. Referring to the section on Dara, he wrote, "Working on it always makes me sick. The two impulses fight so upon it. Self-respect would close it: self-expression seeks to open it. It's a case in which you can't let yourself write as well as you could."[18]

At first Lawrence gave self-expression free rein, describing how "a delicious warmth, probably sexual" swelled through him after the whipping was over.[19] Though this sentence survived his editing, a further admission that the incident had left him with "a fascination and terror and morbid desire, lascivious and vicious perhaps, but like the striving of a moth towards its flame," he eventually excised.[20]

Whether something did happen in Dara to kindle this desire, or whether Lawrence, having initially concocted the story to smear a hated opponent, decided to elaborate on it to express his instincts in a way that would avoid censorship and inspire pity, not condemnation, from his former colleagues, cannot currently be proven. But this new evidence makes it seem likely that Lawrence removed the page from his diary because its contents did not correlate with the tale he would subsequently tell the world.

20

The Balfour Declaration
and Its Aftermath

Lawrence reappeared in Aqaba on 26 November. From the report he had sent on ahead, by the time he arrived at the port his colleagues already knew that he had failed to blow up the bridge in the Yarmuk valley and how lucky he had been to escape more serious injury when he detonated the mine under the train near Minifir. None of them had any inkling of the ordeal Lawrence would say he underwent in Dara, until much later. Almost immediately, he flew from Aqaba to southern Palestine to discuss tactics with Allenby, for he had returned to find that Allenby was on the verge of capturing Jerusalem and to hear news of an unexpected announcement in London that, ninety years later, still has dramatic reverberations around the Middle East.

On 7 November the *Times* had published a letter from Foreign Secretary Arthur Balfour to Lord Rothschild, an MP and prominent British supporter of Zionism, the twenty-year-old campaign to obtain for the Jews a state in Palestine. "I have much pleasure in conveying to you," Balfour theatrically announced to Rothschild, "the following declaration of sympathy with Jewish Zionist aspirations which has been submitted to, and approved by, the Cabinet." It ran,

His Majesty's Government view with favour the establishment in Palestine of a national home for the Jewish people, and will use their best endeavours to facilitate the achievement of this object, it being clearly understood that nothing shall be done which may prejudice the civil and religious rights of existing non-Jewish communities in Palestine, or the rights and political status enjoyed by Jews in any other country.[1]

The Balfour Declaration was, paradoxically, not really about the government of Palestine. It was a plea for support to the Jews worldwide.

At the turn of the twentieth century the belief that the Jews wielded considerable political influence around the world was widespread. Driven by repression from eastern Europe, Jews had migrated westward in large numbers in the years before the war. The Jewish population in Britain, for example, quadrupled to just over 250,000 in the thirty years to 1911. A lobby in New York, meanwhile, bolstered by significant Jewish migration to the United States before the war, found a way to avenge the treatment of Jews by blocking the tsarist government's attempts to raise loans on Wall Street.[2] The Jews were increasingly seen as a cohesive political entity capable of exerting their weight collectively and independently.[3] When Clayton, for example, returned from a visit to Britain in the summer of 1916, he told Wingate,

One impression I gained which confirmed what I have always thought, and which I know you take an interest in, was the wide-

The British foreign secretary, Arthur Balfour (left),
emerging from 10 Downing Street.

spread influence of the Jews. It is everywhere and always on the "moderation" tack. The Jews do not want to see anyone "downed." There are English Jews, French Jews, American Jews, German Jews, Austrian Jews and Salonika Jews—but all are JEWS, and moreover practically all are anti-Russian. You hear peace talk and generally somewhere behind is the Jew. You hear pro-Turk talk and desires for a separate peace with Turkey—again the Jew (the mainspring of the CUP*). I do not mean that the Jews are disloyal in any way, but it seems to me that the ties which bind the Jew to his fellow-Jews all over the world must induce in him an attitude of sort of semi-neutrality. On the other hand of course they are an increasing power as the war becomes more and more a question of who has the deepest pocket and the longest credit.[4]

Strange as it may seem today, Clayton's view was far from extraordinary. The Jews were believed to have a profound ability to influence world affairs, and this was a reputation that the Zionists played on.

Just as the Arab deserter Faruqi had persuaded Clayton two years earlier that the Arabs were a powerful latent force with undecided allegiance, so the Zionists in London similarly depicted the Jewish diaspora as an influential constituency that had to be won over if the Allies were to win the war. One man to whom they spoke frequently was Sykes.

Sykes had been infuriated by the overtures for peace with the Ottomans that had emerged from within the Foreign Office during the summer of 1917. Though no particular supporter of Zionism, he too began to believe that the Zionists were key to sabotaging these peace initiatives. By persuading British Zionists that peace talks threatened their hopes of colonizing Palestine, because they would leave the Ottoman Empire intact, he managed to derail one peace mission to Turkey by a former American ambassador to Constantinople, Henry Morgenthau. Sykes also began to see the Jews as part of an "Arab-Jewish-Armenian barrier between Persia-Egypt-India and the Turco-German combine," which would stop the Germans from marching eastward.[5] He felt that the Zionists should be encouraged to create "a self-supporting Jewish community which . . . should be a proof to the non-Jewish peoples of the world of the capacity of the Jews to produce

* The Committee of Union and Progress: the governing party of the Ottoman Empire.

a virtuous and simple agrarian population."[6] In Sykes's flyaway imagination, Jews across eastern Europe would flock to Palestine to become its milkmaids and apiarists. Sykes, Wingate warned, had become "carried away by the exuberance of his own verbosity."[7]

So much for Sykes's romantic vision. By the summer of 1917 there were two other harder-edged incentives for the British government to reach a settlement with the Zionists. The Foreign Office believed that the enormous Jewish population in Russia, which had been denied equal rights by the tsarist government, was mostly Zionist in outlook. As the situation in Russia deteriorated during the course of 1917, British officials hoped that, if they offered the Jews Palestine, Russian Zionists might, behind the scenes, arrest their country's descent into revolution and probable exit from the war—an outcome that would allow Germany to concentrate its forces on the western front. It was, in retrospect, a preposterous idea, but it appealed to Sykes. Until now, in the face of tsarist oppression, Jews had tended to turn toward socialism and communism for alternatives. He thought that offering the Zionists Palestine might undermine "the extreme Socialist Jews of the underworld who regard Karl Marx as the only prophet of Israel."[8] But time was running out. The same day that the *Times* published the Balfour Declaration, it also reported news of Lenin's Bolshevik coup in Petrograd.

Even if Russia collapsed, there was another good reason for supporting Zionist aspirations. At Russian insistence, under the Sykes-Picot agreement the "Brown zone" of Palestine was to be internationally administered. Anticipating the British capture of Jerusalem, Lloyd George realized that supporting Zionism was a useful tool to deflect American criticism of British imperialism and camouflage his ambition to turn Palestine into a British colony after the war. By helping the Zionists, Britain would also be championing the principle of self-determination.

Vague and halfhearted though the Balfour Declaration was, its significance was immediately grasped in Cairo. Sykes wrote enthusiastically to Clayton, telling him that the declaration emphasized the need for the Arabs to ally themselves with the Zionists. Clayton replied to Sykes that the "prospect of seeing Palestine and even eventually Syria in hands of Jews whose superior intelligence and commercial abilities are feared by all alike" meant that the announcement was received with "little short of dismay."[9] He was even more caustic about Sykes in private to Gertrude Bell, the Arab Bureau's correspondent in Baghdad.

"The Arab of Syria and Palestine sees the Jew with a free hand and the backing of HMG and interprets it as meaning the eventual loss of his heritage. Jacob and Esau once more. The Arab is right and no amount of specious oratory will humbug him in a matter which affects him so vitally," he told Bell.[10] "Experience such as I have gained in this war, impels me to deprecate strongly incautious declarations and visionary agreements. We are like men walking through an unknown country in a fog and it behoves to feel our way and take care of each step we take."

Bell agreed with Clayton. "I hate Mr Balfour's Zionist pronouncement," she later told her mother:

> It's my belief that it can't be carried out; the country is wholly unsuited to the ends the Jews have in view; it is a poor land, incapable of great development and with a solid two thirds of its population Mohammedan Arabs who look on Jews with contempt . . . it's a wholly artificial scheme divorced from all relation to facts and I wish it the ill-success it deserves—and will get, I fancy.[11]

In the Balfour Declaration, Clayton saw just one glimmer of light. "It may perhaps result in consolidating the Arabs, however," he suggested to Bell. "Up to date the Syrian Arab has shown the utmost distaste for any idea of a Government in which Meccan patriarchalism has any influence. Hence a lack of real sympathy with the Sharif. Fear of the Jew may cause a rapprochement."[12]

Clayton's belief reflected the fact that it was slowly dawning on the British that Sharif Husein was very unpopular in Syria. Increasing contact between the Syrian nationalists and the man they had approached to be their advocate in 1915 only revealed the width of the cultural gulf between them. Clayton sensed "a very real fear" among the Syrians: "They realize that reactionary principles from which Sharif of Mecca cannot break loose are incompatible with progress on modern lines."[13]

Husein's "reactionary principles" were clearly visible to anyone who visited Mecca. After seizing power in 1916, Husein had swept away the Turkish legal code and replaced it with religious sharia law. From Jeddah, Cyril Wilson had tried to stop Turkish prisoners' being forced to work chained together in iron collars, and he protested about the amputations of offenders' hands and feet sanctioned by sharia law as punishment for theft. He made little headway. "It is not an easy subject to talk to the King about as he is most impatient of any criticism," he admitted, though he hoped that to avoid aggravating the cosmopolitan inhabitants of Jeddah, "in future such mutilations will only be carried out in the interior."[14]

Husein's style of rule in the Hijaz was all the more awkward for the British because he showed no signs of giving up his claim to Syria, for without that fertile province the Hijaz alone would never be a viable state. As an article in the *Arab Bulletin* admitted, "We have changed the political status of Hijaz, but neither we, nor any others, have changed its economic status. Someone outside must still pay for its government and provide its food."[15] When Wilson gingerly asked Husein about his attachment to Syria, the sharif had replied that any attempt to confine his jurisdiction to the Hijaz "would drive him either to abdicate . . . or to repudiate his connection with us and make the best possible terms with the Turks."[16] Wingate decided that the best way to disguise the growing problem was with money.

Even before the Balfour Declaration was published, Wingate had been planning to counter any Turkish plans to buy the Arabs off with a timely injection of cash. When Husein began to ask for more money that autumn to soothe the increasingly fractious tribesmen of the Hijaz, Wingate was inclined to support him. "Old standing feuds are showing signs of reasserting themselves," he warned London on 2 November, explaining that Husein was "fully alive to this" and had repeatedly suggested "an increase in subsidy which will enable him to placate discontented elements."[17] Aware, too, of the strategic importance to Allenby of Feisal's forces, which, by simply being in southern Syria, were covering his eastern flank, Husein believed that the British government should foot most of the bill for Feisal's army and wanted an increase over and above any extra money allocated to Feisal. Wingate agreed, for a different reason: "It is desirable for political reasons that King Husein should not bear the whole brunt of operations in Maan area and North and thus secure a preponderating voice in regard to future settlement of Syrian problem," he argued, with the concerns of the Syrians and the French in mind.[18]

Extracting more money from London was always difficult. Although the sums involved were relatively trivial, the subsidy was payable entirely in gold—the only currency the Bedu would accept. The Foreign Office even hoped that the money might ultimately be repaid:

"Are these subsidies to be regarded as loans eventually repayable from funds of new Arab kingdom?" one official asked brightly early in 1917.[19] Optimistic though he was, the hope that the payments to Husein might be recoverable never quite disappeared: a Treasury minute of August 1918 noted that a total of £4,520,000 had been "advanced" to the sharif.[20]

It was Allenby who broke the impasse over funding. On 14 November he had captured Junction station, which meant that the Turks could no longer supply Jerusalem, twenty miles farther east by rail. Allenby now planned to cut the road north out of Jerusalem to the nearest railhead still in Turkish hands, at Nablus, forty miles to the north, to isolate the holy city altogether and starve its Turkish defenders out: it was vital that the city not be damaged by fighting. In London the War Cabinet's only worry was that Allenby was advancing so fast that he might overstretch his lines of communication. It was a danger that occurred to Allenby, too, for the following day he contacted Robertson to voice his support for Wingate's request for more money for Feisal, whose forces protected his eastern flank. He was nervous of the consequences if the Arabs went unpaid: "Any slacking on their part will render my position insecure," he warned London.[21] Two days later the Foreign Office approved Wingate's request to raise the authorized amount that could be spent on Arab operations from £200,000 to £500,000, "provided it does not entail further dispatch of gold from here."[22] At the same time payment of the fee promised to Husein if he captured Medina was brought forward, regardless of the lack of success: from January 1918 onward Husein received £225,000 a month from the British.

⁓✻⁓

Early on 9 December—a bright, sunny Sunday—two British soldiers were out looking for eggs in a valley three miles north of Jerusalem. They were surprised when they met a ragtag crowd carrying a large white flag. At its head, Jerusalem's mayor explained that the Turks had made a tactical withdrawal to Jericho and Nablus and, with the holy city undefended, offered both men his surrender. But neither private was willing to return to their officers' mess with the keys to Jerusalem but no breakfast, and so the mayor was forced to trudge onward. It was only later that day that he finally found a British officer willing to accept his surrender.

The British government had been waiting for this moment. Almost three weeks earlier Robertson had contacted Allenby, advising him that "in the event of Jerusalem being occupied, it would be of considerable political importance if you, on officially entering the city, dismount at the city gate and enter on foot. German Emperor rode in and the saying went round 'a better man than he walked.'"[23] Robertson now hoped Allenby would offer a humble contrast.

On 11 December, Allenby entered Jerusalem. It was "a brilliant day; hoar frost here . . . and then iced sunshine, with no wind," he told his wife.[24] "The procession was all on foot," he reassured London in a telegram later that day. Behind, in the multinational force that followed him, walked Clayton and Lawrence, who had come over from Aqaba by airplane to discuss the next stage of the campaign and swapped his Arab robes for a uniform. "The indescribable smell of Jerusalem rose to meet us," wrote another British officer, "a mixture of spices and sweet herbs, strange eastern cooking and dried fruits, camels and native garments and open drains."[25] Film footage from that day shows the large inquisitive crowds that turned out to see the British and, to the sound of distant artillery and rifle fire beyond the city walls, hear Allenby's pledge that he would uphold religious freedom in the holy city. "Great enthusiasm—real or feigned—was shown," Allenby recorded.

The inflexible French negotiator François Georges-Picot was also present. Although the French had played almost no part in the capture of the city, Picot was determined to ensure that his agreement with Sykes was not ignored. At the buffet lunch following the formal declaration in Jerusalem, he raised the topic of the future government of Jerusalem.

"Tomorrow, my dear General, I will take the necessary steps to set up civil government in this town," announced Picot, according to Lawrence. Instantly there was silence. "Salad and chicken mayonnaise and foie gras sandwiches hung in our mouths unmunched," Lawrence remembered, "while we turned our round eyes on Allenby and waited."

Allenby went red.

"In the military zone the only authority is that of the Commander-in-Chief, myself."

The British enter Jerusalem, 11 December 1917. Allenby's advance into Palestine brought the city into Christian hands for the first time since 1187.

"But Sir Edward Grey—"

"Sir Edward Grey referred to the civil government which will be established when I judge that the military situation permits."[26]

Even though Allenby had been warned by Robertson that Picot would press for Palestine to be jointly administered, the British were evidently taken aback by the boldness of his request. On 27 December, Ronald Storrs, who had been quickly commissioned as an army officer, was hurriedly installed as military governor of Jerusalem. "He has had little administrative experience and in this respect may prove a disappointment," remarked Wingate the same day, "but he is well worth a trial and may at any rate serve as a useful stopgap."[27]

The capture of Jerusalem was a remarkable propaganda coup for Lloyd George. The news was announced to the House of Commons on 10 December, and the following day's newspapers were enthusiastic. The *Glasgow Herald*'s editorial suggested, "The taking of Jerusalem marks the end of an epoch of darkness, decay and despair, and the beginning of an era of light and hope such as was dreamed of by prophets long ago."[28] The *Times* of London anticipated "a new order" in the Holy Land, "founded on the ideals of righteousness and justice."[29]

Across Britain church bells pealed the victory. But in the background the Bolshevik revolution—the very outcome the Balfour Declaration had been issued to avert—had caused another problem for the British. For in Russia, within days of taking power, the Bolsheviks released details of the secret treaties to which Russia was a party. Among them was the Sykes-Picot agreement.

The governor of Syria, Jemal Pasha, knew the details of the Sykes-Picot agreement within a week and decided to exploit them as best he could. Through secret contact with Feisal he believed that Feisal's "basic intention was not to find himself on the losing side."[30] On 13 November he wrote directly to Feisal. Pointing at the British advance deep into Palestine, he asked him, "How could you imagine establishing an Arab Government which would be responsible for the administration of the Moslem world independently and with dignity when the Allies have declared that Palestine will be an international religious settlement, Syria will be annexed to France and Iraq to the British Government?"[31] Then he offered Feisal the opportunity for face-to-face talks and, without waiting for Feisal's reply, announced a monthlong amnesty the following day.[32]

On 5 December, Jemal revealed the existence of the Sykes-Picot agreement when he spoke at a meeting in Beirut. Saying nothing about the provision in the treaty that gave France Syria, possibly because this might be welcomed by some in his Lebanese audience, he focused instead on the behavior of Sharif Husein. At first he played on his audience's fears of being ruled from Mecca, but then he suggested that all Husein had done was to make himself the unwitting puppet of the British, who, he claimed, now planned to pare Husein's kingdom down to "Mecca and Medina, towns without those things necessary for independence, namely gold, agriculture and commerce." Britain's aim was to turn the Hijaz into a protectorate, in which "the Sharif, because of his ignorance, will be nothing better than England's slave."[33] Again, Jemal offered to initiate talks:

> I believe that the Sharif began to repent, when he found out the real intention of the British, and I have therefore sent him a letter, pointing out that his dignity, his sincerity and his conscience cannot approve of his conduct towards his country, and asking how he could allow himself to become the slave of England if he has any self-respect.

Jemal's letter to Husein was intercepted before it reached him, how-ever, and it was Feisal who first alerted his father to Jemal's overture. Just before Christmas, Husein in turn forwarded the letter to Wingate. This letter and Jemal's speech in Beirut, a copy of which Wingate appears to have received at about the same time, made sense of another discovery earlier that month, when the Arabs had ambushed a train one hundred miles north of Al Ula, traveling south. Aboard the train was an Arab sheikh, Suleiman Rifada, who was always suspected of colluding with the Turks, £24,000 in gold, and on Rifada they found the letter from Jemal inviting Husein to talks. With evidence suggesting that the Turks were trying to buy the Arabs, Wingate rapidly dispatched Lawrence back from Palestine to Aqaba to talk to Feisal.

Lawrence arrived in Aqaba on Christmas Day. Just how worried he looked is suggested by one soldier who remembered him at the Christ-mas party thrown by the captain of the *Humber*: "Sight of him was quite enough to put the celebrations in their place."[34]

Joyce and Lawrence worked on a denial of Jemal's interpretation of the Sykes-Picot agreement. Jemal, they told Husein, "either from igno-rance or malice" had "distorted its original purpose . . . omitted its stip-ulations regarding consent of native populations and safeguarding their interest and . . . ignored fact that subsequent outbreak and success of Arab Revolt and withdrawal from Russia had for a long time past cre-ated a wholly different situation."[35]

Awareness of the Sykes-Picot agreement caused ripples around the world. In London, Lloyd George also moved to counteract the damage caused by the revelation. Addressing the Trades Union Congress—a group of people more likely than most to be sympathetic to the revo-lutionaries in Russia—at the beginning of January 1918, he said that Arabia, Armenia, Mesopotamia, Syria and Palestine were entitled to "a recognition of their separate national conditions," though, not surpris-ingly, he glossed over what form the recognition would take or whether it would involve self-government. He did, however, say that it would be impossible to restore any of these territories to the Turks.

In Washington, in his celebrated Fourteen Points days later, Presi-dent Wilson went rather further. His twelfth point covered the Ottoman Empire. "The Turkish portions of the present Ottoman

Empire should be assured a secure sovereignty," he advocated, "but the other nationalities, which are now under Turkish rule, should be assured an undoubted security of life and an absolutely unmolested opportunity of autonomous development." It was a clear warning to both Britain and France. It also raised Arab expectations.

21

Fighting De Luxe

The capture of Jerusalem provoked an enthusiastic reaction in Britain that ignited War Office interest in the Palestine campaign. In London the strategists pored over their maps and realized how important control of the country east of the river Jordan was to the security of Allenby's front.

After some thought, on 10 January the official in charge of railway transport at the War Office in London dispatched a telegram to Egypt. The director of railways and roads, he said, "writing demi-officially, asks me to draw attention to the fact that some of the bridges etc. on the Hijaz Railway may now be within distance for bombing by aeroplane. I imagine that this is already known, but write as the War Office suggest it." The Egyptian Expeditionary Force's quartermaster general forwarded the advice to the Arab Bureau. "I think this may interest you," he added in a covering note. "I daresay the D of R and R at W.O. thinks that we are not perhaps aware of the fact that there is a Hijaz Railway."[1]

The Hijaz Railway had already featured highly in Allenby's discussions with Lawrence in December. Allenby's advance to Jerusalem had left his supply lines more exposed than ever, and he explained to London how, while his forces consolidated their position, he hoped "to operate against Hijaz railway during wet season, and while waiting for my railway to overtake me, as there are still 20,000 Turks south of Amman."[2] The presence of so many enemy troops clearly worried him because, shortly afterward, he repeated that it was "advisable before advancing much further north to clear Turkish forces on Medina railway." Allenby might have left the task of cutting the railway to the Arabs, but Lawrence's failure in the Yarmuk valley did not inspire much trust. By the beginning of December he was already mulling over the possibility of raiding the railway in the Amman area with his own forces, once he had captured Jericho.[3]

Like Allenby, Lawrence had also lost confidence in the Arabs. Documents recently seized from the Turks suggested that the Turkish commander in Maan had obtained "considerable, and not altogether inaccurate, information" on the Arabs' plans and whereabouts.[4] With the likelihood that there was a spy among the Arabs, and having discovered that the price on his head had dramatically risen following his devastating raid on the Eighth Corps' General Mehmed Jemal's train at Minifir, Lawrence recruited a bodyguard of Ageyl who were well paid and detached from the internecine tribal structure of western Arabia and whom he felt he could therefore trust not to betray him. Joyce decided that on their next raid they would take no tribesmen at all, but test the armored cars instead. At the beginning of December, Joyce and Lawrence had taken a car and driven up Wadi Itm. Having proved that the vehicles would cope with the new, rough road up the narrow valley, Joyce ordered the Rolls-Royce armored cars and the Talbots, which carried light field guns, to move to Quwayrah, twenty-five miles northeast of Aqaba. He and Joyce then took three lighter Rolls-Royce cars and, leaving the Christmas sports on the beach at Aqaba, set out on 26 December up Wadi Itm and east across the velvety mudflats north of Wadi Ramm to reconnoiter Mudawwarah. After the bone-shaking ride up Wadi Itm, the flats were ideal territory for the cars, which trailed long streams of dust as they raced across the plain. "30–40–50–60–70," wrote one driver, Sam Rolls, remembering his speedometer's clockwise ascent as he tried to satisfy Lawrence's "craze for speed."[5] Following months of waiting in Aqaba, Lawrence recalled, "it cheered up everybody, this twisting in and out among the flats, at top speed, skirting clumps of tamarisk, and roaring along under the great sandstone crags."[6]

After a night of "bully-beef and tea and biscuit, with English talk and laughter round the fire," Joyce and Lawrence established the following day that it was possible to reach Mudawwarah by car, and returned to Quwayrah to collect the other vehicles.[7] On further reconnaissance on the last day of 1917, the two officers discovered that the low, flat-topped hills through which they had driven the day before now petered out.

Armored Rolls-Royce and Talbot cars and their British crews at Quwayrah, 1918. The cars were used on many raids against the railway, including one in April 1918 that cut the line south of Maan permanently.

Ahead lay the railway, in a vast plain of brown stone and drifting sharp yellow sand bounded by pinkish hills in the distance. It was too open for them to dare to mine a train, but open enough for the cars. After more investigation on foot on 1 January 1918, Joyce decided they should attack the small posts defending the railway north of Mudawwarah, using the light artillery mounted on the Talbot cars.

"Armoured car work was fighting de luxe," Lawrence decided, "for all our troops were steel-covered, and could come to no hurt."[8] He and Joyce sat on top of a nearby hill and watched the battle develop through their binoculars. However, the flatness of the plain made it hard to judge distance, and the Talbots ventured too close to the Turkish position and came under what Joyce later described as "a very hot rifle fire."[9] With bullets shrieking off their armor plating, the cars withdrew southward, stopping to bombard Tell Shahm station, where they destroyed a number of freight cars, before driving away. Summing up the raid, Joyce noted with satisfaction that the appearance of the armored cars on the railway for the first time had evidently caught the Turks by surprise, but he realized that the raiders had also been lucky. As Lawrence later admitted, he and Joyce had been so preoccupied by whether the cars could reach the railway that they had given little thought to the tactics they would employ when they got there. And although excellent on the flat, the cars could not cross the steeply sided wadis that crisscrossed the plain, and Joyce observed that further careful reconnaissance was needed to avoid the danger of being cornered in future.

Good news followed Joyce back to Aqaba. On 3 January a force of about 1,000 Bani Sakhr tribesmen and 150 well-armed Arab regulars, led by Sharif Nasir and Nuri Said, had recaptured Abu al Assal, the well on the pass between Aqaba and Maan where Auda's tribesmen had massacred the Turks that summer. Joyce headed there immediately. In the meantime Nasir crossed the railway, skirted around the east side of Maan, and then turned back toward the railway and attacked the station at Jurf ad Darawish, thirty-five miles north of Maan. Jurf, a sleepy, mellow stone halt, with graffiti carved in its parapets by bored sentries, and a station master who welcomed me in with tea, still gives the impression today of a station that was wholly unprepared for the violent attack that overwhelmed it that gray January day.[10]

As I noticed when I visited in September 2004, to the east Jurf station is overlooked by a line of purplish hills. It was from this ridge at dawn that Nasir's 1,000 tribesmen charged down into the valley on their camels, terrifying the garrison, whom they outnumbered by more than three to one. Nuri's men followed and turned the station's only, abandoned field gun on the railway buildings with devastating effect. In the ensuing battle 80 Turkish soldiers were killed, and over 200 more were captured. The Arabs, just two of whom were wounded, held the station for three days until a shortage in supplies forced them to move on.

❧

Storrs had originally been planning to visit Jeddah to reassure Husein about the Balfour Declaration, but his unexpected promotion to Jerusalem meant that he had no time to return to the Hijaz. The task instead fell to Hogarth, whose visit was accelerated by the sudden appearance in Jeddah of another British diplomat, Harry Philby. An envoy of the Government of India, the thirty-two-year-old Philby had come overland from Ibn Saud's capital, Riyadh, and Husein was deeply suspicious of his sudden arrival. He feared, correctly, that he was being pressured to come to an agreement with his fearsome rival.

Hogarth sailed to Jeddah early in January to see Sharif Husein. It was his first visit to the Red Sea port, which he had described years earlier as "before and since notorious for hatred of Christians."[11] With this perhaps in mind, he walked self-consciously though the city's "little dark earthen alleys blocked with Bedouins and camels and watersellers and beggars and hawkers and pilgrims."[12]

It was the first time that Hogarth had met Husein. He assured the sharif that the Arabs would be "given full opportunity of once again forming a nation in the world." He also tried to clarify the Balfour Declaration. Britain, he explained, supported Jewish settlement in Palestine, provided it did not affect the freedom of the existing population.[13] Husein elegantly parried the declaration. He "seemed quite prepared for formula," Hogarth reported back to Cairo, and had replied enthusiastically that "he welcomed Jews to all Arab lands."[14]

The sharif seemed the perfect host, as ever, but he tried his hardest to poison Britain's relationship with Ibn Saud. He argued that Fakhri was holding out so well in Medina because he was receiving surreptitious support from Ibn Saud. Philby, however, had anticipated this and brought with him letters Fakhri had written to Ibn Saud, in which the beleaguered general asked why Ibn Saud never replied. Husein refused to read the letters, and Hogarth concluded that a rapprochement between him and Ibn Saud was, for the time being at least, impossible, as the sharif explained "once more how he loves us all but can't do what we want, and won't!"[15]

As a representative of the Government of India and to emphasize his independence, Philby refused to attend any meetings at the British residency in Jeddah or aboard the *Hardinge*. His behavior annoyed Hogarth, because it emphasized the continuing divide in British policy on the Middle East, which was making Husein feel very exposed. As a consequence of his absence from many of the meetings, Philby— Hogarth felt—had little idea of the magnetic, "Imam-like" personality of the sharif. He was, said Hogarth, "deeply imbued with the idea that Ibn Saud, as his man, is to be championed against a 'Cairo Champion.'"[16]

Hogarth left with a lasting impression that Husein was vulnerable. "His manner to me was most cordial throughout. . . . With Mr Philby he comported himself, even when most contradictory and impracticable, less in anger than sorrow, and ended two of the most heated discussions not only with apologies to us all but an impulsive kiss to Mr

Philby."[17] Hogarth suspected that Husein hoped to force France's hand on the future of Syria at the postwar peace conference, and was anxious to maintain good relations with the British, expecting them to back him. "He is quite firm in his friendship to us," Hogarth concluded, "but none too firm on his throne." This frailty was a theme to which Hogarth would return in a further report on Husein for the *Arab Bulletin*: "He is born to rule, but, probably, not to rule much farther than his eyes can see."[18]

⁂

High in the mountains at Abu al Assal, the Arabs were badly prepared for the atrocious weather that winter in southern Syria. Joyce had warned almost three months earlier that the Meccan troops still fighting with Feisal already looked miserable with the cold. "They hadn't enough blankets and tents to ward off the weather," recalled another British soldier, although the Arabs' Iraqi commander Jafar Pasha blamed this on the troops, who "stubbornly kept to their flimsy attire" and refused to wear more clothing.[19] It was an attitude that was to cost some their lives. On 10 January, Joyce reported that the previous night at Abu al Assal ten men had died from exposure. Many others over that winter suffered a similar fate, being found frozen rigid the following morning by their comrades. Though Lawrence did not yet know it, among the casualties was his servant Ali, who, with Othman, had accompanied him all the way to Aqaba the previous year.

Despite the heavy snowfall Nasir's force made good progress west from Jurf ad Darawish. In the hills southeast of the Dead Sea, his tribesmen attacked first the branch line of the railway to Hishe, where the Turks were cutting down wood to fuel their locomotives, then Shawbak, and finally, on 15 January, captured Tafilah, a quiet town in the hills forty-five miles north of Maan, surrounded by rolling, stony fields. Tafilah was also the southernmost of the hill towns that the Arabs needed to control in order to secure Allenby's right flank. Unfortunately, however, it had taken the arrival of Auda abu Tayi and his confrontational demand—"Dogs, do you not know Auda?"—to persuade the villagers to surrender and, as Lawrence discovered when he arrived shortly afterward, the situation there was far from stable.[20]

"There is shooting up and down the streets every night, and general tension," Lawrence reported to Clayton from Tafilah, seven days after the Arabs arrived.[21] The people of Tafilah were split into two factions, who opposed each other and the appearance of the tribesmen. As a consequence, Lawrence's hope that the Arabs would find food to boost their own supplies proved overly optimistic. By wintertime barley and wheat, which were harvested in March and April, were scarce and dear, and the prospect of imminent fighting between the tribesmen and the Turks led the townspeople to hoard what stocks they had. Lawrence thought that there was little chance that their attitude would change until the tribesmen had taken the towns of Karak and Madaba to the north as well, making Turkish retribution was less likely.

The chance of taking either town was unlikely, Lawrence admitted to Clayton in his letter, because he was acutely short of money. Feisal's younger brother, Zeid, had just arrived to take charge of operations, and he had paid the Bani Sakhr tribesmen a total of £22,000—nearly four times more than they were owed. "We are going to be out of funds perhaps before we take Karak, even," Lawrence confessed. He asked Clayton for a special grant of £30,000 to be sent overland from Palestine for speed. Then he dispatched the letter with a local tribesman who knew the way, and waited. And little did he know that he was about to have to fight to keep Tafilah.

On 24 January the British intercepted an important message from Mehmed Jemal, commander of the Turkish Eighth Corps in Damascus, to one of his officers on the Hijaz Railway south of Amman. It said that Turkish troops from Karak were heading south to retake Tafilah and that he should send troops in the same direction. It turned out to be an expensive demand.

The same day Turkish forces clashed with Arab patrols in Wadi al Hasa, a dramatic canyon a few miles north of Tafilah, which separated the town from Karak to the north. Lawrence decided he would have to stand and fight the pitched battle to defend Tafilah that he had always advised the tribesmen to avoid.

There were two good reasons why Lawrence chose to seek a decisive battle. To relinquish Tafilah without a fight was hardly likely to bolster Allenby's dwindling confidence in his handling of operations east of Wadi Araba. Besides which, to turn and run would only confirm the townspeople's fears that the nomads would leave them to face Turkish retribution on their own. Lawrence also hoped a victory at Tafilah would win the town of Karak over to the Arabs' cause. Days earlier the Arabs had sent messengers north to Karak, but there, as in Tafilah, the political situation was complicated. Two families, the Majali and the Tarawna, controlled the medieval market town and its surrounding lands, but the violent way in which the Turks had crushed a revolt there in 1910 had left its scar. The ringleader of that uprising, Qadar Majali, had mysteriously died on a recent visit to Damascus as the Ottoman government's guest: his kinsmen were understandably reluctant to take up arms.[22] The other family, the Tarawna, offered Lawrence higher hopes. They were "secretly pro-Sharif," he believed, "and may call up enough courage to take a visible plunge."[23] Lawrence hoped that an Arab victory against the Turks at Tafilah would encourage the Tarawna to declare themselves in favor of the sharif, taking the people of Karak with them.

Overnight, following the first skirmish, the Arabs took up a defensive position on the edge of an abrupt valley on the north side of Tafilah. When he returned to the town shortly before dawn, Lawrence found its inhabitants in a state of panic and preparing to flee: "Mounted Arabs were galloping up and down, firing wildly into the air, and the flashes of Turkish rifles were outlining the further cliffs of the Tafilah gorge."[24]

Exactly what happened on 26 January remains unclear. At dawn, after Turkish bullets began to snap through the olive grove where the Arabs were trying to hide, Lawrence sent some lightly armed Arab troops to support the Tafilah peasants who were still holding a low ridge on the north side of the valley. When he made his own way down into the valley and up to that ridge, the peasants counterattacked and drove the Turkish cavalry—the advance guard of the main 600-strong force—back toward Wadi al Hasa. Here, however, they ran into the main Turkish force. Even from a distance Lawrence realized that the fighting had become "very hot": the clatter of machine-gun fire and scream and blast of shells were audible from the town.

On his way toward the battle Lawrence met a man named Abdullah, who was the leader of the small local force that had beaten off the Turkish cavalry, and who was going in the opposite direction. Five of his men were dead, Abdullah explained, and he had run out of ammunition. While Abdullah hurried back to fetch reinforcements, Lawrence headed for a small mound that was being defended by a few Huwaytat and the remaining locals, where he realized that they were about to be outflanked on both sides. Shells from the Turkish field guns were also beginning to fall closer and closer to the Arabs. Leaving a few of the Huwaytat to cover their retreat, Lawrence took the locals back to the ridge just north of the Tafilah valley where they had started the day. Here he found the reinforcements Abdullah had mustered, more machine guns, and an Egyptian army mountain gun.

As he ran back from the exposed mound, Lawrence counted his paces and so, when the Huwaytat finally retired and the Turks occupied the same mound they had just left behind, Lawrence knew they were just over three thousand yards away. This information enabled the Arabs to start firing their mountain gun accurately straightaway. Meanwhile, one of the Arab officers led some soldiers around to the right and attacked the Turks from behind. At about the same time local villagers from Aymah, just northwest of Tafilah, also joined the fighting. Either through luck or judgment, they were in the right place to attack the Turks from behind, from the other side. Caught in a simultaneous attack from three sides on gently undulating, stony ground, which offered no protection from shells or ricocheting bullets, the Turks suffered terrible casualties. By nightfall 200 had been killed, and a further 250 were captured, including the commander, Hamid Fakhri Bey, who later died of his wounds. Many of the wounded froze to death on the battlefield overnight. The Arabs lost 25 men and a further 40 wounded. With Tafilah now secure, Lawrence sent some tribesmen down northward to the Dead Sea to destroy the small Turkish fleet there, which Allenby believed was ferrying supplies across to Jericho, where the Turks were still holding out.

For his role in directing the action Lawrence won a medal and was promoted to lieutenant colonel shortly afterward, both of which reflected the importance Allenby's headquarters now attached to operations east of the Jordan. But he later admitted that his report, the sole basis for the decoration, was "a nearly proof parody of regulation use," in which he portrayed himself as a tyro who had directed the battle with the thumb of one hand marking the relevant page in a copy of Clausewitz's manual *On War*.[25] Headquarters missed the joke. "We should have more bright breasts in the Army," Lawrence laughed, "if each man was able without witnesses, to write out his own despatch."[26] Nor, as he later discovered, would the battle have the positive impact that he hoped it would on the people of Karak. There, he found out in June, the Tarawna made no headway. Their rivals, the Majali, were "pro-Turk" and "now supreme." Not only that; they had raised a force of four hundred locals to defend the town against attack by Feisal's men.[27]

During February the gold that Lawrence had requested arrived in Tafilah. Its escort was a young, tall, and ruthless officer who had grown up in Alexandria, Alec Kirkbride. The six-foot-three Kirkbride clearly impressed Lawrence, who quickly offered him a job as "Intelligence-cum-Demolition officer."[28] After Clayton's concern about his health, Lawrence had been looking for other British officers to share his work, and Kirkbride, though only twenty years old, spoke fluent Arabic and had made the journey back across Wadi Araba with an Arab guide and £30,000 in gold without incident. This, together with the further money Lawrence had gone to beg from Joyce in Quwayrah, would replenish Arab funds, he thought. He set out southward with Kirkbride, accompanying him down through the wild Dana gorge into Wadi Araba. There they parted, Kirkbride for Aqaba to the south, Lawrence to the shore of the Dead Sea, northward.

When, on his return to Tafilah, Lawrence told Zeid of his plans to head north toward Karak and Madaba, Zeid interrupted him.

"But that will need a lot of money," Zeid said.

Lawrence reminded him of the £30,000 Kirkbride had brought, saying the sum would more than cover further operations.

Zeid looked embarrassed. He had spent it all, he said.

"I was aghast; for this meant the complete ruin of my plans and hopes," recalled Lawrence afterward.[29] Gold was by now in short supply in Egypt, and he could not be sure of getting more. He was also deeply disappointed by the Arabs—if they had "any common spirit, they would have been in Damascus last autumn," he complained, condemning them as "the most ghastly material to build into a design."[30] He could not believe that, in just a week, Zeid had managed to spend so much buying tribal support with so little to show for it, and he thought Zeid must be lying. What Zeid had probably done was pass out the cash for the tribesmen's past support and hold none back for future operations. But when he refused to explain his actions further, Lawrence replied that he had no choice but to offer his resignation. On 19 February he hurried away toward Beersheba and the British army's headquarters. "I was going across to Allenby to explain," he told a startled Joyce, who had just arrived in Tafilah, "and to put my further employment in his hands."[31]

22

New Conditions

"Can you identify the individual, sir?" the corporal asked. He directed his question at the officer who had just unexpectedly greeted the short and unusually ruddy "Arab" he had arrested wandering through the tents of British headquarters at Bir Salem, ten miles inland from Jaffa on the Jerusalem road.

"Yes," the officer replied, recognizing the white-robed "Arab" from his time working for Colonel Wilson in Jeddah.

"What name?"

"Lawrence. A British officer."

"Very good, sir," said the corporal, lowering his rifle and turning on his heel.

"It often happens," sighed Lawrence. It was the second time that day he had been stopped.[1] "You see I have ridden over from Karak and am staying with the Chief. I am coming now to see Clayton. Thanks so much for giving me my release. Shall we go in to lunch?"[2]

"Like a bolt from the blue," wrote Alan Dawnay of Lawrence's sudden appearance in Palestine. Colonel Dawnay was the new staff officer who had been given responsibility for bringing a greater degree of organization to "Hijaz Operations" and coordinating them with Allenby's overall plans. He was a precise and diligent man with an "Oxford drawl" who had just been trying, without success, to fly a message to Lawrence in Tafilah, asking him to come to headquarters.[3] Recent developments meant that there was no question that Lawrence would not be needed in the operations that were now being planned.

"I told Clayton a little how I felt," Lawrence would recollect, "but he said that in the new conditions there could be no question of letting me off. In his opinion the East was only now going to begin."[4]

The "new conditions" to which Clayton referred were those that Lloyd George had deftly shaped from the euphoria following the capture of Jerusalem. Bypassing his chief military adviser, Sir William Robertson, the prime minister persuaded the Allies' Supreme War Council—the body comprising the heads of government and senior generals of all the Allies—that the British should unleash another offensive against the Ottomans during 1918. Then he dispatched a member of his War Cabinet, the South African general Jan Smuts, to Egypt to assess whether this strike should come from Palestine or from Mesopotamia. In the meantime in London, Lloyd George finally managed to sideline Robertson, who naturally opposed an eastern offensive. Over breakfast on Monday, 18 February, Robertson read in the newspaper that he had resigned.[5]

Three days later British forces captured Jericho just as Jan Smuts was completing his tour of the Palestine front. On his return to Britain, Smuts endorsed action in Palestine. The capture of Jericho not only solidified political support in London for a further advance but, by giving Allenby direct access to the river Jordan, also made possible another scheme he had been plotting for some time. "If I could destroy 10 or 15 miles of rail and some bridges; and get [in] touch with the Arabs under Feisal—even temporarily—the effect would be great," Allenby had told Robertson late in January, of his hope of raiding the Hijaz Railway.[6] News that Zeid had either misspent or stolen the money only just dispatched to him may have further encouraged Allenby to take matters east of the Jordan into his own hands. In a valedictory letter to Robertson, he commented, "The Arabs, led by Lawrence, have been doing pretty well; but they are an unstable lot."[7] Although he had been reassured by Lawrence that the Arabs would make further headway, given continuing British encouragement and money, Allenby believed that "they cannot run alone, and must have British leaders they know and trust," dismissing at a stroke Lawrence's offer to resign.

Increasingly, Allenby favored an attack on Amman. The beauty of such a scheme was that a break in the railway at that point would not only prevent troops from Medina from reaching the Turkish front line north of Amman but also stop troops from Damascus from launching a surprise attack from Maan behind his lines. Moreover, such an attack would work just as effectively as Arab action farther south.[8] The appearance of British troops east of the Jordan might force the Turks to give up plans to retake Tafilah and finally persuade the farming communities in the hills east of the Jordan to trust the tribesmen.

The threat posed to Allenby's supply lines by the 3,000-strong Turkish garrison at Maan, possibly reinforced by troops from Medina, was to become an increasingly pressing concern as Allenby prepared to advance northward. Dawnay and Joyce had met at the beginning of February to plan an Arab attack on Maan, which Lawrence was optimistic would succeed if the Arabs' own supplies could be improved.[9] Allenby agreed to provide two Egyptian camel transport units to help, but on the condition that they came under Joyce's, and not Arab, command. Then, at a conference at headquarters on 26 February, it was decided that the Arabs should attack Maan at the same time as the British occupied Salt, a picturesque town with a large Christian population thirty-five miles northeast of Jerusalem, high in the hills just east of the Jordan. Salt would be the springboard for a further British attack on the Hijaz Railway at Amman, fifteen miles to the east.

Lawrence advised Allenby against involving Arab forces in the British raid on Amman, but said he would follow up the British incursion by raising a force to occupy the fertile hills around Madaba and Salt immediately afterward. He also seeded an idea—born out of his growing disillusionment with the Arabs—that the Imperial Camel Corps, a 300-strong unit of camel-mounted troops, might be used to attack Dara when Allenby restarted his advance into northern Palestine. Then he left, via Jerusalem, for Cairo and Aqaba.

There was one more task for Lawrence before he could return to Aqaba to prepare for operations. Clayton's concern about his health, the importance of having a replacement ready should he be killed, and the need for someone to manage the Arabs' supplies between Aqaba and Quwayrah meant that Lawrence was looking for a recruit to the campaign. Back in Cairo he went straight to the Arab Bureau's offices at the Savoy Hotel to meet the man he had recommended.

"I had heard vaguely of Lawrence's capture of Aqaba, and of his success with the Sharifian forces, but I did not know for certain that it was he who had sent for me," Hubert Young later recalled. "It was not until

. . . the door opened to admit the familiar little figure, that I was enlightened."[10]

"They asked me to suggest someone who could take my place in case anything happened to me," Lawrence said, smiling mischievously, "and I told them I thought no one could. As they pressed me, I said I could only think of Gertrude Bell and yourself, and they seemed to think you would be better for this participatory job than she would. It is quite amusing, and there is plenty of honour and glory to be picked up without any great difficulty."[11]

Three years older than Lawrence, Young had been meandering home to India through the Middle East before the war when he first met Lawrence, who was working on an archaeological dig at Carchemish, on the Euphrates in eastern Syria. "I have seldom enjoyed a week more than that week of Carchemish," Young declared in his memoirs, remembering drinking coffee from recently excavated Hittite cups and practicing shooting at a matchbox from thirty yards.[12]

Lawrence hoped that Young would be "the right sort of man," he wrote to his mother: "the work is curious and demands a sort of twisted tact, which many people do not seem to possess. We are very short-handed, and it will make things much easier if he fits in well."[13] This was to prove a strange misjudgment, for Young had no tact whatsoever, twisted or otherwise. During the voyage to Aqaba, Young and Lawrence "clashed incessantly," according to Kirkbride, who was aboard the same ship.[14] It may even have been that the wrong Young was sent to Cairo. Lawrence had originally approached Cyril Wilson's assistant, J. W. A. Young, midway through 1917, asking him to join the campaign.[15]

From Aqaba, Dawnay, Lawrence, and Young drove north up Wadi Itm, through Quwayrah, and, occasionally having to get out and push the car, up the steep hill to Abu al Assal on the Arabs' bitterly cold front line. It was raining hard when they arrived, so the three British officers and the Arab commander, Jafar Pasha, ducked into Feisal's tent to discuss the next stage of the campaign. Feisal was already there, twiddling a set of amber worry beads. He looked like "some beautiful thoroughbred quivering at the starting-gate," thought Young.[16] The middle of the tent was uncarpeted and littered with cigarette butts—evidence of the argumentative discussions that often lasted late into the night.

Sitting in a hollow circle on mud-encrusted rugs, with rain pattering on the canvas of the tent, Feisal and the British and Arab officers reviewed the situation. Lawrence soothed Feisal's fears that the Turks were advancing toward Tafilah once more. He explained that, with the British about to attack Amman, and the Arabs Maan, the Turks would quickly be forced to withdraw from Tafilah, where they would be surrounded. But the assault on Maan was easier said than done: "We lacked the means for an immediate frontal attack on the town as we were threatened on both flanks," Jafar Pasha remembered.[17] So, inside the tent, the officers agreed that the Arabs would first cut the railway twenty miles north and south of Maan. To create a further diversion, the British also decided to launch a further raid, south of Mudawwarah, using the armored cars. Only then would the main Arab force assault Maan. Satisfied with this arrangement, Dawnay, the liaison officer, headed back to Aqaba.

Joyce, who was coming down with pneumonia, suggested to Young that he take the Indian machine gunners and reconnoiter the railway south of Mudawwarah to ensure that the route was suitable for the heavy armored cars. The reconnaissance proved otherwise. Young described how, having driven seventy miles to Dhat al Hajj station, twenty miles south of Mudawwarah,

> we had only to look across from the top of the hill to see that our armoured car plan was out of the question. All the way from our look-out post to the line were wind-swept billows of bright yellow sand, through which no armoured car could go, and there was nothing for it but to go back and report failure.[18]

The British did not launch their armored-car attack, and the Arab assault on Maan did not happen either. Jafar Pasha vividly remembered how, as he was descending toward the railway south of Maan, "a torrential downpour soaked us to the skin and further progress became impossible. Camels and pack animals were floundering in mud, and our men were so beset that during the night some of them died of exposure to the bitter cold and rain."[19] He had no choice but to turn back. On 20 March, Feisal was forced to admit defeat. Although he was "quite ready to attack," he told his father, he had been thwarted by the "worst weather."[20] Further snow made a renewed attempt impossible.

The British attack on Amman, which set out on 21 March, also rapidly degenerated into a fiasco. The Turks often successfully decoded British radio traffic and appear to have established that a raid on Amman was about to begin; under no pressure from the Arabs at Maan, they were able to move nine hundred men northward to reinforce the town three days before the British began to cross the Jordan. With any element of surprise already lost, the British then took two days to cross the swollen river, giving the Turks more time to prepare to defend Amman.

By the time the British reached the top of the precarious climb to Salt, the German general, Liman von Sanders, who had been given command of all the Ottoman and German forces in Palestine at the end of February, had established through a second intercept that the British camels were slipping in the mud.[21] "Many of them did the splits with their legs splaying out in either direction," remembered one British soldier on the raid. Others went over the side of the mountain path. The conditions were so treacherous that camels that slipped off the mountain path had to be shot where they lay even if not fatally injured by the fall.[22] The attack on Amman finally began a day late owing to the troops' exhaustion on 27 March, under driving, icy rain. The British suffered heavy casualties, for the Turks' machine gunners were well dug in around the town. Having completed some insignificant railway demolitions south of Amman, the British withdrew after dark on 30 March, spurred in their retreat by misleading intelligence they had received that 15,000 Turkish troops were converging on their position. They abandoned their plans to hold Salt and recrossed the Jordan on 2 April, followed by a gaggle of about 5,000 refugees, mostly Christian, who feared Turkish reprisals. More than 1,200 British soldiers were killed or wounded in the operation, the positive impact of which was then clearly inflated. The *Arab Bulletin* reported that over ten miles of track had been destroyed, more than twice the distance that was actually damaged, and Allenby claimed in a letter to the War Office that his forces had withdrawn simply because the capture of Amman station would have involved considerable losses.[23]

Other disturbing news also curtailed Allenby's operations. The same day that he launched the abortive Amman attack, the Germans began their spring offensive on the western front: the gains they made were devastating. After two days Lloyd George telegraphed the British ambassador in Washington, telling him to try to speed up the deployment of American soldiers in Europe by informing President Wilson that "the situation is undoubtedly critical and if America delays now she may be too late."[24] Within two more days the Germans had taken over 45,000 British and French soldiers prisoner. On 27 March the War Office contacted Allenby to tell him that its plans to send him troops from Mesopotamia were canceled and that British troops and heavy artillery would be taken from him for France as soon as shipping became available. "You will adopt a policy of active defence in Palestine as soon as the operations you are now undertaking are completed," Allenby was told.[25]

In March, Dawnay returned to Aqaba to replace Joyce, whose pneumonia required treatment in Cairo. No amount of staff college training could equip this conscientious officer for life with the Arabs, which was rarely dull. The officers liked Scotch whisky and playing poker for gold sovereigns. There were "incidents when faces got slapped, with those involved reaching for their pistols," Kirkbride remembered, "but they went for their guns slowly enough for bystanders to be able to intervene and induce the combatants to embrace and make friends again."[26]

The charged atmosphere reflected the fact that many of the Arab army's officers were highly political people. Many of them had been associated with the secret nationalist societies formed before the war and now felt that the dream they had of "recreating the wide empire of their forefathers" might now be realized, Kirkbride recalled.[27] They were "not soldiers, but pilgrims, intent always to go a little farther," Lawrence wrote afterward, borrowing a phrase from his late friend the poet James Elroy Flecker.[28] Joyce was not so sympathetic. Before departing to Cairo, he warned Dawnay about the "hopelessly incompetent, ignorant and conceited" Syrians.[29] This uncompromising view probably informed the *Arab Bulletin*'s judgment shortly afterward that the Syrians were "worst in respect of political intriguing" and behind growing "anti-European chauvinism" believed to result from "suspicions about secret agreements among the Allies."[30]

Despite the failure of the Arabs' first attempt, the capture of Maan remained their top priority. When Dawnay discovered that the original plans to isolate the Turkish garrison at Maan by first cutting the railway on either side had been abandoned, he blamed "the influence of Nuri [Said] and the anti-British element among the Arab leaders," who wanted to launch a frontal attack on Maan.[31] Lacking the guidance of Lawrence, who advised his colleagues never to disagree publicly with the Arab leaders, Dawnay on 7 April bluntly asked Feisal how he expected to take on a well-armed and defended garrison and, if he succeeded, hold the town without cutting the rails north and south to prevent the arrival of Turkish reinforcements.[32] After a heated discussion lasting over two hours, "Feisal appeared evidently disconcerted and worried," Dawnay observed, believing him to be "more than half convinced of the error of his decision," but as yet "unwilling to recede, fearing the opposition which such a course might provoke among his Arab advisers."[33] At a further meeting the following day, a compromise was eventually agreed: Jafar and Nuri would attack north and south of the railway, respectively, before turning in and jointly attacking the town.

Jafar's and Nuri's raiding parties set out on 11 April, when there was no moon. That night Nuri attacked Ghadir al Hajj, the first station south of Maan, destroying five bridges and about nine hundred yards of track. Forty miles north of Maan, Jafar's dawn attack on the small station at Abu el Jurdhan quickly lost momentum as a hail of Turkish machine-gun fire swept the open plain around. Renowned for his violent temper, Jafar, Young recalled years later, "used to burst out into torrents of bilingual abuse at the smallest provocation."[34] He now decided that the time had come to harangue his men. "This exhortation had the desired effect," Jafar wrote in his memoirs.[35] His men rushed forward to take the station. It was "a dashing attack culminating in a bomb and bayonet charge," Dawnay reported, which forced the wounded Turkish commander to surrender.[36]

Some way to the north Lawrence could see bright flashes in the distance as Jafar's men started their attack on Abu el Jurdhan. He had spent the previous week escorting an enormous caravan of camels carrying rifles to the area southeast of Amman, to arm the Bani Sakhr tribesmen so that they could assist the British attack on Amman. Though he met the Bani Sakhr, when it eventually became clear that the British attack on Amman had failed—an outcome he criticized as "deplorable"—he turned south again. The return journey should have been straightforward, but the party ran into a Turkish patrol. Lawrence was reluctant to fight, but the tribesmen insisted. In the gun battle that followed, his remaining servant, Othman, was fatally shot.

"We tore his clothes away and looked uselessly at the wound," Lawrence recollected. "The bullet had smashed right through him, and his spine seemed injured."[37] Lawrence's other servant, Ali, had died of the cold that winter. It was clear now that Ali's best friend, Othman, had only hours to live.

Even a few hours was too many. Lawrence knew full well the vengeance the Turks would wreak on Othman if they found him alive—"we had seen them mutilate or burn alive our hapless men"—and he knew he had to escape.[38] But before he could, he would have to kill Othman. Kneeling down beside the wounded man, Lawrence kept his pistol out of Othman's eyeshot near the ground, rather as a dentist hides his pliers, and looked into his eyes.

It was Othman who spoke first.

"Ali will be angry with you."

"Salute him from me," Lawrence replied.

"God give you peace," Lawrence remembered Othman saying before he closed his eyes "to make my work easier."[39]

⁕

On 13 April the Arabs combined in an attack on Simna, a knoll west of Maan. The ease with which they captured this outpost encouraged the Arab officers to press on. Two days later they launched an attack on Maan station, slightly east of the town, a drab and dusty outpost at the edge of the encroaching desert. The station—a cluster of cream stone offices, workshops, and train sheds with terra-cotta pantile roofs—was strongly fortified with concrete machine-gun emplacements. Amid fierce fighting on 17 April, Nuri Said reached the station outbuildings, but the French artillery fire on which he was relying for support suddenly petered out. Even years later Nuri felt let down: "I still remember quite vividly that this battery did not do its job and that it fired a few shells only, to determine distance and direction," he complained.[40] In fact, up on the ridge overlooking Maan, the French officer Pisani had simply run out of ammunition. Lawrence, who had returned to watch the battle, found him "wringing his hands in despair." Pisani told

Lawrence that he had begged Nuri not to attack, given he was almost out of shells.[41]

At nightfall the Arabs were forced to withdraw. Over ninety had been killed and a further two hundred wounded. Lawrence would remember, "The eyes of the wounded men, gone all rich with pain, stared accusingly at us as they were carried past. The human control had gone from their broken bodies, and their torn flesh took free play with its own nerves, and shook them helplessly."[42] Of the officers, whose arguments and intrigue had enlivened the wintry camp at Abu al Assal, Jafar estimated that over half had been either killed or wounded.[43] It was the bloodiest setback the Arabs had suffered.

Now that the attack on Maan had started, Dawnay revived the plan to attack the railway farther south at Tell Shahm with the armored cars, the Egyptian camel corps, which Allenby had sent over, and some tribesmen. His crisp organization for the attack came as a shock to the other officers, who were used to often shambolic operations with the tribesmen. "Gun sites, times for aeroplane co-operation, lines of approach for armoured cars, successive positions for the ECC, even the general direction of the Bani Atiyah camel charge were planned out in the utmost detail," remembered Young, who had accompanied Dawnay on the reconnaissance beforehand. Looking down at the oblivious little garrison of the station, he "could not help feeling that it was really not quite fair of Dawnay to make such up-to-date and elaborate plans for their destruction."[44]

Dawnay's plan also worried Lawrence for more serious reasons. He was wary of mixing the Bedu with the Egyptians because, as experience at Rabigh had shown, each hated the other. The Egyptians looked down on the Bedu, but the superiority they felt was not reflected in their salaries. "The most embarrassing thing," the Egyptian camel corps' British commander, Frederick Peake, recalled, "was to see Lawrence pouring golden sovereigns into the hands of the Bedouin while his Arab Egyptian soldiers only had a few piastres added to their meagre pay."[45] On 18 April, Lawrence decided to accompany the party to try to ease the consequences of the mistake he feared Dawnay was making. "I drove into his camp above Tell Shahm after midnight," he recalled, "and offered myself, delicately, as an interpreter."[46]

Dawnay was pleased to see Lawrence. By torchlight he unfolded a piece of paper and explained his detailed plans—"orthodox-sounding things," Lawrence remembered, "with zero timings and a sequence of movements."[47] The armored cars would attack the first Turkish outpost at dawn the following morning, and a second post while the railway was demolished. After further demolitions "while the force lunched," the combined force would attack a third outpost, before a massed assault on the station, which Dawnay calculated would be taken eleven and a half hours after the dawn attack began.[48]

"It was like picking a ripe peach," Lawrence wrote of the operation afterward.[49] In the lull after the capture of the first outpost, to stop reinforcements arriving from Mudawwarah to the south by train, he and Hornby raced down the line, fastening bricks of guncotton to each length of rail and stuffing the drains of the bridges with explosive. A young British machine gunner standing in the turret of one of the Rolls-Royce armored cars remembered how Lawrence "lit the fuses and ran like a hare down the slope and jumped into the seat of the car. Suddenly there was a hell of a bang, then another, another, another, until hundreds of yards of rails were twisted and bent like cheap hairpins. The great span bridge crashed with a terrific roar onto the ground below."[50] From behind the steering wheel of Lawrence's car, Sam Rolls vividly recalled "the screaming of ripped iron, as great pieces of the rails were torn clean out and sent flying and whizzing over the desert."[51] Lawrence made light of the fact that he had narrowly missed being hit by one of these whirling fragments and summed up the day with the words "we enjoyed ourselves."[52] Later that afternoon the Turks at Tell Shahm surrendered, ten minutes ahead of Dawnay's meticulous schedule, and the force rushed toward the station.

It was only when Peake's Egyptian cameleers tried to stop the Bedu from looting that trouble erupted. "A somewhat dangerous situation arose between the Arabs and the Egyptians; serious consequences were, however, averted by skilful handling of the Bedouin by Colonel Lawrence," Dawnay diplomatically reported afterward.[53] Years later, Lawrence put it rather more frankly: "We were all within a hair's breadth of getting scragged," he told his biographer Robert Graves.[54]

According to plan, the raiders then turned south. The Turks had already abandoned the next station south, and so, the following morning, the British armored cars took a wide loop to approach Mudawwarah from the east from out of the rising sun. But the Turks spotted them and began to fire their howitzers, so the cars swerved southward, completing a demolition on the track about four miles farther down the line toward Medina, before turning around and roaring north up the stony plain, past Tell Shahm, to the next station, Wadi Rethem. Relying on the invincibility of the cars again—to small-arms fire at least—Dawnay ordered one car forward to the station, which was then demolished with explosive. Its battered remains can still be seen today among the sands—the color of old mustard—in the very south of Jordan.

Lawrence and Dawnay left immediately for Allenby's headquarters. Lawrence would spend most of May in southern Palestine and Cairo, planning and resting. It was probably because of him that the Tell Shahm raid was briefly reported in the British newspapers, but as an Arab coup. "Hijaz Railway Cut: Arabs occupy 53 mile section," read the headline in the *Times* of 29 April, before reporting an extract of a communiqué from the War Office: "As a result of operations conducted by the Arab troops of the King of Hijaz against the Hijaz Railway during the week ended April 24 a section of the line extending over some 53 miles to the south of Maan has been occupied effectively." Suddenly, the situation appeared to be improving, but that impression would not last.

23

A Complete Muck-Up

"In the last three days nothing has happened to break the monotony," Hubert Young wrote gloomily on 21 April.[1] Promised honor and glory by Lawrence, he had not expected to be relegated to the role of sentry at one of the important wells by Dawnay for the duration of the Tell Shahm attack, for which he had helped prepare. By the time the attack began, Young was bored and furious. "It seemed to me," he later wrote, "that I was falling between two stools, and I was clearly not wanted to understudy Lawrence."[2]

Never a man to suppress his views, Young confronted Dawnay after the Tell Shahm raid. He told Dawnay how bored he was, referring to a time when he had sat for two and a half hours with Lawrence and Feisal, without once being brought into their conversation. And he attacked Dawnay for arriving from Cairo to take over an operation for which he thought he should have been given responsibility. It was only later that he admitted, "The fact was that Dawnay was getting tired of only doing staff work at Cairo and wanted a little fun for himself, and who shall blame him?"[3]

Dawnay agreed that Young should do more. Both he and Lawrence had just been called to see Allenby in Palestine, and, while they were away, he suggested, Young might act as a liaison officer between Nuri Said and some Bani Sakhr tribesmen in an attack on Jurf ad Darawish station designed to maintain the pressure on the Turkish garrison at Maan.

Cramming his pockets with tins of Maconachie—the British army's staple meat-and-vegetable ration—Young set out immediately north-ward with the band of colorful Ageyl bodyguards whom Lawrence had lent him. He met Nuri Said, who revealed that he planned initially to attack a Turkish *karakul*—one of the intermediate camps between sta-tions that the Turks had established along the line—south of Abu el Jurdhan, and complete the destruction of two bridges damaged in the raid on the station led by Jafar Pasha two weeks earlier.

Nuri Said set off at four the following morning, after a delay when his guides failed to arrive. Discovering that all but one of the Turkish soldiers had already fled their trackside outpost for the relative safety of Abu el Jurdhan, the Arabs set fire to the pile of wooden ties being used to support the track over one of the missing bridge arches, and dynamited the other bridge. Young recommended Lawrence's tech-nique of plugging the drainage duct with explosive: an Arab sapper tamped the charge home and lit the fuse. There was a loud crack, and the arch, cut "as clean as a rasher of bacon," slid into the wadi below.[4]

Nuri Said's plans then went awry when the waterhole east of the rail-way where he was relying on finding water turned out to be dry. Young headed east to Jafr to seek help from Auda abu Tayi. But the great raider who had led Lawrence to Aqaba had fallen out with Feisal, and, after a brief and unfruitful meeting, Young returned northwest to Wadi Mushayyish, to gather the Bani Sakhr, whom Lawrence had been busily arming. There one of the tribe's chief sheikhs, Mirzuq, explained that a few days earlier he had sent envoys directly to Allenby to request help in attacking the Turks. Mirzuq was surprised when these messen-gers returned with a letter from Allenby saying that he proposed to cooperate, and an oral message that, in fact, he intended to cross the Jordan and attack Salt again the following day. Mirzuq was frightened by the scale of the reaction his impromptu appeal had generated. Rather than take action, and since Young knew nothing of the British attack, he decided to send a messenger to Abu al Assal to seek confir-mation of Allenby's plans.

The message from Allenby to the Bani Sakhr turned out to be com-pletely accurate. At four-thirty in the morning on 30 April, Allenby launched a hurried second attack across the Jordan. Political pressure, dwindling time, new intelligence, and a hint of desperation had forced him into action. After the initial panic following the beginning of the German offensive, the War Office had wired him to ask whether there was the "possibility of further raids on Hijaz Railway through Madaba or south of Dead Sea" to relieve the pressure on "the Arab situation, which does not appear to be wholly satisfactory," a reference to the Arabs' failure to capture Maan and British concerns that German gains might cause the Arabs to swap sides.[5]

Two other factors added to the pressure on Allenby. As he explained to Sir Henry Wilson, who replaced Robertson as chief of the Imperial General Staff, an important reason for launching the raid was to "deny to the Turks the grain harvest of the Salt-Madaba area."[6] By the time he wrote, on 20 April, the barley and wheat harvests were imminent; both were expected to be good. It was also Allenby's last chance to use some of his best troops, who had been earmarked by the War Office to return to fight in France.

During the course of April, Allenby had to send two divisions—well over thirty thousand men—back to France; under scrutiny the government recalled further units to the western front in May. The smaller Allenby's force became, the greater his reliance on the Arabs to capture Maan and secure his eastern flank. The Arabs' failure to do so caused escalating concern at British headquarters. In theory the safest solution to the problem was to withdraw to a position that would eliminate the possibility of being outflanked by the Turks from the Maan area—but, since this would mean relinquishing Jerusalem, in practice it was unthinkable. Allenby, in any case, believed that it was more secure to advance than to retire, because his line north of Jerusalem between the Jordan and the Mediterranean would be narrower, and because "any retirement would alienate the Arabs and result in disaster."[7] Knowing that he would soon have even fewer troops to defend his position, Allenby saw no way except forward.

These were the circumstances in which the approach from the Bani Sakhr appeared. The dominant tribe in the region east of the Jordan, the Bani Sakhr had raided the Hijaz Railway during the first British assault on Amman and now seemed to be volunteering to cut off the Turkish supply route between Amman and their front line on the Jordan during a further British attack on Salt. The tribesmen's willingness to act corroborated other promising intelligence Allenby had received that the people of Salt were now "prepared to lay down their lives for the Sharif."[8] Convinced that there was a groundswell of support that would help him retake Salt, Allenby decided to act, but could not tell

Lawrence, because he knew that his wireless communications with Aqaba could be intercepted by the Turks. Lawrence had been anticipating a further attack, though not so soon. He did not appreciate the time constraint, because at this stage he had little, if any, news about the German onslaught in France. He later portrayed the raid as an overhasty gambit conceived by Allenby's short and eager chief of staff, Louis Bols, in a "Eureka" moment in the bath.[9]

The Turks had reinforced their front line on the east bank of the Jordan in anticipation of a further British attack, and although the British force—of mainly Australian and New Zealander troops—successfully reoccupied Salt on 1 May, it soon found itself the target of a ferocious Turkish counterattack. By the third, Liman von Sanders had decided that it was time to make an all-out effort to recapture Salt. "In the evening I issued an order to HQ Fourth Army and to the Third Cavalry Division to penetrate into the town from the north by means of a night attack," he recounted afterward.[10]

By chance the German officer who took Liman von Sanders's call that night was Franz von Papen, the future German chancellor. "By this time my nerves were at breaking point," recalled von Papen, who had narrowly evaded being captured by the British, in his memoirs, "and all I got was the shouted order over the telephone, 'If you have not retaken Salt by tomorrow I will have you court-martialed!'"[11] Liman von Sanders had chosen his angle of attack carefully. Worried that if he boxed the British in he would provoke a fight to the death in which his own troops would be defeated, he deliberately allowed his enemy the opportunity to escape south toward the Jordan.

Allenby received none of the help he had expected from the tribesmen of the Bani Sakhr, who might have stopped the Turkish counterattack. Having suffered over fifteen hundred casualties, the British force recrossed the Jordan late on 4 May; in the words of one British soldier, "the second . . . Salt stunt was a complete muck-up."[12]

Not that either the Arabs or Husein heard as much. The "Raid [was] completely successful," the British hurriedly told them, explaining that the objective all along had been to retain "enemy troops on [the] Jordan front so as to arrest movement of Turkish reinforcements to Maan area."[13] Yet now that the British had withdrawn, the Turks were once again free to reinforce Maan, and news of heavy reprisals in Salt, where over seven hundred townspeople were killed by the returning Turkish forces, undermined what willingness there may have been to support the sharif. In truth, the operation—a military failure—was more significant as a political disaster.[14]

Miles to the south Hubert Young was oblivious to what had happened in Salt, though he spent the following days desperately trying to establish when the planned attack on Jurf ad Darawish would now take place. After further to-ing and fro-ing, he established that the Arabs were planning to congregate just west of Jurf five days later. A disagreement between the Arab soldiers and the tribesmen, however, made Nuri Said abandon his plans to capture Jurf. He decided instead to concentrate on a further attack on Abu el Jurdhan to the south, which was planned for the first day of the new Muslim month—a decision that left the timing dependent on the appearance of the new moon. A dispute over when the new month began led to a day's delay, and it was not until 12 May that the assault was launched. Even so, it was, in Young's words, a "brilliant success." Not only did the Arabs take 150 Turks prisoner, but they also managed to destroy the crucial reservoirs at the station.

Young spent the next few days on an unsuccessful quest to track down guns for the Arabs, during which his car broke down and he was forced to hitch a ride in one of the British armored cars operating with the Arab forces. The commander of the car refused to let Young take his valise with him, and deprived of the padding it contained, which he used as a saddle, he then suffered what he delicately termed "internal damage" from riding a camel over the following days. He was forced to watch another attack on Abu el Jurdhan on 17 May from a distance. The Turks rapidly emerged with their hands in the air. Young was lucky to have been incapacitated. The surrender turned out to be a trap: when the Arabs approached the station, they came under heavy machine-gun fire. Almost all of them were killed or wounded, including their Baghdadi commander, Rashid Ali, and the Turks secured the station itself with reinforcements from the north.[15]

❧

The British failure at Salt had significant political consequences, for it increased British and Arab distrust of one another, which the Turks could then exploit. The failure of the Bani Sakhr to support Allenby during the assault undoubtedly strengthened his existing doubts about the Arabs. Nor was he the only one to wonder about their loyalty. "I'm afraid the Arabs can't be relied upon to any great extent until they are quite certain our side is going to win," Wingate wrote to Allenby in the aftermath of the Salt debacle.[16] Another officer in the Arab Bureau warned that the Arabs' support for the British was waning: German gains on the western front, he suggested, were "causing them furiously to think."[17]

In the circumstances the Turkish commander Mehmed Jemal felt confident that he might yet win the Arabs over simply by offering Husein autonomy in the Hijaz.[18] On 3 May, he wrote—from Salt—to Feisal, offering to open talks in four days' time. "I feel sure we shall be able to fulfill the wishes of all Arabs," he added as a postscript.[19]

When Mehmed's former colleague the governor of Syria, Jemal Pasha, had contacted Feisal late in 1917, Lawrence claimed afterward, he had secretly encouraged Feisal to reply with exorbitant demands. Jemal's objections to these, he calculated, would cause infighting between the Turkish nationalist and pan-Islamic factions within the Young Turk party because the nationalists were willing to countenance an agreement with the Arabs, whereas Jemal—an old-fashioned pan-Islamist—was not. This time, on 10 May, without consulting Lawrence, who spent much of May at Allenby's headquarters and in Cairo, Feisal replied to Mehmed Jemal with a number of demands.[20] The Ottomans should withdraw all their forces deployed down the Hijaz Railway, and in Medina, to Amman. Arab officers serving in the Ottoman army should be freed to serve in the Arab army, which might in the future fight side by side with the Turks, but under Arab command. Syria's future relations with Turkey, he said, should be along the same lines as the close alliance between Prussia and Austro-Hungary. Finally, food in Syria should be placed under the control of the Arab army.

It is difficult to assess how seriously Feisal made these demands, which were certainly steep and which Mehmed Jemal unsurprisingly rejected. But the Turkish overture came at a point when British relations with Sharif Husein were under strain. The situation was not helped by the fact that Cyril Wilson had been absent from Jeddah for almost half of 1918. He had been struck down by a bad attack of dysentery the previous December, and would spend nearly six months recuperating in Cairo. Husein missed Wilson. "He evidently likes Wilson very much and trusts him," reported another British officer, who believed that Wilson's "transparent honesty and shall we whisper stupidity avail where another man's cleverness would fail."[21]

Wilson's replacement, J. R. Bassett, was a rather different quantity. By May 1918 he was engaged in a dispute with Husein after the British asked the sharif's family to use British ciphers in their communications with one another. Husein was suspicious. "Believe me, my dear lord," Bassett wrote to him, "this suggestion was made only to facilitate matters because messages can be put into our cipher in very much fewer groups of figures than is the case in Your Highness's own cipher."[22] British faith in the security of their own communications had been dented earlier that year by the discovery that the Turks in Maan possessed a foreknowledge of Arab movements verging on the clairvoyant. Besides wanting the sharif to swap to more sophisticated British codes, the British also wanted easy access to the traffic between the sharif and his sons, because relations between them were increasingly uneasy. Bassett had already managed to spike a bad-tempered telegram from Husein to Feisal late in April, but the floral language used by the sharif and the unwieldy Arab cipher created a lot of extra work.

Some of Husein's irritable messages got through. Early in May, Feisal was stung by an accusation made by his father that he was wasting money on the Bakri family, prominent Damascus nationalists. The source of this information had in fact been Hogarth, who had remarked to Husein during his January visit to Jeddah—no doubt as a result of Lawrence's own suspicions about Nesib al Bakri during his journey to Aqaba the previous summer—that he thought that spending money on the Bakris was unwise. When Feisal met Joyce and Wilson, who had both now recuperated, at Abu al Assal on 13 May, he raised his father's complaint and said that he had wanted to travel south to the Hijaz to clear the matter up. Husein, however, refused. In a shrill message Bassett forwarded to Aqaba on 8 May, he told Feisal to "die at Maan or capture it," before he would countenance seeing him.[23] With relations between the sharif and Feisal at a new low, Wilson hurried on to Jeddah, promising Feisal he would do his best to persuade the sharif to change his mind.

The British attitude toward Husein had evolved noticeably during Wilson's absence. British officials in Cairo were increasingly critical of Husein. His determination to rule by means of sharia law alienated the more liberal Syrians, while his reliance on a few Hijazi officials, which stemmed from his reluctance to confer power to either Iraqi or Syrian Arabs, led to bad government and further eroded support for him in and beyond the Hijaz. Poor government—which Husein's son Abdullah acknowledged was due partly to the incompatibility of the sharia with modern life—was an ominous advertisement for the Arab state Husein wanted to rule.

On 27 May, Wilson met Husein for the first time that year, in Jeddah. He was touched when, to save his having to climb the stairs, the sharif met him halfway down the house where he was staying, rather than in the airy rooftop chamber where he would usually conduct meetings. "For the most part of the interview the King had an arm round my shoulders, which attitude though affectionate made one rather warm," reported Wilson.[24]

Meetings with Husein, according to Hogarth, involved "inevitable endless preambles and recapitulations before we could get to business," and it was only when Wilson met Husein again the following day that he raised the question of whether the sharif would meet Feisal.[25] When Husein replied that it was an inevitable consequence of war that fathers did not see their sons, Wilson interrupted and asked Husein bluntly why he would not see Feisal. Husein admitted that his real concern was that his son's return to the Hijaz might be interpreted as a sign that he had been defeated. Wilson explained that Feisal wanted to return home to tell his father about his plans and how Ottoman territory would be ruled after the war, and begged Husein to reconsider his decision. Husein relented. Feisal could come home, he said, so long as he returned before the beginning of Ramadan, on 7 June. That afternoon Wilson sent a telegram to Joyce, telling him that Feisal needed to go to Jeddah within the next ten days.

What Wilson did not know was that the British had just agreed to a meeting between Feisal and Chaim Weizmann. Weizmann had arrived in Cairo early in April at the head of a Zionist commission paving the way for Jewish immigration after the war. With his insistence that he wanted not a Jewish government but simply "to provide a home for the Jews in the Holy Land," he greatly impressed the British officers.[26] Even Clayton was positive. "I feel convinced," he wrote to Sykes after meeting Weizmann, "that many of the difficulties which we have encountered owing to the mutual distrust and suspicion between Arabs and Jews will now disappear."[27]

Syrian representatives whom Clayton had met days earlier also seemed amenable to the British government's line that, to realize their own ambitions, the Arabs should support Zionist aspirations too. Though he was adamant that he could not "conscientiously carry out any line of policy which will go against our pledges to the Arabs," Clayton now felt that a rapprochement was possible, "provided we go very easy and don't scare the Arabs."[28] That was the hope behind the British decision to introduce Weizmann to Feisal. "From what I gathered of the Zionist aims, in rather a short conversation, I think there should be no difficulty in establishing a friendly and sympathetic relation between them," Dawnay told Joyce, explaining that Weizmann would soon be on his way.[29]

Wilson was furious when he belatedly found out that Feisal was meeting Weizmann. He had only just persuaded the sharif to write to Feisal to explain that he had never accused him of wasting money, and he now feared that Husein would explode when he found out that Feisal appeared to be negotiating with the Zionists without his prior approval. The matter was so sensitive that the Arab Bureau asked Wilson simply not to tell Husein about what was going on. When he met Husein again on 31 May, two days later, Wilson told Husein that there was no possibility that Feisal could come before the start of Ramadan, because of military plans.

By now something else was bothering Husein. "The King then suddenly began to talk about his title of 'King of the Hijaz' and about his Government being called the Hijaz Government in official correspondence," Wilson reported.

"Why could not it be called the Arab Government?" Husein asked.

The question startled Wilson. "I have no idea what made King Husein suddenly open this subject which he has never before discussed at any great length with me," he wrote to Wingate afterward.[30] He told Husein that the British government could not recognize an Arab government with Husein at its head, unless he was supported by the other Arab chiefs.

It was only when Wilson met Husein again, on 1 June, that slowly the causes of Husein's anxiety began to emerge. In a three-hour meeting that evening, Husein rehearsed the story of his correspondence with Kitchener and McMahon, claiming that, from Kitchener's first tentative communication, in October 1914, he had understood the

British to be in favor of restoring an Arab caliphate. Yet his title, king of the Hijaz, was meaningless, he complained, before threatening to resign. It was a threat he would use repeatedly in the months ahead, for he was well aware of the importance of his support to the British and hoped that he could use it to pursue his ambition to rule the whole of Arabia. "I have never deceived you or His Majesty's Government and never will," Husein said, predicting that if no single ruler of Arabia emerged, the consequences would be "very bad indeed."[31] When Wilson asked what he would do if the other Arab chiefs did not recognize him, Husein said that he would force them to join a united Arabia. It was a heavy hint that he was prepared to fight Ibn Saud.

British officials had already noticed that Husein was diverting an increasing proportion of the British subsidy toward staving off the threat of Ibn Saud, but Husein's suggestion that he was willing to risk armed conflict with his eastern rival was a deeply worrying development, as it raised the possibility that Feisal might go home to help his father, leaving Allenby's eastern flank exposed.[32] The most likely flashpoint that would turn the tension into war was Khurma, an oasis 120 miles east of Mecca. Ibn Saud had accepted Husein's overlordship of this contested part of inner Arabia eight years earlier, but Husein had now heard that Ibn Saud had begun to tax the Utaybah tribesmen in the area, and the sheikh of the village had just announced that he had converted to Ibn Saud's Wahhabi creed. He raised the status of the village with Wilson on 28 May. Faced with a clear challenge to his authority, Husein was blunt. He now wanted a definite answer as to whether the British government still wanted him "to maintain his present noncommittal and friendly attitude towards Ibn Saud."[33]

On 5 June, Wilson wrote to Wingate. He reminded him how, six months earlier, Hogarth had told Husein that Britain and France were "determined that the Arab Race shall be given full opportunity of once again forming a nation in the world." The time was drawing near, he felt, when Britain would have to decide whether to back Husein or Ibn Saud. It seems he was under no illusions that Ibn Saud was the stronger of the two: "If our policy is now to aim at the formation of an Arab Confederation under King Husein's Suzerainty," he said, "we must be prepared for the possibility of a situation developing which would probably prove to be a serious embarrassment to his Majesty's Government."[34] Violence flared at Khurma within weeks. For four years the British tried to prevent a full-scale conflict between their two allies before they grew tired of Husein's intransigence and let events take their natural course.

Feisal had met Weizmann the previous day, at Waheida, just north of Abu al Assal. When Weizmann explained that he had been sent by the British government to discuss the development of the Jewish interests in Palestine, Feisal, though polite, was stubborn. He was, he explained, acting as his father's agent and so unable to discuss the settlement of Palestine in detail and not, in any case, until Arab affairs were "more consolidated." Weizmann went on to say that the creation of a "Jewish Palestine would be helpful to the development of an Arab Kingdom," which the Jews would support.[35] He reiterated that the Jews did not want their own government, but rather to work under British protection. The *Arab Bulletin* put an optimistic gloss on the forty-five-minute encounter. "Some mutual esteem" had been produced, its correspondent claimed, which might help "when the time for bargaining comes."[36]

24

Preparing for the Push

On 28 May 1918 a junior German officer named Lieutenant Thalacker took charge of the Hijaz Railway station at Amman. When he arrived, the station was the target of frequent British air raids. From British records we know that the station was bombed three days after Thalacker arrived, and again eleven days later. Thirteen airplanes took part in that raid, dropping 2,100 pounds of bombs. The pilots claimed twelve direct hits.[1] "The bombs possessed highly sensitive percussion fuses," Thalacker reported, "and, with their splintering effect, almost always led to the loss of lives."[2] The raids on the station, the nearest major depot to the town of Salt, convinced the local Turkish commander that the British were planning to launch another attack across the Jordan shortly. Thalacker's orders were to ensure that, amid the mounting chaos, the trains on the railway ran on time.

What Lieutenant Thalacker discovered on his arrival disturbed his orderly, Germanic mind. While north of Amman the trains ran on schedule, the situation south of Amman could not have been more different. By the end of May only a shuttle service operated between Amman and Al Hasa, seventy-five miles to the south. The frequency of attacks on the railway beyond Al Hasa had made it impossible to travel any farther south by train. Twenty-five bridges were destroyed in Arab raids, orchestrated by Young, Peake, and Hornby, during 1–19 May. "The continued blowing up of bridges and rails was sensibly felt," the German general Liman von Sanders remarked after the war, "because repair material was becoming scarce."[3]

The intensity of the railway raids was not the only problem. An acute shortage of fuel meant that fewer trains ran, at slower speeds. Coal stocks were largely exhausted, and enormous quantities of timber were needed to run the steam engines: a locomotive burned as much as fifteen tons a day. Wood had to be brought in from farther and farther afield, partly as local supplies were felled, partly because the woodcutters were deserting, terrified by the British bombing raids. By the end of the war, olive groves and vineyards were being cut down to keep the trains running.

Water shortages were also a problem. On the 160-mile stretch from Dara south to Al Hasa, there was abundant water only at Amman. South of Amman, Arab attacks and drought meant that the available water was not enough to meet the needs of the troops stationed along the line, let alone the locomotives. The impact of these shortages on the Ottoman army's effectiveness was profound. Between May and August that year, the amount of freight carried by rail fell by two-thirds.[4]

Besides missing bridges and inadequate supplies of fuel and water, there was a further obstacle to a punctual timetable. "Never have I seen such a loathsome crew of debauched, brutalized scoundrels as the permanent staff of the Hijaz railway," Mark Sykes had written following his visit to the region before the war.[5] At around the same time a French archaeologist watched the driver and mechanic of his train polish off a bottle of the fiery aniseed spirit arak in a little over three-quarters of an hour at a halt on the way down to Madain Salih.[6] In Syria the local governor punished miscreants by setting them to work on the track south of Dara. The legacy of this draconian sentencing policy, Thalacker observed, was that the farther south one went, the more unreliable the railway staff became. Trains traveling south would become progressively more delayed because, following the need for tighter security after the increase in Arab attacks, each station telegraphed the next station down the line to let it know a train was on its way. No train was allowed to depart until an answer from that station was received, sometimes hours later, confirming that the line ahead was safe. Dependent on staff whose main characteristic, according to Thalacker, was their "lack of punctuality and interest," this safeguard meant that idling locomotives frequently ran out of steam before they received clearance to continue on their way.

Battling Turkish resistance, Thalacker managed to make some

changes. "Delays which were up to 10 hours could now be reduced to 1–2 hours," he reported proudly. He successfully supervised the delivery of enough water down the line that July to supply a force of three thousand Turkish troops and their pack animals at Qatranah, fifty miles south of Amman, which was being prepared to deal with the Arabs.

Lawrence, who had spent much of May in Cairo and at Allenby's headquarters in Palestine, knew that the continuing Turkish presence at Qatranah threatened the Arabs farther south and Allenby's eastern flank. Allenby shared his fear. Having failed to capture the farming uplands east of the Jordan in time for that year's harvest, he now warned the new chief of the Imperial General Staff, Sir Henry Wilson, that, with replenished supplies, the Turks might now advance southward from Amman. If they recaptured the Dead Sea area, Allenby warned, they would recapture the Hijaz because he believed Husein, who was worried about Ibn Saud, would sue for peace. He feared the reverberations that such a truce would cause in an increasingly unstable Egypt: "Whatever strategical purists may say about side shows, you are committed deeply here," he warned Wilson in mid-June: "and if you lose Egypt, you lose the Empire which hinges thereon."[7]

The reason for this dire warning was that Allenby was deeply concerned about the political situation in Egypt and, in particular, about the enemy propaganda that was circulating, which was designed to exploit the tension between the British and their Egyptian Muslim subjects and the fault line between British and Indian troops within Allenby's army. "It is fairly believed, by the majority in Egypt, that the English and French are beaten in Europe; and that those of our troops who are not removed from Egypt in time, will be made prisoners here at the end of the war," Allenby reported that June.[8] According to the rumors, Allenby would leave behind his Indian troops: they were to be sacrificed to cover his evacuation. And on the front line the Ottoman army's muezzins would loudly proclaim the call to prayer in the direction of the British, to remind those Muslim soldiers in Allenby's army of their divided loyalty, to empire and their faith.

There was disconcerting confirmation that Turkish propaganda was working when a handful of Muslim Indian soldiers defected to the Turks that June. Allenby immediately withdrew the other members of their unit to work behind the front line, but he continued to worry because he knew that in the future he would depend increasingly on

Indian troops, more than a quarter of whom were Muslims. During Lawrence's stay, Allenby had been digesting news that he would have to send back a total of sixty thousand British troops to fight in France. Just one trained, "all white" division would be untouched. Nine out of twelve battalions in each of the other six were recalled to France. The War Office promised that these would be replaced, but with Indian troops whose training and battlefield experience Allenby felt was considerably weaker and who, he feared, were vulnerable to Turkish subversion. Deeply opposed to the changeover, Allenby pleaded to Sir Henry Wilson, "I cannot urge you too strongly; not to carry out this project, in this country, at this time."[9] He was ignored.

Indeed, Allenby was under relentless political pressure to make further territorial gains. As had long been anticipated, the Russians had made peace with the Germans in March that year. Shortly afterward Sir Henry Wilson's predecessor Robertson had raised the need "to establish a barrier to German progress eastwards" through a combination of Japanese intervention in Siberia, continued pressure on the Palestine and Mesopotamia fronts, and support for anti-Bolshevik forces in the Caucasus.[10] Sir Henry Wilson's ambitions were grander still: "I want to see Aleppo joined to Mosul joined to Baku joined to the Urals joined to the Japanese army; and from that base an advance against the Boches," he told Allenby late in May, desperate for pressure on the Germans' eastern front that would curb their seemingly relentless westward advance.[11] There was no way that Allenby could press forward during high summer, but, to meet the demand for rapid headway northward as soon as the hot season had passed, he disbanded the Imperial Camel Corps and increased the number of mounted divisions from three to four.[12]

Having heard about this reorganization, at headquarters one evening over dinner, Lawrence asked Allenby for two thousand camels.

"What do you want them for?" asked Allenby.

"To put a thousand men into Dara any day you please," Lawrence boldly told "The Bull," who rapidly agreed.[13]

In *Seven Pillars of Wisdom* Lawrence outlined the plan he had conceived and put to Allenby. By attacking Dara, he hoped to force the Turks to pull one or even two divisions back from Palestine to secure their line of communications and attack the Arabs at Azraq. This would enable Allenby to press forward and capture Nablus, thirty miles north of Jerusalem. The possession of Nablus, Lawrence believed, would make Salt a dangerous salient, which Mehmed Jemal, the commander of Turkish forces east of the Jordan, would be reluctant to defend. He would be forced to retire to Amman, where his forces would be cut off from Damascus by Arab demolitions on the railway around Dara.

Allenby liked the idea of an Arab raid on Dara, which he thought would help deceive Liman von Sanders into thinking he would attack across the Jordan again. He "quite realizes now that the proposition must be regarded in the light of a gamble," Dawnay explained to Joyce, "and, as a gamble, he is prepared to take it on, so that we can now set to work, and do what we can, with easy consciences."[14]

The problem with the plan was time. It would take about a month to ferry the camels to Aqaba, and a further two to change their diet. In Palestine the camels were fed on barley, and Lawrence knew that to survive on the steppe in Syria, they would have to learn to graze on thorny scrub. While they did so, and while to the west, Allenby prepared to advance, the Arabs would need to keep the Turks in Qatranah at bay and the garrison in Maan isolated by maintaining operations against the railway. These demands dominated the next three months.

At dawn on 23 May, Sharif Nasir's tribesmen, with Peake and Hornby, attacked Al Hasa station, 45 miles north of Maan, and destroyed 4 miles of track, the points, and the station's well and water tower, which provided the only year-round water supply between Amman and Maan stations, 150 miles apart.[15] The following day Nasir moved on and attacked Faraifra, a halt on the line a few miles to the north. While Lawrence ventured into the Madaba area south of Salt to gauge local support for his planned September advance northward, early in June Hornby attacked the bridges north of Faraifra. By now both Hornby and Peake were desperately short of food and explosives. "I am sick with those blasted Bedouin pinching all your rations," Joyce wrote to Hornby on 2 June, in a letter accompanying three tins of Nestlé milk and a packet of tea, in which he urged Hornby to keep going for just a little longer. "If we keep the line cut North I think we must get Maan," he added, promising Hornby a "liberal ration of rum" as soon as he could send it.[16] He had, he admitted, already sent Peake all the cigarettes he could lay his hands on. Peake probably needed them more: on one raid he had escaped being captured by the Turks only by hanging on to the tail of the horse of one of his Arab helpers, and being pulled for half a mile.[17]

With the railway south of Amman effectively wrecked as a result of Hornby's and Peake's exploits, the Arabs now turned their attention to inflicting a decisive blow against Jurf ad Darawish station, where four hundred Turks continued to hold out.[18] Dawnay wrote to Joyce on 12 June, willing the Jurf raid to be a success. The removal of the Turks there, he said, would "very usefully extend our elbow room for future dirty work north of Maan, and it will also add greatly to our own security by compelling the Turk to make his own base, for any operations he may undertake for the relief of Maan, at a respectable distance."[19]

Dawnay had also spent some time reconsidering the question of which British officers should be attached to the Arab forces. Following his run-in with Young, he decided that Young's "present nominal position as understudy to Lawrence has never . . . really panned out entirely satisfactorily, and I am not sure, taking the personal factor into account, that it is ever likely to."[20] Instead, he proposed making Young responsible for the logistics that would now be critical to the Arabs' push north to Dara. At the same time he advocated swapping Maynard, an officer who had been working on demolitions south of Maan, for Frank Stirling. Stirling was a bon vivant on the prewar Cairo social circuit who spoke Arabic and had since worked in intelligence, from where he had followed Lawrence's rise to prominence closely. Earnestly wanting a more exciting job himself, earlier that year he had hosted an extravagant party aboard a houseboat on the Nile with champagne and dancing—which were restricted in Cairo's hotels—until four o'clock in the morning: among his guests were Alan Dawnay and his wife.[21] This memorable hospitality now paid off. Stirling "would be just the fellow to send off stunting with the circus," Dawnay believed, which would free Joyce to concentrate on managing "the whole show" and Lawrence—as ever the loose cannon—to run "his peculiar brand of Lawrentian stunt and carrying on as usual." Joyce was reluctant to lose Maynard, but agreed with Dawnay's suggestion for Young, who, he said, had "put everyone's back up in Aqaba."[22] Young was to play an important, but unglamorous, organizational role for the remainder of the campaign.

❧

Lawrence's clandestine tour through the settled communities in the hills east of the Jordan to gauge their support for Feisal was not encouraging. Likely drawing on his impressions, the *Arab Bulletin* on 11 June reported that, discouraged by the failure of the two raids east of the Jordan, "most of the tribesmen, who own lands, have been compelled to patch up a peace with the Turks and hold their hand till better times."[23] Feisal's failure to attract the people of the settled areas to join the revolt reflected the fundamental rift between the rapacious nomads' and order-loving settled people's ways of life—the desert and the sown—on which his father Husein's dream of an Arabian kingdom that would combine the two was already foundering. It was a difference mirrored within his army: Nuri Said's attack on Jurf ad Darawish, which took place on 10 June, was again handicapped by rivalry between his mixed force of Arab volunteers and Bedu tribesmen. The attack degenerated into an inconclusive artillery duel with the Turks from which Nuri was forced to withdraw.

After further reflection, from Cairo—where he went after his journey through the Jordan uplands—Lawrence wrote a gloomy, longer account. The two Abu Tayi sheikhs, Auda and Mohammed al Dheilan, he reported, had fallen out. Their Huwaytat tribesmen were tired of fighting and rich enough from British gold to be averse to taking further risks.[24] Auda himself had decided that he, too, was a sharif and had begun building a mud-brick palace at Jafr, roofed with telegraph poles from the railway line. The Huwaytat's rivals the Bani Atiyah from the south of Maan were similarly exhausted, and would shortly be retired. To the north the Bani Sakhr, who had let down the British in the second attack on Salt, though not sympathetic to the Turks, were still taking payment from them. They were demanding £30,000 a month from Feisal in return for that year's barley crop, a sum that Feisal simply could not afford. The Rwala sheikh Nuri Shaalan appeared to be profiting from illicit trade between Kuwait and Damascus and showed no signs of warming more to Feisal. Winning the support of Shaalan, the most powerful tribal chief in the region, remained critical, since Lawrence's Dara raid involved crossing his territory. There were also unwelcome signs of sectarianism. In the largely Christian town of Madaba, twenty miles southwest of Amman, Lawrence discovered there had been celebrations at the news that the inhabitants of Salt had been violently punished by the Turks following the British withdrawal. The only way to raise the agricultural communities east of the Jordan, he decided, was to send a force of several thousand Arabs to help them, once Allenby's advance began.

Further work was also needed to reassure several influential Syrians who had approached the Arab Bureau in Cairo with concerns about the future status of their country, by which they meant not just modern Syria but Palestine as well. Relations were tense, for as Hogarth had commented three months earlier, "Nothing hampers so greatly our local relations with the existing non-Jewish inhabitants of Palestine, as the vagueness of our declaration in favour of Zionism."[25]

Following several days of secretive discussions, on 16 June, Lawrence, Hogarth, and Wingate offered the Syrians a commitment from the British government, which they hoped would address their apprehensions. The Declaration to the Seven Arabs, as the document became known, recognized four types of territory in the region and set out British policy on each. The declaration committed the British government to recognize the "complete and sovereign independence" of, first, territories that had been in Arab hands before the war and, second, those that had been liberated by the Arabs since. These two types included much of the interior of Arabia over which the Ottomans had no control even before the war, the Hijaz, and the parts of Arabia north of Aqaba that Arab guerrilla action had forced the Turks to abandon. Third, territory liberated by the Allied armies would be governed according to the "principle of the consent of the governed." This referred to southern Palestine and Mesopotamia, where the British were already in control. This policy, the document declared unequivocally, "will always be that of His Majesty's Government." Fourth, and finally, in territory still under Turkish control, which at that stage still included northern Palestine and much of what is now modern Syria, the British desired that "the oppressed peoples . . . should obtain their freedom and independence," before paying tribute to those engaged in the struggle to liberate those regions and offering them "every support" in their efforts.[26]

On 21 June, Lawrence left for Jeddah in the hope of meeting Sharif Husein. He wanted the sharif's permission to divert some of the Arabs under Abdullah and Ali who were camped around the city of Medina in the Hijaz, to the force he envisaged operating in the settled agricultural belt east of the Jordan. But Husein proved unwilling. Using

Ramadan as his excuse, he refused to leave Mecca to meet Lawrence. All Lawrence could do was write a letter praising Husein's achievements, but obliquely pointing out that Feisal would have to increase his 3,500-strong force by about 7,000 more men if he was to achieve Husein's demand to capture Maan, which was defended by 4,000 well-entrenched Turks. Explaining that the railway south of Maan had now been permanently cut, he tried to encourage Husein to release men from the Hijaz for service farther north. Worried by the rise of Ibn Saud, Husein ignored the hint.

While Lawrence was in Jeddah, exhilarating news arrived from Joyce at Abu al Assal. On 18 June, Turkish airplanes had bombed Nuri Shaalan's camp at Azraq. The bombs caused a few casualties, but the political implications of this mistake were huge. "Situation in North developing rapidly," Joyce's message read, explaining that both Nuri Shaalan and his son had written to Feisal offering their services.[27] Could Lawrence urgently go to Aqaba, Joyce asked, to discuss plans that might require a "large increase in foodstuff and ammunition"?

Dispirited by Husein, whose behavior infuriated him, Lawrence seems to have been strangely ambivalent about this crucial development, for which he and Feisal had been waiting for over eighteen months and which made the risky Dara raid much less likely to fail. He replied that he planned to return to Suez on 6 July and that his plan thereafter was "probably to operate [in] Bani Sakhr country" if Husein continued to block his attempt to draw reinforcements from the Hijaz and the Turks dispatched a relief force to Maan from Qatranah. Even then, he said, he was prepared for a couple of months' delay. In a weary letter to an old friend shortly afterward, he shed light on his mood, suggesting that his increasingly equivocal attitude stemmed from his feeling that what was going on around him was unreal:

> It's a kind of foreign stage on which one plays day and night, in fancy dress, in a strange language, with the price of failure on one's head if the part is not well filled. . . . Whether we are going to win or lose, when we do strike, I cannot ever persuade myself. The whole thing is such a play, and one cannot put conviction into one's day dreams. . . . Achievement, if it comes, will be a great disillusionment, but not great enough to wake one up.[28]

He also described the intense feeling of listlessness that inclined him to be awkward:

> I change my abode every day, and my job every two days, and my language every three days, and still remain always unsatisfied. I hate being in front, and I hate being back and I don't like responsibility, and I don't obey orders. Altogether no good just now. A long quiet like a purge, and then a contemplation and decision of future roads, that is what to look forward to.

Knowing that Hornby and Peake were also exhausted, Joyce was starting to worry that their demolition operations against the railway north of Maan might flag. He was annoyed by Lawrence's languid reply to his urgent call to return to Aqaba and let off steam to Dawnay. He was, he said, annoyed that Dawnay and Lawrence had conceived the Dara raid without involving him at all—although he was in theory in charge of British operations with the Arabs. He was also uncertain whether he would be able to meet the demands of the plan they had concocted with the resources he had to hand.

Jafar Pasha was also becoming restive. He asked the British to supply gas shells in an attempt to end Turkish resistance at Maan more quickly. Dawnay—who had been wounded on the western front—instantly voiced his opposition to the scheme, before predicting that the Turks would only retaliate in kind: "one cylinder let loose on the Arab army unprotected would finish off the whole show for good in half an hour."[29]

Dawnay also belatedly tried to smooth over the situation with Joyce. "You may now feel absolutely assured," he wrote to Joyce, "that in future no scheme or plan will receive official sanction and approval unless and until examined and recommended by yourself."[30] But unexpected events would force him to break this promise within two weeks.

25

Holding Operations

On 13 July, with a mixed German and Turkish force, Liman von Sanders launched a surprise counterattack on Allenby's bridgehead on the east bank of the Jordan, just to the northeast of Jericho. The German general later admitted that the assault, which was beaten off the following day by Australian troops, revealed the decline in the quality of his Turkish forces. But his belligerent move unsettled Dawnay, who feared that if Liman von Sanders were to press an attack of similar strength against the Arabs east of the Jordan, he would annihilate Feisal's force, leaving Allenby's flank exposed and ruining Allenby's plans for an autumn offensive.[1] He began to think urgently about a scheme that would discourage Liman von Sanders from attacking again.

Five days after the German attack was repelled, Frank Stirling landed at Aqaba to join the Arabs' operations. He arrived with a letter for Joyce from Dawnay. "Frankly I am nervous about the next four weeks," Dawnay explained, before gingerly unveiling plans for an ambitious "stunt" using the Imperial Camel Corps to attack Mudawwarah station on the Hijaz Railway and then, 175 miles to the north, demolish the railway viaduct at Kissir, just south of Amman.[2] Having promised just two weeks earlier that he would involve Joyce in any future military planning, Dawnay admitted that the scheme, which he had hurriedly drawn up with Lawrence without consulting Joyce at all, was "simply to keep the Turks occupied on the line and to bridge over the dangerous period till we are ready to set the tribes in motion." The surprise appearance of the Imperial Camel Corps east of the Jordan was designed to force the Turks on the defensive, while the long distance between the two proposed targets would reinforce the impression that more than one British force was scouting the area in advance of an autumn offensive across the Jordan. Interestingly, to ensure that there was no chance that the Turks would receive any prior warning of the attacks, Dawnay asked Joyce not to mention the plans to Feisal, because they feared an Arab spy would pass the information to the enemy.

The urgent need for the Imperial Camel Corps' raid also ran roughshod over the detailed arrangements for Lawrence's raid on Dara, which Hubert Young, now fully recovered from the intimate injury he had acquired from camel riding, had spent the previous two weeks devising. Some of the camels Young had been relying on would now be needed to dump supplies to Azraq for the camel corps. Dawnay tried to soften the impact of the change of plan by advising Joyce to take no action until headquarters had officially approved the scheme, but the telegram from headquarters giving the go-ahead arrived in Aqaba the same day as his letter. "Joyce and I discussed this telegram with some grinding of teeth," Young recalled.[3] It must have been particularly galling to both men. Joyce had just been told, in a throwaway line from Dawnay, "Only the man on the spot can really judge of what the actual situation demands. In that, more power to you—and all good luck."[4] Young had spent days working on a meticulous plan to supply a raiding force of more than 650 men for thirty-five days in the desert, only to watch it be abruptly discarded by Dawnay before it had even been considered at headquarters.

It was up to Lawrence, who flew in to Abu al Assal on 29 July, to give Young's idea the coup de grâce. "Young and Joyce were not best pleased when I returned to say that the great schedule had been torn up," he recalled afterward.[5] Lawrence, however, was able to add the important news that could not be revealed in the telegram: Allenby had just decided to bring forward his offensive into September. Allenby's move was designed to coordinate with a major Allied offensive in France that used fresh American troops, which was to turn the tide of the war against the Germans that August, but it ruined the timescale on which Young's carefully thought-out schedule was based.[6] "This put a different complexion on the matter," Young admitted, "though it did not explain why Joyce had been saddled with the ICC* without having been consulted."[7]

Joyce opposed the appearance of so many white troops in the Arabs' camp at Aqaba, for he worried that they might create tension with the Bedu. Although Lawrence would later snidely remark that Joyce's view was "an untimely victory of my principles so preached from Yanbu," he had himself vetoed Joyce's call for the camel corps a year earlier, and there were good reasons for Joyce's concern.[8] That April a young British soldier had been fatally wounded in Wadi Itm after a dispute with a tribesman over water, and more recently an intelligence officer who had stopped to urinate along the road to Abu al Assal had been stabbed and robbed by a Bedu. Joyce feared that the arrival of the ICC might lead to further casualties. The argument, however, was academic because the ICC had already set out from Suez across the Sinai four days earlier. The following day the 314 men rode into Aqaba on their swift, white Sudanese camels. "As we emerged into the flat Wadi Araba we heard the firing of rifles and wondered if Aqaba was being attacked," one of the ICC's officers recalled. "To our amazement some mounted Arabs galloped towards us on their rough looking ponies, their clothes flying in all directions, greeting us with cries and rifle shots."[9]

Lawrence came to Aqaba from Abu al Assal to meet the men of the ICC and their leader, Robin Buxton. By the time that Lawrence arrived, tension within the camp among the seashore palm groves was already rising—just as Joyce feared it would. Unused to the "rattle of musketry" constant in the Arabs' camp, the soldiers thought they had been shot at while bathing in the sea that afternoon, and, after further gunfire that night, several soldiers had been about to go and deal with the Arabs with some hand grenades when Lawrence suddenly appeared.[10] "He stood in the middle of the square, flung back his aba[†] . . . and, illumined by the countless fires, raised his hand," one soldier remembered. "Immediately the firing ceased, the hubbub died down and we had a peaceful night."[11]

The following evening, "after supper Lawrence gathered the men of the ICC around the fire and gave them the straightest talk I have ever

---

* Imperial Camel Corps.

† A woollen cloak under which Lawrence wore the white wedding robes Feisal had given him.

heard," remembered Frank Stirling, who was accompanying the expedition.[12] According to Stirling, Lawrence told them, with some exaggeration, that they would be going through "a part of Arabia where no white man had set foot since the time of the Crusades." He also explained that, although there was no need to worry about the Bedu, the soldiers should not get between the tribesmen and their loot. To soldiers used to the formal hierarchy of conventional operations, his speech was "a most unusual experience" because only rarely would an officer take his men into his confidence.[13] Early the following morning the ICC left for Mudawwarah on the first leg of their raid to prevent the Arabs from being overwhelmed before Allenby was ready to strike a decisive blow against the Turks.

By 7 August, a scorching day at the height of summer, the ICC was within forty miles of Mudawwarah. During the day some of the officers set out in two cars to reconnoiter the station, crawling up a wadi for the last few hundred yards until they reached a point offering a good view of the Turkish defenses. "We . . . even caught a glimpse of the fat garrison commander as he ambled about on his mule," recalled Stirling.[14] Returning to the ICC camp late that night, the officers briefed the soldiers, and the force set out straightaway. The moon was new, and the ICC was able to approach the station unobserved.

The camel corps' attack began with a noisy diversion west of Mudawwarah in the small hours the following morning that drew Turkish troops away from the station, which was then rapidly captured along with the southernmost of the three fortified outposts guarding the line. By dawn the Turks held out only in the most northerly outpost. They were better defended with artillery and machine guns, and would not be successfully assaulted by the lightly armed raiders alone. The British had allowed for this in their plans, however, and once it was light, aircraft from the Royal Flying Corps appeared from the west to bomb the remaining Turkish position. "I had the job of controlling what must have been one of the first ground-to-air controlled bombardments," claimed Laurence Moore, a signaler with the camel corps. The pilots communicated in Morse code with Moore by blaring a loud horn mounted on their aircraft; Moore replied by arranging large fabric letter signals on the ground in a predetermined code. The biplanes each dropped a couple of bombs in the enemy outpost; "the Turks came streaming out, waving any dirty rag that could serve as a white flag, and I gave the planes the signal 'Cease Fire,'" Moore recalled.[15]

The ICC captured the station and its fortifications at a loss of 6 men dead, and a further 7 wounded, including one of the officers, Joe Lyall, who lost the tip of one thumb to a Turkish bullet that also broke his arm.[16] More than 20 Turks were killed; the remainder, 130 in all, were taken prisoner. Finally, the vital water tower at Mudawwarah was blown up. A copy of a photograph taken in the aftermath, which shows its diced masonry scattered across the desolate valley floor, can be found today among the collection of Lawrence's photographs held at Oxford University, together with his dry caption: "Showing as much of the water tower as could be got into the finder of the camera after Scott-Higgins had finished it."[17] Without this crucial water supply, a railway journey from Maan to Medina was impossible. In Medina, Fakhri was now entirely isolated.

Lawrence had not witnessed the Mudawwarah attack himself. The day before Buxton's men attacked the station, he had flown from Quwayrah to the shimmering mudflat at Jafr for a meeting with Nuri Shaalan to pave the way for the Dara raid the following month. Tested to its limits by the hot summer air, the biplane that was carrying him only narrowly scraped over the Abu al Assal ridge, and for a moment Lawrence wondered whether he might die. He was not looking forward to the encounter, because he faced questioning from Nuri Shaalan on the Sykes-Picot and Balfour agreements, news of both of which had emerged since they had last met at Azraq in June the previous year.

Lawrence was asked the question he expected. "Old Nuri Shaalan, wrinkling his wise nose, returned to me with his file of documents, asking in puzzlement which of them all he might believe."[18]

"The last in date," Lawrence replied, pointing to the Declaration to the Seven Arabs, made in Cairo seven weeks before, which committed the British government to respecting the independence of Arab-liberated territory and self-determination.

Nuri Shaalan's "sense of the honour of his word made him see the humour," Lawrence later wrote. "Ever after he did his best for us, only warning me, whenever he failed in a promise, that he had superseded it by a later intention."[19] The following day Nuri announced his intent to back the Arabs.[20]

"We wanted no rice-converts. Persistently we did refuse to let our abundant and famous gold bring over those not spiritually convinced,"

Lawrence would later claim, flying in the face of all the evidence. For, on top of being bombed by his former allies, the economic grounds for backing the Arab movement were now compelling to Nuri, because the Turks had lost control of trade in the region. The railway raids in May and June had disrupted Turkish influence, and British gold was making Aqaba a magnet for trade to and from the Hauran, the agricultural region east of Dara. By mid-August a German diplomat in Damascus observed, "For about two months an organized caravan traffic has existed from Aqaba across the Hauran. . . . Sugar, coffee and cotton goods are imported, and apricot paste is exported, together with great quantities of grain."[21] The British would buy cereals with gold and could offer goods that had been scarce in Syria for moderate prices. Among the beneficiaries of this traffic was Nuri Shaalan. "Things have got to such a pass," the German noted despairingly, "that it is almost impossible for the Turks to get grain from the Hauran. Only the places on the Western outskirts towards Dara still deliver supplies to us."[22]

৵৶৵

Nuri Shaalan's pledge of support contrasted with the increasingly fraught situation in the Hijaz. Three weeks earlier Husein's dispute with Ibn Saud over the Khurma oasis had looked set to boil over into open warfare, just as the British had feared it would. Husein had arrived in Jeddah on 18 July, demanding to know whether Britain supported his leadership of Arabia. A month earlier Wilson had parried a similar query from Husein, who had wanted to know why the British would not call him king of Arabia. "I personally believe that after this war the world will see some new titles appear and some old titles disappear," Wilson had written ambiguously in reply; "but we must entirely defeat our enemies before such matters can be usefully discussed."[23] Face to face with Husein, Wilson was much blunter. "I told the King," he wrote afterward, "that, so far as I knew, His Majesty's Government, whilst expressing a strong hope and desire for eventual Arab Union, had never guaranteed the formation of an Arab Kingdom under the Kingship or Suzerainty of himself or any other individual."[24] The British, he went on, had approached Husein because he was "accessible" and "renowned" and "well fitted to act as spokesman for the Arabs generally."

This answer was hardly reassuring to Husein, who then threatened to resign again. This situation, already serious, became worse when Wilson discovered that the sharif had dispatched Shakir, the Bedu sharif who had accompanied Lawrence on his first trip to the railway the year before, with a force armed with machine guns to reimpose his authority over the contested oasis at Khurma. Worrying that the Khurma dispute might undermine the Arabs' plans in Syria, Wilson was on 20 July forced to confront Husein about the purpose of Shakir's mission and Husein's willingness to use force.

Husein reacted angrily. According to Wilson, he "said he was sick of the subject, was obstinate in refusing to understand my point and finally lost his temper."[25]

"Am I a fool?" Husein demanded. "I am not a child in politics, and the last thing I want is a state of open hostilities between Ibn Saud and myself." Yet when Wilson suggested he write to Ibn Saud to calm the situation, Husein refused, on the grounds that such an approach would only reduce his own authority in the eyes of his rival, and again offered to resign.[26] Wilson refused to accept his offer, and, following the meeting, on 24 July the British government sent a message to Husein confirming what Wilson had said.[27] Realizing that he could not call on British support to see him recognized as the ruler of all Arabia, Husein four days later yet again submitted his resignation, this time in writing, announcing that he would not do any work not related to his own private affairs.[28]

Wilson's colleague Bassett suspected that the "increasingly nervous and highly-strung" Husein was trying to bluff Britain into backing him, because he knew that the British could not afford to let the Arab movement collapse at such a critical moment.[29] Yet both Bassett and Wilson were well aware that infighting between Husein and Ibn Saud would shatter the illusion of Arab unity, which was so vital to the campaign farther north. An urgent gesture was needed to mollify Husein, who was threatening to withdraw Arab troops from Syria to deal with the situation in Khurma, after Shakir's force was routed by the local tribesmen. Bassett felt that a "definite assurance" from the government that Britain wanted to see a "United Arabia under one supreme Head" would be enough to postpone the friction over Khurma until after the British offensive was under way.

The government in London rapidly obliged. At the beginning of

August, Bassett wrote to Husein, enclosing the text of a declaration that, as he explained, accepted Husein's assurances to Wilson that he simply wanted to restore the situation in Khurma, before warning him not to be distracted by attempts to cause friction with Ibn Saud, since "Turkish influence is probably behind them."[30] Finally, he added, the government could not accept Husein's decision to abdicate on the basis of his "mistaken impression" that he had lost the confidence of the British government when in fact "HMG regard your leadership of the Arab movement in the war as vitally necessary."

"You know, as well as I do, that my operations depend entirely on the cooperation of the Hijaz Arabs," Allenby wrote to Sir Henry Wilson in London on 12 August, commenting on the potential for a shortage of gold to upset his plans. He was just as sensitive to the danger posed by Husein's increasingly belligerent attitude toward Ibn Saud. Having warned Wilson on 14 August that, if further violence flared in Khurma, Ibn Saud would probably give Husein "a hammering" that "might, conceivably, draw Feisal away South; to support his father," Allenby then argued that Britain must openly back Husein and bully Ibn Saud into withdrawing his supporters from the oasis immediately, until the question of the boundary between the men's lands could be settled.[31] The cabinet agreed, accepting that Husein had sent the force "to suppress a rebellious subject," and proposed to arbitrate a frontier between Husein and Ibn Saud after the war was over.[32] Tensions in central Arabia were temporarily papered over.

By this time Lawrence had returned to Jafr to join Buxton's Imperial Camel Corps, which had marched northward after destroying the water supply at Mudawwarah. Buxton confirmed his plan to continue onward to Kissir and arranged for Lawrence to accompany the ICC north into tribal territory. He was already convinced by Lawrence's expertise, writing in his diary, "One has that feeling that things can not go wrong while he is there."[33] Nevertheless, he arrived at Bair to find that half of the rations that Young had arranged had already been pilfered. "Plans had to be quickly revised," wrote Buxton. "I have had to send back one officer and fifty men and a hundred camels as I can't feed them . . . with the remainder we shall make a dash for it."[34] After a second day at Bair—Lawrence's thirtieth birthday—the ICC left for the Kissir viaduct.

Over the next four days the men of the camel corps rode hurriedly north toward the viaduct. They would start at about three or four in the morning, ride until six, stop for two hours, then ride until ten, when they would stop for a long halt during the hottest part of the day, before setting out again at three. During one midday stop Moore, who was sitting under a shelter made from an army blanket, trying to shield himself from the sun, noticed that an armed Arab appeared to be stalking Lawrence, who was sitting under a similar awning, reading.

> The Arab flattened out to take aim and I grabbed for a gun but he beat me to it and fired. The bullet sent up a flurry of sand and feathers about a yard from where Lawrence lay, and the Arab calmly walked forward and picked up the shattered remnants of a small sandgrouse, which he had blown to bits, and carried them away. Lawrence merely raised his head for a moment and then resumed his reading.[35]

On 20 August, as the ICC reached a ruined palace at Muwaqqar, fifteen miles southeast of Amman, they were overflown by two Turkish airplanes. On arrival at the ruins Buxton, Lawrence, and the other officers discussed their options. It seemed likely that the pilots would have identified the soldiers and that the Turks would reinforce Kissir bridge. Arabs who had scouted ahead brought more bad news: Turkish soldiers had arrived in force in the villages between Muwaqqar and the railway to enforce the collection of taxes, which followed each year's harvest. Bedu were also encamped in the area, and Lawrence was concerned that, if the raid went ahead, the tribesmen and their families might become the Turks' target for recriminations, with political consequences that would outweigh the benefits of blowing up the bridge.

Buxton worried that they might be attacked by a large force of cavalry from Amman.[36] The ICC had been lent by Allenby to help the Arabs only on the understanding that, in Lawrence's opinion, the casualties would be "infinitesimal," and Lawrence knew that during a night attack it was inevitable that the force would suffer some, possibly considerable, losses.[37] Reluctantly, they decided to abandon their plan to attack the viaduct and to pull back to Azraq.

One last task remained. "We were to make the Turks aware of our presence and give them the impression that we were a much larger force than in fact we were," recalled Moore. This was to make the Turks assume that significant British activity near Amman was preliminary to a third attack across the Jordan by Allenby.[38] Each man was ordered to open three or four tins of bully beef, eat or burn the contents, and litter the ground with the empty tins. Meanwhile, the cars that accompanied the force drove furiously around the area to leave a muddle of crisscrossing tracks. The cameleers also dropped the animals' dung, which they conserved for fuel, to suggest that there had been many more camels in the vicinity. Then the ICC headed through the darkness east toward Azraq, stopping en route at the ancient Qasr Amrah, where the officers slept under its domed ceilings' frescoes of cavorting, naked women, painted to arouse the Umayyad caliphs thirteen hundred years before.

The following day, 22 August, the ICC arrived at Azraq, but the oasis in midsummer was not as hospitable as Lawrence remembered it. Gray, green-eyed flies with a bite "like the sharp end of a drawing pin" plagued men and camels alike.[39] "Our stay was poisoned by the grey flies, and then ruined by a tragic accident," remembered Lawrence, referring to the moment when Robert Rowan, a young Scottish intelligence officer attached to the ICC, was shot dead.[40] Although Rowan's death was reported as an accident that happened when an Arab dropped his loaded rifle while shooting fish, the signaler Laurence Moore did not agree. "I was close to Rowan at the time and saw and heard him raise his sjambok° and curse them [the Bedu] in what we used to call Cairo Arabic. The Arabs muttered and slunk away and a little later there was a shot from the rim of the crowd which killed him instantly," he later claimed, believing that the real circumstances were covered up for reasons of political expediency.[41]

Accident or not, the ICC left the following morning, heading south toward Bair. By the end of August it had returned to Beersheba. Allenby's great deception plan, of which they were a part, was working. At the end of August a German army officer attached to the Ottoman Eighth Army, which covered the coastal section of the front, concluded, "The general situation leads one to expect that in the event of

° A whip.

not being too pre-occupied on the Western Front, the English will carry out this autumn, like last year, a well-prepared attack, whose strategic objective would be primarily Dara and its political objective Damascus."[42] If, as this assessment seems to imply, its officers thought that the brunt of Allenby's attack would be directed east of its lines, the Eighth Army was in for a terrible surprise. While Allenby made final preparations for his attack, all that was needed was for the Arabs in southern Syria to hold their positions. Yet even that simple ambition was about to be tested, almost to the breaking point. This almost crippling threat would come not from the Turks but from Sharif Husein.

26

The Dara Raid

Far to the south in Mecca, on 19 August the *Qibla* newspaper, which was controlled by Husein, published an unexpected announcement about Jafar Pasha. Jafar, the *Qibla* stated, had never been the commander in chief of Husein's Northern Army. He was "undertaking the supervision of a section of that army and no more."[1]

News of the *Qibla*'s announcement nearly caused the complete collapse of Feisal's army when it became known at Abu al Assal. Though, years later, Jafar airily claimed, "Ranks, titles and appointments had never featured among my ambitions," Alec Kirkbride remembered that at the time Jafar "took deep offence . . . refused to do any work, and spent most of his time in his tent smoking a *nargileh*."[2]

Joyce, who saw translations of every telegram, was "seriously alarmed," according to Kirkbride.[3] The same day that the *Qibla* had been published, he had received a message that the date of Allenby's offensive had again been brought forward and that the Arab raids must take place no later than 16 September. Precise timing for the raid on Dara was crucial. Allenby wanted the Arabs to attack the railway junction three days before the beginning of his own offensive. He hoped that the raid on the railway junction would confirm that the British attack would take place across the Jordan, drawing the Turks in that direction, and away from the Mediterranean coast, where in fact he planned to strike.

The news of the further change of plan was "another fearful shock" to Young because it left his transport arrangements in turmoil yet again.[4] To strike Dara on 16 September, he calculated, the two convoys of baggage camels that were needed to carry supplies to Azraq would have to leave Aqaba on 26 and 28 August—just seven days away.[5] In that short time the political problem created by Husein's announcement in the *Qibla* had to be defused as well.

At Aqaba, while Lawrence and Joyce worked feverishly to undo the damage that Husein had caused, Young hurriedly prepared the supply convoys for their departure to Azraq: "The place was one seething, snarling, sweating mass of camels and Arabs, each as difficult as the other to control," he said, remembering how on the morning of their departure the appearance of two swooping German airplanes temporarily caused chaos.[6]

Young "would have no man hinder him," recalled Lawrence diplomatically.[7] "I am afraid that my eagerness to get things done occasionally offended some of the more sensitive Arab officers," Young acknowledged, before recalling how Nuri Said had once soothed his own officers after they were upset by Young's abrupt treatment of them.[8] "Why worry my dears?" Nuri had asked, before pointing at Joyce and Kirkbride: "He talks to them as he does to us."[9]

On 27 August, while preparing the second convoy, Young realized that he needed ten more camels.

"We know thee not," retorted a tall, black Meccan standing at the head of a small knot of Arabs on the beach in Aqaba, when Young arrived and bluntly explained what he wanted. Young later admitted,

> For the first and I think the last time, I lost control. Having told them all at the top of my voice what I thought of them in the most abusive Arabic I knew, I finished up by spitting almost in the Meccan's face. Funnily enough, this did the trick. The others roared with laughter, hustled the discomfited black man away, and loaded up the camels without more ado.[10]

On 28 August, as planned, a solemn Feisal arrived at the Arab camp at Abu al Assal in his new green motorcar to review his troops before they set out for Azraq. "This advance north is a rather risky venture," he confided to Jafar. "I sincerely hope we may succeed."[11] Past him trooped 450 camel-mounted soldiers, handpicked and led by Jafar's Iraqi chief of staff, Nuri Said, a battery of French mountain guns, three

British armored cars towing tenders full of gasoline cans and other supplies, Peake's Egyptian camel corps, a section of camel-mounted
Gurkhas,° and the bodyguards of Lawrence and his colleague on the
Aqaba march, Sharif Nasir. "They picked their way daintily past him
two by two among the limestone boulders which studded the broad
grass track over the downs," remembered Young. "As each section
saluted Feisal I even felt an absurd lump in my bearded throat at the
greatness of the sight."[12]

Behind the scenes, however, there was uncertainty over whether
the raid would happen at all. When he heard about the report in the
Qibla, Jafar immediately resigned, taking his commanders with him.
Lawrence intervened: "I begged them to pay no heed to the humours
of an old man of seventy, out of the world in Mecca, whose greatness
they themselves had made," he wrote later, though his appeal had no
effect.[13] Pushed by both Iraqi and Syrian factions in his army, who both
resented Husein, Feisal—who had appointed Jafar himself—took
umbrage at his father's intervention and resigned as well on 29 August.
It became clear that Feisal would be satisfied only with an apology
from his father. In a telegram to Cairo the following day, Lawrence
estimated he had just four days to save the situation.[14]

The trouble was that—as Lawrence afterward acknowledged—it
might take weeks to engineer Husein's climb down, and in "three days,
if at all, our expedition to Dara must start."[15] And the likelihood that a
man as patriarchally minded as Husein would relent was growing
smaller. Husein dispatched a telegram to Zeid, describing Feisal as
"rebellious and dishonest" and encouraging him to take command of
the army.[16] With Frank Stirling, Lawrence managed to buy some time
by persuading Nuri Said, who had resigned his commission at the same
time that Jafar did, to set out for Azraq anyway, on the understanding
that he could turn back if there was no apology from Husein. Nuri
Said's force left on 3 September, a day later than planned.

One drastic option remained. Using their knowledge of the Arab
ciphers, Joyce and Lawrence could doctor the angry telegrams traveling back and forth between Husein and Feisal. Lawrence secretly
decoded the incoming messages, and then scrambled the offending
passages and re-encrypted them, before taking them to Feisal. Unable

° Nepalese soldiers who fought (and continue to fight) for the British and Indian armies.

to understand the full text, Feisal would then reply to his father, asking him to resend the telegram.

The result, Lawrence observed, was a gradual détente, as each "fresh version [was] toned down a little from the original harshness."[17] Eventually, "there came a long odd message, whose first half comprised a withdrawal and lame apology of the mischievous proclamation, which the second half repeated in a new and glaring form." Lawrence took the first half, marked it "Very Urgent," and took it into Feisal's tent. Feisal's secretary deciphered the bowdlerized telegram and passed it to his master. Having read it to himself, Feisal glanced suspiciously up at Lawrence, before reading the apology aloud, and announcing that honor had been satisfied.

"The sort of antic cut by King Husein over Jafar ruined any chances he ever had of achieving his ambition to be accepted as King of the Arabs," Kirkbride later wrote.[18] Lawrence himself was incandescent. "It was intolerable," he exploded, "to be at the mercy of so crass a person."[19]

On 5 September, Lawrence left for Azraq by armored car.[20] With him was Lord Winterton, a maverick member of Parliament and an officer in the Imperial Camel Corps who had stayed behind when Buxton returned to Palestine. Tall and thin, with a skeletal face and a love of fox hunting that he had managed to indulge even in the garrison town of Ismailia in Egypt, Winterton was "perhaps the most genuine-looking brigand" of them all.[21] Under a dusty, pale blue sky, Lawrence's Rolls-Royce burned across the dazzling Jafr plain through the streaming mirage to reach Azraq in time for the attack. Rapidly, he began to overtake the Arabs who had set out earlier, passing a stream of men and tribesmen, slowly trekking northward to Azraq.[22] Feisal, who had never really been comfortable in the front line, would follow his supporters up to Azraq some days later, to await events.

Thanks to tarmac, the 180-mile drive to Azraq takes little more than three hours today. Jockeying, hooting gasoline tankers joust along the road, which is scarred black in places where, in head-on collisions, their drivers have met premature, fiery ends. After the flat gray Jafr plain, the road crosses some low hills separating the Jafr basin from the wells at Bair and then climbs gradually toward the three distinct peaks known as the Jabal Thlaithukhwat, before sloping downward, across redder, undulating soil into the bubbling mirage of the Azraq basin.

Lawrence was the first to arrive at Azraq, reaching the ruined castle on 7 September 1918. Three days later two British airplanes, guided by his directions to the mile-long lagoon, landed on a prepared strip at the remote hideout. Then Joyce, with Stirling, Young, and the other armored cars arrived, followed by Peake and his cameleers. The tribesmen—Auda's indigo-cloaked Huwaytat and Nuri Shaalan's Rwala—converged on Azraq from out of the desert. Finally, on the twelfth, the last elements of the Arabs' raiding force arrived. There was no spare time, because of the delays resulting from the uncertainty caused by Husein. The following day the party, 1,000 men in all, set out north for Dara. It was, by contrast to the 10,000-strong "world" that Feisal had led to Wajh the year before, a tiny force. Its impact, however, would prove to be great.

Peake split off to the west, taking his Egyptian camel corps and the Gurkhas to attack the railway south of Mafraq, but his raid was not a success. His own men were tired, and the Gurkhas found camel riding difficult to master and were grumpy for a reason Peake admitted he could not understand. When he arrived at the railway, on the night of the fifteenth, some Bani Sakhr tribesmen who were camped nearby objected to the raid. They had come to an agreement with the Turks not to attack the railway in exchange for water, and did not want to bear the brunt of any Turkish reprisal. Peake was forced to head back toward the main column, which he found at Umtaiye, ten miles northeast of Mafraq and hidden from the railway by a low ridge. This position and a rainwater pool would make Umtaiye the obvious base for operations for the next few days. Lord Winterton had arrived earlier with the armored cars. "We . . . put the cars in a semicircle for defence with the orders 'no lights,'" he remembered.[23] He was unsettled by the Arabs' refusal to follow basic safety drills, though even he was enchanted when Lawrence's Arab escort arrived and lit their fires. Having flitted around the glittering salons of London before the war, Winterton drew on his knowledge of the ballet to describe the Rwala tribesmen who appeared the following morning. "Their blue, brown and saffron cloaks," he believed, "would delight Bakst," a famous set designer of the era.[24]

Peake's failure was a setback. Lawrence knew that he needed to break the railway between Amman and Dara, which would otherwise be used to shuttle Turkish reinforcements rapidly northward to attack the Arabs later. That afternoon—the sixteenth—he took Winterton and Joyce and headed for a stretch of railway north of Mafraq, in the armored cars and tenders packed with guncotton, lurching over the rough ground until they reached a low ridge overlooking the track. While Winterton and Joyce stayed with the tenders on the ridge, Lawrence approached the bridge in one of the armored cars and "took a post of open-mouthed Turks too suddenly for them to realize that we were hostile."[25] He then wrecked the four-arched bridge beside the outpost. It was a perfect demolition, which left the bridge intact but so unsafe that the Turks would have to pull it down before they could start rebuilding.

While the other armored car straddled the track to provide them with cover if the Turks attempted to counterattack, Winterton and Joyce rushed northward up the line to try a devious new demolition technique, which they had christened the "tulip." Each man scraped a hole under the hollow metal tie midway along every pair of rails, placed two fifteen-ounce slabs of guncotton in the space under the tie, ensuring that the charge did not touch the metal, and replaced the ballast before lighting a twelve-inch fuse. The explosion punched each tie about eighteen inches into the air, bending it double into a shape like a tulip bud, and dragging the rails attached to it up, toward each other, and twisting them in opposite directions simultaneously. The three-dimensional distortion, Lawrence noted with satisfaction, was impossible to straighten; the affected lengths of rail had to be cut away and scrapped.[26] Winterton thoroughly enjoyed himself. "We could indulge

A "tulip" exploding on the railway near Dara, September 1918.

in a love of destruction which had lain latent in us since we were small boys," he later reminisced. "We were in fact outside the rules, which is always exhilarating."[27]

Fifteen miles farther south in Amman, at three-fifty that afternoon, Lieutenant Thalacker received the first news of Lawrence's attack. "We were taken by surprise," he later admitted, while the troops stationed nearby, who were supposed to be guarding the bridge, had "simply observed the activity without lifting a finger." Only when the demolitions were complete, he complained, had the railway guards begun shooting.[28] Surprise and the "tulip" technique for wrecking the railway were the two main ingredients of the Arabs' success in the raid.

Nuri Said, meanwhile, was hurrying north toward Dara, leading the bulk of the Arab force. That morning he had agreed with Nasir, Joyce, and Lawrence that he would bypass the town to the east, crossing the embankment of the old railway line to the Roman city of Busra, originally built to collect the grain harvest from the Hauran, and then cross the northern, main line to Damascus and take control of Tell Arar, just to the north of Dara. The tell—one of the area's many distinctive, manmade hills formed by ancient settlements—commanded good views south toward the railway junction. It offered a good base from which Nuri could organize the first attack on the railway running north from Dara, cutting the town off from Damascus, as well as further operations around the railway junction. Nuri was lighthearted and confident. "His great joke," recalled Young, who was with him, "was to offer us what he and his brother officers of the Arab army called 'calories.' These were draughts of a yellow liquid which, to the infidel, smelt and tasted like whisky, but which was by courtesy referred to only as a food value."[29]

By now the Turks were well aware of the Arabs' arrival. When Young and Nuri drank a further "festal calorie" astride the railway line at dawn on 17 September, their celebrations were rudely interrupted by gunfire from the Turkish position on Tell Arar, and they were forced to take cover. After some confusion the Arabs launched a headlong attack against the Turks, capturing the hill with the loss of only one man. Following the Arabs up to the summit, Kirkbride found six dead Turkish soldiers, all of whom had been shot through the head.

Demolitions on the railway below should have begun immediately, but Peake's Egyptians refused to work hungry and sat down to eat in a field of maize beside the railway. One of them had prepared a sumptuous meal for his boss, but breakfast was about to be rudely interrupted.

"I had hardly sat down to my bacon and eggs," Peake recalled, "when Lawrence supercharged with zeal dashed up in his car, and was heard to be asking for the officer in charge." Lawrence had driven overnight from the bridge he had wrecked to catch up with the Arabs, and arrived at Tell Arar that morning. "I wanted the whole line destroyed in a moment," he remembered afterward: "but things seemed to have stopped."[30]

"A moment later," Peake recalled, Lawrence was led through the maize to where he was sitting. "When he saw the table with the white cloth, a certain amount of shiny plate on it and a box of Corona cigars, and all around the Egyptians and Gurkhas eating peacefully, his surprise was such that I shall never forget it."[31]

"It was like Drake's game of bowls,"* Lawrence commented, rather acidly.[32]

Once Peake and the Egyptians had set to work planting the "tulips," Lawrence climbed the tell to survey Dara. Before him the town was clearly visible, with the railway radiating from it like the points of a compass. The line north, linking Dara to Damascus, was now being methodically uprooted by Peake. Out of Dara to the east spiked the short branch line to Busra, which he had negotiated in the night. To the south, the Hijaz Railway disappeared toward Mafraq, where they had destroyed the bridge the day before. And west ran the line through Mezerib, which continued down through the Yarmuk valley toward Palestine, where Lawrence had tried and failed to destroy the bridge at Tell al Shehab the previous November.

So far the Arabs' advance had been almost unopposed. Liman von Sanders heard about the attacks on the railway only during 17 September. "I realized at once that these attacks on our only line of communications were the beginning of serious fighting," he wrote in his memoirs, describing how he had sent a small number of troops to reinforce Dara.[33]

Frantic activity in the town caught Lawrence's eye. Through his binoculars he could see that the aerodrome was "alive with gangs

---

* The sixteenth-century English admiral Sir Francis Drake legendarily refused to let the appearance on the horizon of the invading Spanish Armada blight a game of bowls. He finished the game before going on to thrash the Spanish fleet.

pulling machine after machine into the open. I could count eight or nine lined up."[34] The first airplane appeared over Tell Arar minutes later, just as Peake's first demolitions began. More airplanes, eight in all, followed quickly, bombing and machine-gunning the hill. From among the rocks on the south side of the tell, Nuri's machine gunners fired back at them, while the antique French mountain guns were upended to blast the air with shrapnel.

Of the two British biplanes sent to cover the Arab advance to Dara, the better, a Bristol, had already been badly damaged in a dogfight south of the railway junction. The other, an obsolete BE 12 piloted by Hugh Junor, now lumbered into view, initially causing the enemy aircraft to scatter. Too late, Junor realized he was heavily outnumbered and twisted away, followed by a swarm of hostile aircraft. But he was running low on fuel, and minutes later he turned back toward Tell Arar, dropping a message to the British officers below to say he had to land. The officers rushed down the hill toward the railway, to clear a landing ground. "Junor made straight for the white T which we had put down to mark the beginning of the landing strip, and . . . touched down in what looked like a cloud of tracer bullets," Kirkbride recalled.[35] As he did so, there was a gust of wind, flipping the biplane onto its back. Astonishingly, Junor climbed out unhurt, apart from a cut on the chin. He barely had time to remove his two machine guns from the aircraft before a German plane returned and dropped a bomb on the wreck, which caught fire.

Lawrence turned his attention to the western spoke of the railway lines radiating from Dara, which connected the junction to the Turkish positions in Palestine that Allenby planned to assault the following day. Leaving Joyce behind on top of the tell, he took his bodyguard and headed southwest toward Mezerib, a major depot for rolling stock filled with supplies bound for the Palestine front. Despite being bombed again, Lawrence reached the first of the two stations in the village early in the afternoon, capturing it without loss. A few point-blank shots from the French artillery secured the other station.

While the Arabs ransacked the station and the sidings in what Young described as "an orgy of looting," Lawrence and Young clambered onto the station roof to sever the telegraph link between Palestine and Syria. "Reaching out for the thick wires we cut them one by one," Young wrote.[36] "It was odd to stand looking out over the peaceful landscape . . . and to think of the consternation which the closing of those nippers must have caused in distant Nablus."* Liman von Sanders immediately lost contact with Damascus and Constantinople, but the extent of the breakdown of communications was revealed only several days later when he finally received a message from the capital. "The telegram," he recalled afterward, "inquired whether I was willing to offer a prize for a sack race in a competition in Constantinople on October 8th."[37]

West of Dara, Lawrence and Young split up to continue their devastation. While Lawrence set out to destroy the points, Young went a little east toward Dara to lay a series of "tulips" under the track. "I had planted half a dozen when something made me look along the line towards Dara," recalled Young: "my heart stood still, for a train was crawling slowly out of the town towards Mezerib."[38] His first thought was to warn Lawrence, who was oblivious to the incoming threat. Rushing along the railway line, Young shouted that a train was coming.

"A plane?" asked Lawrence, mishearing and dismissing the threat.

"Not a plane, you damned fool," Young bellowed, "a train."[39]

Young raced back to light the fuse of the nearest of the charges he had already laid beneath the railway ties. Panicking, he could not find the taper he needed and was forced to resort to other means. "One last dab with the glowing cigarette, and I rushed to my camel," he wrote in his memoirs. "It . . . was hardly up before it stumbled and nearly fell, and I realized to my horror that I had forgotten to unhobble it."[40] Luckily for Young, the explosion of the first "tulip," though uncomfortably close, was enough to force the engine to withdraw to safety. Under cover of darkness he returned to complete his demolitions.

For almost a year Lawrence had smarted from his failure to destroy the railway in the Yarmuk valley, and now that he was again within miles of the valley, the opportunity to destroy the bridge arose again that night. Leaving the burning sidings of Mezerib, Lawrence, his bodyguards, Nasir, and some Arabs headed down into the valley. But again they were unsuccessful. Below them a train carrying the German reinforcements Liman von Sanders had dispatched to protect Dara had just arrived. "Nuri was of course quite ready to try it; Lawrence was doubtful; and I was quite definitely against it," Young said afterward.[41]

---

* The headquarters of the Ottoman Seventh Army.

Lawrence, uncharacteristically, decided not to take the risk and abandoned the raid.

On top of Tell Arar, Stirling and Peake were meanwhile recounting the story of their day's destruction on the railway near Ghazale, the first station north of Dara. Stirling had spread out his blanket, gathered the officers, and produced a half bottle of vintage brandy, which he had been keeping for a special occasion. "I enjoyed the drink immensely," Kirkbride recollected, "and I could not help wishing that there had been more brandy and fewer men to drink it."[42] In the darkness Lawrence and Young's work to the west of Dara was easily identifiable. The sky above Mezerib glowed red with flames, and there were intermittent flashes and bangs as Young's "tulips" exploded.

From Mezerib, Sharif Nasir, Nuri Said, Lawrence, and Young set out the following morning, the eighteenth, southeast toward Nesib, a stop on the Hijaz Railway between Dara and Amman, today on the border of modern Syria and Jordan. They sent a message back to Joyce, explaining their plan to continue their counterclockwise circuit of Dara, and told him to return to Umtaiye, where they would meet that night to wait for news of Allenby's offensive, which would begin early on the nineteenth.

The nearness of Dara and its 1,500-strong garrison frightened Young. Behind them, as he had seen the previous night, were German reinforcements, and he feared that ahead they would find the bridge Lawrence had destroyed thirty-six hours earlier strongly defended. "I have never known camels march so slowly, or my own heart beat so fast, as on that sixteen mile ride from Mezerib to Nesib."[43]

To the south Thalacker was struggling to restore the line between Amman and Dara. Under the supervision of his colleague Lieutenant Stuetz, by the evening of the eighteenth a working party had built piers of wooden ties, with girders made of rails laid on top of them to replace the bridge north of Mafraq demolished by Lawrence two days earlier. That night a first repair train passed over the temporary bridge north toward Dara. "Thanks to the indefatigable work of the German railway troops," said Liman von Sanders, "traffic was promptly resumed."[44]

Normal service was to be short-lived. Lawrence's force materialized on the railway near Nesib, ten miles north of Stuetz's working party, late in the afternoon on the eighteenth. The Turks, entrenched around the station and a nearby bridge, were now much more alert: a violent firefight ensued. It was only "after considerable resistance and artillery work," Lawrence reported afterward, that "we were able to carry the post on the big bridge north of the station, and to blow up the bridge."[45]

Knowing Lawrence's tendency to use "unnecessarily large quantities of explosive," Kirkbride, who had caught up with Lawrence's party and was now setting about destroying the track, asked Lawrence to give him plenty of notice before he destroyed the bridge.

"All right, all right, don't fuss!" Lawrence—exhausted—snapped.

Kirkbride was still busy laying charges, he recounted afterward, "when there was a terrific detonation and chunks of the bridge showered down around us from the sky. It was only by the grace of God that none of us was hurt."[46] He went off to protest to Lawrence: "I was tired, hungry and boiling with rage." He was angrier still at Lawrence, who simply "sat on a rock and roared with laughter."[47] Only afterward did Lawrence justify using so much explosive. The bridge was "strategically most critical," he argued, "since we were going to live opposite it at Umtaiye. . . . I was determined to leave not a stone of it in place."[48] Forced to move on the following morning by Turkish shelling from a train-mounted gun, the Arab raiders and their British advisers had to proceed to Umtaiye, just as Allenby's offensive began.

At four-thirty in the morning on 19 September, the British launched their offensive. Convinced that the Arabs' activity around Dara revealed Allenby's true intentions, the German general Liman von Sanders dismissed information received from an Indian deserter just before the attack that the thrust would be up the coast as a clever attempt to deceive him. When, after a short and brutal bombardment, the British advanced at the western end of their front line, the Ottoman army was taken completely by surprise and collapsed. "I made only one mistake in my calculations," Liman von Sanders insisted after the war. "I hoped that individual units would only be pressed back step by step: I did not expect the complete failure of whole divisions."[49] He was not helped by the effectiveness of the Royal Flying Corps, which disrupted his communications with the front line, leaving his units leaderless. Later the same day Allenby wrote to his wife. By now his troops had captured the Turkish Eighth Army's headquarters at Tulkarm, and he knew that the Arabs had cut the railway north, south, and west of Dara. "I am beginning to think that we may have a very great success," he ventured.[50]

The situation for the Arab raiders at their temporary base at the rain pool at Umtaiye, southeast of Dara, was now less promising. Joyce reported that as he and his men withdrew from Tell Arar the previous day, they had been shot at by locals enraged by their presence. When they had stopped at Umtaiye while heading north, the Arabs had the advantage of surprise. Now that the Turks knew exactly where they were, Umtaiye was unsafe and all the more vulnerable, given that neither British airplane was airworthy. Lawrence had seen three German airplanes land nearby and was now worried about the threat they presented. Later that day he and Junor each took an armored car to try to catch the German aircraft on the ground. Though he managed to shoot up one airplane in the valley where it had landed, the other two took to the air. The cars could travel only slowly through the stony ground and arrived back at Umtaiye followed uncomfortably closely by the enemy airplanes. "We crept on defencelessly, slowly . . . feeling like sardines in a doomed tin, as the bombs fell closer," Lawrence wrote.[51] Back, unscathed, in Umtaiye, he decided that the priority was to borrow new airplanes from Allenby to protect the Arabs from further aerial attack.

A British airplane was expected to land at Azraq on 21 September, bringing news from Palestine of Allenby's advance. Lawrence now decided to return to Azraq himself to meet the aircraft and fly to Palestine, where he hoped to persuade Allenby to lend him more planes. It was agreed that day that Joyce should return to Abu al Assal to restore communications with Allenby's headquarters. The Arabs, meanwhile, would retreat farther into the open country southeast of Dara, where it was hoped they would be harder to find.

Lawrence and his Ageyl bodyguards reached Azraq on 20 September. On the twenty-first, as planned, an airplane landed with news from Dawnay of Allenby's early achievements. "On this side," Dawnay had written the day before, "things have gone without the faintest hitch . . . the whole Turkish army is in the net, and every bolt-hole closed, except, possibly, that east of Jordan by way of the Yarmuk valley. If the Arabs can close this, too—and close it in time—then not a man, or gun or wagon ought to escape—some victory!"[52] The aircraft also brought an effusive letter from Allenby for Feisal, praising him for the "great achievement" of his "gallant troops." In his covering note Dawnay asked Lawrence to "deliver this in suitably flowery language to Feisal."[53] Finally, Dawnay communicated three other orders from Allenby:

(1) He wants the railway south of Dara smashed, as completely as you are able to smash it, in order to eliminate that flank once and for all; (2) he wants the tribes to close the gap across the Yarmuk valley between Lake Tiberias and Dara, which may be used by parts of the 8th A[rmy] C[orps] from the Amman area and by remnants of other troops who succeed in making their way across from west of Jordan. (3) Above all, he does NOT wish Feisal to dash off, on his own, to Damascus or elsewhere—we shall soon be able to put him there as part of our own operations, and if he darts off prematurely without Gen A's knowledge and consent, to guarantee his action, there will be the very devil to pay later on, which might upset the whole apple cart. So use all your restraining influence, and get Lawrence to do the same, to prevent F from any act of rashness in the north, which might force our hand, and force it in the wrong direction.[54]

That afternoon Lawrence climbed into the observer's seat, and the aircraft raced down the desert airstrip and climbed west toward Allenby's headquarters at Bir Salem in southern Palestine. There Allenby explained his next steps. There would now be three separate thrusts: one by the New Zealanders, led by General Chaytor, across the Jordan to Amman; a second by the Indians under General Barrow, against Dara; in the third General Chauvel's Australians would cross the northern Jordan valley, toward the Golan Heights. While Chaytor secured the right flank, Barrow and Chauvel would then turn northward for Damascus. "We were to assist them," Lawrence would write in *Seven Pillars of Wisdom*, "but I was not to carry out my saucy threat to take Damascus, till we did it all together."[55]

27

The Road to Damascus

Otto Liman von Sanders only narrowly escaped being captured when British troops entered Nazareth on 21 September. Later that day he reached Dara, where he briefly tried to marshal his dwindling forces before leaving for Damascus. He sent an order to the Fourth Army at Amman to come north to reinforce the Seventh and Eighth Armies on the Palestine front. But, as Thalacker bitterly observed, "due to the destruction of the track around Dara, the railway line . . . was completely paralyzed."[1] The Fourth Army had no choice but to go by road. When he set out for Damascus on 22 September, Liman von Sanders himself had to walk one stretch of the line north of Dara that had still not been repaired since Peake's demolitions six days earlier.

The same morning, at Um Surab in the hills fifteen miles southeast of Dara, Young and Kirkbride were frying sausages together when they heard three airplanes. Having spent two days taking cover every time they heard an aircraft, both men were relieved to see that the planes had British markings. One by one all three landed, and out of one jumped Lawrence.

Lawrence had good news. Two of the aircraft—advanced Bristol fighters from an Australian squadron—had arrived to stay, and Allenby's only Handley Page bomber would follow that afternoon with a payload of food, fuel, and spare parts for the aircraft and the cars. When, shortly afterward, German biplanes appeared from Dara, the Australians scrambled for their airplanes. This time, "the contest was brief and one-sided," Kirkbride remarked.[2] The sausages and tea were

A Bedu inspects the machine gun of a British biplane.
The Arabs were fascinated and heartened by the military
technology that Britain supplied to help them.

still hot, Lawrence claimed, when both Australian pilots returned. A few hundred yards away flames and billowing black smoke marked the point where each German biplane had dived into the ground.

In Amman the atmosphere, Thalacker noted, was "becoming increasingly hostile and violent" as thirsty troops arriving from the south fought over the station's limited supply of water.[3] With the "Turkish troops . . . getting totally out of hand" and panic rising, Thalacker was forced to keep order by waving his pistol at the mob. Having heard that the line north to Dara had finally been repaired, he dispatched on 23 September a hospital train to evacuate the wounded northward out of Amman, which was now being bombed daily. But his plans were to be ruined by the Arabs' determination to smash the railway. That morning, in a sortie in broad daylight, a mixed force of regular Arab soldiers, Rwala tribesmen, armored cars, and tenders returned to Mafraq. There they destroyed the makeshift bridge that had only just been put up to replace the stone bridge that Lawrence had wrecked on 16 September. The hospital train was forced to turn back. To the south the garrison in Maan surrendered. To the west British forces occupied Salt, unopposed. Thalacker left Amman on the last available trolley after dark on 24 September, six hours before British troops arrived. When he reached Mafraq in the early hours of 25 September, he found the station ablaze. Unable to pass through the inferno, he and his colleagues were forced to dynamite their trolley and finish the twenty-mile journey to Dara on foot.

❧

News of the Arabs' exploits was spreading rapidly. Four days earlier a French intelligence officer had passed on "another very important piece of news" to his superiors in Cairo. "Colonel Lawrence," he reported, "with a band of Bedouin, has destroyed the bridges of the railway west of Dara. . . . What's more, he has cut the track south of Dara, between Dara and Amman."[4]

The speed of the British advance through northern Palestine, and the Arabs' significant role in the Ottoman army's collapse, raised French suspicions. On 23 September the French ambassador in London, Paul Cambon, went to see the foreign secretary, Arthur Balfour, to remind him that Syria fell within the French sphere of influence determined by the Sykes-Picot agreement. "It was extremely important," Cambon explained, "that this fact should not be lost sight of in any arrangements that General Allenby . . . might make for the administration of the country he was presumably about to occupy."[5]

The following day an intriguing report on the progress of the Palestine campaign appeared in a French newspaper, the *Echo de Paris*. Having acknowledged Allenby's role in the triumph, the newspaper added, "We must mention Colonel Lawrence as having played a part of the greatest importance in the Palestine victory." With his "experience of the country and his talent for organization," Lawrence would become a household name in Britain, the newspaper predicted—a self-fulfilling prophecy—and went on, "At the head of the cavalry force, which he had formed with Bedouins and Druses, he cut the railway at Dara, thus severing the enemy communications between Damascus and Haifa and the eastern side of the Jordan."[6]

It was the first time Lawrence's—and indeed any British—involvement in the Arabs' northward advance had been acknowledged in public, and it is hard not to detect an ulterior motive behind this apparently magnanimous tribute, which was reprinted the following day in the London press. Until then, as the April report in the *Times* on the

"Arab" destruction of the railway north of Mudawwarah showed, care had been taken to disguise British involvement in the Arab campaign. This sudden revelation that it was a British officer who was the driving force behind the Arabs' success was designed to discredit the Arabs' hopes of independent rule in Syria after the war.

The British remained determined not to give the French more influence in Syria than they had to. On 25 September the director of military intelligence at the War Office contacted Allenby to say that although the government adhered to the Sykes-Picot agreement, Allenby's interpretation of its rules would be final while the country was under military occupation. As to the treaty's stipulation for French officers to be employed for any civilian duties, the director of military intelligence, who had never liked the Sykes-Picot agreement, reminded Allenby, "Discretion rests with you re definition of civilian duties."[7]

Delighted by the havoc that the Arabs had wreaked behind Turkish lines, Allenby made preparations to give them the best possible chance to establish a hold in Damascus. On the twenty-fifth, a member of his staff contacted the British officers with the Arabs to tell Feisal—who had followed the raiders as far as Azraq—that there was "no objection to Your Highness entering Damascus as soon as you consider that you can do so with safety."[8] Allenby ordered his own forces to avoid entering the city "unless forced to do so for tactical reasons."[9]

Lawrence, too, was determined to press home the Arabs' advantage. Realizing on 24 September that the Turks had given up trying to repair the railway between Dara and Amman, he now proposed going north again and stopping just beyond Dara, on the Damascus road. His motive was political as well as strategic. Not only did he hope that the Arabs' presence north of Dara would unsettle the Turks enough to make them leave the town, where they were busy entrenching to fend off a new British attack, but it would also put the Arabs in a position to reach Damascus rapidly. To withdraw before the end of the fighting not only left the brunt of the fighting to Allenby but risked denying the Arabs the right by conquest that he had sought to achieve for over eighteen months.[10] That was why he also wanted the Arabs to be in possession of Dara before British troops arrived, as the town fell just inside the area allocated to France under the Sykes-Picot treaty.

Young, who had ridden with the exhausted Arab regulars and knew how slowly they traveled, was horrified when Lawrence explained his plan. "Our tiny force would be in the position of the hunter who stands in the only line of escape of the driven lion, instead of waiting on a flank to shoot him as he dashes by," he feared, thinking of the Turkish forces that would be fleeing Dara.[11] He preferred to remain in the Hauran, from where escape into the desert would still be possible if the Turks were to regain the upper hand. Like the other officers, he was also fully aware that, following a series of Allied advances, the war in Europe was drawing to a close. With every wish to live to see the peace, he thought that Lawrence's behavior verged on the reckless. Only after the war, having seen President Wilson's public commitment to the principle of self-determination, did he understand that Lawrence's motive for pressing northward was to establish the Arabs in the French zone before the war was over.

Lawrence disagreed, but was forced to temper his initial proposal, offering the village of Sheikh Saad, rather more northwest of Dara, as a compromise. He also contacted Allenby's headquarters to ask if there were large numbers of enemy forces waiting in the Sheikh Saad area, and for Dara to be bombed to reduce the danger that the Arabs would be attacked while they were moving north.

Headquarters obliged, and, covered by a British bombing raid on Dara, the Arabs headed north on 26 September, crossing the railway at Ghazale, ten miles north of Dara between the late afternoon and midnight. "We saw no one, and if anyone saw us, they did nothing about it," remembered a relieved Kirkbride.[12] Then, between the railway and the Dara–Damascus road, the Arabs paused to rest.

Young was too anxious to sleep. "I . . . kept pacing restlessly about with my watch in my hand, torturing myself with visions of the confusion that would be caused by a night attack on our tired force," he remembered afterward.[13] When the moon eventually rose, Young went around waking the party. They crossed the Damascus road at three in the morning and stopped again, only a little farther west, shortly before dawn. "But there was no rest," Lawrence recalled, "for lost men went about the army calling their friends in that sharp full-throated wail of the Arab villager. The moon had gone down, and the world was black and very cold."[14] Dawn on 27 September brought warmth, an unexpected encounter with a straggling column of Turkish, Austrian, and German machine gunners, who were quickly captured, and declarations of support from the villagers of the surrounding country who, sensing an opportunity to avenge years of oppressive Ottoman rule, flocked to join the Arabs.

Young's fears were realized when, later in the day, a British airplane overflew the Arabs' camp and dropped a message warning them that two Turkish columns, of 4,000 and 2,000 men, were approaching from Dara and Mezerib. Lawrence wisely decided to let the larger column pass, and concentrate the Arab forces—about 900 strong—on the smaller, which was approaching the village of Tafas, about halfway between Dara and Sheikh Saad. But, as Young had warned they might be, the Arabs were too slow. By the time they reached the village, the Turks—a regiment of lancers—were there already. Smoke was rising from the village, and there was the ominous sound of gunshots. Outnumbered by the Turks, all Lawrence could do was wait until the Turks had ridden off before he could investigate what had happened. As he walked closer, he gained an inkling of what had happened minutes earlier. "Some grey heaps seemed to hide in the long grass, embracing the ground in the close way of corpses. We looked away from these, knowing they were dead; but from one a little figure tottered off, as though to escape from us."[15] It was a little girl, no more than four years old, whose dirty dress was stained bright red with blood. It looked as though she had been speared by a lance.

"Don't hit me, Baba," she shrieked. When one of the Arabs, himself a local villager, leapt from his saddle to try to comfort the girl, Lawrence recalled, "she threw up her arms and tried to scream; but, instead, dropped in a little heap, while the blood rushed out again over her clothes; then, I think, she died."[16]

There was worse to come. As Lawrence entered the village, he saw "something red and white" sagging over one of the mud walls of the village sheepfolds. "I looked close and saw the body of a woman folded across it, bottom upwards, nailed there by a saw bayonet whose haft stuck hideously into the air from between her naked legs. She had been pregnant, and about her lay others, perhaps twenty in all, variously killed, but set out in accord with an obscene taste."[17]

Talal, the village headman, who had accompanied Lawrence on his ride around Dara the previous November, had ridden into Tafas at the same time. "He gave one moan like a hurt animal," Lawrence remembered, before pulling his headcloth across his face and galloping after the retreating Turks.[18] Lawrence looked on, transfixed. "We sat there like stone while he rushed forward, the drumming of the hoofs sounding unnaturally loud in our ears, for we had stopped shooting and the Turks had stopped shooting," he recalled. As he reached the Turkish rearguard, Talal stiffened in his saddle and shouted his war cry, "Talal, Talal." The Turks turned, there was a rattle of machine-gun fire, and Talal fell dead among their lances.

Auda abu Tayi, who was riding with Lawrence, demanded vengeance, and the tribesmen chased after the disappearing column of Turkish soldiers. Outraged by the cruelty they had witnessed, and fired by the need for revenge, the tribesmen, Lawrence recalled, fought "like devils, the sweat blurring their eyes, dust parching their throats." After the war, he would write, "In a madness born of the horror of Tafas we killed and killed, even blowing in the heads of the fallen and of the animals; as though their death and running blood could slake our agony."[19] Neither Lawrence nor anyone else seemed to retain any control over the swelling Arab army, which was being joined by the peasants living in nearby villages. Liman von Sanders described how, during their retreat, his soldiers discovered that "the inhabitants were armed throughout. . . . Many were killed and mutilated by the Arabs."[20] At the end of the battle in Tafas, the 250 Turkish and German prisoners who had been captured were machine-gunned in cold blood. Lawrence immediately tried to cover up the fact that the tribesmen had run amok, by taking responsibility for what had happened. He claimed that, from the outset, "we ordered 'no prisoners' and the men obeyed," and that the shooting of the prisoners who had not already been killed was triggered by the discovery of one Bedu pinned to the ground by German bayonets "like a collected insect."[21] Other witnesses suggest otherwise. One of the Iraqi officers, Ali Jawdat—a future prime minister of Iraq—described how he and Lawrence had "tried vainly to save a batch of prisoners from being massacred by the Bedouin, whose latent savagery had been aroused by the sight of butchered women and children."[22] Frederick Peake also believed that Lawrence did not give any order to kill the survivors, though he did not arrive in the village until after the killings had ended. "I am certain," he told Lawrence's younger brother, Arnold, in 1965, "that Lawrence did all he could to stop the massacre but was quite unable to do anything as any human mob that has lost its head is beyond control."[23]

An extremely tense evening followed. Young, who was appalled by what had happened, said that the evening was punctuated by "a series of false alarms" that the tribesmen were about to massacre the other prisoners they had captured.[24] Both he and Lord Winterton addressed the Bedu, appealing for the killing to stop. Winterton—who as a member of Parliament perhaps had most to lose if he was subsequently implicated in the killing of prisoners of war—seems to have been particularly effective at defusing the situation. Explaining that, as an MP, he would have an election to fight after the war was over, he provoked immediate laughter among the Arabs. Lawrence, who was translating the speech, turned to Winterton and explained that the MPs who had visited the region before the war were regarded by the Arabs as "comic creatures"—a none too subtle dig at Sykes. Winterton agreed, adding that they were bores as well. More laughter. Winterton then returned to his serious concerns: "The good people of Horsham and Worthing in England whose votes I shall be seeking . . . might think I connived at the shooting and vote against me. In fact," he summed up, "precipitate action . . . might lose me the election."[25] The Bedu killed a sheep rather than their prisoners.

Nuri Shaalan's Rwala tribesmen entered Dara overnight to begin their pillage of the town. Lawrence raced after them, back toward Dara, the following morning with Kirkbride. The sky over Dara was black with acrid smoke from storehouses burning in the town. Lawrence was anxious to beat Barrow and his Indian cavalry to the railway station and raise the Arab flag there, since Dara sat on the border of the French zone agreed by Sykes and Picot. "I felt that politics were starting to complicate a war which had hitherto been fairly straightforward," Kirkbride wrote in his memoirs.[26]

After intense bombing and then ravage by the Rwala overnight, the atmosphere in Dara was apocalyptic. "There was a stench of fire, death and excreta everywhere, with clouds of flies," Kirkbride vividly remembered years later. "It was not easy for us to find a clean place in which to squat. . . . We had to leave our first choice in a hurry when I sat down on a mound of earth which produced a nauseating smell as a purple and swollen hand popped out above the ground."[27] Kirkbride watched a strapping Arab woman walk past, balancing a looted table on her head. A tribesman chased a Turkish cavalryman around and around in circles, whipping him as he went. A Turkish major, the paymaster of his unit, sat in the dirt weeping, stripped of everything but his vest. A little girl, in a grimy, once pretty dress, told Kirkbride that she had been coming home from visiting her aunt in Damascus when the trains stopped running, and she lost her uncle. Kirkbride sat her down on his valise and gave her a cup of tea before finding a doctor who was willing to accompany her home to Amman. In the sidings some Bedu were looting a hospital train, "tearing off the clothing of the groaning and stricken Turks, regardless of gaping wounds and broken limbs, and cutting their victims' throats."[28]

General Barrow arrived soon afterward. He had advanced slowly, uncertain of who controlled the town and scared of being bombed by his own side. "This place is in a bloody awful mess," he told Lawrence when he met him. "My head was working full speed in these minutes," Lawrence remembered, "since now or never was the moment to put the Arabs in control."[29] Greeting Barrow as if he were a guest, Lawrence tried to persuade the general to withdraw his men. Appalled by what he had seen, Barrow, however, refused. Lawrence would later claim that, nevertheless, the general had smartly saluted Sharif Nasir's small silk pennant in the station square—implicitly endorsing the Arabs' control over this contested patch of territory.

The following morning Barrow's Indian cavalry set out for Damascus, with the Arabs on their right, inflicting terrible casualties on the retreating Fourth Army. The Turks, Stirling said, were "now in a pitiful state."[30] He watched as one of their men crawled to a well. "Half an hour later I came back and found him dead. He had died of starvation and exhaustion."

Arab attacks eroded the retreating Fourth Army throughout the next two days. Some 6,000 strong when it left Dara, the column had dwindled to 5,000 by the time it reached Sheikh Miskin, fifteen miles north, 3,000 by Mesmiye, thirty miles farther on, and 2,000 by Kiswe, ten miles outside Damascus, where the Turks were overtaken by Nasir and Nuri Shaalan and trapped between their tribesmen and the advancing British. "In all we killed nearly five thousand of them, captured about eight thousand . . . and counted spoils of about one hundred and fifty machine guns and from twenty-five to thirty guns," Lawrence reported in the *Arab Bulletin* without emotion weeks later.[31]

On 30 September, Allenby confirmed the administrative arrangements for Damascus in a telegram to the War Office. "I shall recognize the local Arab administration which I expect to find in existence, and shall appoint French liaison officer as required," he added, without enthusiasm.[32] He was expecting the Arabs to head into Damascus early the following morning, paving the way for the entrance of his own troops. In fact, his Australian troops would briefly pass through the outskirts of Damascus during that night in their continued pursuit of the Turks northward.

Just as Allenby was preparing his entry into Damascus, Liman von Sanders was hurrying to leave. Armed Arabs, shooting into the air, had been arriving throughout the day, and the atmosphere was becoming menacing. "The four colored flag of the Sharif was displayed from many houses," the German general observed, sensing that the peaceful attitude of the city's inhabitants was on the verge of turning.[33] The situation rapidly deteriorated as the first Arabs, fresh from dispatching the remnants of the Fourth Army, appeared in the city after dark. Fires broke out across the city: the Germans' depots, and both railway stations in the city—at Cadem in the southwest suburbs and the Hijaz Railway terminus itself in the center—were in flames. By the time the Germans left Cadem that night, they found the main street running north through the city blocked with telegraph poles and Arabs shooting at them from all directions.[34]

Thirty miles farther northwest of Damascus, Sharif Ali Haidar, the man who had tried and failed to oust Husein at the outbreak of the revolt over two years earlier, was at a railway station waiting to be evacuated. With him was his nine-year-old daughter, Musbah. The station, which had been bombed the night before, was in darkness, and "on the platform a crowd seethed, fought, prayed and pushed," she remembered years later.[35] A few German soldiers tried to maintain control, but they were losing. With fixed bayonets, her father's bodyguards poked their way through the scrum of soldiers and wailing refugees, enabling Ali Haidar and his daughter to board a waiting train to go north.

Lawrence meanwhile spent that night at Kiswe, on the south side of Damascus. To the north, white flashes instantaneously illuminated the night sky, as the Turks in the city dynamited their remaining ammunition, blasting shells into the night air in lazy yellow parabolas. "Ever since we took Dara, the end has been inevitable," he observed to Stirling, as the two tried to rest beside their Rolls-Royce car, which they had dubbed Blue Mist. "Now the zest has gone, and the interest."[36] It was too noisy to sleep. At dawn he and his danger-seeking colleague Frank Stirling climbed into their car and drove forward to the edge of the hills beyond which lay Damascus. Despite a few palls of black smoke hanging in the still dawn air, below them the ovum of minarets and spires of the old city was visible through a slight dawn mist, gleaming in the morning sunlight, and surrounded to east and west by livid green orchards of orange, almond, and walnut trees.

At about nine in the morning on Tuesday, 1 October, Lawrence and Stirling drove into Damascus to find scenes of jubilation. Nuri Shaalan and Nasir had already entered the city, and the narrow streets of the old city of Damascus were "aflame with joy and enthusiasm," reminisced Stirling in his memoirs, *Safety Last*.[37] "Dervishes danced around us. The horses of the Bedouin, curvetting and prancing, gradually cleared a way for us through the dense crowds, while from the balconies and rooftops veiled women pelted us with flowers and—far worse—with attar of roses. It was weeks before I could get the smell of the essence out of my clothing."

28

A House with No Door

Lawrence went straight into the center of Damascus intending to establish an Arab government in the city. At the headquarters of the Ottoman government, the serail, he forced his way through the scrum that had gathered around the building, only to find that he had been beaten to it. Inside, he discovered not merely Sharif Nasir and Nuri Shaalan but also the Algerian brothers Abdul Qadir and Mohammed Said al Jazairi. The Jazairis sprang forward, announcing that they had taken control of the city, with another Arab nationalist, Shukri al Ayyubi, known as Shukri Pasha. "I was dumb with amazement," Lawrence later wrote.[1] He was suspicious of Abdul Qadir, who had suddenly—and perhaps treacherously—disappeared before his failed Yarmuk valley expedition eleven months earlier. Afterward he would claim that they were "both insane, as well as pro-Turkish and religious fanatics of the most unpleasant sort."[2]

The man whom Lawrence was planning to install as governor of Damascus was Ali Riza al Rikabi, whom he had met during his secret tour of Syria in June 1917. Rikabi was a sensible choice, who would simultaneously provide continuity and change: not only had he been a key figure in the Ottoman government of the city, but he was also secretly an Arab nationalist. The problem was that Rikabi was so discreet about his true political opinions that he was still nominally in command of Ottoman troops who were now hurriedly retreating toward Aleppo, and there was no sign of him.

Time was short, because there were already signs that the fragile Arab coalition was splintering. Lawrence's attention was briefly diverted by

Going their separate ways. Victorious Bedu fighters
and Turkish prisoners pass in the street, Damascus 1918.

a fight that had broken out between two other Arab arrivals, Auda abu
Tayi and Sultan al Atrash, the Druse leader; the fight had begun after
the Druse had hit Auda across the face with a stick. Forcing the two
men apart, Lawrence pushed Auda into a quiet room and held him in
a chair until he had finally calmed down.

No more than thirty minutes after he had arrived, Lawrence found
himself joined by Sir Harry Chauvel, the commander of the Australian
forces waiting west of the city. Chauvel had been told by Allenby that,
when he arrived in Damascus, he should find the Turkish *vali*, promise
him British support, and offer assistance with policing the city, for the
first priority was to try to ensure that anarchy did not break out in
Damascus. If Chauvel had any difficulties with the Arabs, Allenby
directed him to Lawrence. When Chauvel went to see Barrow early that
morning to finalize the plans for their entry into the city, Barrow gave
him the "disquieting information that Lt-Col Lawrence . . . had slipped
off early that morning without saying anything to him and to the best of
his belief had ridden into the city." Chauvel hurried after him.

Chauvel found Lawrence on the steps of the serail when he arrived
at half past nine that morning. "With him," Chauvel recalled ten years
later, was "an individual whom he introduced as Shukri Pasha."[3]

Lawrence explained that his early departure that morning was due
to his concern to find out what was going on inside Damascus. "He

then proceeded to tell me that Shukri was the Governor of Damascus," Chauvel recalled. "Shukri was obviously an Arab so I said I wished to see the Turkish Vali."

Lawrence must have guessed why. On the spur of the moment he replied that the *vali* had fled the previous afternoon with the Turkish general Mehmed Jemal, and that Shukri had been elected governor by the citizens.[4] In fact, Jemal had appointed Mohammed Said al Jazairi governor just before he left the city, and Lawrence's second claim was an outright lie: there had been no time, let alone any attempt, to consult the citizens of Damascus about their future government. Chauvel agreed to Lawrence's request to keep his men out of the city and to allow the Arabs time to consolidate the new administration. His uncertainty over the exact whereabouts of the Turks meant that he was happy not to become embroiled in the running of Damascus.

Having fended off Chauvel, Lawrence returned inside the serail and summoned the Jazairi brothers. "Feisal had begged me to get rid of them," he later told Frank Stirling, "so I told them to go, and that Shukri . . . would be military governor until Ali Riza returned," which Ali Riza did, shortly afterward.[5] Not surprisingly, neither Abdul Qadir nor his brother was enthusiastic at this news. According to Lawrence, Abdul Qadir tried to stab him, but was stopped when Auda abu Tayi punched him to the floor. Both brothers left, threatening revenge.

Thinking that he had seen off the Jazairis and temporarily solved the problem as to who would govern Damascus, Lawrence was in an ebullient mood, and an appropriately symbolic act occurred to him. Walking through the main Hamidiye souk into the heart of the old city, he passed behind the ancient mosque and went into Saladin's tomb. There he pried away the gilt wreath presented to the sultan by the kaiser twenty years before. He would give it shortly afterward to the Imperial War Museum in London, where it is displayed today. On an accompanying chit, kept by the museum, he recorded that the wreath was "removed by me, as Saladin no longer required it."[6]

In the evening Lawrence turned his attention to the administration of the city. "My reading of history," he later wrote, "told me that the steps were humdrum:—appointments, organization, departmental routine."[7] The city's electricity had failed; prices stood at ten times prewar levels; and diseases, including typhus, dysentery, and influenza, were scything through the malnourished inhabitants. "It was a busy evening," Lawrence commented afterward with some understatement, admitting that it was only by "sweeping delegation of office (too often, in our haste, to hands unworthy)" that a frail façade of local government was erected.[8] As the evening call to prayer sounded across the city, and Lawrence prepared to hand power over to the Arabs, he realized that his role in Damascus was coming to an end.

✦

Frank Stirling's first thought the following morning was that he needed a bath—his first in six weeks. With Sharif Nasir he headed to one of Damascus's Turkish baths. "We sweated and were rubbed and soaped and pummelled until for my part I felt I was being flayed alive," he remembered. Finally cleansed of desert grime, they lay drinking coffee and smoking cigarettes.[9]

It was only when they left the *hammam* three hours later to find fresh corpses in the streets that Stirling and Nasir discovered what had happened. The Jazairis had "tried to stage a counter-revolution to put themselves in power. Lawrence had been obliged to turn the machine-guns on them," Stirling later wrote.[10]

Lawrence had been told during the night that the Jazairis had called on the Druses to back them in an armed uprising against the sharif, whom they described as a British puppet. Suddenly Lawrence feared that he would be the target of the very Druse revolt he had envisaged helping the Arabs' cause. Early that morning, while Nasir and Stirling were sweating in the *hammam*, Lawrence contacted Chauvel to ask for support before he and Kirkbride toured the streets. The shops were shut, and the Druses were busy looting. "We must have looked an ill-assorted couple, he short and in Arab robes with no arms but an ornamental dagger, and myself long and lanky in khaki, wearing a large Service revolver," Kirkbride reflected afterward.[11] "When we found anyone butchering Turks he went up and asked them in a gentle voice to stop, while I stood by and brandished my firearm. Occasionally, someone turned nasty and I shot them at once before the trouble could spread." But you can still gain a sense of just how wild the unrest was, if you look up from the spicy fug of the Hamidiye souk today into its arched, iron roof, and see the bullet holes that puncture it.

It was during this tour that Lawrence also gained a truer sense of the terrible condition of the city. Entering one hospital, "we were met in the corridor by the most appalling stench which set me retching," Kirkbride remembered.[12] The dead and the living were lying side by side. Some of the dead were so decomposed that the only way to bury them "was to pick them up in the sheets on which they lay and dump the bundle in the long trench which had been dug by Turkish prisoners in the garden." The regular army doctors who followed were appalled. "Indescribably hideous and inhuman" was the verdict of an Australian medical officer the following day.[13]

Order was restored when Chauvel marched his troops through the city center. Reluctant to admit that stability depended not on the Bedu but on the occupying British force, Lawrence asked Chauvel first to salute the Arab flag at the serail and then, when he refused, to allow a body of Arabs to lead the British troops. It was "quite a reasonable request," Chauvel thought, until he saw the size of the flags with which the Arab contingent arrived to join the march.[14] Nevertheless, the demonstration went ahead, and the violence appears to have been short-lived. A photograph taken soon thereafter depicts a decidedly more subdued crowd contemplating the two makeshift gallows that had been erected in front of the serail.[15] Neither, according to Kirkbride, had to be used. By nightfall electric light and a semblance of calm had both been restored across the city. Blaming the proximity of the hotel accommodating the campaign's war correspondents to the scene of the shooting for the vivid press reports that followed, Lawrence later claimed that only five had been killed and a further ten wounded during the two days' unrest, of whom Kirkbride accounted for three.

Allenby arrived in Damascus the following day, 3 October. Two days earlier he had been told in a telegram from London that he should recognize the authority of "the friendly and allied Arabs" in the areas over which the British and French were to have influence according to the Sykes-Picot agreement. In line with the Declaration to the Seven Arabs that summer, the telegram explained that areas liberated by the Arabs "should properly be treated as Allied territory enjoying the status of an independent State, or confederation of States, of friendly Arabs" and "not as enemy provinces in temporary military occupation." Wherever possible, the War Office advised, Allenby should encourage

Arab administration and work through local Arab officials, "so as to give rise to no inconvenient claim to the employment where unnecessary of French civilians."[16]

In the light of the unrest in Damascus perhaps, Allenby ignored the order from London. He preferred to rely on his authority as the commander of Allied forces and on the military hierarchy that had incorporated the Arab forces under his command after the capture of Aqaba. Presumably he deemed this the easiest way to give practical authority to the Arabs without surrendering any of the powers he had as the senior military commander on the spot, which also enabled him to limit French influence. When Allenby heard that Feisal, who had arrived from Azraq, now belatedly wanted a triumphal entry into Damascus, he refused to wait. He sent Hubert Young, in a bright red Mercedes left behind by the Germans, to fetch the Arab sharif. Feisal, though, refused to be driven into town. Instead, he spurred his horse on and galloped into the city center to meet Allenby for the first time.

Chauvel's recollection of Allenby's meeting with Feisal was that it had been uncomfortable.[17] Allenby had made it very clear that he remained in charge and that Feisal would administer the Arab territory just as another British general would run Palestine. Chauvel remembered that Feisal had reacted badly when Allenby informed him that "France was to be the Protecting Power over Syria" and that Feisal would administer Syria—excluding Palestine and Lebanon—with French guidance and financial backing. Feisal said that he knew nothing about France's right to be involved in Syria, claimed that Lawrence had told him that the Arabs were to have all of Syria, and flatly rejected French assistance.[18] Chauvel said that Lawrence stalked off after the meeting, having denied any knowledge of the Sykes-Picot agreement; Lawrence claimed he parted amicably with Allenby that day. Certainly Allenby left the meeting more upbeat, telling his wife that evening that he had had "a long and satisfactory talk with Feisal," but his optimism gradually evaporated. "The future, when martial law no longer prevails, is not so cloudless," he told the chief of the Imperial General Staff, Sir Henry Wilson, a month later.[19]

The exhausted Lawrence felt he was now useless in Damascus and believed he could do more for the Arabs elsewhere. He left for Cairo the following day, 4 October. In his campaign notebook there is an odd

Feisal leaves the Victoria Hotel in Damascus,
3 October 1918, after his meeting with Allenby.

but resonant phrase that seems to articulate his feelings two days earlier, as he hurriedly sketched out the arrangements through which the
Arabs would govern the city. "In Damascus when prayer silence came,
I knew I was [a] worn tool lying in darkness under [the] bench, rejected
for ever by the master."[20]

The men Lawrence left behind were forced to grapple with an
impossible situation caused by the contradictory promises Britain had
made to Husein and then to the French. In the port of Beirut, which
was always the strongest center of Arab nationalist support but within
the "Blue" zone, which, under Sykes-Picot, France would be allowed
to rule directly, the Arabs announced their independence and raised
the Arab flag before British troops arrived. Anticipating French opposition, Allenby quickly warned the War Office. With the war not yet
over he, too, was uncomfortable about the development, which might
threaten his own supply arrangements. He told London he intended to
overturn the Arabs' decision. The Arabs quoted back at Allenby the
Declaration to the Seven Arabs made to them that summer, in which
the British government had accepted that the Arabs should govern
what they conquered and that, in areas under Allied occupation, the
"future government of these regions would be based principally on
consent of those governed."[21] Allenby was furious: "I was not consulted
before this assurance was given; further, Arab leaders have never been
officially notified of terms of Anglo-French Agreement."

An exhausted Lawrence, on 3 October 1918 in Damascus.
The following day he left for London to continue
his efforts to keep the French out of Syria.

As the contradictions of the various promises the British had made
became apparent, Stirling described the confused atmosphere: "My
office was now thronged with frenzied and almost despairing Arabs
who could not believe that we had signed an agreement which would
hand them over to the French."[22] Early in November he wrote to his
sister:

> The situation here bristles with difficulties. As you know we have
> fanned the flames of the Arab Revolt and sympathized with
> money and men in the Sharif's attempt to form a free Arab nation.
> Up to now the Arabs have a blind confidence in all the English-
> men who have been in contact with them. They almost literally
> eat out of our hands. The Arab cause has been successful beyond
> the wildest dreams of anybody. That is just the trouble. Mark
> Sykes MP never probably believing that the Arab Revolt would
> ever really reach further north than Aqaba, formed a compact
> with the French, known as the Sykes-Picot Agreement, whereby
> Beirut and the entire littoral northward of there should be under
> French administration and that Damascus, Homs, Hama and
> Aleppo should be allowed to fall to the Arabs (if they can get
> there) but should be under French influence. . . . But in this pres-
> ent temper the Arab won't have the French at any price. Already

the Americans in Beirut are saying that we have sold the Arabs to the French. The results will be as follows—If we keep our part with the French the Arabs will rightly say we have sold them, that we have raised them up only to cast them down. . . . News of this will spread through the Mohammedan World and do us unutterable harm. Also it will entail certain interior chaos and probably war between the French and the Arabs. If we don't keep our pact with France the world will say "Oh Yes! England land grabbing again." We don't in the least want any of this country but we simply cannot let the Arabs down. If only we could buy French interests out by the session of land say in the Cameroons it would save so much. Otherwise our name will be mud.[23]

Feisal's behavior grew increasingly desperate. He had promised Bertie Clayton that he would not issue any proclamations before consulting Allenby, but then announced without warning that the independent government formed in the name of his father "embraced all Syrian towns." When he refused to withdraw Shukri Pasha, whom he had sent as his governor to Beirut, Allenby tried another trick to encourage him to toe the line. He suggested that all the arrangements were temporary and would undoubtedly be discussed at the forthcoming peace conference. He warned Feisal that any attempt he made to take control of the coastal "Blue" area allotted to France under the Sykes-Picot agreement would prejudice his case at the conference, to which he would be invited as a belligerent.[24] This did not please Feisal. "What he feels most is that all access to the sea is barred," Allenby reported to Sir Henry Wilson in London. "I am in a house with no door," Feisal reputedly complained.[25]

Feisal also told Allenby that he did not trust the French and feared that their military governors would "take advantage of their official positions to carry on propaganda" to manipulate any settlement supposedly founded on self-determination. Allenby responded, telling Feisal that he would remove any military governor he found dabbling in politics. Bertie Clayton proposed a more active approach. "We should now relax local censorship to enable those holding opposite views to French, whose press and other propagandist activity is increasingly active, to state them in moderation," he advised three days later.[26] For Feisal had a point. On his tour around the region following the armistice, the French intelligence officer Antonin Jaussen carefully catalogued towns and Christian communities where he found opposition to British or Arab rule for future reference.[27] Shortly afterward the French would begin a campaign to win support from the Syrian diaspora for their claim to Syria.

In Cairo, Lawrence was trying a little propaganda of his own. Before leaving for Britain, he wrote an article on the capture of Damascus, which was published in the *Times* on 17 October. In it he seeded a revised version of the final days of the campaign, claiming that "the Arab Camel Corps formed the extreme right of the Allied advance upon Damascus, which was entered on the night of the 30th, Arabs being the first troops in."[28] Privately, he told the cabinet on his return to London that Allenby's "Arab alliance enabled him to throw his cavalry, without lines of communication or the usual precautions, from Jaffa to Aleppo in pursuit of the Turks."[29]

Suddenly, it looked as if the situation was turning in the Arabs' favor. A week after the *Times* article appeared, the director of military intelligence in London contacted Allenby with news that Sykes and Picot were being sent to Syria to assess the need for political officers to ease the tension between the British, French, and Arabs. "Don't take Mark at his own valuation," Hogarth—now himself back in Britain—whispered to Clayton days later, telling him he could safely ignore Sykes. "His shares are unsaleable here and he has been sent out (at his own request) to get him away."[30] Hogarth also brought news of the effect of Lawrence's return to Britain:

> Our whole attitude towards the French is hardening here. TEL has put the wind up everybody and done much good. . . . He is trying to get the principle accepted that Arabs and Zionists are to be called in to any such "Conversations" on the S.P. business as Cambon admits must take place eventually. Meanwhile S.P. is considered scrapped here, but not so by Paris.

The British government had considerable bargaining power with the French, who needed British support for their campaign to claim their eastern provinces of Alsace and Lorraine back from the Germans. Britain now tried to dilute the Sykes-Picot agreement. At British insistence on 7 November the British and French governments issued a joint declaration committing both to "the complete and definite emancipation of the peoples so long oppressed by the Turks and the establishment of national governments and administrations deriving their authority from the initiative and free choice of the indigenous populations."[31] In Damascus the Arabs greeted news of the statement enthusiastically. "Roughly 200,000 rounds of ball ammunition [were] fired into the air," Young remembered afterward.[32] The British were also quietly satisfied with their diplomatic maneuver. "When we are counting up the various weapons we have in our hands for dealing with the Sykes-Picot Agreement later on, I think we shall find ourselves laying very great stress upon the general spirit, if not upon the actual terms, of the declaration," a member of the War Cabinet, Lord Curzon, asserted in London.[33]

It was not until 10 January 1919 that Fakhri finally emerged from Medina to surrender. He had defiantly held out in Medina since the beginning of 1917 and for over ten weeks after the Ottoman armistice. He had mustered such a brave defense partly, perhaps, because he had been needled in its latter stages by Sharif Husein. Husein had ill-advisedly written to the Turkish general the previous summer mocking him for having to feed his men on *hibnah*, an herb more usually eaten by goats. As the *Arab Bulletin* commented, this attack on Fakhri was unjustified, and only likely to stiffen his will to hold out in Medina, which it did. "As all reports show that the prolonged resistance of the garrison is in no small measure due to this man's proud and resourceful spirit, it is, perhaps, a pity that he was not spared these pinpricks."[34] Fakhri, who had already circulated recipes for cooking locusts among his men, defiantly replied to Husein a fortnight later, telling him about a dream in which the Prophet Muhammad had appeared before him. "As I am now under the protection of the Prophet," he wrote to Husein, "I am busying myself with strengthening the defenses and building roads and squares in Medina. Trouble me not with useless requests."[35]

Fakhri's religious faith, however, proved no antidote to the influenza outbreak that crossed the world at the end of the war and depleted his garrison. Fakhri's men began to desert, and finally he was overthrown by his junior officers. Three days later Husein's son Abdullah entered Medina for the first time since the outbreak of the revolt. He went straight to the mosque containing the tomb of Muhammad, to pray. He had entered the city first to try to preserve order, but the city was ransacked by the Arab forces who followed him in.

Except in its finality, the fall of Medina had little significance, because the revolt had no bearing on who would win the wider war. Just as the British had intended when they backed Husein in an effort to avert the jihad, the revolt's major significance was political, though not in the way that the British imagined. For the revolt had grown far beyond its original defensive purpose, into a belligerent support of the British army's invasion of Palestine; because of this, its long-term repercussions were to prove far more significant than anyone had ever envisaged.

⁓⚜⁓

At Lawrence's suggestion, Husein approved Feisal as his representative at the peace conference that would open in Paris. Feisal left Beirut for France late in November 1918. After he had boarded the ship, his chauffeur was stopped by the French and arrested and the Arab flag removed from his car.[36] It was a sign of what was to come.

Colonel Brémond was assigned to look after Feisal during his stay in France. His instructions were to treat Feisal as "a person of distinction, but not to recognize in him any diplomatic status," and he took him on a tour of the French battlefields to keep him away from Paris.[37] Finally, on 3 December, Feisal took Brémond to one side. He pleaded,

> We fought the war together, we were brothers in arms. I'm trusting your feelings of friendship and loyalty: tell me frankly what is going on. If the French Government doesn't want me to go to Paris, tell me point blank. I left my brother Zeid, who is young and inexperienced, to replace me in Damascus. The situation there is difficult and I am uneasy. If I am wasting my time here, it would be better for me to return to Damascus.

The last thing the French wanted was for Feisal to return to Damascus, where he might stir up opposition to French rule. Time was suddenly found for a meeting between Feisal and the French president, Poincaré, which took place four days later.

Feisal traveled on to London in December. There, at the beginning of 1919, he signed an agreement with Chaim Weizmann, in which the two men agreed to set a definite boundary between the Hijaz and

Palestine, after the peace conference was over. Arabs in Palestine would be "protected in their property and rights, and shall be assisted in forwarding their economic development," and the "Mohammedan Holy Places" would come "under Mohammedan control."[38] The agreement is often produced today as a freely given Arab acknowledgment of the legitimate existence of the state of Israel. However, Feisal—who still depended on a British subsidy of £150,000 a month and believed he could still rely on British help to counterbalance French influence in the Middle East—signed reluctantly under British pressure. As he signed, he added the caveat that he would honor the deal only "provided the Arabs obtain their independence," defined by conditions set out in a memorandum he had just completed. Drafted with Lawrence's help, Feisal's memorandum maintained that, although the Arabs needed outside assistance, "we cannot sacrifice for it any part of the freedom we have just won for ourselves by force of arms."[39]

In his memorandum Feisal also yielded to British ambitions in the region, however. "The world wishes to exploit Mesopotamia rapidly," he acknowledged, arguing that there was a need for local government, which should be "Arab, in principle and spirit," although "buttressed by the men and material resources of a great foreign Power." This concession reflected the fact that, in London, the India Office had never abandoned its hope of colonizing Mesopotamia. But, in the climate of self-determination created by American criticism of British and French imperialism, it argued its case in an extraordinarily elliptical manner. At the India Office a senior official held that, given Arab aspirations of independence, if the French wanted Syria, the British should not embarrass their ally by encouraging the Arabs and should therefore keep Mesopotamia.

> If we support the Arabs in this matter, we incur the ill-will of France; and we have to live and work with France all over the world. We have no interests of our own in Syria at all commensurate with those in Mesopotamia; and if we had, and could eliminate the French in our own favour, could we possibly undertake the control of Syrian politics and administration in addition to our responsibilities in Mesopotamia and the Arabian peninsula?[40]

The interest in Mesopotamia to which the official alluded, and the real reason for the India Office's keenness to control the region, was oil. Although oil had not been the motive for Britain's overtures to Husein in 1915, it was certainly the major factor in Britain's determination to remain in the Middle East after the war was over. By the middle of 1918 the British government had secretly acknowledged that the country was overdependent on the United States for oil. "Fuel oil is now essential to the maintenance of British sea power," a British intelligence report concluded early in 1919: "Our power to control the world's shipping in time of war is likely in the future to be measured largely by the proportion of the world's oil supply that we shall command."[41] The question of where this oil could be obtained independently had already been answered by Maurice Hankey, the secretary to the War Cabinet, who had bluntly told Balfour before the war was over, "The only big potential supply that we can get under British control is the Persian and Mesopotamian supply."[42] By the beginning of 1919 it was not only the India Office that recognized what a vital addition Mesopotamia would be to the British Empire. Prime Minister Lloyd George rapidly demanded from Clemenceau Mosul in the north of modern Iraq and its rich oil fields. Clemenceau would agree that February. He also accepted that the British would continue to run Palestine.

Feisal found that in war-torn Europe Middle Eastern matters were peripheral, when the long-anticipated peace conference finally opened in Paris on 18 January 1919. He discovered that his name was omitted from the official list of delegates. The French told him he should blame the British for failing to explain that he had no formal standing at the conference. The British hit back, arguing that France should accept the two Hijazi delegates because the Arabs had been allies, and had been recognized as independent by the French late in 1916. Feisal was finally offered a seat. It was only on 6 February, toward the end of the main session, that he finally had the chance to speak, with Lawrence interpreting. It was "one of the most interesting and statesmanlike speeches," the top Foreign Office official, Lord Hardinge, noted. When the French foreign minister, Stéphen Pichon, interrupted Feisal, asking what France had done to help him, Feisal had politely begun by praising the French government for its support before mentioning that the French had sent "a small contingent with four antiquated guns and two new ones to join his forces," Hardinge recalled. "Pichon was sorry he had spoken and looked a fool."[43]

While Clemenceau seems to have been largely unbothered about whether or not his country colonized Syria, others in France were much more exercised. In Syria the French military attaché told Stirling, "Though Clemenceau and many thinking Frenchmen are dead against him taking Syria yet the temper of the French People is such that any govt. which gave up Syria would inevitably fall—more particularly if it were given to Britain. There is a strong Anglophobe campaign being waged in France at present."[44] Under increasing domestic pressure not to give ground to Lloyd George, Clemenceau hardened his views; having obtained the oil fields he wanted in northern Iraq, and believing that there was nothing of similar strategic value in northern Syria, Lloyd George was willing to concede. The outbreak of nationalist unrest in Egypt—stoked by public awareness of the promises Britain had made to the Syrians and Husein, as well as Feisal's invitation to the peace conference—and a collapse in British army morale in Egypt because of the slow pace of demobilization forced the British to consider pulling out of Syria. That September, Lloyd George made the decision to withdraw. Balfour reputedly told Lloyd George that it was "preferable to quarrel with the Arab rather than the French."[45] By "preferable" he meant easier. It was easier to ignore the various commitments to Husein and to the Syrians in the Declaration to the Seven Arabs than to risk a confrontation with the French.

Thanks to French obstinacy, the Sykes-Picot agreement survived, having already outlived its ebullient British negotiator who had died from influenza at the peace conference. Along the lines of his agreement, in 1920, Britain was awarded the mandates for Palestine, including Transjordan and Iraq, and France for Syria, including Lebanon. According to the mandates each of these territories had "reached a stage of development where their existence as independent nations can be provisionally recognized subject to the rendering of administrative advice and assistance by a Mandatory until such time as they are able to stand alone. The wishes of these communities must be a principal consideration in the selection of the Mandatory." Yet although the wording looked forward to a time when each territory would be independent, in practice they were colonies.

Feisal had already returned to Syria, where he found himself caught between the French and the increasingly vocal Arab nationalists in Syria. While Feisal was realistic and willing to come to an agreement with the French, the nationalists wanted him to be king of a greater Syria. This crown he was offered on 7 March 1920. It was to prove his undoing, for the move was unacceptable to both the French and the British, who were worried that escalating tensions in the region might lead to war. The French would take control of inland Syria and force Feisal into exile that July. The French general responsible is reputed to have gone to Saladin's tomb in Damascus afterward and announced, "Nous revoilà, Saladin"—Saladin, we're back.[46] And with that, Lawrence's dream to "biff the French out of all hope of Syria" was finally crushed.

Britain, meanwhile, clung on to Palestine for strategic and sentimental reasons. But the major strategic justification, to secure the Suez Canal, was fast diminishing. In 1922 Egypt was given independence following three years of intermittent violence. In India a wiry, persistent lawyer, Mohandas Gandhi, began his campaign to end British rule, which would cease with Indian independence in 1947. The eastern empire that Britain had originally backed Sharif Husein to save was, slowly but surely, beginning to unravel. And in its place a new legacy, of increasingly bitter relations between the British and the Arabs, was only just beginning.

Epilogue

Having been awarded the mandate for Iraq, Britain was immediately forced to deal with an uprising there in the summer of 1920 that persisted for much of the rest of the year. Among those killed during the disturbances was Muhammad al Faruqi, whose desertion to the British five years earlier had formed a significant catalyst for McMahon's overtures to Sharif Husein. The uprising infuriated Lawrence. In an article for the *Sunday Times* that August, in which he was described in his byline as the leader of "one of the outstanding romances of the war," he publicly blamed the uprising on the Government of India officials who had run the country since the capture of Baghdad and given the Iraqis almost no say in the character of their government: "Things have been far worse than we have been told, our administration more bloody and inefficient than the public knows. It is a disgrace to our imperial record, and may soon be too inflamed for any ordinary cure. We are to-day not far from a disaster."[1]

The decision to make Feisal king of Iraq was taken at a conference in Cairo convened by the colonial secretary, Winston Churchill, in March the following year. Feisal's coronation changed the nature of the government, but Britain remained the financial and military power behind his throne. The choice of Feisal was to lead to a close association between many of those involved in the Arab revolt and the new country. The pressure on Churchill to save money led him to reduce the British military presence in Iraq to the Royal Air Force alone, and in 1921 Pierce Joyce was posted to Baghdad to advise the Iraqis on the creation of an army—continuing much the same role that he had played at Aqaba.

Lawrence, who worked for Churchill during 1921–22, was immensely proud of his role at Cairo in setting up the Iraqi state. When, in 1928, his former chief Sir Gilbert Clayton was appointed British high commissioner in Baghdad, Lawrence wrote to him to offer his congratulations, and asked him to pass on his regards to Feisal: "Tell him that I thought a great deal of him during the war: and that I think far more of him now. He has lasted splendidly."[2] Clayton was to die less than a year later, from a heart attack while playing polo in Baghdad.

Many of the Iraqis who had joined the Arab revolt also returned to Baghdad. Jafar Pasha was appointed minister of defense before being named Iraq's diplomatic representative in London in 1922. In November the following year Feisal recalled him to serve, for the first of two occasions, as prime minister. Jafar was murdered in 1936, trying to use his popularity within the armed forces to forestall a military coup. Jafar's brother-in-law and former chief of staff, Nuri Said, followed him to the Ministry of Defense in 1921, and became prime minister for the first time in 1930. In a statistical testimony to the region's volatility, he served as prime minister a further thirteen times, up until 1958, when he, too, was murdered in a coup. Feisal would not have been surprised. After twelve years as king, in March 1933 he reflected on his unruly subjects: "There is still—and I say this with a heart of sorrow—no Iraqi people but unimaginable masses of human beings, devoid of any patriotic idea, imbued with religious traditions and absurdities connected by no common tie, giving ear to evil, prone to anarchy and perpetually ready to rise against any government whatever."[3]

That September he died of a coronary thrombosis.

Feisal's brother Abdullah fared not much better. Following an appeal from the Arab nationalists in Damascus for assistance against the French, he had gone northward from the Hijaz in 1920 and stopped at Maan, where he made the railway station his headquarters. It is today a rather melancholy museum, with an almost empty visitors' book. In April the following year the British offered him a subsidy to rule "Transjordan." Abdullah accepted the position while his father was consulted. Ultimately he hoped to reunite Transjordan with Palestine. He was assassinated outside the Al-Aqsa Mosque in Jerusalem in July 1951. His dynasty, however, has proved robust. Still closely allied to the

West, Jordan is today ruled by Abdullah's great-grandson, Abdullah, and is so far the least unstable of the Middle East's regimes. King Abdullah's great-great-uncle Feisal's Iraq is, of course, a different story.

Pragmatically, Lawrence believed that the settlement of Iraq and Transjordan to Feisal and Abdullah meant that Britain was "out of the Arab affair with clean hands."[4] He went to Jeddah in the summer of 1921 to persuade Husein to endorse his sons' appointments, in return for an ongoing subsidy of £100,000 a year. The timing was unfortunate: July was, he said, "the most stinking month of the year,"[5] and Husein, patriarchal as ever, refused to accept that his sons were anything more than his viceroys. Less than eighteen months later, the British government, which had tried to mediate between Husein and Ibn Saud, gave up, exasperated, and left political natural selection to take its course. When Ibn Saud attacked the Hijaz and captured Mecca late in 1924 to create the modern Saudi Arabia, Husein was forced to abdicate. He was not missed by Lawrence, who later wrote, "Husein's usefulness did not extend beyond 1916. He was a nuisance after that, till he fell."[6]

Husein spent much of the rest of his life in exile on the Mediterranean island of Cyprus. After suffering a stroke, he was allowed to go to Amman to see his son Abdullah. He never lost his trusting opinion of the English, blaming his treatment on the political change that had taken place in Britain between 1915 and 1918. "The English, my son, are an honorable kind, in word and in deed, in fortune and in adversity," he told an interviewer in 1931. "I say honorable," he emphasized, before continuing, "Only his Excellency the estimable, energetic Luweed Jurj° is something of an acrobat and a fox. I say a fox, saving your presence. God have mercy on the soul of his Excellency Kitchener."[7] Husein died in Amman that July.

The crash that would kill Lawrence occurred late in the morning on 13 May 1935. Recently retired from the Royal Air Force, in which he had enlisted under a pseudonym, Lawrence was returning from the post office to his tiny Dorset cottage on his motorcycle, when he was forced to swerve to avoid two young cyclists in a lane. He lost control, flew over his handlebars, and hit the road headfirst. Six days later he died, having never regained consciousness. By the time of his death "Lawrence of Arabia" had already assumed near-legendary status for

---

° As Husein pronounced "Lloyd George."

his central role in directing the Arab uprising of almost twenty years before. Reacting to the news of his former adviser's death, Churchill described Lawrence as "one of the greatest beings of our time."[8]

Lawrence's death cleared the way for the publication of *Seven Pillars of Wisdom*. A general edition was published two months later, that July. It is a pleasingly substantial book, more family bible than war memoir, bound in tan canvas with golden lettering on its face and spine. "SEVEN PILLARS OF WISDOM" reads the title page inside; below, the simple assertion "a triumph."

"A triumph" aptly summarized the British view of the revolt, from which Lawrence was inseparable. Largely thanks to the Chicago journalist Lowell Thomas, who had briefly met Lawrence at Aqaba during the revolt and who went on to lionize him in a postwar illustrated slide show, Lawrence's fame obscured that of his other colleagues, whose obituaries in later years would identify their wartime association with T. E. Lawrence. Lawrence was the perfect British hero: an eccentric amateur whose unorthodox methods brought victory with an economy and fluidity that had been absent from the western front. "Our duty," he had written, "was to attain our end with the greatest economy of life, since life was more precious to us than money or time."[9] It was this aim—and its success—that resonated around a land now studded with bright new war memorials.

The success of Lawrence's strategy caused a complete change in the perception of guerrilla warfare, which up until that point, and with the notable exception of the Boers, tended to be seen as the desperate resort of an enemy too weak or disorganized to risk an open confrontation. Lawrence's achievement, together with the advent of motorized warfare, was about to change that. "Military history cannot dismiss him as merely a successful leader of irregulars," the outspoken military thinker Basil Liddell Hart argued. "He is . . . a strategist of genius who had the vision to anticipate the guerrilla trend of civilized warfare that arises from the growing dependence of nations on industrial resources."[10] A mobile army could advance faster, but its supply lines were longer, and so more vulnerable to the deadly hit-and-run tactics Lawrence had popularized. The strategy described in detail in *Seven Pillars of Wisdom* would inspire the generation of men who fought in the following war. One of them, the future leader of the Long Range Desert Group, which operated behind enemy lines in the North

African campaign of World War Two, would afterward recall, "Lawrence had lit the flame which fans the passion of those who lead guerrilla warfare and I wanted more than anything to experience it."[11]

The irony is that it is precisely because of the unorthodox origins of the revolt, and its subsequent success, that it raises completely different emotions for the Arabs.

When the idea that the British could support Sharif Husein in a revolt against the Turks was first conceived, no one expected the revolt to break out of the Hijaz. As Ronald Storrs admitted years later, the attempt to wrest the caliphate from the Ottoman sultan and transfer it to the sharif was attractive precisely because, in "uniting the strongest religious with the weakest material power, it would be greatly to our interest."[12] His attitude, that the sharif, though a powerful religious influence around the Islamic world, was a political dwarf, encouraged McMahon to take a cavalier approach in the letters that he wrote to him. "I had necessarily to be vague as on the one hand HMG disliked being committed to definite future action, and on the other any detailed definition of our demands would have frightened off the Arab," McMahon explained at the end of 1915:

> I do not for one moment go to the length of imagining that the present negotiations will go far to shape the future form of Arabia or to either establish our rights or bind our hands in that country. What we have to arrive at now is to tempt the Arab people onto the right path, detach them from the enemy and bring them on to our side.[13]

His successor, Wingate, saw the revolt in similar terms. At the end of the war he admitted

> to having been sufficiently opportunist to take the fullest advantage of the situation to treat the Sharif's revolt rather as a really useful war measure than as a means to an end for the renaissance of a great united Arab Empire. . . . There are others who may still retain such beliefs and hopes and I admire their enthusiasm, but, personally . . . as long as the movement served its purpose in knocking out one or two stones of the arch of the Central Powers,

I am satisfied that its object (as far as my intervention is concerned) has been achieved.[14]

Had the revolt never reached Syria, the cynicism of these calculations
would never have become so clear. Had his forces never reached
Damascus in October 1918, Husein would have found it hard to
make a strong claim for Syria, which the British then had to deny. It
was precisely because the revolt was so successful—greatly thanks to
Lawrence—that the extent of British bad faith would inevitably be
revealed.

Not that the British had no premonition of what would follow.
Throughout the war, when Husein had repeatedly told them that he
trusted Britain to honor the commitments made by McMahon before
the revolt, he caused discomfort. They knew that Husein was misin-
terpreting the strength of the assurances they had given him; but they
were frightened to confront the problem in case it caused a collapse in
Arab support, which would have initially exposed them to the nebulous
threat of jihad and, later and more materially, greatly affected the security of Allenby's operations in Palestine. Husein "has read into the
terms of that 'pledge' very wide territorial boundaries, and professes
the most implicit trust in the intention and ability of Great Britain to
redeem the 'pledge' as he reads it," Cyril Wilson's colleague Colonel
Bassett warned early in 1918. "Anything that would mean for him a
'rude awakening,' I dread."[15]

The farther northward Allenby pushed into Palestine, the stronger
the argument for inertia became. Nothing should be done to disabuse
Husein, in case the sharif reacted by breaking off his support and leaving Allenby exposed to a Turkish attack from the Maan area. Allenby,
who had originally justified his campaign for its value in supporting the
Arab movement, also recognized that the British alliance with the sharif was a powerful piece of propaganda. In the autumn of 1917 he wrote
to his wife, enclosing a copy of a leaflet dropped by the British over
Palestine. "The enclosed photograph of the Sharif of Mecca—and the
proclamation by him—is one of the means we have of inducing the Arabs
to desert the Turks. We drop these papers—and packets of cigarettes—
over the Turkish lines, from aeroplanes," he explained. The proclamation encouraged the Arabs to desert and join the war "for the freedom

and independence of Arabia. . . . A good many come in, as a result of our propaganda."[16] The use of this sort of tactic only fueled later Arab claims that they had been misled by Britain. Other leaflets—presumably of British origin—depicted Husein embodying the entire Arab peninsula: a commitment rapidly dropped in the 1920s as the British lost faith in the sharif.[17]

Debate over the meaning of the correspondence between Husein and McMahon intensified after Lawrence's death. During the 1920s the Arabs had not seen Jewish immigration to Palestine as a threat. They were "annoyed and insulted by Zionist immigration, but not alarmed by it," Sharif Husein's son Abdullah later stated.[18] "It was steady, but fairly small, as even the Zionist founders thought it would remain. Indeed for some years, more Jews left Palestine than entered it—in 1927 almost twice as many." Two, linked events upset this equilibrium. The first was the economic depression triggered by the stock-market crash of 1929; the second, the rise to power of Hitler. Both caused thousands of mostly reluctant Jews to leave central and eastern Europe in search of work and safety. They might have gone to the United States or western Europe, but immigration controls had been tightened there. Instead, some went to Palestine. The growth in the Jewish population during the 1930s startled the Arabs. "In 1932," Abdullah told an audience in 1947, "only 9,500 Jews came to Palestine. We did not welcome them, but we were not afraid that, at any rate, our solid Arab majority would ever be in danger. But the next year—the year of Hitler—it jumped to 30,000! In 1934 it was 42,000! In 1935 it reached 61,000!"

In 1936 the Arabs in Palestine reacted violently. Fears that another world war was imminent prompted a collapse in economic confidence in Palestine, where a rather precarious reliance on credit had previously sustained growth. The Arabs were acutely affected, and Jewish immigration began to aggravate them. Strikes called in the spring of 1936 evolved into widespread insurgency, which died away only at harvest time. Two years of sporadic violence followed.

Looking for ways to undermine the basis for the Jewish influx into Palestine, the Arabs began to focus their attention on the correspondence between Husein and McMahon before the outbreak of the revolt in Mecca, because it seemed to undermine the basis of the Balfour Declaration. The British government refused repeated requests to publish the letters. There were "valid reasons, entirely unconnected with the question of Palestine, which render it in the highest degree undesirable in the public interest to publish the correspondence," a junior minister informed Parliament in August 1930.[19] This was rather disingenuous. Behind the scenes civil servants worried that, if printed in their entirety, the letters would reveal an uncomfortable degree of British meddling in the issue of the caliphate—still then a sensitive issue in India—and do nothing to clarify whether or not Palestine was excluded from the area offered to the Arabs by McMahon. This position was untenable because versions of the letters in Arabic were already circulating. In 1937 the government granted the royal commission it had appointed to seek a solution to the situation in Palestine permission to quote from the Husein-McMahon correspondence in its report. "It was in the highest degree unfortunate that, in the exigencies of war, the British Government were unable to make their intention clear to the Sharif," was the commission's verdict.[20]

Exactly what McMahon promised in his letters to Husein has never satisfactorily been made clear, just as McMahon intended. But his studied ambiguity, which seemed so suitable at the time, was counterproductive in the long run. British officials went to enormous lengths to interpret what McMahon had said, to try to exclude Palestine from the area the Arabs claimed was theirs. The problems mounted when, after being missing for nearly fifteen years, copies of the Arabic versions of the two most significant letters were found in a clearing out of Ronald Storrs's office in Cairo.[21] Their discovery only increased British discomfort. In his letter to Husein of 24 October 1915, McMahon had tried to qualify his commitment with the proviso that he could give assurances in places "in which Britain is free to act without detriment to the interests of her ally France." Designed to be ambiguous—as chapter 2 of this book related—the phrase as it was then translated into Arabic read as a confirmation that, except in the areas he had vaguely defined, Britain was able to confirm Husein's demands, without affecting French interests. "This careless translation completely changes the meaning of the reservation, or at any rate makes the meaning exceedingly ambiguous," the lord chancellor decided, in a secret legal opinion on the strength of the Arab claim.[22] Storrs later acknowledged that the way in which the letters had been translated, by his secret agent Ruhi, was imperfect. Ruhi, he admitted, was "a better agent than scholar."[23]

The refusal to admit that McMahon's true purpose was to string Sharif Husein along drew the controversy out, into what the *Times* described in McMahon's obituary, with wonderful British understatement, as "a disagreeable aftermath."[24] By the late 1930s, with war looming yet again, the British needed to curry the Arabs' support. In 1939, on the sidelines of a London conference on Palestine, the British agreed to a full examination of the correspondence by a committee comprising British and Arab representatives. A single sentence in their report summed up the story: "Both the Arab and the United Kingdom representatives have tried (as they hope with success) to understand the point of view of the other party, but they have been unable to reach agreement upon an interpretation of the Correspondence."[25] By then the British, recognizing that arguing that McMahon had never meant to include Palestine in his offer to Husein on the words he chose was fruitless, had resorted to claiming that the French interest in Palestine had meant that Britain could not have ceded the region to the Arabs. This was why McMahon had been reluctant to go into detail in the first place, but it was an astonishing argument, given that the thrust of British policy throughout the war had been to contain and undermine French influence.

The two sides of the revolt—the triumph personified by Lawrence and the betrayal felt by the Arabs—are inextricably intertwined. Without the correspondence there would have been no British involvement in the revolt, and without the triumph the insincerity of the letters to Husein would never have been so starkly revealed. Both sides of this legacy—of triumph and betrayal—survive today. A new generation of military advisers in Iraq pore over Lawrence in search of inspiration that might help them achieve some sort of victory. Meanwhile, in the Arab mind Britain's failure to honor its initial promise to Husein has created a reservoir of deep resentment on which opponents of the West continue regularly to draw. This is regardless of the fact that without British arms and money, the Arabs would have had none of the success that gives them grounds for complaint.[26] Here there is a striking parallel. Just as Husein was armed by the British government in 1916, Osama bin Laden was one of those armed by the

U.S. government in the 1980s to fight a war against the Soviet Union in Afghanistan. The supply of gold and guns to both recipients has had disturbing and unforeseen consequences: such are the dangers of war by proxy. And today these two examples are closely interlinked. In his first public statement after the terrorist attacks of 11 September 2001, bin Laden—who was born in Riyadh and educated in Jeddah—reminded the world, "Our nation has been tasting humiliation and contempt for more than eighty years."[27] In 2003 he added, "As I speak, our wounds have yet to heal . . . from the Sykes-Picot Agreement of 1916 between France and Britain, which brought about the dissection of the Islamic world into fragments. The Crusaders' agents are still in power to this day, in light of a new Sykes-Picot agreement, the Bush-Blair axis, which has the same banner and objective."[28] With these reminders of the recent past, to the Arabs today the British role behind their uprising ninety years ago remains unforgotten, and largely unforgiven.

Notes

BL	British Library, London
CCC	Churchill College, Cambridge
IOR	India Office Records, London
IWM	Imperial War Museum, London
LHCMA	Liddell Hart Centre for Military Archives, London
MAE	Ministère des Affaires étrangères, Paris
MEC	Middle East Centre, Oxford
PCC	Pembroke College, Cambridge
SAD	Sudan Archive, Durham
TNA	The National Archive, London
Vincennes	Château de Vincennes

PROLOGUE

1. Photographs taken in 1964 show that the locomotive has in fact been righted and turned around since its derailment, possibly during one of the abortive attempts to rebuild the railway after its destruction during the First World War. "Tracking the Train That Lawrence Wrecked," *Times* (London), 4 Dec. 1964, and Phillip Knightley and Colin Simpson, *The Secret Lives of Lawrence of Arabia* (London, 1969), photograph, pp. 94–95.

2. LHCMA, Joyce Papers, 1/264, Dawnay to Joyce, 3 July 1918. Dawnay had been wounded on the western front and walked with a stick.

3. SAD, Wingate Papers, 139/2, Robertson to Wingate, 8 Aug. 1916.

4. IOR, L/PS/10/609, Hirtzel, minute, 15 Aug. 1916.

5. Valentine Chirol, *Pan-Islamism* (London, 1906), p. 2.

6. Ronald Storrs, *Orientations* (London, 1937), p. 98. The letter was dated 10 May 1906.

7. Quoted in Jacob M. Landau, *The Politics of Pan-Islam* (Oxford, 1990), p. 47.

8. IOR, L/PS/10/12, piece 2181; G. B. Jathar and S. G. Beri, *Indian Economics* (London, 1933), p. 120. William Ochsenwald, *The Hijaz Railroad* (Charlottesville, 1980), however, believes that Western governments overestimated the sums their Muslim subjects gave.

9. TNA, WO 158/987, *Handbook of Hejaz* (Cairo, 1917), p. 9.

10. Chirol, *Pan-Islamism*, p. 9.

1. A CLEAR-THINKING HATCHET MAN

1. PCC, Storrs Papers, diary, 15 Oct. 1916.

2. PCC, Storrs Papers, diary, 14 Oct. 1916.

3. PCC, Storrs Papers, diary, 13 Oct. 1916.

4. Baroness Elles, interview, July 2004.

5. Ronald Storrs, *Orientations* (London, 1937), p. 220.

6. Egypt, Ministry of Finance, Survey Department, *A Short Note on the Design and Issue of Postage Stamps Prepared by the Survey of Egypt for His Highness Husein Emir and Sharif of Mecca and King of the Hejaz*, Nov. 1918.

7. Quoted in Jeremy Wilson, *Lawrence of Arabia: The Authorised Biography of T. E. Lawrence* (London, 1989), p. 138.

8. Malcolm Brown, ed., *Lawrence of Arabia: The Selected Letters* (London,

2005), p. 81, Lawrence to E. T. Leeds, 16 Nov. 1915.

9. David Garnett, ed., *The Letters of T. E. Lawrence* (London, 1938), pp. 195–96, Lawrence to Hogarth, 22 March 1915.

10. Brown, ed., *Lawrence of Arabia: The Selected Letters*, p. 40, Lawrence to Sarah Lawrence, 24 June 1911.

11. SAD, Wingate Papers, 135/1, Lawrence, "The Politics of Mecca," 8 Feb. 1916.

12. SAD, Clayton Papers, 693/10, Clayton to Hall, 2 Feb. 1916.

13. T. E. Lawrence, *Seven Pillars of Wisdom* (London, 1935), p. 57.

14. TNA, FO 141/736, Lawrence to Arab Bureau, 9 April 1916, quoting Shakespeare to Cox, 17 Jan. 1915. Shakespeare's letter was reprinted in *Arab Bulletin*, no. 25 (7 Oct. 1916).

15. SAD, Wingate Papers, 137/7, Lawrence's report, "Intelligence, IEF D," cover note dated 12 June 1916.

16. W. F. Stirling, *Safety Last* (London, 1953), pp. 66–67.

17. Lawrence, *Seven Pillars of Wisdom* (1935), p. 58.

18. Storrs, *Orientations*, p. 220.

19. Ibid., p. 200.

20. Ibid., p. 143.

21. Thomas W. Arnold, *The Caliphate*, 2d ed. (London, 1965), p. 47.

22. PCC, Storrs Papers, Storrs to Abdullah, n.d.

23. PCC, Storrs Papers, letter to Philtate [i.e., "Dearest"], 22 Feb. 1915.

24. TNA, FO 882/4, note on a conference at Ismailia, 12 Sept. 1916.

25. SAD, Wingate Papers, 134/2, Clayton to Wingate, 29 May 1915.

26. Geoffrey Lewis, "The Ottoman Proclamation of Jihad in 1914," in *Arabic and Islamic Garland: Historical,*

Educational and Literary Papers presented to Abdul Latif Tibawi (London, 1977).

27. John Buchan, *Greenmantle* (London, 1916), p. 6.

28. CCC, Marsh Papers, Storrs to Marsh, 7 Sept. 1914.

29. PCC, Storrs Papers, leaflet, n.d., by the Ottoman minister of marine, Jemal Pasha.

30. George Wyman Bury, *Pan-Islam* (London, 1919), p. 35.

31. Storrs, *Orientations*, p. 165.

32. Buchan, *Greenmantle*, p. 9.

2. WILL THIS DO?

1. MEC, Hogarth Papers, Hogarth to Billy Hogarth, 10 Jan. 1918.

2. Ibid.

3. Victoria Wester Wemyss, *The Life and Letters of Lord Wester Wemyss* (London, 1935), p. 354, and MEC, J. W. A. Young Papers, "A Little to the East," 29 Dec. 1945.

4. MEC, Hogarth Papers, Hogarth to Billy Hogarth, 10 Jan. 1918.

5. TNA, FO 882/13, *Arab Bulletin Supplementary Papers*, no. 2 (1 March 1918), Hogarth, "Position and Prospects of King Hussein."

6. MEC, J. W. A. Young Papers, "A Little to the East," 29 Dec. 1945.

7. Sandra Mackey, *The Saudis* (New York, 2002), pp. 195–96.

8. TNA, FO 371/3054, Wingate to Balfour, enclosing reports from Lawrence, 16 Aug. 1917; FO 882/27, *Arab Bulletin*, no. 76 (13 Jan. 1918).

9. Evidence of serious drought in the region at this time is provided in Ramzi Touchan, David Meko, and Malcolm K. Hughes, "A 396-Year Reconstruction of Precipitation in Southern Jordan," *Journal of the American Water Resources Association* 35, no. 1 (Feb. 1999).

10. TNA, FO 371/2486, piece 154423, McMahon to FO, 20 Oct. 1915.

11. TNA, FO 882/25, *Arab Bulletin*, no. 33 (4 Dec. 1916).

12. MEC, J. W. A. Young Papers, "Three Months in Jedda," n.d.

13. TNA FO 882/25, *Arab Bulletin* 33, and Sharif Husein's Proclamation of Independence, 27 June 1916.

14. IOR, L/PS/11/117, piece 353. The proclamation in which this complaint was made was issued before 14 Nov. 1916.

15. Edouard Brémond, *Le Hedjaz dans la Guerre Mondiale* (Paris, 1931), p. 128; T. E. Lawrence, *Seven Pillars of Wisdom: The Complete 1922 "Oxford" Text*, rev. ed. (Fordingbridge, 2004), p. 51.

16. Thomas W. Arnold, *The Caliphate*, 2d ed. (London, 1965), p. 48.

17. IOR, L/PS/11/117, piece 353, dated before 14 Nov. 1916.

18. Sharif Husein's Proclamation of Independence, 27 June 1916.

19. Husein to McMahon, 14 July 1915, in George Antonius, *The Arab Awakening* (London, 1938), p. 414.

20. TNA, FO 371/2486, piece 117236, McMahon to Grey, 22 Aug. 1915.

21. Antonius, *Arab Awakening*, p. 167.

22. McMahon to Husein, 30 Aug. 1915; Husein to McMahon, 9 Sept. 1915, in Antonius, *Arab Awakening*, p. 417.

23. Eliezer Tauber, *The Arab Movements in World War I* (London, 1993), p. 76.

24. SAD, Wingate Papers, 135/2, Clayton to Wingate, 9 Oct. 1915.

25. TNA, FO 371/3486, piece 150309, Kitchener to Maxwell, 13 Oct. 1915.

26. TNA, FO 371/2486, piece 153045, McMahon to Grey, 18 Oct. 1915.

27. TNA, FO 371/2486, piece 155203, McMahon's draft, 20 Oct. 1915.

28. Ronald Graham, quoted in Elie Kedourie, *In the Anglo-Arab Labyrinth* (Cambridge, 1976), p. 35.

29. Lord Hardinge, quoted in Kedourie, *In the Anglo-Arab Labyrinth*, p. 35.

30. TNA, FO 882/2, Clayton to Tyrrell, 30 Oct. 1915.

31. TNA, FO 371/2486, piece 152729, minute by George Clerk, 19 Oct. 1915.

32. The vagueness of McMahon's approach contrasts revealingly with the careful way in which he had previously delineated contested borders as an Indian civil servant before the war. See, e.g., coverage of his work in U.S. Department of State, International Boundary Study No. 6, Afghanistan-Iran Boundary, 20 June 1961.

33. TNA, FO 371/2486, piece 163832, McMahon to Grey, 26 Oct. 1915. An earlier draft (piece 153045) uses the clearer phrase "in so far as England is free to act without detriment to the interests of her present Allies."

34. TNA, FO 371/2486, piece 163832, McMahon to Grey, 26 Oct. 1915.

35. SAD, Clayton Papers, 469/11, Wingate to Clayton, 15 Nov. 1915.

36. Quoted in Roger Adelson, *Mark Sykes* (London, 1975), p. 246.

37. MEC, Sykes Papers, War Committee Minutes, 16 Dec. 1915.

38. SAD, Wingate Papers, 148/4, Lloyd to Wingate, 2 Feb. 1918.

39. TNA FO 882/2, minutes of the second meeting of the Committee discussing the Arab question and Syria, 23 Nov. 1915.

40. SAD, Wingate Papers, Sykes to Director of Military Operations, 21 Nov. 1915.

41. MEC, Sykes Papers, War Committee Minutes, 16 Dec. 1915.

42. Quoted in Adelson, *Sykes*, p. 200.

43. Quoted in ibid., p. 201.

44. Cyril Falls, "Turkish Campaigns," in *A Concise History of World War I* (New York, 1964), p. 208. Falls was co-author of the official British history of the campaign.

45. Mark Sykes, *The Caliphs' Last Heritage* (London, 1915), p. 596.

46. SAD, Wingate Papers, 135/6, Sykes to Director of Military Operations, 21 Nov. 1915.

47. Husein to McMahon, 1 Jan. 1916, in Antonius, *Arab Awakening*, p. 426.

48. TNA, FO 882/19, Husein to McMahon, 18 Feb. 1916.

49. SAD, Clayton Papers, 693/10, Clayton to Director of Military Intelligence, 3 March 1916.

3. THE UPRISING STARTS AND STUTTERS

1. TNA, FO 882/25, *Arab Bulletin*, no. 29 (8 Nov. 1916).

2. TNA, FO 882/25, *Arab Bulletin*, no. 21 (15 Sept. 1916).

3. Ibid.

4. Djemal Pasha, *Memories of a Turkish Statesman* (London, 1922), p. 215.

5. D. G. Hogarth, "Mecca's Revolt against the Turk," *American Century Magazine* (1920), in *Journal of the T. E.*

Lawrence Society 1, no. 1 (Spring 1991).

6. TNA, FO 882/4, Clayton to Wingate, 22 April 1916.

7. PCC, Storrs Papers, Storrs's report, 14 June 1916.

8. IOR, L/PS/10/598, piece 3040, Storrs's telegram, 6 June.

9. Hogarth, "Mecca's Revolt against the Turk."

10. TNA, FO 882/25, *Arab Bulletin*, no. 22 (19 Sept. 1916).

11. LHCMA, Joyce Papers, 1/43, 1–5 Feb. 1917.

12. T. E. Lawrence, *Seven Pillars of Wisdom* (London, 1935), p. 94.

13. Philip P. Graves, ed., *Memoirs of King Abdullah* (London, 1950), p. 144.

14. Ibid., p. 148.

15. Earl of Cork and Orrery, *My Naval Life, 1886–1941* (London, 1942), p. 94.

16. IWM, F. Hayward Papers, Hayward to Lawrence, 6 Sept. 1936.

17. Earl of Cork and Orrery, *My Naval Life*, p. 97.

18. Proclamation of Sharif Husein, 26 June 1916, and TNA, FO 686/149, evidence of Sayyid Mehdi Hasan.

19. BL, Mss Eur E 264/7, Chelmsford to Chamberlain, 13 June 1916.

20. Ronald Storrs, *Orientations* (London, 1937), pp. 188–89.

21. IOR, L/PS/10/599, piece 2506, Chelmsford to Chamberlain, 29 June 1916.

22. IOR, L/PS/10/599, piece 3113.

23. IOR, L/PS/10/597, piece 2394, McMahon to FO and response, 19 and 21 June 1916.

24. TNA, FO 882/4, Sayid Ali's report, 9 July 1916.

4. THE BLAME GAME BEGINS

1. Malcolm Brown, ed., *T. E. Lawrence: The Selected Letters* (London, 2005), p. 87, Lawrence to Sarah Lawrence, 1 July 1916.

2. TNA, FO 882/25, *Arab Bulletin*, no. 5 (18 June 1916); ibid., no. 9 (9 July 1916).

3. TNA, FO 882/4, memorandum, 25 June 1916.

4. Rupert Smith, *The Utility of Force: The Art of War in the Modern World* (London, 2005), pp. 23–24.

5. BL, Add 52463, *Egypt 1916–17, Private Letters between General Sir William Robertson and General Sir Archibald Murray* (privately printed, 1932), Robertson to Murray, 16 Oct. 1916.

6. PCC, Storrs Papers, Ruhi's report, 15 June 1916.

7. Brown, ed., *T. E. Lawrence: The Selected Letters*, p. 87, Lawrence to Sarah Lawrence, 1 July 1916.

8. SAD, Wingate Papers, 143/6, Cornwallis to Wingate, 30 Nov. 1916.

9. MEC, Hogarth Papers, Hogarth to Laura Hogarth, 7 Nov. 1916.

10. MEC, Hogarth Papers, Hogarth to Laura Hogarth, 19 Jan. 1917.

11. SAD, Wingate Papers, 143/6, Cornwallis to Wingate, 30 Nov. 1916.

12. SAD, Wingate Papers 138/3, Parker to Wingate, 6 July 1916; TNA, WO 158/625, piece 42A, Murray to Robertson, 29 June 1916.

13. SAD, Wingate Papers, 137/4, Wingate to Clayton, 15 June 1916.

14. MEC, Hogarth Papers, Hogarth to "Mary," 19 Jan. 1918.

15. TNA, FO 882/4, Cornwallis's report, 8 July 1916.

16. SAD, Wingate Papers, 138/5, Wilson's report, 7 July 1916.

17. PCC, Storrs Papers, note on the pilgrimage, n.d.

18. MEC, JWA Young Papers, "A Little to the East," completed 29 Dec. 1945.

19. SAD, Wingate Papers, 147/6, Beryl Wilson to Wingate, 28 Dec. 1917.

20. N. N. E. Bray, *Shifting Sands* (London, 1934), p. 75.

21. PCC, Storrs Papers, Storrs to "Colum," 21 Dec. 1916.

22. SAD, Wingate Papers, 135/1, Lawrence, "The Politics of Mecca," 8 Feb. 1916.

23. SAD, Wingate Papers, 139/2, Clayton to Wingate, 7 Aug. 1916.

24. TNA, FO 686/10, note dated 1 Aug. 1916.

25. BL, Add 52463, Robertson to Murray, 1 Aug. 1916.

26. BL, Add 52463, Robertson to Murray, 29 Aug. 1916.

27. IOR, L/PS/10/599 and TNA, FO 686/11, Ali Haidar's proclamation, 9 Aug. 1916.

28. IOR, L/PS/11/113, Chamberlain to Asquith, 16 Aug. 1916.

29. SAD, Clayton Papers, 470/3, Wingate to Clayton, 6 Aug. 1916.

30. SAD, Clayton Papers, 470/3, Wingate to Clayton, 14 Sept. 1916.

31. TNA, FO 882/4, Ibrahim Dmitri's report, written after 17 Aug. 1916.

32. SAD, Wingate Papers, 139/5, Wilson to Wingate, 23 Aug. 1916.

33. TNA, FO 882/4, Wilson's report, 1 Sept. 1916.

34. SAD, Clayton Papers, 470/4, Wingate to Clayton, 30 Nov. 1916.

35. IOR, L/PS/10/600, piece 4238, Wilson to McMahon, 24 Aug. 1916.

36. SAD, Clayton Papers, 693/10, Clayton to Hall, 10 Sept. 1916.

37. TNA, FO 882/4, note on the Conference at Ismailia, 12 Sept. 1916.

38. Victoria Wester Wemyss, *The Life and Letters of Lord Wester Wemyss* (London, 1935), p. 236.

5. THE FRENCH ARRIVE

1. Ronald Storrs, *Orientations* (London, 1937), p. 204.

2. Edouard Brémond, *Le Hedjaz dans la Guerre Mondiale* (Paris, 1931), p. 35.

3. Pierre de Margerie, "Note to the President of the Council," 19 July 1916, quoted in Christophe Leclerc, "The French Soldiers in the Arab Revolt," *Journal of the T. E. Lawrence Society* 9, no. 1 (Autumn 1999).

4. SAD, Clayton Papers, 694/4, "Notes on a Conference held at the Commander in Chief's house on 5th September 1916, with regard to the French military mission to the Hedjaz."

5. IOR, L/PS/10/615, piece 3768, McMahon to Grey, 13 Sept. 1916.

6. BL, Add 52463, Murray to Robertson, 5 Sept. 1916.

7. Storrs, *Orientations*, p. 192.

8. Ibid., p. 193.

9. PCC, Storrs Papers, diary entry, 27 Sept. 1916.

10. Ibid.

11. Storrs, *Orientations*, p. 193.

12. PCC, Storrs Papers, diary entry, 27 Sept. 1916.

13. Ibid.

14. Brémond, *Le Hedjaz dans la Guerre Mondiale*, p. 52.

15. MEC, J. W. A. Young Papers, "Three Months in Jedda," n.d.

16. Storrs, *Orientations*, p. 194.

17. IOR, L/PS/10/600, piece 4160, Parker to McMahon, 3 Oct. 1916.

18. IOR, L/PS/10/600, piece 4054, McMahon to Grey, 29 Sept. 1916.

19. IOR, L/PS/10/600, piece 3977, Wilson to FO, 28 Sept. 1916.

20. SAD, Wingate Papers, 140/8, Wigram to Wingate, 28 Sept. 1916.

21. IOR, L/PS/10/600, piece 4238, War Committee Minutes, 3 Oct. 1916.

22. Quoted in H. V. F. Winstone, ed., *The Diaries of Parker Pasha* (London, 1983), p. 137.

23. SAD, Wingate Papers, 142/11, McMahon to Wingate, 6 Oct. 1916.

24. IOR, L/PS/10/600, piece 4209, Wingate's telegram, 11 Oct. 1916.

6. THIS WAS THE MAN

1. IOR, L/PS/10/600, piece 4238, 14 Oct. 1916.

2. Ronald Storrs, *Orientations* (London, 1937), pp. 200–201.

3. T. E. Lawrence, *Seven Pillars of Wisdom* (London, 1935), p. 63.

4. SAD, Clayton Papers, 470/3, Wingate to Clayton, 13 Sept. 1916.

5. SAD, Clayton Papers, 693/10, Clayton to Wingate, 12 Oct. 1916.

6. BL, Add 52463, *Egypt 1916–17, Private Letters between General Sir William Robertson and General Sir Archibald Murray* (privately printed, 1932), Murray to Robertson, 14 Nov. 1916.

7. Lawrence, *Seven Pillars of Wisdom* (1935), p. 65.

8. David Garnett, ed., *The Letters of T. E. Lawrence* (London, 1938), p. 97, Lawrence to his parents, 24 Jan. 1911.

9. BL, Add 45914, "Haud Rediturus," *Times* (London), 15 March 1916.

10. T. E. Lawrence, *Seven Pillars of Wisdom* (1935), p. 6.

11. SAD, Clayton Papers, 470/5, Wilson to Clayton, 22 Nov. 1916.

12. SAD, Clayton Papers, 693/11, Lawrence to Clayton, 18 Oct. 1916.

13. PCC, Storrs Papers, diary entry, 16 Oct. 1916.

14. PCC, Storrs Papers, letter to "Colum," 21 Dec. 1916.

15. PCC, Storrs Papers, diary entry, 16 Oct. 1916.

16. Storrs, *Orientations*, p. 203.

17. Philip Graves, ed., *Memoirs of King Abdullah* (London, 1950), p. 157.

18. Ibid., p. 158.

19. Storrs, *Orientations*, p. 203.

20. SAD, Clayton Papers, 470/5, Wilson to Clayton, 18 Oct. 1916.

21. Lawrence, *Seven Pillars of Wisdom* (1935), p. 71.

22. Ibid., p. 73.

23. Graves, ed., *Memoirs of King Abdullah*, p. 158.

24. PCC, Storrs Papers, diary entry, 17 Oct. 1916.

25. IOR, L/PS/10/602, piece 5195, Wilson's report, 20 Oct. 1916.

26. MEC, J. W. A. Young Papers, "Three Months in Jedda," n.d.

27. T. E. Lawrence, *Seven Pillars of Wisdom: The Complete 1922 "Oxford" Text*, rev. ed. (Fordingbridge, 2004), p. 57.

28. Storrs, *Orientations*, p. 208.

29. BL, Add 45914, f. 22.

30. PCC, Storrs Papers, Lawrence to Clayton, 17 Oct. 1916.

31. Ibid.; SAD, Clayton Papers, 693/11, Lawrence to Clayton, 18 Oct. 1916.

32. SAD, Clayton Papers, 693/11, Lawrence to Clayton, 18 Oct. 1916.

33. Storrs, *Lawrence of Arabia* (London, 1940), p. 13.

34. TNA, FO 882/25, *Arab Bulletin*, no. 32 (26 Nov. 1916).

35. BL, Add 45915, 19 May 1917, f. 50.

36. Lawrence, *Seven Pillars of Wisdom* (1922), p. 75.

37. TNA, FO 882/25, *Arab Bulletin*, no. 32 (26 Nov. 1916).

38. Lawrence, *Seven Pillars of Wisdom* (1935), p. 91.

39. Ibid.

40. Ibid.

41. TNA, FO 882/25, *Arab Bulletin*, no. 32 (26 Nov. 1916).

42. Ibid.

43. Ibid.

44. MEC, Newcombe Papers, Lawrence to Newcombe, 17 Jan. 1917.

45. Lawrence, *Seven Pillars of Wisdom* (1935), p. 67.

46. SAD, Wingate Papers, 138/5, Wingate to Robertson, 9 July 1916.

47. TNA, FO 882/25, *Arab Bulletin*, no. 32 (26 Nov. 1916).

48. H. V. F. Winstone, ed., *The Diaries of Parker Pasha* (London, 1983), p. 173, report to Arab Bureau, 8 Nov. 1916.

49. TNA, FO 882/25, *Arab Bulletin*, no. 32 (26 Nov. 1916).

50. Charles Callwell, *Small Wars*, 2d ed. (London, 1899), p. 3.

51. Ibid., p. 105.

52. Earl of Cork and Orrery, *My Naval Life* (London, 1942), p. 99.

7. CRISIS OVER RABIGH

1. IOR, L/PS/10/637, piece 4932, Wilson to McMahon, 31 Oct. 1916.

2. PCC, Storrs Papers, diary, 17 Oct. 1916.

3. IOR, L/PS/10/637, piece 5321, Wilson to McMahon, 5 Nov. 1916.

4. IOR, L/PS/10/637, McMahon to Grey, 21 Nov. 1916.

5. SAD, Wingate Papers, 143/6, Clayton to Wingate, 23 Nov. 1916.

6. Philip Graves, ed., *Memoirs of King Abdullah* (London, 1950), p. 161.

7. IOR, L/PS/10/637, piece 5235, FO to Wingate, 11 Dec. 1916.

8. IOR, L/PS/10/602, Wingate to FO, 7 Nov. 1916.

9. Even Sir Mark Sykes, who had previously opposed the dispatch of troops, was wavering. He had been swayed by Norman Bray, a junior officer who had also visited Rabigh and who took the view that a brigade could successfully defend the wells there.

10. T. E. Lawrence, *Seven Pillars of Wisdom* (London, 1935), p. 111.

11. SAD, Clayton Papers, 694/4, "Observations by Lt Lawrence," 18 Nov. 1916.

12. Ibid.

13. TNA, FO 882/26, *Arab Bulletin*, no. 60 (20 Aug. 1917), Lawrence's "Twenty-seven Articles."

14. SAD, Clayton Papers, 694/4, "Observations by Lt Lawrence," 18 Nov. 1916.

15. Edouard Brémond, *Le Hedjaz dans la Guerre Mondiale* (Paris, 1931), p. 98.

16. PCC, Storrs Papers, Storrs to Sybil Graham, 21 Nov. 1916.

17. IOR, L/PS/10/602, Wingate to Grey, 22 Nov. 1916.

18. SAD, Wingate Papers, Wingate to Wilson, 23 Nov. 1916.

19. TNA, FO 882/6, Lawrence's diary of his visit to Feisal, 2–5 Dec. 1916.

20. Lawrence, *Seven Pillars of Wisdom* (1935), p. 119.

21. TNA, FO 882/6, Lawrence's diary of his visit to Feisal, 2–5 Dec. 1916.

22. Ibid.

23. After the war Lawrence presented the rifle to King George V, who in turn gave it to the Imperial War Museum in London, where it is displayed today.

24. TNA, FO 882/6, Lawrence to Hogarth, 5 Dec. 1916.

25. Ibid.

26. Ibid.

27. BL, Add 45914, entry dated 5 Dec. 1916.

28. TNA, FO 882/6, Lawrence to Hogarth, n.d.

29. BL, Add 45914, entry dated 6 Jan. 1917; TNA, WO 158/625, P184A.

30. Lawrence, *Seven Pillars of Wisdom* (1935), p. 129.

31. IWM, H. Garland Papers, lecture, n.d. (but before April 1921). Garland's draft lecture notes contain a great deal of criticism about the Bedu, some of which he then crossed out, but which is still legible. I have quoted freely from this material, on the basis that it appears to represent Garland's heartfelt views, even if he did not wish to share them with an audience.

32. IWM, H. Garland Papers, lecture, n.d.

33. T. E. Lawrence, *Seven Pillars of Wisdom: The Complete 1922 "Oxford" Text*, rev. ed. (Fordingbridge, 2004), p. 121.

34. TNA, FO 882/6, Lawrence to Director, Arab Bureau, n.d.

35. Lawrence had just written to Hogarth, "One of the things not fixed when I came down here was my chief, and my manner of reporting. It is probably through Colonel Wilson." TNA, FO 882/6, Lawrence to Hogarth, 5 Dec. 1916.

36. David Garnett, ed., *The Letters of T. E. Lawrence* (London, 1938), p. 213, Lawrence to Wilson, 6 Dec. 1916.

37. LHCMA, Joyce Papers, 1/7, Joyce to Wilson, 9 Dec. 1916.

38. LHCMA, Joyce Papers, 1/1, Joyce to Wilson, 15 Nov. 1916.

39. Brémond, *Le Hedjaz dans la Guerre Mondiale*, p. 88.

40. LHCMA, Joyce Papers, 1/3, Joyce to Wilson, 26 Nov. 1916.

41. LHCMA, Joyce Papers, 1/11, Joyce to Rees-Mogg, 21 Dec. 1916.

42. TNA, FO 141/736, Joyce to Arab Bureau, 24 Jan. 1917.

43. IWM, T. Henderson, *The Hejaz Expedition, 1916–17—A Narrative of the Work Done by the Arabian Detachment of No. 14 Squadron RFC While Attached to the Hejaz Expedition*, n.d.

44. TNA, FO 882/6, Wilson to Arab Bureau, 12 Dec. 1916.

45. PCC, Storrs Papers, "Visit to Grand Sharif," 13 Dec. 1916.

8. TURNING POINT

1. BL, Add 52463, Robertson to Murray, 1 Dec. 1916.

2. IOR, L/PS/10/602, Hirtzel, minute, 8 Dec. 1916.

3. IOR, L/PS/10/602, piece 5213, Chamberlain, note, 11 Dec. 1916.

4. LHCMA, Robertson Papers, 4/4/63, Robertson to Murray, 11 Dec. 1916.

5. IOR, L/PS/10/602, FO to Wingate, 11 Dec. 1916.

6. IOR, L/PS/10/602, piece 5230, Wingate to FO, 11 Dec. 1916; TNA, FO 686/6, George Lloyd's report, 22 Dec. 1916.

7. TNA, FO 882/6, Wilson to Arab Bureau, 12 Dec. 1916.

8. IOR, L/PS/10/602, Wingate to Wilson, 11 Dec. 1916.

9. Ronald Storrs, *Orientations* (London, 1937), p. 212.

10. PCC, Storrs Papers, "Visit to Grand Sharif," 13 Dec. 1916.

11. Storrs, *Orientations*, p. 213.

12. TNA, FO 686/6, Report on the Hijaz, 22 Dec. 1916.

13. Otto Liman von Sanders, *Five Years in Turkey* (Nashville, 2000), pp. 144–45.

14. Ibid., p. 231; George Stitt, *A Prince of Arabia: The Emir Shereef Ali Haider* (London, 1948), pp. 174–75.

15. Stitt, *Prince of Arabia*, p. 171.

16. TNA, FO 882/26, *Arab Bulletin*, no. 39 (19 Jan. 1917).

17. T. E. Lawrence, *Seven Pillars of Wisdom: The Complete 1922 "Oxford" Text*, rev. ed. (Fordingbridge, 2004), p. 124.

18. Philip P. Graves, ed., *Memoirs of King Abdullah* (London, 1950), p. 165.

19. TNA, T 1/12249.

20. Earl of Cork and Orrery, *My Naval Life* (London, 1942), p. 108.

21. TNA, FO 882/25, *Arab Bulletin*, no. 32 (11 Nov. 1916).

22. TNA, FO 686/6, Garland's report, 6 March 1917.

23. TNA, FO 882/26, *Arab Bulletin*, no. 39 (19 Jan. 1917).

24. TNA, FO 882/26, *Arab Bulletin*, no. 37 (4 Jan. 1917.)

25. TNA, WO 158/625, piece 171A, 11 Dec. 1916.

26. Stitt, *Prince of Arabia*, p. 171.

27. TNA, FO 882/28, *Arab Bulletin*, no. 110 (30 April 1919).

28. TNA, FO 882/6, Lawrence to Cornwallis, 27 Dec. 1916.

29. H. V. F. Winstone, ed., *The Diaries of Parker Pasha* (London, 1983), Parker's report, 10 Oct. 1916, p. 141.

30. Lawrence, *Seven Pillars of Wisdom* (1922), p. 131.

31. TNA, FO 686/6, Lawrence to Wilson, 8 Jan. 1917.

32. Ibid.

33. IOR, L/PS/11/116, piece 243, Hirtzel's memorandum, 15 Jan. 1917.

34. SAD, Wingate Papers, 145/1, Murray to Wingate, 5 Jan. 1917.

35. SAD, Clayton Papers, 694/5, draft orders for GOC Rabegh, 7 Jan. 1917.

36. TNA, FO 141/736, Wilson to Arab Bureau, 7 Jan. 1917.

37. IOR, L/PS/11/116, piece 243, Hirtzel's memorandum, 15 Jan. 1917.

38. SAD, Wingate Papers, 145/1, Wingate to FO, 12 Jan. 1917.

39. SAD, Wingate Papers, 145/1, Murray to Wingate, 19 Jan. 1917.

40. IOR, L/PS/11/118, piece 585, Wingate to Balfour, 24 Jan. 1917.

41. Malcolm Brown, ed., *Lawrence of Arabia: The Selected Letters* (London, 2005), p. 106, Lawrence to Sarah Lawrence, 16 Jan. 1917.

42. Cork and Orrery, *My Naval Life*, p. 102.

43. Ibid.

44. Lawrence, *Seven Pillars of Wisdom* (1922), p. 137.

45. Edouard Brémond, *Le Hedjaz dans la Guerre Mondiale* (Paris, 1931), p. 120.

46. MEC, Newcombe Papers, Lawrence to Newcombe, 17 Jan. 1917. Newcombe seems to have taken the advice to heart, for he carried the letter around with him in the Hijaz.

47. TNA, FO 686/6, Lawrence's report to Wilson, 8 Jan. 1917.

48. BL, Add 45914, entry for 22 Jan. 1917, f. 49.

9. WAJH

1. Victoria Wester Wemyss, *The Life and Letters of Lord Wester Wemyss* (London, 1935), p. 346, diary entry for 21 Jan. 1917.

2. N. N. E. Bray, *Shifting Sands* (London, 1934), p. 119.

3. TNA, FO 882/27, *Arab Bulletin*, no. 41 (6 Feb. 1917).

4. Bray, *Shifting Sands*, pp. 128–29.

5. TNA, FO 882/27, *Arab Bulletin*, no. 41 (6 Feb. 1917).

6. Bray, *Shifting Sands*, p. 123.

7. Ibid., p. 131.

8. BL, Add 45914, f. 7.

9. T. E. Lawrence, *Seven Pillars of Wisdom* (London, 1935), p. 163.

10. Malcolm Brown, ed., *Lawrence of Arabia: The Selected Letters* (London, 2005), p. 108, Lawrence to Sarah Lawrence, 31 Jan. 1917; TNA, FO 141/736, Weldon to Arab Bureau, 25 Jan. 1917.

11. TNA, FO 882/6, Vickery, "The General Situation in Arabia (Hedjaz) and the Policy and Organisation of the British Mission to Grand Sharif," 2 Feb. 1917.

12. Bray, *Shifting Sands*, p. 132.

13. TNA, FO 882/26, *Arab Bulletin*, no. 41 (6 Feb. 1917).

14. H. V. F. Winstone, ed., *The Diaries of Parker Pasha* (London, 1983), p. 97, quoting notes written by Parker but titled "Oct. 1915, TEL Arab Tribes in Arabia."

15. TNA, FO 882/17, Gertrude Bell, "Northern Arabia," and FO 882/4, Dmitri Ibrahim, report, after 17 Aug. 1916; Winstone, ed., *Diaries of Parker Pasha*, p. 97.

16. TNA, FO 882/6, Bray, report, n.d. but before 4 Jan. 1917.

17. SAD, Clayton Papers, 694/4, Salmond to Clayton, 12 Nov. 1916.

18. Musbah Haidar, *Arabesque* (London, 1945), p. 91; Eugene Rogan, *Frontiers of the State in the Late Ottoman Empire* (Cambridge, 1999), p. 228; George Stitt, *A Prince of Arabia* (London, 1948), p. 180. The reward was reputed to be £20,000, or roughly $1.8 million today.

19. SAD, Clayton Papers, 693/11, Lawrence to Sykes, 9 Sept. 1917 (unsent).

20. MEC, Hogarth Papers, Hogarth to Laura Hogarth, 3 Feb. 1917.

21. BL, Add 45914, f. 26.

22. LHCMA, Joyce 1/78, Joyce to Wilson, 23 March 1917.

23. TNA, FO 882/6, Joyce to Wilson, 1 April 1917.

24. Quoted in Henry Laurens, "Jaussen en Arabie," *Photographies d'Arabie, Hedjaz 1907–1917* (Paris, 1999), p. 30.

25. BL, Add 45914, f. 21.

26. Ibid.

27. BL, Add 45914, f. 19.

28. Alois Musil, *The Northern Hegaz* (New York, 1926), p. 7.

29. University of Newcastle, Gertrude Bell Archive, letter, 25 Jan. 1914.

30. TNA, FO 882/6, Lawrence to Clayton, 28 Feb. 1917.

31. TNA, FO 882/6, Pearson to Clayton, n.d., and Clayton to Pearson, 2 March 1917.

10. THE FIRST
RAILWAY RAIDS

1. TNA, WO 158/987, *Handbook of Hejaz* (Cairo, 1917), p. 15.
2. SAD, Wingate Papers, 132/5, "G," "The Hedjaz Railway," filed 23 Dec. 1907.
3. A. J. B. Wavell, *A Modern Pilgrim in Mecca*, 2d ed. (London, 1918), p. 72.
4. TNA, WO 158/987, *Handbook of Hejaz*, p. 9.
5. TNA, FO 882/4, Garland's report, 6 March 1917.
6. IWM, H. Garland Papers, postwar lecture, n.d.
7. Ibid.
8. Touchan et al., "A 396-Year Reconstruction of Precipitation in Southern Jordan," *Journal of the American Water Resources Association* 35, no. 1 (Feb. 1999).
9. IWM, H. Garland Papers, postwar lecture, n.d.
10. IWM, T. Henderson, *The Hejaz Expedition*.
11. Earl Winterton, *Fifty Tumultuous Years* (London, 1955), p. 8.
12. IWM, H. Garland Papers, postwar lecture, n.d.
13. TNA, FO 882/4, Garland's report, 6 March 1917.
14. It is impossible to be certain whether the train was traveling north or south. In a lecture after the war Garland claimed it was heading south. However, after the attack Wingate reported that a train had been mined

heading north in the same area (TNA, FO 882/6, Wingate to Robertson, 21 Feb. 1917).
15. IWM, H. Garland Papers, postwar lecture, n.d.
16. Ibid. and TNA, FO 882/4, Garland's report, 6 March 1917.
17. TNA, FO 882/4, Garland's report, 6 March 1917.
18. Ibid.
19. IWM, H. Garland Papers, postwar lecture, n.d., and TNA, FO 882/4, Garland's report, 6 March 1917.
20. IWM, H. Garland Papers, Joyce to Garland, 3 March 1917.
21. *Photographies d'Arabie, Hedjaz 1907–1917* (Paris, 1999), p. 51.
22. IWM, Henderson, *Hejaz Expedition*.
23. George Stitt, *A Prince of Arabia* (London, 1948), p. 177.
24. Ibid., p. 178.
25. Ibid., pp. 178–79.
26. TNA, FO 882/6, Wingate to Robertson, 19 March 1917; FO 141/736, Wingate to Pearson, 6 March 1917.
27. MEC, Hogarth Papers, Hogarth to Laura Hogarth, 7 Nov. 1917.
28. MEC, Karadogan Papers, Karadogan to Monroe, 17 Sept. 1971.
29. TNA, FO 686/6, Newcombe's report, 12 March 1917.
30. Ibid.
31. BL, Add 45914, f. 23.
32. David Garnett, ed., *The Letters of T. E. Lawrence* (London, 1938), p. 222, Lawrence to Wilson, 9 March 1917.
33. BL, Add 45915, f. 22.
34. BL, Add 45915, f. 25.
35. T. E. Lawrence, *Seven Pillars of Wisdom* (London, 1935), pp. 186–87.
36. Edouard Brémond, *Le Hedjaz dans la Guerre Mondiale* (Paris, 1931),

p. 72. The Field of Cloth of Gold was the name given to the place of a meeting between Henry VIII of England and Francis I of France in 1520. Each king had tried to outdo the other in the splendor of his camp.

37. BL, Add 45983A, entries for 17–25 March 1917.

38. TNA, FO 882/6, Newcombe to Hogarth, 3 April 1917.

39. Quoted in Suleiman Mousa, *T. E. Lawrence: An Arab View* (Oxford, 1966), p. 55.

40. Philip P. Graves, ed., *Memoirs of King Abdullah* (London, 1950), p. 170.

41. TNA, FO 686/6, Lawrence's report, 24 April 1917.

42. Lawrence, *Seven Pillars of Wisdom* (1935), p. 199.

43. Ibid., p. 202.

44. TNA, FO 686/6, Lawrence's report, 24 April 1917.

45. Ibid.

11. DIFFERENCES OVER TACTICS

1. TNA, FO 686/6, Lawrence's report, 16 April 1917.

2. T. E. Lawrence, *Seven Pillars of Wisdom* (London, 1935), pp. 192–93.

3. TNA, FO 686/6, Newcombe's report, 4 May 1917.

4. BL, Add 45915, reverse f. 48.

5. SAD, Clayton Papers, 470/6, Wilson to Clayton, 16 Jan. 1917.

6. Lawrence, *Seven Pillars of Wisdom* (1935), p. 194.

7. BL, Add 45914, f. 13.

8. Lawrence, *Seven Pillars of Wisdom* (1935), p. 221.

9. Alois Musil, *The Northern Hegaz* (New York, 1926), p. 7; Richard Burton, *Personal Narrative of a Pilgrimage to Al-Madinah and Meccah* (London, 1893), p. 119.

10. Musil, *Northern Hegaz*, p. 8, and MAE, Guerre 1914–1918, 878, 173–81, Defrance, "Le mouvement arabe à la frontière du désert syrien," 30 Aug. 1917.

11. Lawrence, *Seven Pillars of Wisdom* (1935), p. 221. It was not until that autumn that the British supplied him with a replacement set. SAD, Clayton Papers, 694/5, George Lloyd, "Diary of a Journey with TEL to El Jaffer."

12. TNA, FO 882/7, Lawrence to Clayton, 27 Aug. 1917.

13. MEC, Sykes Papers, Clayton's report on Feisal's plans, 29 May 1917.

14. TNA, FO 686/6, Lawrence's report, late April 1917.

15. TNA FO 882/6, Clayton's note, n.d., but after 5 April 1917.

16. MEC, Sykes Papers, Clayton's report on Feisal's plans, 29 May 1917.

17. TNA, FO 686/6, Lawrence to Wilson, 8 Jan. 1917.

18. BL, Add 45914, f. 29.

19. TNA, FO 882/6, Lawrence to Wilson, 16 April 1917.

20. BL, Add 45914, f. 29.

21. MEC, Sykes Papers, Clayton's report on Feisal's plans, 29 May 1917.

22. MEC, Sykes Papers, minute of Sykes's interview at 10 Downing Street, 16 Dec. 1915.

23. BL, Add 52463, Murray to Robertson, 29 Feb. 1917.

24. MEC, Sykes Papers, note of a conference held at 10 Downing Street, 3 April 1917.

25. Ibid.

26. MEC, Sykes Papers, Sykes to Wingate, 5 May 1917.

27. Ibid.

28. IOR, L/PS/11/119, Wingate to Balfour, 28 April 1917.

29. Quoted in Roger Adelson, *Mark Sykes* (London, 1975), p. 230.

30. TNA, FO 686/6, Lawrence to Wilson, 8 Jan. 1917.

31. TNA, FO 686/6, Lawrence's report, 24 April 1917.

32. MEC, Sykes Papers, Sykes to Wingate, 5 May 1917.

33. Edouard Brémond, *Le Hedjaz dans la Guerre Mondiale* (Paris, 1931), pp. 137–38.

34. SAD, Clayton Papers, 693/12, Clayton to Storrs, 7 May 1917.

12. FIGHTING FOR US ON A LIE

1. SAD, Clayton Papers, 693/11, Lawrence to Sykes (unsent), 7 Sept. 1917.

2. T. E. Lawrence, *Seven Pillars of Wisdom* (London, 1935), p. 148.

3. Alec Kirkbride, *An Awakening* ([Tavistock, Eng.], 1971), p. 51.

4. BL, Add 45983A, 11–12 May 1917.

5. BL, Add 45915, reverse f. 47.

6. Lawrence, *Seven Pillars of Wisdom* (1935), p. 237.

7. Woodrow Wilson, speech to Congress, 2 April 1917.

8. Charles Seymour, ed., *The Intimate Papers of Colonel House*, vol. 3 (London, 1928), p. 47.

9. IOR, L/PS/10/609, Wingate to Balfour, 23 April 1917; Wingate to Balfour, 10 May 1917; Balfour to Wingate, 14 May 1917.

10. MEC, Sykes Papers, Sykes to Wingate, 22 Feb. 1917.

11. MEC, Sykes Papers, Sykes to Wingate, 23 May 1917.

12. IOR, L/PS/11/124, Wemyss's report, 13 June 1917.

13. MEC, Sykes Papers, Sykes to Cox, 23 May 1917.

14. TNA, FO 882/12, Lawrence to Wilson, 30 July 1917.

15. IOR, L/PS/11/124, Wemyss's report, 13 June 1917.

16. MEC, Sykes Papers, Sykes to Wingate, 23 May 1917.

17. TNA, FO 371/3054, Wingate to Balfour, enclosing reports from Lawrence, 16 Aug. 1917.

18. George Antonius, *The Arab Awakening* (London, 1938), pp. 423–24, McMahon to Husein, 13 Dec. 1915.

19. SAD, Clayton Papers, 693/13, Clayton to "George," 2 March 1918.

20. MEC, Sykes Papers, Sykes to Wingate, 23 May 1917.

21. Ibid.

22. BL, Add 45915, 20 May 1917, f. 50.

23. BL, Add 45915, reverse f. 49.

24. Ibid.

25. BL, Add 45915, 22 May 1917, f. 53.

26. Lawrence, *Seven Pillars of Wisdom* (1935), p. 248.

27. BL, Add 45915, 23 May 1917, reverse f. 52.

28. Lawrence, *Seven Pillars of Wisdom* (1935), p. 253.

29. TNA, FO 882/26, *Arab Bulletin*, no. 60 (20 Aug. 1917), Lawrence's "Twenty-seven Articles."

30. Lawrence, *Seven Pillars of Wisdom* (1935), p. 255.

31. Ibid.
32. BL, Add 45915, f. 53.
33. Lawrence, *Seven Pillars of Wisdom* (1935), p. 254.
34. BL, Add 45915, f. 54.
35. Lawrence, *Seven Pillars of Wisdom* (1935), p. 270.
36. Ibid., p. 265.
37. BL, Add 45915, f. 54.
38. Lawrence, *Seven Pillars of Wisdom* (1935), p. 266.
39. BL, Add 45915, f. 55.
40. BL, Add 45983A, 5 June 1917.
41. BL, Add 45915, reverse f. 55.

13. STALEMATE IN THE HIJAZ

1. MEC, Sykes Papers, Clayton's report on Feisal's plans, 29 May 1917.
2. IWM, H. Garland Papers, postwar lecture, n.d.
3. TNA, FO 686/6, Newcombe's report on raids of 4–10 May 1917.
4. TNA, FO 686/6, Garland's report, 22 May 1917.
5. LHCMA, Joyce Papers, 1/F/16–17, Hornby to Newcombe, 17 May 1917.
6. TNA, FO 686/6, Garland's report, 22 May 1917.
7. TNA, FO 686/6, Newcombe's report on raids of 4–10 May 1917.
8. Alec Kirkbride, *An Awakening* ([Tavistock, Eng.], 1971), p. 39.
9. William Facey and Najdat Fathi Safwat, eds., *A Soldier's Story—From Ottoman Rule to Independent Iraq: The Memoirs of Jafar Pasha Al-Askari* (London, 2003), p. 105.
10. IWM, Henderson, *The Hejaz Expedition 1916–17.*
11. LHCMA, Joyce Papers, 1/243, Joyce to Wilson, 3 July 1917.

12. Facey and Safwat, eds., *Memoirs of Jafar Pasha Al-Askari*, p. 122.
13. LHCMA, Joyce Papers, 1/245, Joyce to Wilson, 15–16 July 1917. Joyce had ordered 200 pairs of boots in May 1917, asking for "7s, 8s, 9s and a few 10s," Joyce Papers, 1/204.
14. Facey and Safwat, eds., *Memoirs of Jafar Pasha Al-Askari*, p. 122.
15. LHCMA, Joyce Papers, 1/245, Joyce to Wilson, 15–16 July 1917.
16. TNA, WO 339/125412, H. S. Hornby, Army record.
17. T. E. Lawrence, *Seven Pillars of Wisdom* (London, 1935), p. 239.
18. IWM, Henderson, *Hejaz Expedition.*
19. Ibid.
20. TNA, FO 686/6, Newcombe's report, 18 July 1917.
21. LHCMA, Joyce Papers, 1/245, Joyce to Wilson, 15–16 July 1917.
22. Facey and Safwat, eds., *Memoirs of Jafar Pasha Al-Askari*, p. 119.
23. TNA, FO 686/6, Davenport's report, 8 Aug. 1917.
24. Facey and Safwat, eds., *Memoirs of Jafar Pasha Al-Askari*, p. 158.
25. Malcolm Brown, ed., *Lawrence of Arabia: The Selected Letters* (London, 2005), p. 123, Lawrence to Sarah Lawrence, 27 Aug. 1917.

14. TRIUMPH AT AQABA

1. David Garnett, ed., *The Letters of T. E. Lawrence* (London, 1938), p. 225, Lawrence to Clayton, 10 July 1917.
2. T. E. Lawrence, *Seven Pillars of Wisdom* (London, 1935), p. 546.
3. BL, Add 45915, reverse f. 57.
4. TNA, FO 882/27, *Arab Bulletin*, no. 44 (12 March 1917).

5. BL, Add 45915, f. 57.

6. Lawrence, *Seven Pillars of Wisdom* (1935), p. 293.

7. Ibid., p. 298.

8. Ibid., p. 301.

9. Ibid., p. 302.

10. Ibid.

11. Ibid., p. 303.

12. Ibid.

13. T. E. Lawrence, *Seven Pillars of Wisdom* (Oxford, 1922), p. 336. The moment was caught by Lawrence in the photograph used on the cover of this book.

14. BL, Add 45983A, 7 July 1917.

15. THE IMPACT OF AQABA

1. MEC, Sykes Papers, Clayton's report, 10 July 1917.

2. T. E. Lawrence, *Seven Pillars of Wisdom: The Complete 1922 "Oxford" Text*, rev. ed. (Fordingbridge, 2004), p. 347.

3. BL, Add 45915, f. 59.

4. IOR, L/PS/11/124, Wingate to Robertson, 10 July 1917.

5. TNA, FO 882/26, *Arab Bulletin*, no. 57 (24 July 1917).

6. IOR, L/PS/11/124, Wingate to Robertson, 13 July 1917.

7. TNA, WO 33/935, Allenby to Robertson, 13 Oct. 1917.

8. MAE, Guerre 1914–1918, 879, 25–57, Defrance to Ribot, enclosing report by Jaussen, 8 Oct. 1917.

9. Lawrence, *Seven Pillars of Wisdom* (1922), pp. 295 and 305.

10. T. E. Lawrence, *T. E. Lawrence to His Biographers: Robert Graves and Liddell Hart* (London, 1963), pp. 88–89.

11. Jeremy Wilson, *Lawrence of Arabia: The Authorised Biography of T. E. Lawrence* (London, 1989), p. 413. Reference to a "little revolt lately" in the area north of Acre is also made by Jaussen, in a report dispatched by Defrance to Ribot, MAE, Guerre 1914–1918, 879, 25–57, 8 Oct. 1917.

12. Eugene Rogan, *Frontiers of the State in the Late Ottoman Empire* (Cambridge, 1999), p. 231.

13. Basil Liddell Hart, *"T. E. Lawrence": In Arabia and After* (London, 1934), pp. 206–7.

14. IWM, W. F. Stirling Papers, Stirling to his sister, 12 Sept. 1917.

15. MEC, Sykes Papers, Wingate to Balfour, 3 July 1917.

16. MEC, Sykes Papers, Sykes to Clayton, 22 July 1917. TNA, FO 371/3054, Hogarth's memorandum, 10 July 1917.

17. MEC, Hogarth Papers, Hogarth to Clayton, 20 July 1917.

18. MEC, Sykes Papers, Sykes to Clayton, 22 July 1917; Sykes to Drummond, 20 July 1917.

19. MEC, Hogarth Papers, Hogarth to Clayton, 20 July 1917.

20. David Garnett, ed., *The Letters of T. E. Lawrence* (London, 1938), pp. 228–30, Lawrence to Clayton, 10 July 1917.

21. MEC, Sykes Papers, Clayton's report, 16 July 1917.

22. LHCMA, Allenby Papers, 1/8/6, Allenby to Lady Allenby, 9 July 1917.

23. T. E. Lawrence, *Seven Pillars of Wisdom* (London, 1935), p. 322.

24. Anthony Bruce, *The Last Crusade* (London, 2003), p. 116.

25. TNA, WO 106/718, Allenby to Robertson, 16 July 1917.

26. TNA, WO 158/634, Allenby to Robertson, 19 July 1917.

27. TNA, FO 882/16, Clayton to Sykes, 22 July 1917.

28. MEC, Sykes Papers, Sykes to Clayton, 22 July 1917.

29. Edward Robinson, *Lawrence the Rebel* (London, 1946), p. 92.

30. TNA, WO 158/634, piece 24A.

31. LHCMA, Robertson Papers, 8/1/67, Robertson to Allenby, 1 Aug. 1917.

16. IMPOLITIC TRUTHS

1. TNA, WO 158/611, Robertson to Allenby, 10 Aug. 1917.

2. Quoted in Jeremy Wilson, *Lawrence of Arabia: The Authorised Biography of T. E. Lawrence* (London, 1989), p. 427.

3. LHCMA, Robertson Papers, 8/1/69, Robertson to Allenby, 10 Aug. 1917.

4. TNA, WO 158/634, Lawrence's report, 6 Aug. 1917; T. E. Lawrence, *Seven Pillars of Wisdom* (Oxford, 1922), p. 355.

5. LHCMA, Robertson Papers, 8/1/70, Allenby to Robertson, 21 Aug. 1917.

6. TNA, WO 158/634, piece 41B, Arab Bureau to GHQ, 16 Aug. 1917.

7. Malcolm Brown, ed., *Lawrence of Arabia: The Selected Letters* (London, 2005), pp. 126–27, Lawrence to Clayton, 27 Aug. 1917.

8. William Facey and Najdat Fathi Safwat, eds., *The Memoirs of Jafar Pasha Al-Askari* (London, 2003), p. 132.

9. TNA, WO 158/634, MacIndoe's report, 27 Aug. 1917.

10. TNA, WO 158/634, piece 91A, Joyce to Clayton, 12 Sept. 1917, reported by Clayton to GSO, 20 Sept. 1917.

11. Brown, ed., *Lawrence of Arabia: The Selected Letters*, p. 125, Lawrence to Clayton, 27 Aug. 1917.

12. MEC, Sykes Papers, Sykes to Clayton, 22 July 1917.

13. SAD, Clayton Papers, 693/11, Lawrence to Sykes, 9 Sept. 1917 (unsent).

14. SAD, Clayton Papers, 693/11, Lawrence to Clayton, 7 Sept. 1917.

15. SAD, Clayton Papers, 694/5, Lloyd, "Diary of a Journey with TEL to El Jaffer."

16. T. E. Lawrence, *Seven Pillars of Wisdom* (London, 1935), p. 359.

17. TNA, FO 882/4, Clayton to General Staff, enclosing Lawrence's report, 29 Sept. 1917.

18. T. E. Lawrence, *Seven Pillars of Wisdom: The Complete 1922 "Oxford" Text*, rev. ed. (Fordingbridge, 2004), p. 399.

19. Lawrence, *Seven Pillars of Wisdom* (1935), p. 361.

20. Ibid., p. 367.

21. A. W. Lawrence, ed., *T. E. Lawrence by His Friends* (London, 1954), p. 167.

22. Lawrence, *Seven Pillars of Wisdom* (1935), p. 368.

23. David Garnett, ed., *The Letters of T. E. Lawrence* (London, 1938), pp. 237–38, Lawrence to Leeds, 24 Sept. 1917.

24. LHCMA, Liddell Hart Papers, 9/13/42, Lawrence to Stirling, 25 Sept. 1917.

25. BL, Add 45903, Lawrence to Charlotte Shaw, 29 March 1927, with a copy of a letter to Vyvyan Richards, 15 July 1918, on the reverse.

26. MEC, Hogarth Papers, Hogarth to Laura Hogarth, 14 Oct. 1917.

27. Lawrence, ed., *T. E. Lawrence by His Friends*, p. 167.

28. LHCMA, Joyce Papers, 1/258, Joyce to Clayton, 25 Sept. 1917.

29. SAD, Wingate Papers, 146/3, Lloyd to Wingate, 17 Aug. 1917.

30. Garnett, ed., *Letters of T. E. Lawrence*, p. 236, Lawrence to Wilson, 2 Sept. 1917.

17. DIFFICULT TIMES

1. SAD, Clayton Papers, 693/12, Clayton to Lawrence, 20 Sept. 1917.

2. LHCMA, Joyce Papers, 1/254, Joyce to Clayton, 17 Sept. 1917.

3. Malcolm Brown, ed., *Lawrence of Arabia: The Selected Letters* (London, 2005), p. 125, Lawrence to Clayton, 27 Aug. 1917.

4. L. Schatkowski Schilcher, "The Famine of 1915–1918 in Greater Syria," in John Spagnolo, ed., *Problems of the Modern Middle East in Historical Perspective* (Reading, 1996).

5. LHCMA, Joyce Papers, 1/255, Joyce to Clayton, 18 Sept. 1917.

6. LHCMA, Joyce Papers, 1/255, Joyce to Clayton, 25 Sept. 1917.

7. T. E. Lawrence, *Seven Pillars of Wisdom: The Complete 1922 "Oxford" Text*, rev. ed. (Fordingbridge, 2004), p. 98.

8. TNA, WO 158/634, Snagge's report, 1 Oct. 1917.

9. Ibid.

10. MEC, Sykes Papers, Sykes to Cox, 23 May 1917.

11. LHCMA, Joyce Papers, 1/258, Joyce to Clayton, 25 Sept. 1917.

12. Edouard Brémond, *Le Hedjaz dans la Guerre Mondiale* (Paris, 1931), p. 179.

13. Ibid., p. 177.

14. TNA, WO 158/634, Jeddah to Arab Bureau, 26 Nov. 1917.

15. TNA, FO 686/6, Davenport's report, 8 Aug. 1917.

16. TNA, WO 158/611, Robertson to Allenby, 5 Oct. 1917.

17. TNA, WO 158/611, Allenby to Robertson, 9 Oct. 1917.

18. MEC, Sykes Papers, Clayton to Sykes, 20 Sept. 1917.

19. TNA, FO 371/3054, note on the situation in Egypt, 10 July 1917.

20. SAD, 146/7, FO to Wingate, 19 Oct. 1917; Wingate referred to the report from Bern (dated 25 Oct.) in a telegram on 2 Nov. 1917 (IOR, L/PS/10/609, piece 4396).

21. Alec Kirkbride, *An Awakening* ([Tavistock, Eng.], 1971), p. 17.

22. Brémond, *Le Hedjaz dans la Guerre Mondiale*, p. 215.

23. TNA, FO 882/26, *Arab Bulletin*, no. 66 (21 Oct. 1917).

24. Ibid.

25. Quoted in Christophe Leclerc, "The French Soldiers in the Arab Revolt," *Journal of the T. E. Lawrence Society*, 9, no. 1 (Autumn 1999).

26. TNA, FO 882/26, *Arab Bulletin*, no. 66 (21 Oct. 1917).

27. Lawrence, *Seven Pillars of Wisdom* (1922), p. 423.

28. SAD, Clayton Papers, 693/12, Clayton to Lawrence, 20 Sept. 1917.

29. LHCMA, Robertson Papers, 8/1/73, Allenby to Robertson, 17 Oct. 1917.

30. Ibid.

31. TNA, FO 371/3054, Hogarth to Ormsby-Gore, 26 Oct. 1917.

32. MEC, Sykes Papers, Clayton to Sykes, 18 Oct. 1917.

18. GAZA AND YARMUK:
VICTORY AND FAILURE

1. TNA, FO 882/26, *Arab Bulletin* no. 67 (30 Oct. 1917).
2. Ibid.
3. William Facey and Najdat Fathi Safwat, eds., *The Memoirs of Jafar Pasha Al-Askari* (London, 2003), p. 130.
4. MEC, Sykes Papers, extract from Pearson to Clayton, 5 Oct. 1917, in Clayton to Sykes, 18 Oct. 1917.
5. SAD, Clayton Papers, 693/12, Clayton to Joyce, 30 Oct. 1917.
6. IWM, Lawrence Papers, notes on the campaign dictated by Lawrence to Edward Robinson, Sept. 1917.
7. SAD, Clayton Papers, 693/11, Lawrence to Clayton, 24 Oct. 1917.
8. Ibid.
9. T. E. Lawrence, *Seven Pillars of Wisdom* (London, 1935), p. 388.
10. CCC, Lloyd Papers, GLLD 9/10, Clayton to Lloyd, 25 Oct. 1917.
11. SAD, Clayton Papers, 693/12, Clayton to Lawrence, 20 Sept. 1917.
12. SAD, Clayton Papers, 694/5, Lloyd, "Diary of a Journey with TEL to El Jaffer."
13. Ibid.
14. Ibid.
15. Lawrence, *Seven Pillars of Wisdom* (1935), p. 401.
16. CCC, Lloyd Papers, GLLD 9/10, Lloyd's notes, n.d.
17. Lawrence, *Seven Pillars of Wisdom* (1935), p. 398.
18. SAD, Clayton Papers, 694/5, Lloyd, "Diary of a Journey with TEL to El Jaffer," n.d.
19. Ibid.
20. Lawrence, *Seven Pillars of Wisdom* (1935), p. 401.
21. The bombardment, designed to divert Turkish attention away from Beersheba, where the main thrust of the offensive was aimed, in fact began on 27 Oct., the previous day.
22. SAD, Clayton Papers, 694/5, Lloyd, "Diary of a Journey with TEL to El Jaffer," n.d.
23. MEC, Hogarth Papers, Hogarth to Laura Hogarth, 11 Nov. 1917.
24. MEC, Hogarth Papers, Hogarth to Billy Hogarth, 2–3 Nov. 1917.
25. TNA, FO 882/7, Joyce to Clayton, 4 Nov. 1917.
26. Lawrence, *Seven Pillars of Wisdom* (1935), p. 411.
27. Ibid., p. 423.
28. David Garnett, ed., *The Letters of T. E. Lawrence* (London, 1938), p. 239, Lawrence to Joyce, 13 Nov. 1917.
29. Lawrence, *Seven Pillars of Wisdom* (1935), p. 425.
30. Ibid., p. 428.
31. T. E. Lawrence, *Seven Pillars of Wisdom: The Complete 1922 "Oxford" Text*, rev. ed. (Fordingbridge, 2004), p. 483.
32. Malcolm Brown, ed., *Lawrence of Arabia: The Selected Letters* (London, 2005), p. 140, Lawrence to his parents, 14 Dec. 1917.
33. TNA, FO 158/634, Joyce to Arab Bureau, 25 Nov. 1917.
34. MEC, Hogarth Papers, Hogarth to Laura Hogarth, 26 Nov. 1917.
35. MEC, Hogarth Papers, Hogarth to Laura Hogarth, 29 Nov. 1917.
36. TNA, FO 882/26, *Arab Bulletin*, no. 73 (5 Dec. 1917).

19. DARA OR AZRAK: WHERE WAS LAWRENCE?

1. T. E. Lawrence, *Seven Pillars of Wisdom* (London, 1935), p. 442.
2. Malcolm Brown, ed., *Lawrence of Arabia: The Selected Letters* (London, 2005), p. 175, Lawrence to W. F. Stirling, 28 June 1919.
3. TNA, FO 141/510/7.
4. T. E. Lawrence, *Seven Pillars of Wisdom: The Complete 1922 "Oxford" Text*, rev. ed. (Fordingbridge, 2004), p. 496.
5. Ibid., p. 497.
6. Ibid., p. 498.
7. Ibid., p. 499.
8. BL, Add 45983A. An unusual change in the style of Lawrence's capital As for 27–28 Nov. (both entries are for "Akaba") suggests that he wrote up the earlier entries no later than 26 Nov.
9. Quoted in Lawrence James, *The Golden Warrior* (London, 1990), p. 252.
10. I would never have bothered requesting this test had I already known, as I subsequently discovered, that a similar test had been commissioned by J. N. Lockman during research for his book *Scattered Tracks on the Lawrence Trail* (Whitmore Lake, Mich., 1996). Lockman said his test revealed nothing.
11. Brown, ed., *Lawrence of Arabia: The Selected Letters*, p. 138, Lawrence to Sarah Lawrence, 14 Nov. 1917; p. 139, Lawrence to his parents, 14 Dec. 1917.
12. BL, Add 45903, Lawrence to Charlotte Shaw, 19 July 1924.
13. Lawrence, *Seven Pillars of Wisdom* (1935), p. 30.
14. Ibid.
15. Ibid., p. 496.
16. Ibid., p. 348.
17. BL, Add 45903, Lawrence to Charlotte Shaw, 28 Sept. 1925.
18. BL, Add 45903, Lawrence to Charlotte Shaw, 26 Dec. 1925.
19. Lawrence, *Seven Pillars of Wisdom* (1935), p. 445.
20. Lawrence, *Seven Pillars of Wisdom* (1922), p. 502.

20. THE BALFOUR DECLARATION AND ITS AFTERMATH

1. Reproduced in Leonard Stein, *The Balfour Declaration* (London, 1961), frontispiece.
2. Hew Strachan, *The First World War*, vol. 1 (Oxford, 2003), p. 957.
3. Robert Gildea, *Barricades and Borders: Europe 1800–1914* (Oxford, 1987), p. 284.
4. MEC, Clayton Papers, Clayton to Wingate, 3 Aug. 1916.
5. MEC, Sykes Papers, 19 July 1917.
6. Quoted in Stein, *Balfour Declaration*, p. 275, Sykes to Sokolow, 12 April 1917.
7. SAD, Wingate Papers, 166/3, Wingate to Allenby, 17 Dec. 1917.
8. Quoted in Stein, *Balfour Declaration*, p. 275, Sledmere Papers, no. 66, ca. Sept. 1917.
9. MEC, Sykes Papers, Clayton to Sykes, 28 Nov. 1917.
10. SAD, Clayton Papers, 693/13, Clayton to Bell, 8 Dec. 1917.
11. University of Newcastle, Gertrude Bell Archive, Bell to Mary Bell, 25 Jan. 1918.
12. SAD, Clayton Papers, 693/13, Clayton to Bell, 8 Dec. 1917.

13. MEC, Sykes Papers, Clayton to Sykes, 28 Nov. 1917.

14. TNA, FO 686/38, Wilson's notes of conversation with King Husein, 6 June 1918.

15. TNA, FO 882/26, *Arab Bulletin*, no. 68 (7 Nov. 1917).

16. MEC, Sykes Papers, Wingate to FO, 29 Nov. 1917.

17. IOR, L/PS/10/609, Wingate to FO, 2 Nov. 1917. Husein was reported to have stopped paying the Harb, in *Arab Bulletin*, no. 70 (21 Nov. 1917).

18. IOR, L/PS/10/609, Wingate to FO, 15 Nov. 1917.

19. IOR, L/PS/10/609, FO to Wingate, 6 Feb. 1917.

20. TNA, T 1/12249, piece 33669, note, n.d.

21. TNA, WO 33/946, Allenby to Robertson, 15 Nov. 1917.

22. IOR, L/PS/10/609, piece 4753, FO to Wingate, 17 Nov. 1917.

23. TNA, WO33/946, Robertson to Allenby, 21 Nov. 1917.

24. LHCMA, Allenby Papers, 1/8/32, Allenby to Lady Allenby, 11 Dec. 1917.

25. IWM, H. V. Gilbert Papers.

26. T. E. Lawrence, *Seven Pillars of Wisdom: The Complete 1922 "Oxford" Text*, rev. ed. (Fordingbridge, 2004), p. 510.

27. SAD, Wingate Papers, 147/6, Wingate to Allenby, 27 Dec. 1917.

28. "Jerusalem Delivered," *Glasgow Herald*, 11 Dec. 1917.

29. "Jerusalem," *Times* (London), 11 Dec. 1917.

30. Franz von Papen, *Memoirs* (London, 1952), p. 80.

31. TNA, FO 686/38, Jemal to Feisal, Nov. 1917.

32. Donald M. McKale, *War by Revolution* (Kent, Ohio, 1998), p. 213.

33. SAD, Wingate Papers, 147/2, *El Balagh*, 6 and 12 Dec. 1917, reporting Jemal's speech to the Beirut Club, 5 Dec. 1917.

34. Edward Robinson, *Lawrence the Rebel* (London, 1946), p. 123.

35. Quoted in ibid., p. 119.

21. FIGHTING DE LUXE

1. TNA, WO 158/634, Macauley to EEF, 10 Jan. 1918, forwarded by Campbell on 12 Jan. 1918.

2. LHCMA, Robertson Papers, 4/5/10, Allenby to Robertson, 14 Dec. 1917 and 20 Dec. 1917.

3. IWM, Dawnay Papers, 69/21/2, Allenby to Robertson, 26 Nov. 1917.

4. SAD, Wingate Papers, 148/1, Lt.-Col. for Brig. Gen. Hejaz Ops to Dir. Mil. Int., 5 Jan. 1918.

5. A. W. Lawrence, ed., *T. E. Lawrence by His Friends* (London, 1954), p. 170.

6. T. E. Lawrence, *Seven Pillars of Wisdom: The Complete 1922 "Oxford" Text*, rev. ed. (Fordingbridge, 2004), p. 515.

7. T. E. Lawrence, *Seven Pillars of Wisdom* (London, 1935), p. 458.

8. Lawrence, *Seven Pillars of Wisdom* (1922), p. 518.

9. TNA, FO 882/27, *Arab Bulletin*, no. 77 (27 Jan. 1918).

10. Siddons in his flight log (IWM, V. D. Siddons Papers) mentions low clouds.

11. David Hogarth, *The Penetration of Arabia* (London, 1904), p. 46.

12. MEC, Hogarth Papers, Hogarth to "Mary," 19 Jan. 1918.

13. SAD, Wingate Papers, 148/1, Arab Bureau to Bassett, 6 Jan. 1918.

14. Quoted in Leonard Stein, *The Balfour Declaration* (London, 1961), p. 633.

15. MEC, Hogarth Papers, Hogarth to "Billy," 10 Jan. 1918; TNA, FO 882/27, *Arab Bulletin*, no. 77 (27 Jan. 1918).

16. SAD, Wingate Papers, 148/2, Hogarth to Wingate, 19 Jan. 1918.

17. TNA, FO 882/13, Hogarth to Wingate, 15 Jan. 1918.

18. TNA, FO 882/27, *Arab Bulletin*, no. 77 (27 Jan. 1918).

19. Edward Robinson, *Lawrence the Rebel* (London, 1946), p. 130; William Facey and Najdat Fathi Safwat, eds., *The Memoirs of Jafar Pasha Al-Askari* (London, 2003), p. 154.

20. Lawrence, *Seven Pillars of Wisdom* (1935), p. 472.

21. TNA, WO 158/634, Lawrence to Clayton, 22 Jan. 1918.

22. Eugene Rogan, *Frontiers of the State in the Late Ottoman Empire* (Cambridge, 1999), p. 238.

23. TNA, WO 158/634, Lawrence to Clayton, 22 Jan. 1918.

24. TNA, FO 882/27, *Arab Bulletin*, no. 79 (18 Feb. 1918).

25. Lawrence, *Seven Pillars of Wisdom* (1935), p. 483.

26. Ibid.

27. TNA, FO 882/27, *Arab Bulletin*, no. 92 (11 June 1918).

28. Alec Kirkbride, *An Awakening* ([Tavistock, Eng.], 1971), p. 14.

29. Lawrence, *Seven Pillars of Wisdom* (1935), p. 500.

30. TNA, FO 882/7, Lawrence to Clayton, 12 Feb. 1918.

31. Lawrence, *Seven Pillars of Wisdom* (1922), p. 568.

22. NEW CONDITIONS

1. MEC, Hogarth Papers, Hogarth to "Billy," 25 Feb. 1918.

2. MEC, J. W. A. Young Papers, "A Little to the East," 29 Dec. 1945.

3. Edward Robinson, *Lawrence the Rebel* (London, 1946), p. 133.

4. T. E. Lawrence, *Seven Pillars of Wisdom: The Complete 1922 "Oxford" Text*, rev. ed. (Fordingbridge, 2004), p. 572.

5. Matthew Hughes, *Allenby and British Strategy in the Middle East* (London, 1999), p. 60.

6. LHCMA, Robertson Papers, 7/5/84, Allenby to Robertson, 25 Jan. 1918.

7. LHCMA, Robertson Papers, 7/5/86, Allenby to Robertson, 23 Feb. 1918.

8. TNA, FO 882/3, Clayton to Wilson, 17 Dec. 1917.

9. LHCMA, Joyce Papers, 1/265, Dawnay to Joyce, 22 Feb. 1918.

10. Hubert Young, *The Independent Arab* (London, 1933), pp. 141–42.

11. Ibid.

12. Ibid., p. 18.

13. Malcolm Brown, ed., *Lawrence of Arabia: The Selected Letters* (London, 2005), p. 153, Lawrence to Sarah Lawrence, 8 March 1918.

14. Alec Kirkbride, *An Awakening* ([Tavistock, Eng.], 1971), p. 22.

15. SAD, Clayton Papers, 470/7, Wilson to Clayton, 6 Oct. 1917.

16. Young, *Independent Arab*, p. 150.

17. William Facey and Najdat Fathi Safwat, eds., *The Memoirs of Jafar Pasha Al-Askari* (London, 2003), p. 138.

18. Young, *Independent Arab*, p. 160.

19. Facey and Safwat, eds., *Memoirs of Jafar Pasha Al-Askari*, p. 138. The year 1918 was the wettest in the region since 1798.

20. TNA, WO 158/634, Hedgehog Cairo to Jeddah, 20 March 1918.

21. Otto Liman von Sanders, *Five Years in Turkey* (Nashville, 2000), p. 211.

22. Geoffrey Inchbald, *Imperial Camel Corps* (London, 1970), p. 107.

23. TNA, FO 882/27, *Arab Bulletin*, no. 84 (7 April 1918), and WO 33/946, Allenby to WO, 31 March 1918.

24. Quoted in Martin Gilbert, *First World War* (London, 1994), p. 408.

25. TNA, WO 33/946, WO to Allenby, 27 March 1918.

26. Kirkbride, *Awakening*, pp. 42–43.

27. Ibid., p. 41.

28. Lawrence, *Seven Pillars of Wisdom* (1922), p. 586. See James Elroy Flecker's "The Golden Journey to Samarkand" (1915).

29. LHCMA, Joyce Papers, 2/6, Joyce to Dawnay, 6 Jan. 1918.

30. TNA, FO 882/27, *Arab Bulletin*, no. 80 (26 Feb. 1918).

31. LHCMA, Joyce Papers, 1/270, Dawnay's report, 1 May 1918.

32. TNA, FO 882/26, *Arab Bulletin*, no. 60 (20 Aug. 1917).

33. LHCMA, Joyce Papers, 1/270, Dawnay's report, 1 May 1918.

34. Young, *Independent Arab*, p. 151.

35. Facey and Safwat, eds., *Memoirs of Jafar Pasha Al-Askari*, p. 139.

36. LHCMA, Joyce Papers, 1/270, Dawnay's report, 1 May 1918.

37. T. E. Lawrence, *Seven Pillars of Wisdom* (London, 1935), p. 516.

38. Lawrence, *Seven Pillars of Wisdom* (1922), p. 598.

39. Ibid. Lawrence gave Ali and Othman the names Daud and Farraj in *Seven Pillars of Wisdom*. In this quotation "Daud" has been replaced with "Ali."

40. Quoted in Suleiman Mousa, *T. E. Lawrence: An Arab View* (Oxford, 1966), p. 163.

41. Lawrence, *Seven Pillars of Wisdom* (1935), p. 520.

42. Lawrence, *Seven Pillars of Wisdom* (1922), p. 604.

43. Facey and Safwat, eds., *Memoirs of Jafar Pasha Al-Askari*, p. 143.

44. Young, *Independent Arab*, pp. 165–66.

45. IWM, F. G. Peake Papers, DS/Misc/16.

46. Lawrence, *Seven Pillars of Wisdom* (1935), p. 521.

47. Ibid.

48. Ibid.

49. Ibid., p. 522.

50. IWM, Beaumont Papers, 12 Dec. 1936. In his account, written from memory after the events, Beaumont associates this incident with another raid. However, the detail about the stone striking the turret seems to correlate with Lawrence's description of this raid.

51. S. C. Rolls, *Steel Chariots in the Desert* (London, 1937), p. 176.

52. Lawrence, *Seven Pillars of Wisdom* (1935), p. 522.

53. LHCMA, Joyce Papers, 1/270, Dawnay's report, 1 May 1918.

54. T. E. Lawrence, *T. E. Lawrence to His Biographers: Robert Graves and Liddell Hart* (London, 1963), p. 100.

23. A COMPLETE MUCK-UP

1. MEC, H. W. Young Papers, note, 21 April 1918.

2. Hubert Young, *The Independent Arab* (London, 1933), p. 166.

3. Ibid., p. 165.

4. Ibid., p. 174.

5. TNA, WO 33/946, WO to Allenby, 2 April 1918.

6. IWM, Wilson Papers, HHW 2/33A/2, Allenby to Wilson, 20 April 1918.

7. LHCMA, Robertson Papers 4/4/108, Allenby to Robertson, 7 Dec. 1917.

8. TNA, WO 158/634, Report by E. D. Machray, 24 April 1918.

9. T. E. Lawrence, *Seven Pillars of Wisdom: The Complete 1922 "Oxford" Text*, rev. ed. (Fording-bridge, 2004), p. 611.

10. Quoted in C. T. Atkinson, "General Liman von Sanders on His Experiences in Palestine," *Army Quarterly* 3 (1921–22): 266.

11. Franz von Papen, *Memoirs* (London, 1952), p. 79.

12. IWM, D. H. Calcutt, diary 6 May 1918, quoted in Eugene Rogan, *Frontiers of the State in the Late Ottoman Empire* (Cambridge, 1999), p. 238.

13. TNA, WO 158/634, Hedgehog to Aqaba, 5 May 1918.

14. TNA, WO 158/634, Joyce's report, 31 May 1918, and LHCMA, Joyce Papers, 1/Q/8, testimony of Ibn al-Najdawi, 8 Shaaban, 1336 [ca. 17 May 1918].

15. TNA, WO 158/634, Joyce's report, 31 May 1918.

16. SAD, Wingate Papers, 148/3, Wingate to Allenby, 7 May 1918.

17. MEC, Sykes Papers, Ormsby-Gore to Sykes, 9 April 1918.

18. Count Bernstorff, *Memoirs* (Berlin, 1936), p. 179, quoted in Efraim Karsh and Inari Karsh, "Myth in the Desert, or Not the Great Arab Revolt," in *Middle Eastern Studies* 33, no. 2 (April 1997): 267–312.

19. TNA, WO 158/634, Jemal to Feisal, reported in intelligence notes, 5 June 1918.

20. TNA, FO 371/3881, quoted in Karsh and Karsh, "Myth in the Desert."

21. SAD, Clayton Papers, 470/7, Cornwallis to Clayton, 28 Nov. 1917.

22. TNA, FO 686/38, Bassett to Husein, 2 May 1918.

23. LHCMA, Joyce Papers, 1/271, Bassett to Arab Bureau, 8 May 1918.

24. TNA, FO 686/38, Wilson, note on conversation with King Husein, 27 May 1918.

25. MEC, Hogarth Papers, Hogarth to "Mary," 19 Jan. 1918.

26. TNA, FO 882/27, *Arab Bulletin*, no. 87 (30 April 1918).

27. SAD, Clayton Papers, 693/13, Clayton to Sykes, 4 April 1918.

28. SAD, Wingate Papers, 148/8, Clayton to Wingate, 21 April 1918.

29. LHCMA, Joyce Papers, 1/272, Dawnay to Joyce, 27 May 1918.

30. TNA, FO 686/38, Wilson to Wingate, 5 June 1918.

31. Ibid.

32. IWM, Wilson Papers, HHW2/33A/18, Allenby to Wilson, 14 Aug. 1918.

33. TNA, FO 686/38, Wilson, note of meeting with Husein, 28 May 1918.

34. TNA, FO 686/38, Wilson to Wingate, 5 June 1918.

35. LHCMA, Joyce Papers, 1/O/14, Joyce's notes on the Feisal-Weizmann meeting.

36. TNA, FO 882/27, *Arab Bulletin*, no. 93 (18 June 1918).

24. PREPARING FOR THE PUSH

1. TNA, WO 158/634, pieces 123 and 135, for 31 May and 11 June 1918.
2. "The Hijaz Railway 1918: A German Report," in *Journal of the T. E. Lawrence Society* 12, no. 2 (Spring 2003).
3. Otto Liman von Sanders, *Five Years in Turkey* (Nashville, 2000), p. 231.
4. Ibid., p. 258.
5. Mark Sykes, *The Caliphs' Last Heritage* (London, 1915), p. 471.
6. Antonin Jaussen, *Mission Archéologique en Arabie*, vol. 2 (Paris, 1914), p. 7.
7. IWM, Wilson Papers, HHW2/33A/7, Allenby to Wilson, 15 June 1918.
8. IWM, Wilson Papers, HHW2/33A/12, Allenby to Wilson, 22 June 1918.
9. Ibid.
10. SAD, Clayton Papers, 693/13, Robertson to India, copied to Clayton, 14 March 1918.
11. IWM, Wilson Papers, HHW2/33A/3A, Wilson to Allenby, 29 May 1918.
12. Anthony Bruce, *The Last Crusade* (London, 2003), p. 205.
13. T. E. Lawrence, *Seven Pillars of Wisdom* (London, 1935), p. 527.
14. LHCMA, Joyce Papers, 1/272, Dawnay to Joyce, 27 May 1918.
15. IOR, L/PS/10/12, F. R. Maunsell, Detailed Report on Hejaz Railway, 1907.
16. LHCMA, Joyce Papers, 1/282, Joyce to Hornby, 2 June 1918.
17. C. S. Jarvis, *Arab Command: The Biography of Lieutenant-Colonel F. W. Peake Pasha* (London, 1942), p. 37.
18. Malcolm Brown, ed., *Lawrence of Arabia: The Selected Letters* (London, 2005), p. 155, Lawrence to Husein, 25 June 1918.
19. LHCMA, Joyce Papers, 1/300, Dawnay to Joyce, 12 June 1918.
20. Ibid.
21. IWM, W. F. Stirling Papers, Stirling to his sister, 16 April 1918.
22. LHCMA, Joyce Papers, 1/308, Joyce to Dawnay, 20 June 1918.
23. TNA, FO 882/27, *Arab Bulletin*, no. 92 (11 June 1918).
24. TNA, FO 882/13, *Arab Bulletin Supplementary Papers*, no. 5 (24 June 1918), Lawrence, "Tribal Politics in Feisal's Area."
25. TNA FO 882/27, *Arab Bulletin*, no. 83 (27 March 1918), "Palestine Letter." Hogarth was the Arab Bureau's representative in Palestine at the time.
26. George Antonius, *The Arab Awakening* (London, 1938), p. 434.
27. TNA, FO 686/10, Joyce to Lawrence, 28 June 1918.
28. David Garnett, ed., *The Letters of T. E. Lawrence* (London, 1938), pp. 243–46, Lawrence to Richards, 15 July 1918.
29. LHCMA, Joyce Papers, 1/264, Dawnay to Joyce, 3 July 1918.
30. Ibid.

25. HOLDING OPERATIONS

1. TNA, WO 158/639B, Bartholomew to Chief of General Staff, 15 July 1918.
2. LHCMA, Joyce Papers, 1/311, Dawnay to Joyce, 15 July 1918.
3. Hubert Young, *The Independent*

Arab (London, 1933), p. 203.

4. LHCMA, Joyce Papers, 1/264, Dawnay to Joyce, 3 July 1918.

5. T. E. Lawrence, *Seven Pillars of Wisdom* (London, 1935), p. 540.

6. Allenby informed the CIGS of his intention to attack in Sept. on 24 July 1918; IWM, Wilson Papers, HHW2/33A/14.

7. Young, *Independent Arab*, p. 203.

8. T. E. Lawrence, *Seven Pillars of Wisdom: The Complete 1922 "Oxford" Text*, rev. ed. (Fordingbridge, 2004), p. 642.

9. IWM, Pearman Papers, 78/21/1, Lecture: 'The Imperial Camel Corps with Col. Lawrence," n.d.

10. IWM, H. Garland Papers, postwar lecture, n.d.

11. Laurence Moore, quoted in Geoffrey Inchbald, *The Imperial Camel Corps* (London, 1970), pp. 131–32.

12. W. F. Stirling, *Safety Last* (London, 1953), p. 86.

13. Moore, quoted in Inchbald, *Imperial Camel Corps*, p. 132.

14. Stirling, *Safety Last*, p. 87.

15. Moore, quoted in Inchbald, *Imperial Camel Corps*, pp. 133–34.

16. TNA, WO 374/43340, Lyall's army record.

17. BL, MS Photogr. c.123/2 f. 130.

18. Lawrence, *Seven Pillars of Wisdom* (1935), p. 555.

19. Lawrence, *Seven Pillars of Wisdom* (1922), p. 667.

20. TNA, FO 882/27, *Arab Bulletin*, no. 100 (20 Aug. 1918).

21. Otto Liman von Sanders, *Five Years in Turkey* (Nashville, 2000), p. 262.

22. LHCMA, Bartholomew Papers, 1/9, translation of a document dated 29 Aug. 1918, written by a German army liaison officer attached to the Turkish Eighth Army, addressed to the Military Plenipotentiary in Constantinople.

23. TNA, FO 686/9, Wilson to Husein, 21 June 1918.

24. TNA, FO 686/9, Wilson's report, 19 July 1918.

25. TNA FO 686/10, Wilson's report, 21 July 1918.

26. TNA, FO 686/9, Wilson's report, 21 July 1918.

27. TNA, FO 686/10, Bassett to Director, Arab Bureau, 30 July 1918.

28. TNA, FO 686/10, Husein's letter, 28 July 1918.

29. TNA, FO 686/10, Bassett to Arab Bureau, 30 July 1918.

30. TNA, FO 686/10, Bassett to Husein, 3 Aug. 1918.

31. IWM, Wilson Papers, HHW2/33A/18, Allenby to Wilson, 14 Aug. 1918; TNA, WO 33/960, Allenby to WO, 16 Aug. 1918.

32. Quoted in Joseph Kostiner, "Prologue of Hashemite Downfall and Saudi Ascendancy: A New Look at the Khurma Dispute, 1917–1919," in Asher Susser and Aryeh Shmulevitz, eds., *The Hashemites in the Modern Arab World* (London, 1995).

33. Buxton, note dated 4 Aug. 1918, quoted in Jeremy Wilson, *Lawrence of Arabia: The Authorised Biography of T. E. Lawrence* (London, 1989), p. 534.

34. Buxton, note dated 16 Aug. 1918, quoted in ibid., p. 537.

35. Moore, quoted in Inchbald, *Imperial Camel Corps*, p. 135.

36. TNA, WO 158/639B, Bartholomew to Chief of General Staff, 15 July 1918.

37. Ibid.

38. Moore, quoted in Inchbald, *Imperial Camel Corps*, p. 136.

39. Alec Kirkbride, *An Awakening* ([Tavistock, Eng.], 1971), p. 62.

40. Lawrence, *Seven Pillars of Wisdom* (1935), p. 574.

41. Moore, quoted in Inchbald, *The Imperial Camel Corps*, p. 137.

42. LHCMA, Bartholomew Papers, 1/9, translation of a document dated 29 Aug. 1918, written by a German army liaison officer attached to the Turkish Eighth Army, addressed to the Military Plenipotentiary in Constantinople.

26. THE DARA RAID

1. TNA, FO 882/27, *Arab Bulletin*, no. 104 (24 Sept. 1918).

2. William Facey and Najdat Fathi Safwat, eds., *The Memoirs of Jafar Pasha Al-Askari* (London, 2003), p. 149. A *nargileh* is a traditional Arab water pipe; Alec Kirkbride, *An Awakening* ([Tavistock, Eng.], 1971), p. 47.

3. Kirkbride, *Awakening*, p. 47.

4. Hubert Young, *Independent Arab* (London, 1933), p. 204.

5. Ibid.

6. Ibid., p. 206.

7. T. E. Lawrence, *Seven Pillars of Wisdom: The Complete 1922 "Oxford" Text*, rev. ed. (Fordingbridge, 2004), p. 700.

8. Young, *Independent Arab*, p. 197.

9. Ibid., p. 198.

10. Ibid., pp. 208–9.

11. Facey and Safwat, eds., *Memoirs of Jafar Pasha Al-Askari*, p. 150.

12. Young, *Independent Arab*, p. 211.

13. T. E. Lawrence, *Seven Pillars of Wisdom* (London, 1935), p. 576.

14. TNA, FO 882/13, Lawrence via Commandant Aqaba to Hedgehog Cairo, 30 Aug. 1918, quoted in Jeremy Wilson, *Lawrence of Arabia: The Authorised Biography of T. E. Lawrence* (London, 1989), p. 540.

15. Lawrence, *Seven Pillars of Wisdom* (1935), p. 577.

16. LHCMA, Joyce Papers, 1/Q/20, n.d.

17. Lawrence, *Seven Pillars of Wisdom* (1922), p. 703.

18. Kirkbride, *Awakening*, p. 47.

19. Lawrence, *Seven Pillars of Wisdom* (1922), p. 702.

20. BL, Add 45983B.

21. Earl Winterton, *Fifty Tumultuous Years* (London, 1955), p. 179. The comment was made by the Chicago journalist Lowell Thomas.

22. Lawrence, *Seven Pillars of Wisdom* (1935), p. 581.

23. Winterton, *Fifty Tumultuous Years*, p. 182.

24. Ibid.

25. TNA, FO 882/27, *Arab Bulletin*, no. 106 (22 Oct. 1918).

26. Ibid.

27. Winterton, *Fifty Tumultuous Years*, pp. 64–65.

28. "The Hijaz Railway 1918: A German Report," in *Journal of the T. E. Lawrence Society* 12, no. 2 (Spring 2003).

29. Young, *Independent Arab*, p. 219.

30. Lawrence, *Seven Pillars of Wisdom* (1935), p. 594.

31. C. S. Jarvis, *Arab Command: The Biography of Lieutenant-Colonel F. W. Peake Pasha* (London, 1942), p. 48.

32. Lawrence, *Seven Pillars of Wisdom* (1935), p. 594.

33. Otto Liman von Sanders, *Five Years in Turkey* (Nashville, 2000), p. 274.

34. Lawrence, *Seven Pillars of Wisdom* (1935), p. 594.

35. Kirkbride, *Awakening*, p. 69.

36. Young, *Independent Arab*, p. 227.

37. Liman von Sanders, *Five Years in Turkey*, p. 290.

38. Young, *Independent Arab*, p. 228.

39. Ibid.

40. Ibid., pp. 228–29.

41. Ibid., p. 230.

42. Kirkbride, *Awakening*, p. 71.

43. Young, *Independent Arab*, p. 231.

44. Liman von Sanders, *Five Years in Turkey*, p. 274.

45. TNA, FO 882/27, *Arab Bulletin*, no. 106 (22 Oct. 1918).

46. Kirkbride, *Awakening*, p. 72.

47. Alec Kirkbride, *A Crackle of Thorns* (London, 1956), p. 8.

48. Lawrence, *Seven Pillars of Wisdom* (1935), p. 608.

49. C. T. Atkinson, "General Liman von Sanders on His Experiences in Palestine," *Army Quarterly* 3 (1921–22): 257–75.

50. LHCMA, Allenby Papers, 1/9/1, Allenby to Lady Allenby, 19 Sept. 1918.

51. Lawrence, *Seven Pillars of Wisdom* (1935), p. 612.

52. LHCMA, Joyce Papers, 1/263, Dawnay to Joyce, n.d. but from context 20 Sept. 1918.

53. MEC, H. W. Young Papers, Allenby to Feisal, 20 Sept. 1918.

54. LHCMA, Joyce Papers, 1/263, Dawnay to Joyce, n.d. but from context 20 Sept. 1918.

55. Lawrence, *Seven Pillars of Wisdom* (1922), p. 754.

27. THE ROAD TO DAMASCUS

1. "The Hijaz Railway 1918: A German Report," in *Journal of the T. E. Lawrence Society* 12, no. 2 (Spring 2003).

2. Alec Kirkbride, *An Awakening* ([Tavistock, Eng.], 1971), p. 77.

3. "The Hijaz Railway 1918."

4. Vincennes, SS Marine Q86, Jaussen's report, 20 Sept. 1918.

5. Quoted in Jeremy Wilson, *Lawrence of Arabia: The Authorised Biography of T. E. Lawrence* (London, 1989), p. 553.

6. Translated in the *Evening Standard*, 25 Sept. 1918.

7. TNA, WO 33/960, DMI to Allenby, 25 Sept. 1918.

8. TNA, WO 95/4371, Allenby to Feisal, 25 Sept. 1918.

9. TNA, WO 95/4551, Special Instruction to the Australian Mounted Division, quoted in Matthew Hughes, *Allenby and British Strategy in the Middle East* (London, 1999), p. 98.

10. T. E. Lawrence, *Seven Pillars of Wisdom* (London, 1935), pp. 623–24.

11. Hubert Young, *The Independent Arab* (London, 1933), p. 245.

12. Kirkbride, *Awakening*, p. 81.

13. Young, *Independent Arab*, p. 248.

14. T. E. Lawrence, *Seven Pillars of Wisdom: The Complete 1922 "Oxford" Text*, rev. ed. (Fordingbridge, 2004), p. 770.

15. Lawrence, *Seven Pillars of Wisdom* (1935), p. 631.

16. Ibid.

17. Ibid.

18. Ibid.

19. Ibid., p. 633.

20. Otto Liman von Sanders, *Five Years in Turkey* (Nashville, 2000), p. 292.

21. TNA, FO 882/27, *Arab Bulletin*, no. 106 (22 Oct. 1918).

22. Young, *Independent Arab*, p. 251.

23. LHCMA, Joyce Papers, 2/20/1, Peake to A. W. Lawrence, 4 Aug. 1965.

24. Young, *Independent Arab*, pp. 251–52.

25. Earl Winterton, *Fifty Tumultuous Years* (London, 1955), pp. 71–72.

26. Kirkbride, *Awakening*, p. 82.

27. Ibid., pp. 84–85.

28. Sir G. de S. Barrow, *The Fire of Life* (London, n.d.), p. 211.

29. Lawrence, *Seven Pillars of Wisdom* (1922), p. 782.

30. W. F. Stirling, *Safety Last* (London, 1953), p. 93.

31. TNA, FO 882/27, *Arab Bulletin*, no. 106 (22 Oct. 1918).

32. TNA, WO 33/960, Allenby to WO, 30 Sept. 1918.

33. Liman von Sanders, *Five Years in Turkey*, p. 304.

34. Ibid.

35. Musbah Haidar, *Arabesque* (London, [1945]), p. 147.

36. Stirling, *Safety Last*, p. 94.

37. Ibid.

28. A HOUSE WITH NO DOOR

1. T. E. Lawrence, *Seven Pillars of Wisdom* (London, 1935), p. 645.

2. TNA, FO 882/27, *Arab Bulletin*, no. 106 (22 Oct. 1918).

3. MEC, Allenby Papers, Chauvel to Bean, 8 Oct. 1929.

4. Ibid.

5. Malcolm Brown, ed., *Lawrence of Arabia: The Selected Letters* (London, 2005), p. 176, Lawrence to W. F. Stirling, 28 June 1919.

6. IWM, certificate, dated 8 Nov. 1918, accompanying EPH 4338.

7. T. E. Lawrence, *Seven Pillars of Wisdom: The Complete 1922 "Oxford" Text*, rev. ed. (Fordingbridge, 2004), p. 799.

8. Lawrence, *Seven Pillars of Wisdom* (1935), p. 651.

9. W. F. Stirling, *Safety Last* (London, 1953), p. 95.

10. Ibid.

11. Alec Kirkbride, *A Crackle of Thorns* (London, 1956), p. 9.

12. Alec Kirkbride, *An Awakening* ([Tavistock, Eng.], 1971), p. 97.

13. TNA, WO 95/4553, War Diary of ADMS, Australian Mounted Division, for Oct. 1918.

14. MEC, Allenby Papers, Chauvel to Bean, 8 Oct. 1929.

15. IWM, Q12377.

16. TNA, WO 33/960, WO to GHQ Egypt, 1 Oct. 1918.

17. This impression was corroborated by Kirkbride, who had heard about the meeting from Tahseen Qadri, an Arab who was present. Kirkbride, *Awakening*, p. 99.

18. MEC, Allenby Papers, Chauvel, note, 31 Oct. 1935.

19. SAD, Wingate Papers, 170/2, Allenby to Lady Allenby, 3 Sept. [Oct.] 1918; IWM, Wilson HHW2/33A/29, Allenby to Wilson, 9 Nov. 1918.

20. BL, Add 45914, f. 42.

21. TNA, WO 33/960, Allenby to WO, 6 Oct. 1918.

22. Stirling, *Safety Last*, p. 97.

23. IWM, Stirling Papers, Stirling to his sister, 5 Nov. 1918.

24. TNA, WO 33/960, Allenby to WO, 12 Oct. and 13 Oct. 1918.

25. IWM, Wilson Papers, HHW2/33A/28, Allenby to Wilson, 19 Oct. 1918.

26. TNA, FO 882/17, Clayton to FO, 19 Oct. 1918.

27. MAE, Nantes, Jerusalem, B, 114, SS Marine Q86, Jaussen's report, 15 Nov. 1918.

28. *Times* (London), 17 Oct. 1918.

29. David Garnett, ed., *The Letters of T. E. Lawrence* (London, 1938), p. 266, "The Reconstruction of Arabia," 4 Nov. 1918.

30. MEC, Hogarth Papers, Hogarth to Clayton, 1 Nov. 1918.

31. Quoted in Margaret Macmillan, *Peacemakers* (London, 2002), p. 397.

32. Hubert Young, *The Independent Arab* (London, 1933), p. 280.

33. Quoted in Matthew Hughes, *Allenby and British Strategy in the Middle East* (London, 1999), p. 118.

34. TNA, FO 882/27, *Arab Bulletin*, no. 102 (3 Sept. 1918).

35. MEC, Tibawi Papers, Fakhri to Husein, 4 Sept. 1918, and S. Tanvir Wasti, "The Defence of Medina, 1916–19," *Middle Eastern Studies* 27, no. 4 (Oct. 1991).

36. TNA, WO 33/960, GHQ to WO, 22 Nov. 1918.

37. Edouard Brémond, *Le Hedjaz dans la Guerre Mondiale* (Paris, 1931), p. 310.

38. SAD, Clayton Papers, 694/6, the Weizmann-Feisal Agreement, 3 Jan. 1919.

39. Quoted in Jeremy Wilson, *Lawrence of Arabia: The Authorised Biography of T. E. Lawrence* (London, 1989), p. 596.

40. TNA, CAB 27/37, Hirtzel, "Policy in Arabia," 20 Nov. 1918.

41. TNA, FO 608/97/371/5/3, Intelligence Department of the Naval Staff, 26 Feb. 1919, quoted in Hughes, *Allenby and British Strategy*, p. 121.

42. TNA, CAB 21/119, Hankey to Balfour, 1 Aug. 1918, quoted in Hughes, *Allenby and British Strategy*, p. 120.

43. Lord Hardinge of Penshurst, *Old Diplomacy* (London, 1947), p. 232.

44. IWM, W. F. Stirling Papers, letter, 26 April 1919.

45. Quoted in Hughes, *Allenby and British Strategy*, p. 158.

46. Ross Burns, *The Monuments of Syria* (London, 1992), p. 91.

EPILOGUE

1. "A Report on Mesopotamia," *Sunday Times*, 22 Aug. 1920.

2. SAD, Clayton Papers, 693/11, Lawrence to Clayton, 8 Oct. 1928.

3. Quoted in Hanna Batatu, *The Old Social Classes and the Revolutionary Movements of Iraq* (Princeton, 1978), p. 25.

4. David Garnett, ed., *The Letters of T. E. Lawrence* (London, 1938), p. 345.

5. Ibid., p. 330, Lawrence to Kennington, 12 June 1921.

6. BL, Add 45903, Lawrence to Charlotte Shaw, 24 Nov. 1927.

7. George Antonius, *The Arab Awakening* (London, 1938), p. 183.

8. *Times* (London), 20 May 1935.

9. T. E. Lawrence, *Revolt in the Desert* (New York, 1927), p. 66.

10. Basil Liddell Hart, *"T. E. Lawrence" in Arabia and After* (London, 1934), p. 438.

11. D. L. Lloyd Owen, *The Desert My Dwelling Place* (London, 1957), p. 46.

12. Ronald Storrs, *Orientations* (London, 1937), p. 177.

13. Quoted in Elie Kedourie, *In the Anglo-Arab Labyrinth* (Cambridge, 1976), p. 119.

14. SAD, Wingate Papers, 171/6, 28 Dec. 1918, quoted in M. W. Daly, *The Sirdar* (Philadelphia, 1997), p. 27.

15. SAD, Wingate Papers, 148/4, 11 Feb. 1918.

16. LHCMA, Allenby Papers, 1/8/15, Allenby to Lady Allenby, 3 Oct. 1917.

17. Amin Rihani, *Around the Coasts of Arabia* (London, 1930), frontispiece.

18. King Abdullah, "As the Arabs See the Jews," *American Magazine*, Nov. 1947.

19. *Hansard*, 1 Aug. 1930, cols. 902–3.

20. *Times* (London), 8 July 1937.

21. Kedourie, *In the Anglo-Arab Labyrinth*, p. 228.

22. IOR, L/PS/12/3349, memoranda respecting the McMahon-Husein correspondence of 1915 and 1916 and certain subsequent statements made on behalf of His Majesty's Government in regard to the future status of Palestine. Dec. 1939: Lord Chancellor's opinion, circulated to Cabinet on 23 Jan. 1939.

23. Storrs, *Orientations*, p. 179.

24. *Times* (London), 30 Dec. 1949.

25. *Report of a committee set up to consider certain correspondence between Sir Henry McMahon and the Sharif of Mecca in 1915 and 1916*, March 16, 1939, Cmd. 5974.

26. "In Iraq, Lawrence Is a Must Read," *Christian Science Monitor*, 8 Dec. 2004; "Lessons We Should Learn from Lawrence," *Miami Herald*, 5 Dec. 2004.

27. Osama bin Laden, http://news.bbc.co.uk/1/hi/world/south_asia/1585636.stm.

28. Bruce Lawrence, ed., *Messages to the World: The Statements of Osama bin Laden* (London, 2005), p. 187, "Among a Band of Knights," 14 Feb. 2003.

Bibliography

1. ARCHIVES

BODLEIAN LIBRARY, OXFORD
T. E. Lawrence Papers

BRITISH LIBRARY
Egypt 1916–17, Private letters between General Sir William Robertson and General Sir Archibald Murray, privately printed in 1932 (Add 52463)
T. E. Lawrence papers, diaries, letters, and photographs (Add 45914, Add 45915, Add 45983A and B, Add 45903, Add 50584)

THE GERTRUDE BELL PROJECT (ONLINE ARCHIVE),
ROBINSON LIBRARY, UNIVERSITY OF NEWCASTLE
G. Bell letters

CHURCHILL COLLEGE, CAMBRIDGE
G. Lloyd Papers
E. Marsh Papers

INDIA OFFICE RECORDS, BRITISH LIBRARY, LONDON
Files from series:
L/PS/10
L/PS/11
L/PS/12
L/PS/18
Mss Eur D660, Sir A. H. Grant Papers
Mss Eur D613, Sir G. Roos-Keppel Papers
Mss Eur E264/7, telegrams between the Viceroy and the Secretary of State for India, 1916

IMPERIAL WAR MUSEUM
T. W. Beaumont Papers
Sir P. W. Chetwode Papers
G. Dawnay Papers
H. Garland Papers
H. V. Gilbert Papers
F. Hayward Papers
T. Henderson, The Hejaz Expedition, 1916–17—A Narrative of the Work done by
    the Arabian detachment of No 14 Squadron RFC while attached to the Hejaz
    expedition
F. G. Peake Papers
D. G. Pearman Papers
V. D. Siddons Papers
W. F. Stirling Papers
Sir H. H. Wilson Papers

LIDDELL HART CENTRE FOR MILITARY ARCHIVES,
KING'S COLLEGE, LONDON
Sir E. H. H. Allenby Papers
Sir W. H. Bartholomew Papers
P. C. Joyce Papers
Sir W. R. Robertson Papers

MIDDLE EAST CENTRE, ST ANTONY'S COLLEGE, OXFORD
Sir E. H. H. Allenby Papers
N. Barbour Papers
E. Baring Papers
Sir G. F. Clayton Papers
D. G. Hogarth Papers
I. Karadogan Papers
T. E. Lawrence Papers
S. F. Newcombe Papers
H. St.J. Philby Papers
Sir M. Sykes Papers
A. Tibawi Papers
W. Yale Papers
Sir H. W. Young Papers
J. W. A. Young Papers

THE NATIONAL ARCHIVES, KEW
Files from series:
FO 141 Embassy and Consulates, Egypt: general correspondence
FO 371 Political Departments: general correspondence
FO 686 Jeddah Agency papers

FO 882 Arab Bureau papers
T1 Treasury files
WO 33 War Office: Reports, Memoranda and Papers
WO 95 War diaries
WO 106 Directorate of Military Operations and Military Intelligence: correspondence and papers
WO 158 War Office, Military Headquarters' correspondence and papers
WO 374 Officers' service records

PEMBROKE COLLEGE, CAMBRIDGE
Sir R. Storrs Papers

SUDAN ARCHIVE, UNIVERSITY OF DURHAM LIBRARY
Sir G. F. Clayton Papers
Sir F. R. Wingate Papers

2. BOOKS AND ARTICLES

Abdullah, "As the Arabs See the Jews," *American Magazine*, November 1947.
Adelson, R., *Mark Sykes: Portrait of an Amateur*, London, 1975.
Antonius, G., *The Arab Awakening*, London, 1938.
Armstrong, K., *Islam: a Short History*, London, 2001.
Arnold, T. W., *The Caliphate*, second edition, London, 1965.
Asher, M., *Lawrence: The Uncrowned King of Arabia*, London, 1999.
Asprey, R. B., *War in the Shadows*, London, 1994.
Atkinson, C. T., "General Liman von Sanders on His Experiences in Palestine," *Army Quarterly* 3 (1921–22).
Ayalon, A., "The Hashemites, T. E. Lawrence and the Postage Stamps of the Hijaz," in Susser, A., and Shmuelevitz, A., eds., *The Hashemites in the Modern Arab World: A Festschrift in Honour of the Late Professor Uriel Dann*, London, 1995, pp. 15–30.
Baker, R., *King Husain and the Kingdom of the Hejaz*, Cambridge, 1979.
Barrow, Sir G. de S., *The Fire of Life*, London, n.d.
Batatu, H., *The Old Social Classes and the Revolutionary Movements of Iraq*, Princeton, 1978.
Bell, Gertrude, *The Desert and the Sown*, New York, 1907.
Bernstorff, Count, *Memoirs*, Berlin, 1936.
Birdwood, Lord C. B. B., *Nuri As-Said*, London, 1959.
Bray, N. N. E., *Shifting Sands*, London, 1934.
Brémond, E., *Le Hedjaz dans la Guerre Mondiale*, Paris, 1931.
Brodrick, A. H., *Near to Greatness: A Life of the Sixth Earl Winterton*, London, 1965.
Brown, M., ed., *Lawrence of Arabia: The Selected Letters*, London, 2005.

Bruce, A., *The Last Crusade*, London, 2002.

Buchan, J., *Greenmantle*, London, 1916.

Burdett, A. L. P., ed., *Arab Dissident Movements*, Slough, 1996.

Burns, R., *Monuments of Syria*, London, 1999.

Burton, R. *Personal Narrative of a Pilgrimage to Al-Madinah and Meccah*, London, 1893.

Cain, P. J., and Hopkins, A. G., *British Imperialism 1688–2000*, second edition, Edinburgh, 2002.

Callwell, C. E., *Small Wars*, second edition, London, 1899.

Charmley, J., *Lord Lloyd and the Decline of the British Empire*, London, 1987.

Chirol, V., *Pan-Islamism*, London, 1906.

———, *Fifty Years in a Changing World*, London, 1927.

Churchill, W. S., *Great Contemporaries*, London, 1937.

Clayton, Sir G. F., *An Arabian Diary*, ed. Collins, R. O., Berkeley, 1969.

Cork and Orrery, Earl of, [Boyle, W.], *My Naval Life, 1886–1941*, London, 1942.

Cumming, H. H., *Franco-British Rivalry in the Post-War Near East*, Oxford, 1938.

Daly, M. W., *The Sirdar: Sir Reginald Wingate and the British Empire in the Middle East*, Philadelphia, 1997.

Daly Metcalf, B., *Islamic Revival in British India: Deoband 1860–1900*, Princeton, 1982.

Dawisha, A., *Arab Nationalism in the Twentieth Century*, Princeton, 2003.

Dawn, C. E., *From Ottomanism to Arabism: Essays on the Origins of Arab Nationalism*, Illinois, 1973.

Djemal Pasha, *Memories of a Turkish Statesman 1913–1919*, London, 1922.

Dowson, Sir E. M., *A Short Note on the Design and Issue of Postage Stamps Prepared by the Survey of Egypt for His Highness Husein, Emir & Sherif of Mecca & King of the Hejaz*, El-Qahira, 1918.

Douglas-Hamilton, J., *From Gallipoli to Gaza: The Desert Poets of World War One*, London, 2003.

Erickson, E., *Ordered to Die: A History of the Ottoman Army in World War One*, London, 2001.

Erskine, Mrs S., *King Faisal of Iraq*, London, 1933.

Esin, E., *Mecca the Blessed, Madinah the Radiant*, London, 1963.

Facey W., with Grant, G., *Saudi Arabia by the First Photographers*, London, c. 1996.

Facey, W., and Safwat, N. F., eds., *A Soldier's Story: The Memoirs of Jafar Pasha Al-Askari*, London, 2003.

Ferguson, N., *Empire: How Britain Made the Modern World*, London, 2003.

Field, M., *The Merchants*, London, 1984.

Fisher, J., *Curzon and British Imperialism in the Middle East*, London, 1999.

———, "The Rabegh Crisis 1916–17: 'A comparatively Trivial Question' or 'A Self-Willed Disaster'," *Middle Eastern Studies* 38, no. 3 (July 2002), pp. 73–92.

———, *Gentlemen Spies*, Stroud, 2002.

Fitzherbert, M., *The Man Who Was Greenmantle: A Biography of Aubrey Herbert*, London, 1983.

Fletcher, D., *War Cars: British Armoured Cars in the First World War*, London, 1987.

Freedman, I., *The Question of Palestine*, London, 1973.

Fromkin, D., *A Peace to End All Peace*, paperback edition, London, 2000.

Gilbert, M., *First World War*, London, 1994.

———, *Israel*, London, 1999.

Gildea, R., *Barricades and Borders: Europe 1800–1914*, Oxford, 1987.

Graves, P., *The Pursuit*, London, 1930.

———, *Briton and Turk*, London, 1941.

———, ed., *Memoirs of King Abdullah of Transjordan*, London, 1950.

Graves, R., *Lawrence and the Arabs*, London, 1927.

Grey, Sir E., *Twenty-Five Years — 1892–1916*, London, 1925.

Gubser, P., *Politics and Change in Al-Karak*, Oxford, 1973.

Haidar, M., *Arabesque*, London, 1944.

Hardinge of Penshurst, Lord, *Old Diplomacy*, London, 1947.

Hardy, P., *The Muslims of British India*, Cambridge, 1972.

Henderson Stewart, F., *Honor*, Chicago, 1994.

Hogarth, D. G., *The Penetration of Arabia*, London, 1904.

———, "Mecca's Revolt against the Turk," *Century Magazine* 100 (1920), pp. 403–9

Hogue, O., *The Cameliers*, London, 1919.

Hughes, M., *Allenby and British Strategy in the Middle East*, London, 1999.

———, ed., *Allenby in Palestine: The Middle East Correspondence of Field Marshal Viscount Allenby, June 1917–October 1919*, Stroud, 2004.

Inchbald, G., *Imperial Camel Corps*, London, 1970.

James, L., *Imperial Warrior—The Life and Times of Sir Edmund Allenby*, London, 1993.

———, *The Golden Warrior: The Life and Legend of Lawrence of Arabia*, revised edition, London, 1995.

Jarvis, C. S., *Arab Command: The Biography of Lieutenant-Colonel F. W. Peake Pasha*, London, 1942.

Jathar, G. B., and Beri, S. G., *Indian Economics*, London, 1933.

Jaussen, A., *Coutumes des Arabes au pays de Moab*, Paris, 1908.

Jaussen and Savignac, *Mission Archéologique en Arabie*, Volume II, Paris, 1914.

Karsh, E., and Karsh, I., "Myth in the Desert, or Not the Great Arab Revolt," *Middle Eastern Studies* 33, no. 2 (April 1997).

Keay, J., *Sowing the Wind: The Seeds of Conflict in the Middle East*, London, 2003.

Kedourie, E., *In the Anglo-Arab Labyrinth*, Cambridge, 1976.

Khoury, P. S., *Urban Notables and Arab Nationalism*, Cambridge, 1983.

Kidwai, M. H., *Pan-Islamism and Bolshevism*, London, [1937].

Kinross, J. P. D. B., *Ataturk: The Rebirth of a Nation*, London, 1964.

Kirkbride, A., *A Crackle of Thorns*, London, 1956.

———, *An Awakening*, University Press of Arabia, 1971.

Knightley, P., and Simpson, C., *The Secret Lives of Lawrence of Arabia*, London, 1969.

Kostiner, J., "Prologue of Hashemite Downfall and Saudi Ascendancy: A New Look at the Khurma Dispute, 1917–1919," in Susser, A., and Shmuelevitz, A., eds., *The Hashemites in the Modern Arab World*, London, 1995.

Landau, J. M., *The Politics of Pan-Islam*, Oxford, 1990.

Lancaster, W., *The Rwala Bedouin Today*, Cambridge, 1981.

Larès, M., *T. E. Lawrence, la France et les Français*, Paris, 1980.

Laurens, H., "Jaussen et les services de renseignement français (1915–1919)," in Chatelard, G., and Tarawneh, M., eds., *Antonin Jaussen: Sciences sociales occidentales et patrimoine arabe*, Centre d'Études et de Recherches sur le Moyen-Orient Contemporain, 1999, pp. 23–35.

Lawrence, A. W., ed., *T. E. Lawrence by His Friends*, London, 1937.

Lawrence, B., ed., *Messages to the World: The Statements of Osama bin Laden*, London, 2005.

Lawrence, T. E., *Seven Pillars of Wisdom*, London, 1935.

———, *The Letters of T. E. Lawrence*, ed. Garnett, D., London, 1938.

———, *Letters to His Biographers Robert Graves and Liddell Hart*, London, 1963.

———, *Crusader Castles*, Oxford, 1988.

———, *Seven Pillars of Wisdom (The Complete 1922 Oxford Text)*, Fordingbridge, 2004.

Leclerc, C., "The French Soldiers in the Arab Revolt," *Journal of the T. E. Lawrence Society* IX, no. 1 (Autumn 1999).

Lewis, B., *The Crisis of Islam*, London, 2003.

Lewis, G., "The Ottoman Proclamation of Jihad in 1914," in *Arabic and Islamic Garland: Historical, Educational and Literary Papers Presented to Abdul Latif Tibawi*, London, 1977.

Liddell Hart, B., *"T. E. Lawrence" in Arabia and After*, London, 1934.

Liman von Sanders, O., *Five Years in Turkey*, Nashville, 2000.

Lloyd Owen, D. L., *The Desert My Dwelling Place*, London, 1957.

Lockman, J. N., *Scattered Tracks on the Lawrence Trail*, Michigan, 1996.

———, *Meinertzhagen's Diary Ruse*, Michigan, 1995.

MacMillan, M., *Peacemakers*, London, 2001.

Manual of Field Engineering 1911, General Staff, War Office (1914 reprint)

Margoliouth, D. S., "Pan-Islamism," *Proceedings of the Central Asian Society* 12 (January 1912).

Massey, W. T., *Allenby's Final Triumph*, London, 1920.

McKale, D. M., *War by Revolution*, Ohio, 1998.

Meeker, M., *Literature and Violence in North Arabia*, Cambridge, 1979.

Morgenthau, H., *Ambassador Morgenthau's Story*, New York, 1919.

Morris, J., *The Hashemite Kings*, London, 1959.

Mousa, S., *T. E. Lawrence: An Arab View*, Oxford, 1966.

Mundy, M., and Musallam, B., *The Transformation of Nomadic Society in the Arab East*, Cambridge, 2000.

Musil, A., *The Northern Hegaz*, New York, 1926.

Nelson, B., *Azraq: Desert Oasis*, London, 1973.

Nevakivi, J., *Britain, France and the Arab Middle East, 1914–1920*, London, 1969.

Nevo, J., "Abdallah's Memoirs as Historical Source Material," in Susser, A., and Shmuelevitz, A., eds., *The Hashemites in the Modern Arab World: A Festschrift in Honour of the Late Professor Uriel Dann*, London, 1995, pp. 165–82.

Nicholson, J., *The Hejaz Railway*, London, 2005.

Nicolson, N., ed., *Harold Nicolson, Diaries and Letters, 1907–1964*, London, 2004.

Ochsenwald, W., *The Hijaz Railroad*, Charlottesville, 1980.

———, *Religion, Society and the State in Arabia—The Hijaz under Ottoman Control, 1840–1908*, Ohio, 1984

O'Dwyer, M. F., *India as I Knew It*, London, 1925.

Özcan, A., *Pan-Islamism: Indian Muslims, the Ottomans and Britain 1877–1924*, Leiden, 1997.

Peake, F. G., *History of Jordan and Its Tribes*, Miami, 1958.

Photographies d'Arabie, Hijaz 1907–1917, Paris, 1999.

Pierard, P., and Legros, P., *Off-Road in the Hejaz*, Dubai, 2001.

Prasad, Y. D., *The Indian Muslims and World War I: A Phase of Disillusionment with British Rule, 1914–1918*, New Delhi, 1985.

Reid, F., *The Fighting Cameliers*, Sydney, 1934.

Robertson, Sir W., *From Private to Field Marshal*, London, 1921.

Robinson, E. H. T., *Lawrence the Rebel*, London, 1946.

Rogan, E., *Frontiers of the State in the Late Ottoman Empire*, Cambridge, 1999.

Rolls, S. C., *Steel Chariots in the Desert*, London, 1937.

Schatkowski Schilcher, L., "The Famine of 1915–1918 in Greater Syria," in Spagnolo, J., ed., *Problems of the Modern Middle East in Historical Perspective*, Reading, 1996.

Segev, T., *One Palestine, Complete*, paperback edition, London, 2001.

Seymour, C., ed., *The Intimate Papers of Colonel House*, London, 1928.

Smith, J. A., *John Buchan, A Biography*, London, 1965.

Stein, L., *The Balfour Declaration*, London, 1961.

Stevenson, D., *1914–1918: The History of the First World War*, London, 2005.

Stirling, W. F., *Safety Last*, London, 1953.

Stitt, G., *A Prince of Arabia, The Emir Shereef Ali Haider*, London, 1948.

Storrs, R., *Orientations*, London, 1937.

Strachan, H., *The First World War, Volume I: To Arms*, Oxford, 2001.

Sykes, M., *The Caliphs' Last Heritage*, London, 1915.

Tanvir Wasti, S., "The Defence of Medina," *Middle East Studies* 27, no. 4 (October 1991).

Tauber, E., *The Arab Movements in World War I*, London, 1993.

"The Hijaz Railway 1918: A German Report," *Journal of the T. E. Lawrence Society* XII, no. 2 (Spring 2003).

Thesiger, W., *Arabian Sands*, London, 1959.

Tibawi, A. L., *A Modern History of Syria*, London, 1969.

Touchan, R., Meko, D., and Hughes, M. K., "A 396-year reconstruction of precipitation in Southern Jordan," *Journal of the American Water Resources Association* 35, no. 1 (February 1999).

Tourret, R., *Hedjaz Railway*, Abingdon, 1989.

Travers, T., *Gallipoli*, Stroud, 2001.

Travis, A., *Bound and Gagged: A Secret History of Obscenity in Britain*, London, 2000.

Vansittart, Lord, *The Mist Procession*, London, 1958.

Von Papen, F., *Memoirs*, London, 1952.

Wallach, J., *Desert Queen*, paperback edition, London, 1997.

Wavell, A. J. B., *A Modern Pilgrim in Mecca*, second edition, London, 1918.

Weldon, L. B., *Hard Lying*, London, 1925.

Wemyss, V. Wester, *The Life and Letters of Lord Wester Wemyss*, London, 1935.

Westrate, B., *The Arab Bureau: British Policy in the Middle East, 1916–1920*, Pennsylvania, 1992.

Wilson, J., *Lawrence of Arabia: The Authorised Biography of T. E. Lawrence*, London, 1989.

Wilson, M. C., *King Abdullah of Jordan: A Political Biography*, Oxford, 1983.

———, *King Abdullah, Britain and the Making of Jordan*, Cambridge, 1987.

Winstone, H. V. F., ed., *The Diaries of Parker Pasha*, London, 1983.

Winterton, Earl, [Turnour, E.], *Fifty Tumultuous Years*, London, 1955.

Woodward, D. R., *Lloyd George and the Generals*, Newark, 1983.

Wyman Bury, G., *Pan-Islam*, London, 1919.

Yapp, M. E., *The Making of the Modern Near East, 1792–1923*, London, 1987.

Young, H., *The Independent Arab*, London, 1933.

Zeigler, P., *Edward VIII*, London, 1990.

Zeine, Z. N., *The Emergence of Arab Nationalism*, Beirut, 1966.

Acknowledgments

This book would not exist without the efforts of my agents, George Lucas and Catherine Clarke, and my editor, Maria Guarnaschelli, whose determination to make this book the best it could be has been extraordinary. I am very grateful to them all, as well as to Sarah Rothbard and Laura Timko at W. W. Norton for their work in putting the book together. I would particularly like to thank Richard Spring for his constant encouragement since our visit to Syria in 2002, which sparked my interest in Britain's involvement in the Middle East, and Steve Boyle and Tom Tugendhat, who accompanied me into the desert on the field trips to Jordan and Saudi Arabia.

For a wide range of help during my research, including expertise, research, recollections, suggestions, and hospitality, I am grateful to Attayak Ali, the late St. John Armitage, Ray Benitez, Michael Binyon, Jenny Carter-Manning, Anna Checkley, Derek Cooper, Rob Crothers, Richard Drayton, Baroness Elles, Ed Erickson, William Facey, Mark Goodwin, David Grisenthwaite, Jane Hogan, Patrick Kidd, Robert Knight, Henri Laurens, Alysa Levene, Sami Nawar, Tamsin O'Connell, Harold Orlans, Patrick Pierard, Andrew Reynolds, Eugene Rogan, Avi Shlaim, Charlie Sykes, Ramzi Touchan, Mesut Uyar, Debbie Usher, George Williamson, and Harvey Woods. That I was able to enter Saudi Arabia at all was due largely to the then British Ambassador, Sir Sherard Cowper-Coles. I am very grateful to him and his wife, Bridget, for welcoming me to Riyadh. I must also thank the staffs of the India Office Library, The National Archive, the Liddell Hart Centre for Military Archives, the Imperial War Museum, the Sudan Archive, the Middle East Centre and the Modern Papers Reading Room at the Bodleian Library for their help. Dr. Christopher Wright and Dr. Barry Knight at the British Library enabled me to have T. E. Lawrence's diary forensically examined by George Jenkinson. I would like to thank all three for their time and I should add that my interpretation of the films that resulted is my own.

Finally, I would also like to thank my colleagues at work, especially Meladie Blackshaw, Caroline Denton, James Dunseath, and Juliette Proudlove, for their forbearance, and my parents, Valerie and Stuart, for their endless support.

Permissions

For permission to quote from copyrighted published and unpublished records I would like to thank: Omar Ziad al Askari for Jafar Pasha al Askari; Rutters Solicitors of Shaftesbury for T. W. Beaumont; Patricia Bettany for D. H. Calcutt; Patience Marshall for Sir Gilbert Clayton; Mena Garland O'Connor for Herbert Garland; Dr. Caroline Barron for David Hogarth; The Seven Pillars of Wisdom Trust and Random House Inc. for T. E. Lawrence; Sir Tatton Sykes for Sir Mark Sykes; and Martin Dane for Sir Reginald Wingate. Extracts from Gertrude Bell's letters are reprinted by permission of the Special Collections Librarian, Robinson Library, University of Newcastle upon Tyne; and from Sir Ronald Storrs's papers by permission of the Master and Fellows of Pembroke College, Cambridge. I would like to thank the Trustees of the Liddell Hart Centre for Military Archives and the Imperial War Museum for permission to quote from the papers held in their respective archives. Quotations from Crown copyright records held by the India Office Records, The National Archive, the Sudan Archive, and the British Library appear by permission of Her Majesty's Stationery Office. Efforts have been made to contact every copyright holder for material contained in this book. If any owner has been inadvertently overlooked, the publisher would be glad to hear from them and to make good in future editions any errors or omissions brought to their attention.

Photograph Credits

p. 96   "Not an army but a world": Reproduced courtesy of the Imperial War Museum, London. Photograph by T. E. Lawrence.

p. 107 Herbert Garland: Reproduced courtesy of the Imperial War Museum, London.

p. 112 Toweira Station: Photograph by James Barr.

p. 113 An abandoned railway car: Photograph by James Barr.

p. 115 Stewart Newcombe: Reproduced courtesy of the Imperial War Museum, London. Photograph by T. E. Lawrence.

p. 119 Sharif Abdullah: Reproduced courtesy of the Imperial War Museum, London.

p. 122 A typical Hijaz railway station: Photograph by James Barr.

p. 126 Auda abu Tayi: Reproduced courtesy of the Bodleian Library, University of Oxford.

p. 147 Turkish repairs to the railway line: Reproduced courtesy of the Imperial War Museum, London.

p. 149 Sahl al Matran: Photograph by James Barr.

p. 159 Wadi Itm, 5 July 1917: Reproduced courtesy of the Imperial War Museum, London. Photograph by T. E. Lawrence.

p. 196 The bridge over the Yarmuk: Reproduced courtesy of the Imperial War Museum, London.

p. 199 The southern gate of Azraq: Photograph by James Barr.

p. 208 Arthur Balfour: Reproduced courtesy of the Imperial War Museum, London.

p. 215 The British enter Jerusalem: Reproduced courtesy of the Imperial War Museum, London.

p. 221 Armored cars at Quwayrah: Reproduced courtesy of the Bodleian Library, University of Oxford.

p. 278 A "tulip" exploding: Reproduced courtesy of the Imperial War Museum, London.

p. 288 A Bedu inspects the machine gun of a British biplane: Reproduced courtesy of the Imperial War Museum, London.

p. 299 Going their separate ways: Reproduced courtesy of the Imperial War Museum, London.

p. 304 Feisal leaves the Victoria Hotel: Reproduced courtesy of the Imperial War Museum, London.

p. 305 An exhausted Lawrence: Reproduced courtesy of the Imperial War Museum, London.

Index

Page numbers in *italics* refer to illustrations.